Hawker Siddeley Aviation and Dynamics
1960–77

Hawker Siddeley Aviation and Dynamics
1960–77

Stephen Skinner

The Crowood Press

First published in 2014 by
The Crowood Press Ltd
Ramsbury, Marlborough
Wiltshire SN8 2HR

www.crowood.com

British Library Cataloguing-in-Publication Data
A catalogue record for this book is available from
the British Library.

ISBN 978 1 84797 739 7

Frontispiece: Hawk T.1. XX247. The Hawker
Siddeley Hawk first flew in 1974 and is still in
production by BAE Systems at its Brough and
Warton plants. (BAE Systems)

Typeset by Shane O'Dwyer, Swindon, Wiltshire

Printed and bound in India by Replika Press Pvt Ltd

Acknowledgements

There are many people and organizations I
wish to thank for the assistance they have
given me in the writing of this history.

I would like to thank the following individuals and organizations for their help:
Barry Guess and Trevor Friend of BAE
Systems Archives at Farnborough; Peter
Hotham and his colleagues at BAE Systems
Archives at Brough; George Jencks *et al*:
Avro Heritage Centre; Ray Williams at the
Armstrong Whitworth Collection; Chris
Farara of the Hawker Archive; Jeremy
Close, Director of Communications &
CSR, Astrium and Nikki Standing, Astrium; Brian Riddle of the National Aerospace
Library at Farnborough; the RAF Museum
Archives; Alistair Scott, President of the
British Interplanetary Society; Gary Noone
of MBDA; Mike Phipp; Derek Ferguson;
and Ken Haynes.

I should like to note the assistance and
excellent service provided by the Hertfordshire Public Library Service and the speedy
provision of books available from its wide
catalogue, especially when such services
are under threat in the UK.

My special thanks are rightly reserved
for the continued enthusiasm, support and
editorial help that my wife Jane provided
throughout the writing of this book.

Contents

Preface

The inspiration for writing this book arose quite naturally as it is a companion title to my *British Aircraft Corporation – A History* (Crowood, 2012). Although Hawker Siddeley and BAC were very different groupings, they were the predominant UK aerospace manufacturers from 1960 until nationalization in 1977. Hawker Siddeley was the greater of the two as it had become a Group in 1935 and was already the largest aviation company in the UK and Europe. Yet today many aviation enthusiasts remain unaware of this British company's significance, and regard enterprises such as Avro and Hawker as being wholly separate entities when this was far from the case. The firms within the Hawker Siddeley Group did maintain a high level of autonomy until the late 1950s, but they were not independent and were wholly owned by the Group. In order to set the record straight I felt compelled to write a history of Hawker Siddeley and give the company its due worth.

The book begins with an overview of the firm's background from its beginning until 1960 and then goes on to make a detailed examination of the period between the company's takeover of Folland, de Havilland and Blackburn in 1959–60 until its nationalization as part of British Aerospace in 1977.

All the aircraft types that fell under the aegis of the Hawker Siddeley Aviation and Dynamics umbrella in 1960 have been described, so this book embraces older types such as the Hunter and Comet as well as the Blue Streak missile and satellite launcher. I have written in more depth about those projects begun post-1960 and have con-

The Sopwith Aviation Company's Canbury Park Rd premises in Kingston, Surrey; aircraft manufactured here were taken by road to Brooklands to fly. The extensive Hawker Siddeley Group grew from these small premises. BAE Systems

tinued the history of those aircraft and weapons beyond nationalization in 1977.

Until only short time ago Hawker Siddeley Dominies, Harriers and Nimrods were all flying with the Royal Air Force until they were felled in the 2010 Strategic Defence Review, leaving only the Hawk still serving and in production. Harriers fly with several foreign forces and many variants of the 125 executive jet still grace the skies.

Hawker Siddeley was not only concerned with aerospace, but began diversifying in the 1950s into other forms of engineering such as diesel engines, electrical engineering, agricultural and forestry equipment, power stations, sewerage works, and locomotive and railway carriage manufacture. Generally these non-aerospace interests made greater profits than the aerospace divisions. The Group continued its policy of diversification and this enabled it to remain in existence well after the nationalization of its aircraft and dynamics divisions, until it was taken over in 1991.

CHAPTER ONE

Hawker Siddeley from 1910 until the End of the 1950s

Beginnings

In September 1910 Thomas Octave Murdoch Sopwit (*see* Appendix I) visited Brooklands Airfield in Surrey, paid £5 and was taken for a sedate cruise of two circuits of the airfield in a Henri Farman biplane. From that moment, Sopwith decided he was going to be a pilot. He began by buying a little Howard Wright Avis monoplane though, as there were no dual controls, he would just have to get into the thing and teach himself to fly. It was not only the aviator's, but also the machine's, maiden flight. After a few runs he guided the machine into the air and, after two or three hundred yards, he rose suddenly to forty feet and for a moment looked like he was going to fall

backwards, so steep was the angle. Fortunately he righted the plane, but in landing he came down sideways, smashing the propeller and chassis, and damaging one wing.

Undaunted, Sopwith sought new worlds to conquer. The next month he bought a bigger Howard Wright biplane for £630; on 26 November he flew it 107 miles (172km) in 3 hours 20 minutes to establish British distance and duration records – and this within a week or so of qualifying for his aviator's certificate. He then competed for the £4,000 Baron de Forest prize for the longest non-stop flight from anywhere in England to anywhere on the Continent. On the morning of 18 December 1910 he took off from Eastchurch, in Sheppey. His compass went unserviceable, so he steered by the sun

until it was hidden by cloud and then carried on by instinct. As he crossed the Belgian frontier the wind became so gusty that he was nearly thrown out of his aircraft; soon it became too strong to make headway, and he landed in a field near Beaumont. He had flown in a straight line for 169 miles (272km) and was declared winner.

The early years of the century saw the beginnings of British flying. Others whose firms were to become part of the Hawker Siddeley Group were making their first flights at this time. A.V. Roe (later Sir Alliott Verdon-Roe) made a short hop at Brooklands in 1907, and Geoffrey de Havilland (later Sir Geoffrey) was experimenting at Newbury with a biplane built in a shed off Fulham Palace Road. In 1912 he was designer-pilot to the Royal Aircraft Factory at Farnborough, where he produced the famous BE biplane. Associated with him at the Factory was Harry Folland, who later joined Hawker Siddeley as designer for Gloster Aircraft and later formed Folland Aircraft, which itself joined the Group in 1959. Bob Blackburn, too, was flying a monoplane on Filey sands in 1909.

Sopwith Aviation Company

Sopwith established an aircraft firm of his own at the end of 1912. Fred Sigrist, who had been employed in 1910 as an engineer on Sopwith's yacht, was soon helping adapt and design aircraft. A year later the Sopwith Aviation Company Ltd was formed. About this time a young Australian, Harry Hawker, came to England to study flying and went to Brooklands, where Sopwith taught him to fly: he had a natural flair so soon took over the test flying. Thereafter, the driving force behind the Sopwith Company in producing the famous line of Sopwith aircraft in World War One was the triumvirate of Sopwith as salesman and promoter, Sigrist controlling production,

Tom Sopwith's 1910 Howard Wright biplane. Author's collection

and Hawker designing and flying. As the firm expanded Sopwith invested money in proportion, so maintaining control of it.

The first Sopwith aeroplane, the Sopwith-Wright, was built in a disused skating rink at Kingston-on-Thames. It had an openwork fuselage for pilot and passenger, wings copied from Sopwith's Wright, and was powered by the 70hp Gnome from the Blériot. Eventually it was bought by the Admiralty – the first of many thousands of Sopwith aircraft for the Services.

World War One gave the Sopwith Company its big chance. Seven different aircraft types were ready for immediate service and were snapped up by the Royal Naval Air Service. But it was the subsequent series of fighters that brought fame and fortune to the firm. First came a two-seater fighter-bomber known as the 1½ Strutter, then a line of single seaters: the Pup, Camel, Triplane and others, finishing with the Snipe, which remained in service with the RAF for many years after the war.

ABOVE: **The Sopwith Aviation Company logo.**
BAE Systems

RIGHT: **The Sopwith Triplane, one of Sopwith's successful World War One fighter designs.**
BAE Systems

Sopwith Snipe and Salamander production at Richmond Road, Ham, Kingston. BAE Systems

At the beginning of the War two other figures entered the aircraft industry who were to hold major roles in the years ahead: Tom Sopwith employed Frank Spriggs to help with the books, while A.V. Roe employed Frank Dobson; both these men were to have a major influence in the years ahead (*see* Appendix I).

When peace came the Sopwith Company carried on for a year or so. They built the Atlantic biplane in which Harry Hawker and his navigator, Kenneth Mackenzie-Grieve, attempted the first direct crossing of the Atlantic in May 1919. Forced down, they were rescued in mid-Atlantic after being missing for a week and given up for lost.

Hawker

By 1920, with no orders for aircraft in hand and threatened with a demand from the government to pay substantial Excess War Profits Duty, Sopwith told his board they must wind up the company while still solvent. But soon afterwards a new firm was

ABOVE: **Harry Hawker.** Author's collection

RIGHT: **The Hawker Hurricane prototype K5083 at Brooklands, which made its maiden flight on 6 November 1935.** BAE Systems

formed, named H.G. Hawker Engineering after Harry, both as a tribute to his work as test pilot during the war and to avoid confusion with the former Sopwith company. Hawker Engineering took over Sopwith's patent rights and support for Sopwith aircraft in the RAF. The original directors were Tom Sopwith, Harry Hawker, Fred Sigrist and Bill Eyre.

The intention was to keep Hawker a small firm, making aircraft whenever there was a demand and keeping going the rest of the time by making motorcycles and other things. This plan fell by the wayside, however, and it blossomed over the years to become Hawker Siddeley Group, comprising about a half of the entire British aircraft industry and becoming the largest aerospace group in Europe by the 1960s.

The first aeroplane built by the Hawker firm was a military monoplane, the Duiker. But Harry did not live to see it fly: before it was ready he was killed testing a Nieuport Goshawk at Hendon. Thereafter the Hawker firm built many aircraft for the RAF, from the Woodcock fighter to the big Horsley

bomber. The latter was the first military aircraft to be developed by Sir Sidney Camm, who joined the firm in 1922 and was destined to become Chief Engineer of Hawker Aircraft. During the 1930s the mainstays of the RAF's fighter and bomber strength were Camm's Harts and Furies.

In 1934 Camm produced his masterpiece, the Hurricane. Hawker directors, inspired by Tom Sopwith, saw they had a winner and laid down a production line even before they had an Air Ministry order. This decision was a key factor in the Battle of Britain, in which more Hurricanes took part than any other fighter.

The Formation of Hawker Siddeley Aircraft Ltd

The British aircraft industry consisted of about twenty aircraft and aero-engine manufacturers until 1928, when Vickers acquired control of Supermarine. This set the pattern for future mergers in that Vickers let Supermarine carry on as a separate entity until 1957: so it was to be with firms in the Hawker Siddeley Group until 1960.

After World War One, many other aircraft firms ran into financial trouble. Alliott Verdon Roe had to sell a majority holding

Avro Anson G-AGPG. Though the Anson dated back to the 1930s, this one only flew after the war, in August 1945. It was used as an Avro/Hawker Siddeley communications aircraft for many years; in 1969 it was sold to Pye Telecom and received a new nose to accommodate radar. BAE Systems

in Avro to Crossley Motors in 1920, but by 1928 Crossley's car-manufacturing business was in serious trouble so Avro was sold to Sir John Siddeley. He was the owner of the Armstrong Siddeley Development Company, which also owned Armstrong Whitworth Aircraft, Armstrong Siddeley Motors and High Duty Alloys (see Appendix II). Roe and his closest associates then decided to join forces with Sam Saunders of Cowes to build flying boats, and formed Saunders-Roe. Meanwhile, in May 1934 Hawker Aircraft – as H.G. Hawker Engineering had become the previous year – bought the Gloster Aircraft Co., which enabled Hawker to double its production potential and provided extra finance for Gloster to continue independent design and construction.

On 25 June 1935 the Armstrong Siddeley Development Company was purchased by a newly formed company, Hawker Siddeley Aircraft under the chairmanship of Tom Sopwith. All that weekend Sopwith had carried around a cheque for £1m (= £60m in 2013), awaiting the call from Sir John Siddeley to clinch the deal.

After the merger, Tom Sopwith was less concerned with daily affairs and more engrossed in business strategy, while Frank Spriggs was Managing Director. Hawker Siddeley remained an association of eight firms, each with a separate identity though with tight financial control from the centre. These firms were: Avro, A.W. Hawksley (a manufacturer of aircraft during wartime and prefabricated housing post-war), Air Service Training (training pilots and engineers and aircraft repair and conversion), Armstrong Siddeley Motors (making aero-engines and cars), Armstrong Whitworth Aircraft, Gloster Aircraft, Hawker Aircraft and High Duty Alloys. In November 1937 the firm's capital was doubled to £4m and it thus became the largest aeronautical business in the world.

The Hawker Siddeley Aircraft Company at War

At the outbreak of war, the Avro Anson was in quantity production as a general reconnaissance aircraft, and development of the twin-engined Avro Manchester bomber was under way. Owing to its unreliable Rolls-Royce Vulture engines the Manchester was not a success, but it was developed to the superb four-engined Lancaster, of which 7,374 were built. Its York transport derivative mated the same wings and tail, plus a central fin, with an entirely new fuselage seating twelve passengers. The Lincoln bomber was built as a replacement for the Lancaster, entering RAF service soon after VJ Day. Armstrong Whitworth, which had been producing the Whitley bomber at the start of the war, assisted Avro with Lancaster and Lincoln manufacture.

During the war Hawker produced Hurricanes, which bore the brunt of the Battle of Britain and were still in use at D-Day in 1944 when production ended. Its descendants, the Typhoon and Tempest, became ground attack aircraft and fighter, respectively. Hurricane production reached a peak of one every four hours during the critical period in the autumn of 1940.

At the outbreak of war the Gloster Gladiator biplane fighter was still in production, but Hurricanes and Typhoons were constructed in increasing numbers. Practically all the Typhoons were produced by Gloster. It was the Gloster company which was entrusted with the task of building, in association with jet engine pioneer Frank Whittle, Britain's first jet aircraft, the E.28/39, which flew in May 1941. The E.28/39 led to the Gloster Meteor, the first practical jet fighter with offensive armament and an appreciable range, which broke the world speed record in both 1945 and 1946.

Armstrong Siddeley Motors played a major part in the war effort and Air Service Training undertook management of specialized centres in the training of no fewer than 40,000 pupils as pilots and supernumeraries.

Avro Lancaster production at the Chadderton plant in June 1944. BAE Systems

Britain's first jet aircraft, the Gloster E.28/39 powered by a Whittle jet engine, which made its maiden flight at Cranwell on 15 May 1941. A second E.28/39 crashed. W4041 is preserved at the Science Museum in London. BAE Systems

This map of England indicates all the Hawker Siddeley plants involved in the war effort in 1944. There were the main groupings of Hawker Siddeley factories at Yeadon, Manchester, Coventry, Gloucester, Langley, Kingston and Hamble. The numbers indicate the number of factories involved in each place. The other places were not company-owned. Note the ten-fold increase in aircraft production from 1938–44. Author's collection

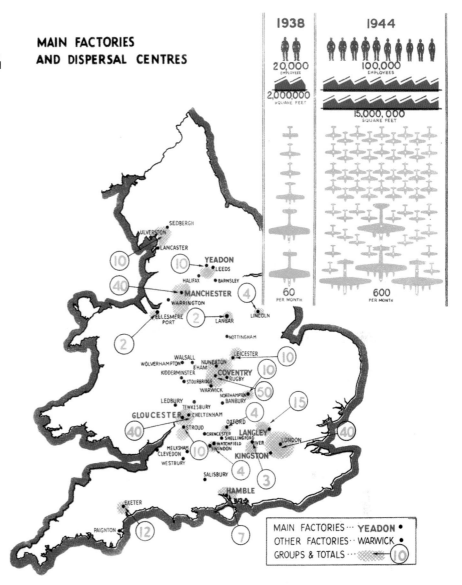

Hawker Siddeley Aircraft Post-War

From 1948 Hawker Siddeley was formally called a Group, but this indicated very little and the companies wholly owned by it continued to function with significant autonomy. The management style of the Chairman, Tom Sopwith, was very 'hands off' – even in the 1930s he had rarely been seen, though he chaired the Board meetings and quarterly meetings of the Chief Designers. With the success of Hawker Siddeley he had become a very wealthy man, and received a knighthood in 1953. He spent some winters in South Africa, and spent time during the summer at his castle and estate at Amhuinnsuidhe on the Isle of Harris, which he owned from 1944–61. (Jimmy Orrell, Avro's chief test pilot, would collect Sir Thomas and Lady Phyllis Sopwith from Chilbolton near the Sopwiths' Manor House in King's Somborne, Hampshire, and fly them to Stornaway in Avro's 'hack' Anson, G-AGPG.)

Although production contracts were slashed with the end of hostilities, the technological advances made in the war such as the introduction of the jet engine and the fruits of German aeronautical research stimulated new designs. Immediately after the war, Armstrong Whitworth and Avro produced airliners, but neither the former's Apollo nor the latter's Tudor were a success, the Apollo never even going into production, so Hawker Siddeley decided to concentrate its resources on military aircraft and weapons. This policy continued until the late 1950s, when it became clear that there would be fewer military orders, so the Armstrong Whitworth Argosy civil freighter and Avro 748 airliner were put into production.

In the post-war years Avro produced two contrasting major military aircraft, one a conservative design and the other at the cutting edge of development. These were the Shackleton maritime reconnaissance aircraft, a final development of Avro's large wartime piston-engined bombers, and con-

The wartime Hawker Siddeley logo referring to all of the firms that were owned by the Group. Author's collection

trastingly the world's first four-jet delta-winged aircraft, the Vulcan bomber.

Gloster continued to build and export large numbers of Meteors, passing development and production of the night fighter variant to Armstrong Whitworth. Hawker enjoyed considerable success both at home

and with export orders for its Sea Hawk and, in particular, Hunter fighters, to the extent that production of the Sea Hawk also had to be passed to Armstrong Whitworth. Gloster followed Avro with the delta wing on its large Javelin fighter, which was designed to follow on from the Meteor but

Hawker Siddeley – employment, deliveries and wages during World War Two[1]

Wartime statistics	1939–40	1943–44	Total 1939–45
Employees – male	29,700	56,600	n/a
Employees – female	4,000	35,400	n/a
Deliveries of aircraft	3,362	8,795	40,089
Deliveries of aero-engines	4,378	7,763	38,564
Productive output	£37.0m	£123.5m	£507.5m (= £18.5bn 2013)
Wages	£9.4m	£26.5m	£123.2m

A 1948 advertisement showing the major aircraft and engines built by Hawker Siddeley and its predecessors since the Avro 504 and the Sopwith Camel, including the Hart, Gladiator, Lancaster and the Meteor. Author's collection

Gloster Meteor F.8 WA820 fitted with Armstrong Siddeley Sapphire engines, which made four time-to-altitude records from Moreton Valence in August 1951. F.8s were made in greater numbers than any other mark of Meteor. Almost 4,000 Meteors were made. Ray Williams

failed to echo its predecessor's success and was only ordered by the RAF.

The Group's newly formed Canadian subsidiary, Avro Canada, had quickly established itself as a major player in the aviation world by producing the world's second jet airliner, which was only just beaten into the air by the De Havilland Comet, and followed it with the large CF-100 jet fighter. Their designers then produced the supersonic CF-105 Arrow fighter, which was regrettably cancelled by the Canadian Government in 1959, crippling Avro Canada.

Aero Engines, Missiles and Training

Armstrong Siddeley's range of piston aero engines was gradually superseded and replaced by the Sapphire turbojet, which competed with Rolls-Royce Avon to become the UK's dominant turbojet. The Sapphire had to settle for a strong second place and powered the Javelin, and some marks of the Handley Page Victor, English Electric Canberra and Hawker Hunter. It was also licence-built in the USA for the Martin B-57, itself a licence-built Canberra. Armstrong Siddeley was unable to challenge the lead Rolls-Royce had established in the turboprop market with the Dart, but its small Viper jet was very successful, powering a wide range of aircraft including the Jet Provost trainer and its Strikemaster development, the Italian Aermacchi MB-326 trainer and early marks of the Hawker Siddeley 125 executive jet. Its Gamma rocket powered the Saunders-Roe Black Knight, and the Stentor rocket was installed in the Avro Blue Steel stand-off bomb carried by the Vulcans and Victors of the RAF.

Hawker Siddeley companies only started development of guided missiles in the 1950s. Avro was contracted to produce Blue Steel, which had a troubled development through the 1950s but eventually saw service with Bomber Command during the 1960s until the nuclear deterrent was passed to the Royal Navy. Indicating the wastefulness of autonomy, its sister company Armstrong Whitworth developed the Navy's first anti-aircraft missile, the Seaslug, both teams working in isolation.

Air Service Training at Hamble continued with its flying, navigation, radio and engineering schools at a reduced scale postwar. Seventy per cent of its students were from overseas, and it operated technical training schools in India and Pakistan for their respective air forces. Air Service Training was also engaged in aircraft design, repair and modification; it carried out a number of conversions of Lancasters and Lincolns to become engine test beds, and designed the trainer version of the Javelin, the T.3.

Hawker Siddeley at Twenty-One

At the Hawker Siddeley Group's twenty-first annual general meeting in 1957 the Chairman, Sir Thomas Sopwith, made special reference to the achievements of the past twenty-one years. During that period, he said, the Group's companies had produced over 44,000 aircraft, including 13,000 Hurricanes, more than 8,000 Ansons, 5,000 Lancasters and over 3,500 Meteors.

Sir Thomas said that the largest single factor in the growth of the Group was Avro Canada – formed in 1945 with only 300 employees – which had in the previous eleven years become one of Canada's major industrial enterprises, employing some 20,000 people. Avro Canada was seen as a strategic foothold in the lucrative American military and civil aircraft market.

The Group had had another satisfactory year's trading, both in the UK and in Canada, and its profits for the year 1956–57 amounted to £12.8m before taxation, compared with £12.7m the previous year. Of this 1956–57 profit, over £6m was contributed by Canadian members of the Group.

An Avro Canada CF-100 for the RCAF. Avro Canada had speedily established itself as the predominant aircraft manufacturer in Canada. However, the company collapsed when its later CF-105 was cancelled. Author's collection

Burgeoning Hunter wing production at Kingston in 1954. BAE Systems

The 1957 Defence White Paper and Rationalization

The 1957 Defence White Paper produced by Duncan Sandys, the Minister of Defence, envisaged missiles as providing the method of both attack and defence for the UK, though no timescale for their introduction was indicated. All future fighter aircraft programmes bar the English Electric Lightning would cease and the industry would need to concentrate on guided weapons. The Hawker Siddeley Group board debated the ramifications of this and considered withdrawing from any new investment in aviation to concentrate on its non-aviation interests, but Sir Tom Sopwith unequivocally decided that the firm would remain in aviation and would have to invest more itself.

Despite the axing of most manned aircraft projects by the White Paper there was one specification still in hand, for a bomber to replace the Canberra: Operational Requirement OR339, which later became OR343 and led to the TSR2 aircraft. The Government made it plain that this contract would only be awarded to a consortium of firms. Though Hawker Siddeley already existed as a consortium, the individual firms guarded their autonomy jealously and despite the Government's ruling, Avro, Gloster and Hawker all separately offered proposals for OR339. Eventually Sopwith and Spriggs forced these firms to put forward a sole group proposal based on the Hawker offering.

Management Reshuffle

In June 1958, in a boardroom coup caused by growing friction between Sir Roy Dobson (*see* Appendix I) and Sir Frank Spriggs, Sir Tom Sopwith asked Spriggs to leave, which he did that day with what was then

ABOVE: An Armstrong Siddeley Sapphire jet engine, which was a rival to the Rolls-Royce Avon and powered not only British types but also the Martin B-57, an American licence-built version of the Canberra. Author

BELOW: In 1957, as part of its programme of diversification, Hawker Siddeley bought Brush Traction, which manufactured railway locomotives. HS4000, named Kestrel, was a prototype high-power mainline diesel locomotive built by Brush in 1967. It had a power rating of 4,000hp. It is seen at Barrow Hill in 1971. Author

each other, as exemplified by three Group companies offering proposals for OR339. Sopwith now favoured a more central control and knew that Dobson would tighten the Group's structure.

Tighter Control and Diversification

Following the multiple OR339 proposals, all designs had to be considered by Hawker Siddeley Design Council before receiving the go-ahead. The Council was headed by Sir Roy Dobson with representatives of all the Group's aircraft companies, including Armstrong Siddeley and High Duty Alloys. As part of their role the Council visited and held discussions with 'movers and shakers' in their business, not only in the UK but also worldwide.

To direct operations more strategically in 1959 the Hawker Siddeley Aviation and Hawker Siddeley Industries Divisions were formed. These became necessary as, mindful of the future and the need for diversification, from the early 1950s Hawker Siddeley had been buying firms outside the aviation business. These were quickly added to with the establishment in 1955 of Hawker Siddeley Nuclear Power and two years later the purchase of the Brush Group, which itself included several engineering firms. In Canada Sir Roy Dobson vigorously pursued the same policy, and by 1956 a total of forty-four companies were held within the Avro Canada subsidiary (later Hawker Siddeley Canada). Thirty-three of these had been acquired with the takeover of the Dominion Steel and Coal conglomerate, which included various steel mills, coal mines and manufacturing plants, as well as Halifax Shipyards.

'The Twelfth Largest Industrial Concern outside the USA'

As the new decade loomed, demands by the Government were to lead to an increase in the size of the Group and to a period of rapid change and reorganization. However, at the annual general meeting of the Hawker Siddeley Group in 1958 Sir Tom Sopwith announced that the Group was now the twelfth largest industrial concern outside the USA. Assets had climbed to £200m (2013 = £3,798m), sales stood at £250m (2013 = £4,748m) and the total number of staff was approaching 100,000.

the UK record payoff of £75,000 (£1.52m at 2013 prices). In a press release Sir Tom praised Sir Frank for his forty-four years of service to the firm, and when interviewed the latter amicably maintained it was time for him to retire. Dobson took over Sprigg's role as Group Managing Director.

Sir Arnold Hall, (*see* Appendix I) who had joined the Group as Technical Director in 1955, proposed a close-knit operation very different from the loose federation that existed under Spriggs. Though Spriggs was on the Board of each subsidiary, he had allowed the companies to compete against

CHAPTER TWO

Hawker Siddeley from 1960 to Nationalization

Takeovers

The Government had made it plain in an official statement of policy in May 1958 that it sought a rationalized aircraft industry and would refuse aid to any firm that stood out from this. The industry was slow to react so, even though the Government had no legal power to force them to merge, in mid-December 1959 Duncan Sandys – who had become Minister of Aviation the previous October – informed the industry chiefs that there was only room for two major aviation manufacturers and that they alone would be eligible for Government aid.

With Government policy set on reducing the plethora of aviation companies in the UK, the Hawker Siddeley Group with assets of over £200m (approximately £4bn = 2013) was in the perfect position to take over other aircraft firms. In September 1959 it bought the comparatively small Folland Aircraft based at Hamble, Hampshire, which was then building the Gnat fighter/trainer.

De Havilland Merges with Hawker Siddeley

De Havilland had been engaged in talks with Vickers and English Electric (which had already agreed to merge their aviation interests to eventually form the British Aircraft Corporation) from July 1959, but in late November withdrew from these, much to the displeasure of Duncan Sandys. He informed de Havilland's Chairman, Sir Aubrey Burke, that de Havilland would receive no Government support henceforward. Throughout November de Havilland had been arguing that the Airco grouping established with Fairey and Hunting to build the DH121 airliner (which became the Hawker Siddeley Trident) could be the basis for a third grouping in British aviation, but this was rejected by the Minister.

Vickers-Armstrongs and English Electric pondered a hostile bid for de Havilland with the support of the Minister, but on 17 December the boards of Hawker Siddeley and de Havilland announced that they had agreed to recommend a merger of the two companies; Hawker Siddeley was offering to buy de Havilland's share capital for £14.2m.

Clearly matters were now moving very quickly, as only two days earlier Sir Aubrey Burke had reported to the de Havilland board about the situation with Vickers and English Electric, and about informal conversations he had held with Hawker Siddeley's Managing Director, Sir Roy Dobson. The de Havilland board decided that they could not remain independent and authorized their chairman to open negotiations with Hawker Siddeley. They accepted that if de Havilland merged with Hawker Siddeley, then de Havilland Engines could join Bristol Siddeley Engines and de Havilland Propellers would be associated with Armstrong Whitworth's missile division. The Board minutes stated that

> The aim would be to ensure sufficient DH representation on the new parent board and in the management of the new company. It was agreed that the merger with Hawker Siddeley represented a greater possibility of DH continuing as an entity than on any other basis.

Negotiations

Following discussions between Sir Aubrey Burke and Sir Roy Dobson on 18 December 1959, the new structure was noted down. There would be a Hawker Siddeley Group Board with Sir Tom Sopwith as Chairman, Sir Roy Dobson as Deputy Chairman and Managing Director, and Sir Aubrey Burke as Deputy Managing Director. There would be two subsidiaries: Hawker de Havilland with Sir Aubrey Burke as Chairman/Chief

Executive, dealing with all aviation interests; and Hawker Siddeley Industries for non-aviation interests.

However, at a meeting between the interested parties on 6 January, that previously agreed new structure was appreciably altered. Sir Roy Dobson said that some of the matters he had agreed to in the hurried negotiations with de Havilland had now been deemed to be unacceptable to his Hawker Siddeley and Blackburn colleagues (Blackburn was also merging with the Group, as outlined below). Sir Aubrey Burke would be Deputy Managing Director of the Group Board, and there would be one additional de Havilland Group Board member and one from Blackburn. The Aviation subsidiary would have Dobson as Chairman and Burke as Deputy Chairman, plus other Directors. Sir Aubrey Burke had wanted the Aviation subsidiary to be called Hawker de Havilland, but Sir Tom Sopwith and Sir Roy Dobson refused to consider it. Sir Aubrey Jones reported all this to the de Havilland board at a special meeting the following day. They were dismayed by this and considered abandoning the merger, but then decided to invite Sopwith and Dobson to Hatfield to discuss the matter further; that discussion never happened, but eventually the de Havilland board accepted it.

In mid-January 1960, Hawker Siddeley sent out the prospectus for the purchase of the de Havilland and Blackburn shares to the company's shareholders. It stated 'It is the intention that the de Havilland companies will, as part of Hawker Siddeley, continue to enjoy a considerable degree of autonomy and independence.'

Blackburn Joins the Group

Like de Havilland, Blackburn Aircraft knew that it could not continue to maintain its independence within the British aircraft industry. The Vickers–English Electric grouping – which was to become BAC – had little interest in Blackburn, so Blackburn's directors opened talks with Hawker Siddeley, where they felt they could maintain some autonomy as other companies such as Avro had. Unaware of the negotiations taking place with de Havilland, in early December Hawker Siddeley's bid for the ownership of the Blackburn Group was accepted. When the Blackburn management heard of the de Havilland merger, they realized that they would now have even less influence within the Group.

By May 1960 purchase of de Havilland and Blackburn shares had been finalized, and the two companies began to feel the effect of being part of Hawker Siddeley. Blackburn's Dumbarton factory was sold in June, and in October Sir Roy Dobson became Chairman of Blackburn. At the same time Dobson announced that all companies within the Group would now need to submit budgets to the Group Board for capital expenditure in 1961. Smaller items, if urgent, might be approved by the local Boards for approval by the parent Board.

Other Possible Merger Targets – Bristol and Handley Page

The Group had little interest in Bristol Aircraft, which was in a sorry state, its factories empty, with no prospect of work apart from the Supersonic Transport – later Concorde – project. Hawker Siddeley would have taken over the design team and closed the site had it bought the firm. In the event, Bristol Aircraft had no choice other than to join Vickers-Armstrongs and English Electric as a minority partner as part of BAC.

There was a number of meetings between Hawker Siddeley and Handley Page, but Sir Frederick Handley Page never agreed to a merger. In his talks with Hawker Siddeley in 1960, Sir Frederick asked for 16/- per share when the market price was 13/-; Hawker Siddeley offered 10/-, which he turned down. At this point the Government cancelled twenty-eight Handley Page

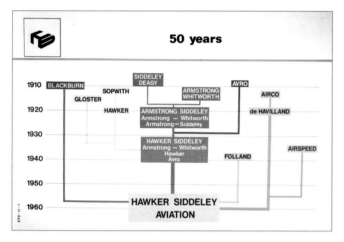

LEFT: A Hawker Siddeley diagram indicating when the various companies became part of the Group. BAE Systems

BELOW: An Argosy promoting its car transporter credentials at Bitteswell. The three Armstrong Siddeley Sapphires arrayed in front of it were produced at the Armstrong Siddeley factory in Coventry. Ray Williams

Victor B.2 bombers, so Hawker Siddeley reduced their offer to about 8/- when the shares were trading at 10/-. Then the RAF selected the Handley Page Herald rather than the Avro 748 for a military freighter contract, but the Government would not pay Handley Page its full Victor contract cancellation claim, and the merger talks collapsed. Next Hawker Siddeley offered 5/-; this was rejected and, with no prospect of a merger, the Government cancelled the Herald order and ordered a version of the 748 in 1962. Handley Page Aircraft struggled on for another eight years, but then went into receivership.[2]

The Expanding Group

With its purchase of Folland, Blackburn and de Havilland, Hawker Siddeley had greatly increased its aviation, aero-engine and missile interests, and the number of employees and sites under its control. These acquisitions strengthened its predominance in the UK military aircraft market, as it now produced the Folland Gnat with its potential as a trainer for the RAF, and the de Havilland Sea Vixen fighter and Blackburn Buccaneer bomber for the Royal Navy.

Hawker Siddeley had been weak in the civil airliner market, and in 1960 only had the new Avro 748 feeder airliner and Armstrong Whitworth Argosy freighter, which it had funded entirely from its own resources. However, it now inherited the large de Havilland range of civil airliners, though three of these were toward the end of their production lives. The small Dove stayed in limited production until 1968, though manufacture of the larger Heron ceased in 1961. More significantly, the de Havilland Comet 4 jet airliner remained in limited production until early 1964. However, already under construction at Hatfield was the first Trident tri-jet airliner, of which high sales were expected. Another bright star on the horizon was the DH125 executive jet, which was to prove its potential and remained in production until 2012.

Though the purchase of Folland brought nothing of significance other than the Gnat, Blackburn had in addition to the Buccaneer a range of small engines, while de Havilland possessed the mighty de Havilland Propellers with its Firestreak and Red Top air-to-air missiles, the Blue Streak rocket and propeller manufacture. The de Havilland Engine Division's range included rocket, piston and jet engines.

ABOVE: The second prototype Hawker Siddeley 748, G-ARAY, demonstrating its sprightly take-off performance at the 1964 Farnborough Air Show. It was in Queen's Flight livery but with 'Hawker Siddeley 748' titling. Alex Christie

BELOW: The first Trident, G-ARPA, bearing the colours of BEA as it makes a taxi run prior to its maiden flight on 9 January 1962. BAE Systems

The second prototype HS125 executive jet, G-ARYB, at Hatfield where it made its maiden flight in December 1962. It had a fuselage 1ft (30cm) shorter than that of the standard production model and was fully instrumented for performance testing. BAE Systems

In purchasing de Havilland, Hawker Siddeley also became owners of important overseas aircraft firms, most notably de Havilland Canada, which had grown from wartime manufacture of Mosquitoes to manufacture successful, rugged, indigenous

The thirteenth Buccaneer, XK529, one of the twenty development aircraft. While engaged in catapult launch trials in August 1961 on HMS *Hermes*, XK529 stalled and crashed into the sea with the loss of the two crew. BAE Systems

designs: the Chipmunk, Beaver, Otter and Caribou. De Havilland Australia had distinguished itself with a single design, the Drover, which was a cross between a Dove and a Heron.

Though the Group now had a significant presence in the civil market, the reality was that the profitability of military programmes was in the order of double that of civil aircraft.

The Hawker Siddeley Group at the Beginning of the 1960s

The Hawker Siddeley Group was a mighty combine with sales in 1961 of £320m (at 1961 prices), exports of £34m and a trading profit of £19m. The Group had 101,479 employees, with 31,212 overseas. The founder of the Group, Sir Thomas Sopwith

was the Chairman; Sir Roy Dobson was Vice-Chairman and Managing Director while Sir Aubrey Burke was Deputy Managing Director (*see* Appendix IV).

An immediate and major problem for the company was the virtual collapse of the innovative Avro Canada with the cancellation of the Avro CF-105 Arrow fighter project and huge redundancies in February 1959. Avro Canada had been bought by Hawker Siddeley Group in 1945 from a shadow factory established during the war and had manufactured successful designs such as the Avro Canada CF-100 fighter. Avro Canada made a loss after tax of £812,000 and was merged with the Group's other engineering interests, and renamed as Hawker Siddeley Canada. Hawker Siddeley tried to maintain the huge Avro Canada plant at Malton by diversifying into other work, but with little success. In 1962 Sir Roy Dobson sold the virtually empty yet exceedingly well-equipped factory to another subsidiary, de Havilland Canada, for the CDN$12.5m it had in the bank.

Some tidying up ensued in the UK: Armstrong Siddeley Motors merged with Bristol Aero-Engines to form Bristol Siddeley Engines in 1959, and abandoned car production (*see* Appendix II) Air Service Training at Hamble was sold in 1960.

ABOVE: Vickers Vanguard G-APEA at Weybridge prior to its first flight. The Vanguard had de Havilland propellers for its Rolls-Royce Tyne engines. Propellers had been a very profitable market, but with the greater use of jet engines demand was falling. BAE Systems

RIGHT: The Blue Streak rocket at the Spadeadam test centre in Cumbria. Blue Streaks were not actually launched from Spadeadam, but were tested there before transport to Woomera in Australia, where they were launched. Author

Whitworth Gloster was formed by the merger of Gloster and Armstrong Whitworth in 1961 and, with the end of Javelin production, Gloster's factories at Hucclecote and Brockworth were closed in mid-1962. De Havilland announced redundancies at Christchurch in November 1961, running up to closure in 1962, and its Portsmouth factory was put up for sale, in August 1961 but only finally closed in 1968.

Tom Sopwith Stands Down as Chairman

In 1963 Sopwith retired as Chairman to become the Group's President; Sir Roy Dobson stepped into his shoes, with Sir Arnold Hall as Vice-Chairman. That year from sales of £327m the company only made a profit of £5.2m, but almost £9.3m was set aside for Research and Development. Orders in hand at the end at 1962 amounted to £390m, a substantial increase on the previous year-end.

Initial Rationalization, 1960–63

Over the three years following the takeover of Folland, Blackburn and de Havilland the Group had instigated only minor changes to the management of any of its companies: investment decisions were centralized, but each firm still had its own Board. In fact, it seemed much as Tom Sopwith had written in the first edition of *Hawker Siddeley News* of February 1948:

> The Hawker Siddeley Group is a free association of companies teamed together to provide a pool of technical experience, technique, resources and facilities which would be beyond the scope of any individual firm. Each company manages its own affairs entirely, but has behind it the resources and facilities of all the other firms and is able to call upon the research and production resources of the Group.

Sopwith chaired Board meetings and quarterly meetings of Chief Engineers, but other than that he was not a 'hands-on' manager.

It is possible that, had Sopwith remained at the helm, major rationalization would not have occurred. As it was, in 1963 the Board under Dobson and Hall set to work to shape their wide range of aircraft and missile assets. For those firms taken over in 1959–60, the loss of their heritage and independence was a mighty shock.

The fifth de Havilland Canada Caribou, temporarily registered CF-LKF-X. It was later delivered to the US Army. BAE Systems

ABOVE: The last Armstrong Siddeley car built was a Star Sapphire used by Sir Arnold Hall as his chauffeur-driven transport from 1960 to 1967. It is now in private ownership. With the merger of Armstrong Siddeley Motors with Bristol Aero-engines in 1959, car manufacture was abandoned in 1960. via Mark Nelson

BELOW: The Hawker Siddeley logo adopted in 1963. BAE Systems

Hawker Siddeley Group

The Establishment of Hawker Siddeley Aviation and Hawker Siddeley Dynamics

With nearly 55,000 employees in the UK concerned with development and production of aircraft, missiles and related equipment, Hawker Siddeley Group's aviation interests were then the largest in Europe. Its design and production interests spanned a range of aeronautical hardware, varying from the latest ideas in V/STOL strike fighters to space booster vehicles for the first European satellites.

A major reorganization was set in train to rationalize all the Group's activities. The Board recognized the need to refine and

The former de Havilland headquarters at Hatfield under the HSA banner. BAE Systems

Hawker Siddeley Aviation 1963

Division	Production in 1963	Present status
Avro-Whitworth Division		
Baginton, Coventry	Production of Argosy	Closed by HSA 1965
	Development of 681	
	Production of 748 and Vulcan assemblies	
	Spares	
Bitteswell, Leics	Assembly and flight test of Argosy	Closed by BAe 1983
	Modification and flight test of other HSA types	
Bracebridge Heath, Lincs	Repair and stores	Closed by BAe 1982
Chadderton, Lancs	Production and development of 748,	
	Andover and Vulcan	Closed by BAE Systems 2012
	Shackleton support	
Langar, Notts	Repair and stores	Closed by HSA 1968
Whitley, Coventry	Design of HS681	Closed by HSA 1968
Woodford, Cheshire	Assembly and flight test of 748,	
	Andover and Vulcan	Closed by BAE Systems 2011
de Havilland Division		
Chester, Cheshire	Production of Comet, Dove, 125 and Sea Vixen	Now Airbus UK
Hatfield, Herts	Flight test, production and development of Trident	Closed by BAe 1992
	Flight test of Comet, 125 and Sea Vixen	
Portsmouth, Hants	Production of Trident front fuselages	Closed by HSA 1968
Hawker Blackburn Division		
Brough, Yorks	Production and development of Buccaneer	BAE Systems
Dunsfold, Surrey	Assembly and flight test of Gnat and P1127	Closed by BAE Systems 2000
	Refurbishment of Hunters	
Hamble, Hants	Production of Gnat, Trident tails and wings	GE Aviation Aerostructures
Holme-on-Spalding Moor, Yorks	Flight test of Buccaneer	Closed by BAe 1982
Kingston, Surrey	Production and development of P1127 and P1154	Closed by BAe 1992
	Hunter assemblies	

promote its image in line with other large manufacturers, and to reduce administrative overheads by the centralization of back office functions such as marketing, sales, finance, manufacturing policies and so on. On 1 July 1963, the establishment of Hawker Siddeley Aviation (HSA) as the parent body of the many aircraft firms taken over by the Group meant the disappearance of many time-honoured pioneering company names, although most of these were still perpetuated in the titles of the three main divisions within HSA. From that date, all the various aircraft then in production or under development became known as Hawker Siddeley types in order better to communicate the Group's identity to the world at large. The chairman of Hawker Siddeley Aviation was Sir Arnold Hall, and the Vice-Chairman and Managing Director was John Lidbury.

Avro Whitworth Division

Avro Whitworth Division encompassed the former factories of Avro and Whitworth Gloster, then employing around 15,000 people. In the Manchester area, Woodford and Chadderton produced the Vulcan B.2, the HS748 and the 748MF, this last a military version of the 748 for the RAF that was later named the Andover. Sets of 748 components were being made for licence production by Hindustan Aeronautics at Kanpur, for the Indian Air Force. In addition, refurbishing work was in hand on Shackletons for RAF Coastal Command, and revising earlier models of the Vulcan to advanced standards. Final assembly of the 748s and Vulcans, together with test flying and some design work, took place at Woodford, Cheshire, which also had wind tunnel and other facilities. The Bracebridge Heath, Lincolnshire and Langar, Nottinghamshire sites carried out overhaul and repair.

At its other main centre, in Coventry, Avro Whitworth had factories and design offices at Baginton, Bitteswell and Whitley; Bitteswell was also engaged in modification and assembly work for other parts of the Group. Argosies were built at Baginton and then transported to Bitteswell for assembly and flight test. With delivery of the RAF's Argosies due for completion in early 1964 and other sales being very slow, the success of the follow-on project, the Hawker Siddeley 681, was vital for the factories.

De Havilland Division

Further south was the second large component of Hawker Siddeley Aviation, the de Havilland Division. This employed approximately 12,500 people in factories at Hatfield, Chester (Broughton) and Portsmouth, plus a design office at Edgware. The Division was mainly concerned with civil aircraft, although work was continuing on deliveries of its final military design, the Sea Vixen FAW.2 for the Royal Navy from Chester. Also at Chester, production was tapering off of Doves and Comet 4s, with five Comets on the line against poten-

tial orders and Doves being produced when required. Hatfield was busy flight testing the Trident tri-jet airliner and developing new versions for export customers. By May 1963 there were firm orders for thirty-six of the 125 executive jet built at Chester, from the batch of sixty that had been authorized by Hawker Siddeley. Fully equipped price to full airline standard was approximately £210,000. The Christchurch factory had closed in mid-1962, but Portsmouth was engaged in forward fuselage manufacture for the Trident.

Hawker Blackburn Division

The third component of Hawker Siddeley Aviation, the Hawker Blackburn Division, comprised five separate and widely distributed factories with 11,500 personnel engaged solely on military production and projects. In the south, the former Folland factory at Hamble continued production of the Gnat trainer, of which 105 were on order for RAF Flying Training Command. Licence production of the single-seat Gnat was also underway in India. The factory also built Trident wings and tails and HS748 wings.

At Kingston work was progressing on the P1127 and the P1154 V/STOL fighters. The P1154 was intended as a replacement for the RAF's Hunters and the Royal Navy's Sea Vixens (final examples of which were delivered in 1962), though in the event the Navy rejected the P1154 and ordered McDonnell Douglas Phantoms instead. Development and manufacture of the P1127 Kestrels for the tripartite V/STOL evaluation squadron was conceived. Dunsfold in

Surrey handled flight-testing of the Gnats and the Kingston-built Hawker types.

At the former Blackburn factory at Brough, near Hull, production was tapering off of the Buccaneer S.1, which equipped two squadrons of the Royal Navy, while the S.2 was in production for the RN and the South African Air Force. Final assembly and flight-testing of the Buccaneer was at nearby Holme-on-Spalding Moor, where the prototype S.2 had started trials following its first flight in May 1963.

Hawker Siddeley Dynamics

All the missiles, aerospace equipment and associated activities were grouped together as Hawker Siddeley Dynamics (HSD), which also took over the design, development and production of airscrews, air conditioning systems and electronic gear. All products were branded as 'Hawker Siddeley'. The Chairman was Sir Arnold Hall, Vice-Chairman and Managing Director Sir Aubrey Burke. The new company employed about 15,500 people, taking on the missile, aerospace and accessory projects and facilities of the former Avro, Whitworth Gloster and de Havilland Propeller companies. Headquarters were at Manor Road, Hatfield, which was concerned with Blue Streak satellite launcher and aerospace communications projects. The Stevenage factory was also involved with Blue Streak production, together with propeller contracts. Spadeadam in Cumbria was operated in conjunction with Rolls-Royce for the static testing of the Blue Streaks' RZ.2 engines before their long journey to the Woomera Launch Centre in Australia. At Whitley, Coventry, HSD has taken over Seaslug surface-to-air missile production. Manufacture of the Firestreak and Red Top missiles took place at Lostock, near Bolton.

One of the final Comets built was this Mk 4C, SA-R-7, delivered to the Saudi Arabian Government in June 1962. It crashed into the Italian Alps on 20 March 1963. BAE Systems

The Grouping of Hawker Siddeley's Non-Aerospace Industries

Simultaneously with the establishment of HSA and HSD, the Group set up Hawker Siddeley Industries, Hawker Siddeley International and Hawker Siddeley Holdings. Hawker Siddeley Industries was the holding company for the Group's industrial power interests (Brush, Fuller Electric, Mirrlees National, Petters and McLaren Fabrications), its metals companies (High Duty Alloys, Norstel and Templewood Hawksley) and Activated Sludge. Hawker Siddeley International was established to co-ordinate the export sales and promotion of all Hawker Siddeley Group products. Hawker Siddeley Holdings was formed to manage a number of the smaller companies trading in industrial products. Hawker Siddeley Canada was not affected, and remained a self-standing organization.

A Change of Government – Projects under Threat

The Labour Party won the General Election of 15 October 1964, but with an exceedingly slim majority of just four parliamentary seats. Confronted with a dire economic situation, the new Government decided to seriously trim expenditure and within days announced that prestige projects such as Concorde might be scrapped. The Ministry of Defence was known to be examining alternatives to Hawker Siddeley's HS681 military airlifter and P1154 V/STOL supersonic fighter.

On 14 January 1965, more than 5,000 workers from Hawker Siddeley's plants at Kingston, Dunsfold and Coventry, joined by BAC workers worried about the TSR2, gathered near Waterloo Station to take part in a protest march. They marched across Waterloo Bridge, along the Strand and Whitehall to Parliament Square, bringing much of central London to a halt. On leaving Parliament Square they marched on to Speaker's Corner in Hyde Park, where they were addressed by trade union representatives.

The *Evening Standard*'s headlines were 'We backed you at the poll they say' and 'The angry men are marching.' The paper continued:

> The giant protest march today by thousands of aircraft workers brought much of London to a halt. Traffic was brought to a standstill in Trafalgar Square and long queues stretched back along the Strand, Charing Cross Road, Whitehall and the Mall. As the first column reached Trafalgar Square police split it up. The marchers carried a coffin with the slogan 'The body of British aircraft' [actually with P1154 painted on it]. The first of the four batches of marchers had passed Trafalgar Square before the final one moved off.

Workers from Hawker Siddeley Kingston with placards and a coffin 'The body of British Aircraft' during their protest against the expected cancellation of P1154 on 14 January 1965. Author

Government Cancellation of Contracts

In the House of Commons on 2 February 1965, the Prime Minister, Harold Wilson, made a statement about the P1154, the P1127 and the HS681.

> The House will recall the ... many changes of policy about replacements for the RAF Hunter and the Royal Navy's Sea Vixen. In July 1963 the P1154 was going to meet both requirements ... In February 1964, this was all changed and the then Government decided to buy American Phantom aircraft as the Sea Vixen replacement ... Meanwhile, the P1154 was to go on to provide a replacement for the Hunter when that was withdrawn from service. I have to tell the House that this is not a practicable proposition. It is not so much the question of cost, though the present estimate, made when the aircraft is still only in the design stage, is a very heavy estimate indeed ... the problem here is that on these present estimated requirements, and on the latest realistic estimate of the remaining life of the Hunter aircraft, the P1154 will not be in service in time to serve as a Hunter replacement...
>
> In these circumstances, on defence grounds alone, quite apart from the cost argument, it will be necessary to extend the late Government's purchasing programme for Phantoms and to use this aircraft as a partial replacement for the Hunter. This is the only way to close the time gap. All of us regret it, but this has been forced on us by the facts. They will have British engines and will incorporate as many British components as possible. We are urgently examining the possibility of manufacturing or at any rate assembling them, and making some of the parts in this country...
>
> We have been urgently surveying the needs of our forces in the light of present revised estimates of commitments. We believe that there is an urgent need for an operational version of P1127 ... As soon as it can be negotiated, a contract will be placed for a limited development programme so that the RAF can have by the time they need it ... an aircraft which will in fact be first in the field, with vertical take-off for close support of our land forces...
>
> [The HS681 was also cancelled because] ...its development was authorized so late [by the previous Conservative Government] that it cannot enter service at a date which will meet the real needs of the Forces ... there appears to be no alternative to buying the American C-130 which, though offering a lower performance than the HS681, can be ready much earlier. The problem is having them there when they are needed.

There is, of course, a very considerable saving to the Exchequer. Each C-130 costs ... about one-third of the present very early estimate of the cost of the HS681, one-third per plane ... I do not think that the House can really ignore the saving ... but, even if that were not the issue at all, the question of timescale, having it for the right time, is the important one.

So, for the loss of two major projects – the HS681 and the P1154 – there would be a limited development programme for an operational version of the P1127 (which became the Harrier) and a development of the Comet (the Nimrod) to replace the Shackleton, which was also announced in Wilson's speech.

The American aircraft industry was a major beneficiary of these decisions, though eventually offset work was contracted to British firms. For example, BAC (Preston Division) manufactured tails for Phantoms while Hawker Siddeley at Brough became the British-based design organization qualified to clear modifications and technical instructions for the Phantom without reference to the manufacturers. Marshall of Cambridge became the UK completion centre for the C-130 Hercules.

Mass Redundancies

On the same day Hawker Siddeley announced 'On the basis of our knowledge today the redundancies in Hawker Siddeley Aviation will be in the region of 14,000 to take effect during 1965. The process will start immediately.' A few days later came the announcement that Hawker Siddeley's Baginton (Coventry) factory was to close. This was then followed by redundancies at Kingston and Hamble.

The Government – stung by Hawkers' announcement and the huge press coverage it received – reacted strongly. Roy Jenkins, Minister of Aviation, met Sir Arnold Hall and informed him that the Government could not accept the statement apparently made by the company that 14,000 redundancies would follow directly from the HS681 and P1154 cancellations. Jenkins estimated that, including indirect workers, about 3,000 people were employed at HSA on the HS681 and P1154, and that had they proceeded this would have built up to about 9,000 by the end of 1965. Other work announced by the Prime Minister would provide employment for about 1,300 by the end of the year, so that the direct net effect

of the changes on Hawker Siddeley Aviation workforce requirements over the next eleven months would be a reduction of some 7,700. This figure, not 14,000, was clearly the relevant one.

The Government had not been at fault in challenging Hawker Siddeley's figures, as the company in response amended their original statement, explaining that about 4,000 men would have been redundant in any case as a result of a rundown in Hawker Siddeley's aviation work over the past two years, quite apart from the cancellation of the HS681 and the P1154. The figure of 14,000 was based on a survey of all the companies within the Group and their workload expectations for the forthcoming year. This showed that the volume of factory space and number of employees substantially exceeded the amount of work in hand and in prospect. The new Nimrod and Harrier work would be on a much smaller scale than the cancelled HS681 and P1154 production programmes.

The Effect of the Cancellations

However, in its Annual Results for 1965 the Group stated it had 92,000 employees including HSA's 40,000 employees. So what were the true redundancy figures? It is unclear. At the same time it was reported that HSD had 15,000 staff. The cancellations had ramifications not only for HSA but for Hawker Siddeley Dynamics, High Duty Alloys (a Group subsidiary producing high-tech alloys for aero-engines and other specialized uses) and Bristol Siddeley. The Group further endeavoured to turn away from its dependency on aviation.

Sir Roy Dobson said that Hawker Siddeley was left with a considerable volume of work for the three or four years after the cancellations, but the changes removed the longer-term developments that would have provided production work in the future and kept the company at the forefront of military aeronautical technology in the 1970s – typically, throughout the early to mid-1960s Hawker Siddeley was spending £9m per year on research (c. £165m at 2012 prices).

The gloomier aspects of the cancellations and redundancies were mitigated not only by the orders for what eventually became the Nimrod and Harrier, but also by further Buccaneer and Trident orders, while the HS125 and HS748 had by that time each sold more than 100. Additionally, substantial programmes of modernization, repair

and spares supply for existing types were received.

Hawker Siddeley Dynamics suffered from the cancellation of the two HSA projects and BAC's TSR2, as it was due to supply equipment for all of them. In a change of strategy Hawker Siddeley Dynamics wisely decided to reduce its dependence on defence contracts, and to further diversify its activities into mechanical and electrical technologies.

De Havilland Canada Losses and Douglas

In 1965 De Havilland Canada made a loss, after Research and Development charges of £1.1m. This situation arose because the newer projects – the Turbo-Beaver, Twin Otter and Buffalo – incurred large R & D charges at a time when sales of older types had declined and sales of the new were not yet replacing them.

Meanwhile, the opportunity to manufacture aircraft components for Douglas Aircraft brought new life to the former Avro Canada's Malton plant in March 1963. DHC entered into a joint venture with Douglas to manufacture wings and tail assemblies for the DC-9 jetliner. The Douglas DC-9 sub-contract programme rose rapidly in size and complexity until it was producing more than double the amount of work originally contemplated, and by September 1965 DHC could not fund its part of the work. In the event, Douglas leased the plant from DHC with an option to buy it and would purchase the equipment and machinery needed for the DC-9 work.

By 1967 DHC had moved back into substantial profitability (CDN$5m), reflecting the income from the lease of the Malton plant and from sales of the new Buffalo and Twin Otter.

Further Rationalization in 1965

Quickly after the cancellations took effect on 1 April 1965, the historic HSA names were finally expunged: the de Havilland Division became the Hatfield Chester Division, Avro Whitworth the Manchester Division and Hawker Blackburn the Kingston-Brough Division. At the same time, HSA's headquarters moved back from the parent group's offices at Hawker Sidde-

Shortly after the cancellation of the P1154 and HS681 on 1 April 1965, the historic HSA names were finally expunged. At the same time HSA's headquarters moved back from the parent group's offices in St James's Square, London to Kingston-upon-Thames.
BAE Systems

ley House, 18 St James's Square, London SW1, to Richmond Road, Kingston-upon-Thames. The Group, which had moved to St James's Square in 1949, remained there.

As management was streamlined, Sir Arnold Hall, Managing Director of Hawker Siddeley Group, announced that the management structure of HSA was to be reorganized. He became Chairman of HSA while the divisional directors became executive directors of HSA, and boards of the Divisions were scrapped.

Sir Roy Dobson stood down as Chairman of the Group in 1967, remaining as a Director until his death the following year. He had been a commanding figure in the Hawker Siddeley Group, especially at Avro where he had started work as a mechanic in 1914, and had risen through the firm to Group Director level. Sir Arnold Hall, a far less ebullient and much more private figure, replaced him as Chairman and remained in that role until 1986, nine years after Hawker Siddeley's aviation interests had been nationalized.

For all the loss of identity by the UK-based parts of HSA, De Havilland Canada continued to trade under its name while the former Australian subsidiary was renamed Hawker De Havilland Australia.

The Plowden Report

On 16 December 1965 the report of the 'Committee of Inquiry into the Aircraft Industry', chaired by Lord Plowden, was published, which had been set up under the auspices of the Government to examine the aviation industry. Hawker Siddeley was uneasy about the conclusions of the report: Plowden acknowledged that the Group was one of the largest engineering groups in Britain, but still concluded that all major aviation projects would have to be collaborative and recommended a Government equity interest in industry. Whereas Plowden did not refer to an actual merger, a Government statement in the House of Commons recommended that a merger of Hawker Siddeley Aviation and Dynamics and BAC would be in the public interest. Throughout the late 1960s the Labour Government toyed with a merger between the two major UK aircraft and guided weapons manufacturers, with the Government having a holding of its own in any such arrangement.

In February 1967 the *Daily Mail* reported that the Government planned to buy the whole of BAC as the first stage of the planned BAC/Hawker Siddeley merger. It was expected to have a final holding of about 35 per cent in the merged company, the article stated; the cost to the taxpayer was expected to be not more than £40 million, and no parliamentary legislation would be needed. In the event, both firms managed to hold this off at the time, though it simmered in the background and eventually came to fruition with full-scale nationalization in 1977.

1967 – Devaluation and Other Developments

In the same year that Sir Roy departed his role on the HSG Board, future defence cuts were a cause for further concern. Work continued at a satisfactory level, but there was a worrying increase in costs caused by the Labour Government's devaluation of the exchange rate between the pound sterling and the US dollar rate on 19 November 1967. The devaluation raised import prices

By the end of 1967, 184 Hawker Siddeley 748s had been sold. G-AVRR, a 748 Series 2A fitted with the uprated Dart 532 engine, first flew at Woodford on 5 September 1967 and replaced G-ARAY as the company demonstrator. It is seen at Cape Town Airport in 1970.
Avro Heritage

but correspondingly reduced export prices, so the price of the HS125 executive jet fell, stimulating interest following a slowdown in sales earlier in the year. The sales record of the HS125 was already impressive: 146 had been ordered since its maiden flight five years earlier. Meanwhile, Manchester's HS748 was doing well with 184 sold and more orders received during the year.

HSA's workload was dominated by the thirty-eight Nimrods on order at Chester and Manchester, and by improved Harriers and the two-seater variant under development at Kingston. At Hatfield production of the Trident 2 for BEA was gathering pace and the company expected an order for the Trident 3B. Substantial refurbishment and modernizing business was continuing with Shackletons, Vulcans, Hunters (for export) and Sea Vixens. As a result of the rise of the number of the firm's aircraft in service, there had been a corresponding increase in the number of spares sold.

Production at Chester of the fuselages for the initial order for thirty-eight Nimrod MR.1s. XV258 and XV260 are at the front of the line. BAE Systems

LEFT: An Iraqi Air Force Hunter FGA.59 registered 585, refurbished at Kingston and Dunsfold in 1965. Author's collection

BELOW: The Buccaneer S.2 production line at Brough in 1965. Aircraft visible are nos 3–6 of the South African Air Force's order for sixteen, and no. 14 for the Royal Navy. The SAAF wanted to order an additional sixteen aircraft, but the Labour Government put an embargo on the order. BAE Systems

Redundancies and Factory Closures

The Labour Government's refusal to grant an export order to South Africa for a further sixteen Buccaneers owing to the apartheid policy of the South African Government, and the cancellation of eight for the Royal Navy, had resulted in the threat of redundancies at Brough, though the latter order was later reinstated. The Group determined to close two small factories: in 1968 the former Airspeed factory at Portsmouth latterly building Trident fuselages and that at Langar, Nottinghamshire, used for repair and modification by Avro, were closed. The

Trident work was transferred to Brough while Bitteswell inherited Langar's work.

Airbus

Most significantly in 1967, the HSG Board first started discussing Airbus. This was the first phase of a design study for the European Airbus project, which was nearing completion with French and German partners. The Annual Report stated:

Provided that the respective Governments agree late this year that the project should proceed HSG 'were confident that a highly competitive and commercially successful aircraft will be produced as a result of this international co-operation'.

These were prescient words, and evidence of the wisdom of the people in the commanding heights of the British aviation industry in those days! However, on 16 April 1969 Tony Benn, Minister of Technology, stated in the House of Commons that he had met the French and German Governments on 10 April, and:

[I] had to make it clear that Her Majesty's Government were not yet satisfied with all aspects

of the project, in particular with the market and economic prospects development costs and recovery, and the lack of a firm commitment to a European engine ... we have not pulled out of the Airbus project, but we were not satisfied that sufficient progress had been made to justify us in going ahead with it ... The position of Hawker Siddeley as a member of the [Airbus] consortium is not necessarily affected by this.

So after collaborating for two years with French and German firms in the design of what become known as the European Airbus, and which all three Governments had indicated an interest in supporting, the British Labour Government unilaterally withdrew from it. Hawker Siddeley was left with trying to find a way to benefit from the considerable contribution it had made to the project from 1967–69.

Hawker Siddeley Dynamics Refocuses at the End of the 1960s

Business in the company's well-established guided weapons divisions was diminishing as changes in the UK's Defence Programme took effect. Research and development

into guided weapons was curtailed, and the former Armstrong Whitworth factory at Whitley, Coventry, closed in 1968. With increased rationalization and diversification, staff numbers fell to 10,000 by 1969. Nevertheless, production continued at a high level and work was in hand on the development of two major guided missiles, the Martel air-to-surface missile and the Sea Dart shipborne air defence missile.

At the Space Division the IRIS satellite had been launched and gone into satisfactory operation and, as part of the MESH international consortium, the division was developing the TD satellite for ESRO and had won new contracts. As stage 1 of the European Space Launch Vehicle (Europa 1), Blue Streak had nine successful launchings from Woomera in 1967–70. However, in 1968 the Government decided it saw no economic justification for continuing investment in ELDO beyond the programme ending in 1971–72, resulting in the end of the development of space launcher vehicles.

The Industrial Automation division was selling simulators to the RAF, the Royal Australian Air Force and – for Concorde and Boeing 747 training – British Airways, which was formed by the merger of BOAC and BEA in 1974.

Recognizing that with changes of defence commitments the traditional business would diminish to some extent, HSD endeavoured to apply its electronic and mechanical technology to new commercial applications. These included electron beam welding equipment and electronic controls for industrial engines. Development of the air conditioning system for Concorde had been completed, and British Rail placed a design and development contract for the suspension and braking system for the Advanced Passenger Train. Automatic Test Equipment (TRACE) was in use with a number of important airlines in Europe and the USA. Hawker Siddeley Dynamics entered into an agreement with McDonnell Douglas to work jointly on a proposal for the NASA Space Shuttle project.

The model of the TV-guided HS-Matra Martel missile, which was employed on the Buccaneer. Author

De Havilland Canada in the late 1960s

De Havilland Canada sales for 1969 were $78m, substantially down from the 1968 figure of $108m (Canadian Dollars). Profit before interest of $3m was depressed by the lower turnover and the reduced utilization of facilities, and the final payments from McDonnell Douglas under the 1965 agreement produced only a small amount of revenue compared with the substantial receipts in preceding years. The tight credit situation in Canada seriously affected the amount of capital available for financing export orders, which had always represented an important part of the company's business.

Sales of Twin Otter aircraft in 1969, especially in the USA, were at a reduced level, the shortage of credit particularly affecting operators of this class of aircraft. Development of the type continued and a steady market was expected to continue for several years. The company was continuing to manufacture the Buffalo, which had received new orders from the Brazilian and Peruvian air forces, and deliveries to these customers would keep production running until 1972.

Building on their experience with the Buffalo, from 1967 DHC had been considering building a 48-seater turboprop STOL aircraft for short haul inter-city work. This caused a conflict of interest within the Hawker Siddeley Group as the project was in competition with the HS748 and the projected HS146, and the Group was not willing to invest in it. The Canadian Government, recognizing the importance of the company to the country's economy, encouraged the company to proceed with it. This aircraft eventually emerged as the Dash 7.

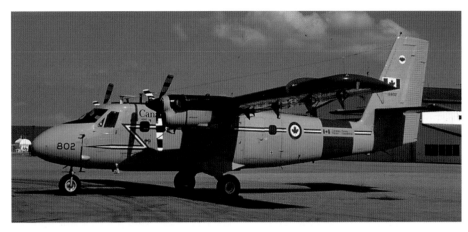

DHC Twin Otter 13802 of the Canadian Armed Forces. The Twin Otter sold well, especially in the USA, but was seriously affected by the peaks and troughs of the feederliner market. Author's collection

DHC Buffalo 5483 delivered to the Canadian Armed Forces in 1966. The Buffalo was not adopted by the US Army and did not emulate the Caribou's success. Author's collection

Hawker de Havilland Australia

Though the former de Havilland Australia (from 1965 Hawker de Havilland) was much smaller than DHC, it had built aircraft in World War Two and after, for example Vampires for the RAAF in the 1950s and its own design, the Drover. However, it ploughed a very different furrow from that of HSA's other companies.

In the 1960s Hawker de Havilland (HdH) contracted to maintain several RAAF types including the DHC-4 Caribous, and subsequently maintained aircraft for the Singapore Air Force. The Macchi jet trainers chosen for the RAAF were assembled in Australia by Commonwealth Aircraft, with HdH manufacturing parts for the airframe and the Bristol Siddeley Viper engines. The company also provided staff for the operation and maintenance for a deep space tracking station in Northern Australia to monitor the ELDO programme launches from Woomera.

Divisional Performance in 1969

HSA and HSD joint sales for 1969 totalled £200.7m with a profit of only £5.6m, or 2.8 per cent. (At 2012 prices: sales £2.75bn, profit £76.5m.) In contrast, Hawker Siddeley Group's Electrical Engineering Division had sales of £93.4m and profits of £5.7m, while the Mechanical and Metal Division equivalent figures were £84.5m and £5.7m. These other divisions were making proportionally much higher profits.

In 1969 HSA had received a large order from BEA for the Trident 3B and a small order from Cyprus Airways for the Trident 2E, too. By then BEA Tridents were making 300 autolands per month on regular services in normal weather as part of the work leading to its use in bad visibility. The HS125 had received fifty orders in the year, mainly for export against keen competition. In contrast, the HS748 had a disappointing sales year but the Chadderton and Woodford factory were fully employed on dealing with the large backlog of orders. HSA was also looking into a VTOL inter-city airliner with the possibility of a wider future military application; this manifested itself as the HS141 proposal and was Hatfield's last VTOL airliner proposal.

The Harrier had successfully entered service with the Royal Air Force and a first order was obtained from the United States Marine Corps in December 1969. The agreement with McDonnell Douglas was directed to servicing and widening this important achievement. The award of this order validated the company's technical supremacy in vertical take-off.

Finally, the aged Shackletons would be replaced as delivery of Nimrods to the RAF started in late 1969. As it was the only jet maritime reconnaissance aircraft in the world there were hopes of overseas sales, though none ever materialized. As these new types were introduced into service, orders for refurbished Hunters continued to be received from many air forces throughout the world, providing continuing work for Kingston and Dunsfold.

HSA's Major International Agreements in 1969

During 1969 HSA entered into three agreements with overseas interests that were of considerable and long-lasting importance:

- An arrangement with French, German and Dutch associates for the design, development and production of a large regional civil aircraft, the European Airbus A300B, to go into airline service towards the end of 1973.
- An arrangement with the Beech Aircraft Corporation in the USA for joint design, development, manufacture and marketing of the Hawker Siddeley 125 business jet.
- An agreement with the McDonnell Douglas Corporation in the USA for the marketing and manufacture of the Harrier.

Under the Airbus arrangements, the company moved from being a partner with 37.5 per cent share to become a subcontractor responsible for the complete design of the wing in detail, and the manufacture of the greater part of it. The company was also involved in the overall design of the aircraft, so ensuring that its expertise in this important class of aircraft would be maintained despite the Government's withdrawal from the project. HSA shared the view of the consortium of which it was a part, in that a substantial market existed for the aircraft over the next fifteen years, and the new arrangement meant that the amount of work accruing to its factories would be considerable. The launch costs of the project were some £180m and these were provided, for the greater part, by the French, German and Dutch governments. HSA was convinced that to secure a sound basis for funding development and to create the possibility of a 'home' market substantially greater than the UK could provide, it was

necessary to handle projects of this size on an international basis.

The Board felt that the level of commercial risk the company had in this project was in no way abnormal, and was well within the area in which it had successfully handled aerospace ventures in the past.

The Group at the Beginning of the 1970s

At the beginning of the new decade HSD was in a healthy position, making sales of

£454m with a gross profit of £21.2m and a net profit of £8.1m; exports from the UK were £90m (2012 equivalents: £5.9bn, £275m, £105m and £1.17m). The Group had 80,000 employees, of which 15,000 worked abroad. With sales of £226.8m, the Aviation and Dynamics Divisions represented approximately half of the Group's sales, but they produced the lowest returns: only £5.6m (see Appendix IV).

Substantial deliveries were achieved during the year, but the company's activities were unlikely to continue at that level as – apart from the Nimrod and Harrier – HSA

ABOVE: **In December 1969 the US Marine Corps placed an order for the Harrier. This is the fourth aircraft, 158387, which made its first flight in February 1971.** BAE Systems

BELOW: **In December 1969 Hawker Siddeley and the Beech Aircraft Corporation agreed the joint production and marketing of the Hawker Siddeley 125. The US registration N125BH reflects this arrangement.** BAE Systems

had not received a Government contract for a new airframe since 1963. By the end of 1971 the Group would need work to replace the Buccaneer and to fill the gap as HS748 and Trident production slowed down. HSA was planning to reduce its workforce by 2,000, but in the event further Buccaneer and Nimrod orders precluded this.

ABOVE: Hawker Siddeley's major military programmes in the 1970s were the Harrier, Buccaneer and Nimrod. The three aircraft brought together for this publicity shot are Harrier GR.1 XV753, Buccaneer S.2 XV350 and Nimrod MR.1 XV229.
BAE Systems

Civil Aircraft Progress

By the end of 1970 good progress was being made in the design and development of the Airbus A300B with HSA's European associates and manufacture of prototypes was gathering impetus. It had become evident that no European competitor to the A300B would emerge, and marketing efforts indicated that the aircraft had good prospects for substantial sales into the 1980s. Hatfield with its workforce of 5,500 was the technical design centre for the company's participation in the A300B programme; Hatfield was also completing two Trident 3Bs per month for BEA. Chester, the production site for the A300B wings, had a workforce of 4,200 and was building three HS125 per month, plus Nimrod fuselages.

In only eight years since its first flight the HS125 business jet had rung up 243 sales; 1970's results were disappointing, but this was mainly due to the difficult financial climate in the USA, which had been depressing the sales of all classes of executive aircraft. A new development with greater range and seating capacity, the HS125-600, had made its first flight. Although the market for executive aircraft was far from buoy-

RIGHT: An Airbus advertisement showing the A300 prototype under construction in Toulouse. Even though Hawker Siddeley had been relegated to the position of a subcontractor, it received equal billing with France and Germany. Author

ant, it was expected that the HS125 would continue to sell for many years. The HS748 had retained its appeal; of the 246 sold, thirty-one were ordered during 1970. HSA Manchester at Woodford and Chadderton had a workforce of 8,800, building 748s and Nimrods.

Military Programmes

Deliveries of Buccaneers, Nimrods and Harriers were being made to the RAF. Boosting Harrier production even more, an order was received from the US Marine Corps for delivery in 1972, with advanced material

Airbus A300s nos 2–5 on the production line at Toulouse in January 1973. From the left: F-WUAC in Air France livery, F-WUAD in Lufthansa livery, F-WUAD for Air Inter and F-BVGA for Air France. BAE Systems

of US commuter operators, worsening in the second half of 1971, caused Twin Otter orders to lag and the assembly line was again temporarily stopped until new orders justified a restart of production.

After encouraging DHC to continue to work on the DHC-7 STOL airliner in the face of opposition from the UK Group Board, from mid-1970 the Canadian Government provided twelve months' funding of research and development.

Continuing Success in 1971

Despite continuing uncertainties about the future, the aerospace divisions maintained their sales performance in 1971 and for the first time included deliveries of Harriers to the United States Marine Corps; the USMC had placed an order for Harriers for delivery in 1973, with advance material provisioning for an additional supply of these aircraft in 1974.

In competition with the British Aircraft Corporation, HSA had been awarded the contract to design, develop and produce a new jet trainer, the HS1182 (later named the Hawk) for the Royal Air Force. This aircraft was accurately predicted to have a good export potential and a correspondingly long production run. Elsewhere, the Government had placed additional orders for the Buccaneer and Nimrod, and HSA was awarded a contract to carry out the conversion of the Victor B.2s to the tanker role.

On the civil side, a major breakthrough was achieved when an order was received in 1971 from the People's Republic of China for six Trident 2Es, opening up a significant

provisioning for further deliveries in 1973. Substantial export orders for refurbished Hunters were continuing, including orders for thirty aircraft from the Swiss Government and for twenty-five from Singapore.

Following the sad demise of their manufacturer in 1970, some twenty-four Handley Page Victor B.2s were gathered at Woodford so that HSA could develop conversions for them into the flight refuelling role. At the same time, responsibility for the supply of spares for Handley Page's Victors and Hastings in the Royal Air Force was passed to the company.

The Kingston Brough division had a workforce of 9,900. At Brough the factory was busy with Buccaneer production, Harrier wings and centre sections, Trident 3 fuselages and heavy machining on the A300B Airbus, along with support work for the RAF's American-built Phantoms. Production of Harriers and refurbished Hunters remained at Kingston/Dunsfold. There were two other small HSA facilities: Hamble with a workforce of 1,700 working on Harrier and other group products, and Bitteswell employing 1,200 on refurbishing Hunters and Gnats, and group subcontract.

RIGHT: The delivery ceremony for the first Trident 2E for China at Hatfield in November 1972. In the front row on the left is Sir Arnold Hall, Chairman of the Hawker Siddeley Group from 1967 until 1986, and on the right is Michael Heseltine, then a Minister of State for the Department of Transport. BAE Systems

DHC

De Havilland Canada sales were low in 1970 and the company was obliged to suspend manufacture of Twin Otter aircraft for several months. The reduction in turnover and the consequent under-utilization of manufacturing facilities resulted in a trading loss. However, sales increased in 1971, mainly due to the higher volume of Twin Otter production and spares deliveries, which more than offset a reduction in the number of Caribou and Buffalo aircraft delivered. The company recorded a substantially improved result compared with the previous year. The continuing problems

The second Trident 2E for China with delivery registration G-AZFU, which later became B-2202 Trident 3B for BEA at Hatfield in January 1973.
BAE Systems

new market. Sales of both the HS748 and HS125 passed the 250 mark. Although the market for executive aircraft remained far from buoyant, in 1971 new orders for the HS125 had showed a slight improvement compared with the preceding year. The HS748 continued to be ordered in modest numbers and remained popular with its fifty operators throughout the world. Lastly, in what was to prove to be a momentous step for the company and the UK aircraft industry, the first Airbus wing, designed and manufactured by HSA, was delivered in 1971.

Improved Profits

In 1972 HSA and HSD had improved profits of £15.6m (2013 = £186m) generated by sales of £183.1m (2013 = £2.2bn), though these were reduced on the previous year. Deliveries continued of the Aviation division's aircraft and the order book stayed strong: there was a marked increase in sales of the HS125 and orders were finalized for Harriers for the US Marine Corps for delivery in 1974. Work was proceeding on the design of the HS1182 (Hawk) jet trainer and a contract to supply 175 to the RAF was agreed in March 1972.

The maiden flights of the first and second prototype Airbus A300Bs were a step change for the programme. Excellent progress was made in the flight development work and with the accumulation of data required for the certification of the aircraft by the airworthiness authorities. The early flight experience was satisfactory and early indications were that no problems of a serious nature were likely to be encountered in bringing the aircraft to certification

standard, or in meeting performance requirements. The full Certificate of Airworthiness for the Airbus was awarded in 1973 and scheduled services started by Air France on the London–Paris route. A series of long-distance flight tests in January 1974 demonstrated that the A300 was a very fuel-efficient aircraft, a characteristic of some importance in view of the scarcity and rising cost of fuel. It also set a new standard in quietness.

Throughout the 1970s HSA and other firms researched into quiet transport aircraft with steep gradient operations and vertical take-off. As a result, an agreement was reached with VFW-Fokker and Dornier in Germany to explore the joint development of a new generation of quiet short/medium-haul passenger aircraft; in the event, this never came to fruition.

Restructuring at HSD

Aware of the continuing weakness in the defence market, HSD been developing new products making use of the technology derived from their guided weapon activity. Early in 1971, it judged that the time had come to set up some of these products in a separately managed business, so while Hawker Siddeley Dynamics concentrated on weapon, space and aircraft equipment activities, Hawker Siddeley Dynamics Engineering managed the build-up of the business in electronic controls, automatic test and handling equipment and electron beam welding machines. Hawker Siddeley Dynamics Holdings was established as a supervisory company over the two separate businesses.

1973 Queen's Award to Industry

The company was a consistent exporter of its aircraft, with over fifty sold to export customers in 1973. During the year, HSA's design, research and production activities continued at much the same level as in the previous year, with a stable workforce of 32,000, the order book remaining very strong. The fourth and final Trident order was received from China for fifteen Trident 2E aircraft worth some £50m, bringing the total Chinese order to thirty-five aircraft worth £120m (£125bn at 2012 prices). By the end of 1973 the first six of these had been delivered. Demand for the HS125 and the HS748 continued at a satisfactory level and a total of 346 HS125s and 296 HS748s had been sold by then.

In 1973 the Queen's Award to Industry was awarded to HSA Kingston for export achievement with the Harrier, deservedly so as the United States Marine Corps had ordered a further batch of twenty for delivery in 1975–76, completing their planned programme for a total of 110 aircraft. At Kingston, Harrier designs under development included the first mention of what went on to become the Sea Harrier and, with McDonnell Douglas, the Harrier 2. Also at Kingston, design and development of the new Hawk was proceeding.

HS146

After a long gestation under de Havilland and then Hawker Siddeley involving considerable technical and market research, a

In 1973 the Queen's Award to Industry was awarded to HSA Kingston for export achievement with the Harrier, marking its special achievement in selling it to the US Marines. BAE Systems

design for a new jet feeder-liner, the HS146, had evolved. It was designed to replace the Viscount and similar aircraft and was able to operate in its smaller seventy-seat version from unpaved and short airfields, while a larger version would operate from conventional longer runways and carry about 100 passengers.

In 1971 talks had begun with the Conservative Government requesting support to develop the HS146 and two years later the Government agreed to make an investment fixed at 50 per cent of the launch costs, which totalled £46m, and with an according share in profits. The remainder of the finance needed to be found by Hawker Siddeley Group. The aircraft was then planned to make its first flight about December 1975 and enter service in 1977 to neatly follow on from the Trident on the Hatfield production line.

Canadian Nationalization of DHC

Problems beset DHC throughout 1972, operations being affected by a strike of manufacturing employees from mid-January to mid-September. The company management and supervisory staff made an outstanding effort during the period of the strike and, by completing a number of aircraft and delivering spares, were able to help keep the company afloat.

The dispute between Hawker Siddeley in the UK and DHC about the DHC-7 had continued: the Canadian Government was still encouraging the firm to develop the aircraft, having offered financial support until December 1971, while HSG argued that it had its own HS748 in production and the jet 146 under development. In October 1972 the Canadian Government granted substantial financial assistance to the building of two DHC-7 pre-production prototypes to fly in late 1974. As the Canadian Government did not feel able to enter into an arrangement of this kind with a foreign-owned (i.e. British) company, an agreement was reached with HSG that Canada would have an option to acquire either the whole of the Group's shareholding or a minority interest in DHC, a clear threat to the Group's ownership, which would expire at the end of June 1974. Just before the option ran out the Canadian Government acquired 99.7 per cent of de Havilland Canada from Hawker Siddeley for CDN$38.8m (£16m, or £163m at 2012 prices).

In its Annual Report for 1974 Hawker Siddeley expressed a deep sense of injustice at the enforced nationalization of its aviation interests by the Canadian Government, though according to some sources HSG was actually glad to sell. The Board emphasized to its shareholders that it was diversifying and now held a significant place in the mechanical and electrical engineering world. It continued to own 60 per cent

The Hawker Siddeley Group and its divisions in 1971. BAE Systems

of Hawker Siddeley Canada with its large engineering concerns, including Orenda aero-engines that had originally been an Avro Canada firm.

The Threat of Nationalization in the UK

During 1973 the oil crisis and the UK miners' strike resulted in a three-day working week being enforced by the Conservative Government on all employers. While this had disrupted production, demand for products continued to run at a high level as the Group weathered the storm.

The Conservative Government was narrowly defeated in a General Election in February 1974, and Labour returned to power with a minority government. A second election was held in October and Labour was returned with a wafer-thin parliamentary majority of three. However, Labour felt able to announce that the aircraft industry (and others) would be nationalized. Naturally, the Group regarded this as a major threat to its future even though it had substantial non-aviation interests that accounted for 34 per cent of its sales and 41 per cent of its profit in 1974 (£188.1m and £18.8m, or £1.8bn and £179m at 2012 prices).

Hawker Siddeley and the British Aircraft Corporation compared in 1974[3]

	HSA & HSD	HSG in total	BAC
Employees	34000	82400	34000
Sales	£201.9m	£553.9m	£174.3m
Net profit	£18.8m	£23.4m	£5.87m

The Chairman Argues against Nationalization

In a leaflet distributed in early September to all HSA and HSD employees about the nationalization, Sir Arnold Hall wrote:

This is an issue of a personal kind for everyone who will be affected by it, not to be left to the whims and dogma of a few ... I can see no evidence that nationalization has led to improvement in the efficiency of industry, or in the earnings in industry or in conditions of work – can you?

The report of a joint working party of the Labour Party, TUC and CBI published the previous month had said that the industry's performance was poor and that large Government investment in it justified

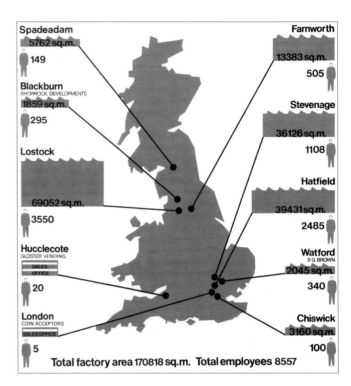

The Hawker Siddeley Dynamics and Hawker Siddeley Dynamics Engineering sites in 1971. The Stevenage and Lostock plants are still in aerospace, the former with Astrium and the latter with MBDA. Astrium

BELOW: The Hawker Siddeley Aviation sites in 1974. Only the Brough site is still an aerospace factory, as part of BAE Systems. BAE Systems

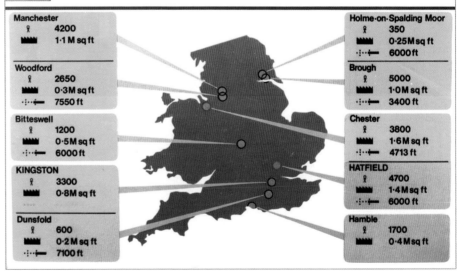

nationalization. Sir Arnold replied that the industry's performance in export had been exemplary and that putting a lot of money into an industry is no justification for owning it. Of every £1 spent by Government on civil aviation over the last ten years, 92p had gone on Concorde and the Rolls-Royce RB.211 engine, a little under 3p went to HSA and 5p went elsewhere in the industry.

Individual workers in HSA should take pride in their achievements, Sir Arnold continued:

If you are working on HS748, HS125 or Airbus A300B, keep in mind that you wouldn't be working on them except for the enterprise of the company, because there isn't a penny of Government money in any of them, and the Government wanted nothing to do with them anyway.

Ask yourself whether you believe that we really made the mess of it that those who wrote the Working Party Papers ... have the nerve to suggest.

Sales Maintained

During 1974 the number of HSA employees increased marginally over that of 1973, with production and design activities at much the same level as the previous year, despite difficulties caused by energy restrictions and shortages of materials. The oil price shock of 1973 also affected sales of the HS125 and HS748 aircraft, but the company was confident that as the economic and business climate improved, demand for the HS125 would return. They were proved right, as by the end of 1975, sales of the 125 totalled 348. The increase in fuel prices accelerated the development of the turbofan-powered series 700, which first flew in 1976 powered by the Garrett AiResearch TFE731, and production of which was due to reach three per month by the end of 1977.

Harrier deliveries to the US Marine Corps continued through 1974 against their total order for 110 aircraft. The Royal Navy was maintaining its interest in a naval Harrier, and although no decision on this project had yet been taken by the Government, HSA assessed it would have a strong appeal to a number of overseas navies. Work on possible Harrier developments funded by the USA and UK continued with the company's American

licensee, McDonnell Douglas. The Hawk trainer for the RAF had made a successful first flight in August and was demonstrated for the first time (the first of many) at the 1974 Farnborough International Air Show.

The HS146

In June 1974 HSA informed the Government that the HS146 was no longer financially viable, and on 21 October announced that all work on the HS146 would cease and that about 250 redundancies could be expected. HSA had no firm price to offer its customers so there was simply no basis for a contract and no reasonable hope of orders. In August the HS146 project status review had indicated that the development costs would far surpass £92m and might exceed £200m. Although the British Government's share of development costs was adjusted for inflation, Hawker Siddeley was not prepared to continue spending on the project.

The unilateral HSA announcement of a halt to work on the HS146 led to a dispute with the Government and involved the unions, who mobilized support from the local MP and Tony Benn, the Minister for Technology who oversaw aviation. Anxious to present their case, the workers demonstrated outside Parliament, while a delegation led by Hatfield shop stewards went to 10 Downing Street to hand in a petition. After lengthy negotiations in the House of Commons, on 9 December Tony Benn

announced that the project would be kept in being: all jigs, tools, drawings and design capacity would be maintained until the nationalized aircraft industry was fully established and could review the project and consider where to proceed with it. The Hawker Siddeley Annual Report 1974 stated:

> Meantime, keeping the design [the 146] on the back burner has absorbed several million pounds of Government funding since October 1974, when Hawker Siddeley decided to stop spending on it. A small team has been kept working on the HS146 ... to give colour to Government statements that a nationalized corporation will retain the option of reactivating this project.

Hawker Siddeley Aviation up to Nationalization

The aerospace sales of HSA and HSD together totalled £242.5 million in 1975 (up more than 20 per cent from 1974), on which the pre-tax profit was £22.5 million (up 6.6 per cent).

Completion of the thirty-five Tridents ordered by the Chinese civil aviation authority was continuing to occupy the Hatfield production line and new orders thereafter seem unlikely. As work on the HS146 was only continuing on a Government-sponsored basis, there was a likelihood of substantial redundancies as the Trident production line ran down.

The HS748 continued to sell well with 185 airliner sales and 130 military transport sales. The company had high hopes that the maritime surveillance version of the 748 – the Coastguarder, which flew in early 1977 – would sell well and give a new lease of life to the military HS748. Production at Chadderton and Woodford was running at two per month. The 125 executive jet continued to sell well despite the 1973 oil crisis, the turbofan-powered series 700 giving a boost to sales.

The Airbus wing production contract maintained its importance, not only because it had kept the British industry involved in the Airbus programme after the Government elected not to participate, but also because it has brought Hawker Siddeley to the forefront of latest wing technology, including supercritical wing aerodynamics. In 1974 further orders for wing sets had been received for the Airbus, which by then had orders and options covering over forty aircraft. The A300 entered service with Air

HB-VFA, a Hawker Siddeley 125-700, which first flew in September 1977. The 125-700 was the first turbofan-powered version of the 125: the Viper engines were replaced by the American-built Garrett TFE731. BAE Systems

An early Hawk T.1, XX168, flying over Dunsfold. It made its maiden flight from there on 4 April 1977 and was probably the last aircraft completed by Hawker Siddeley prior to nationalization.
BAE Systems

France in May 1974 and demonstrated a high degree of reliability and economy. The B4 version with increased range received its type certification and entered service with a charter company, Germanair, in June that year.

Production of the Harrier was maintained with a batch of twenty-four Sea Harriers for the Royal Navy, and the forthcoming US Marine Corps order for some 345 of the AV-8B model would involve HSA, Rolls-Royce and certain equipment manufacturers in approximately 48 per cent of the total contract value, with HSA being responsible for making the fuselages from the air intakes aft.

The trials programme for the Hawk was almost complete at Dunsfold, and with 175 ordered by the RAF, this would be an important product for many years to come; higher performance variants for the 1980s were already on the drawing board. A small number of Nimrods were still being built at Woodford and in 1976 the first Nimrod MR.1s returned to the factory for conversion to MR.2 standard. Design work on the airborne early warning (AEW) version of the Nimrod was continuing and a contract was placed to build it just before nationalization. Finally, production of the long-serving Buccaneer (which had first flown in 1958) was gradually coming to an end, while the Victor K.2 tanker conversions were only finally completed in 1978.

In the last few years prior to nationalization the number of those employed by HSD had fallen from 15,500 when it was established in 1963 to 7,000. The Division had expanded its skills into non-aviation

sectors owing to a rightful concern about aerospace's vulnerability as a political football.

Following lengthy trials production had begun on the Linescan infra-red camera and was continuing on Martel, a television-guided air-to-surface weapon. Design and development of what became the Sky Flash missile was proceeding and was rightly predicted as having good potential.

Notwithstanding the cancellation of the Blue Streak launch vehicle programme by the European Launcher Development organization, the Space division was heavily involved in consortium manufacture of satellites. The volume of work connected with aircraft and hovercraft propellers had increased, but prospects for aircraft air-conditioning were less promising, due in part to the dearth of new types of aircraft being developed.

Nationalization and Afterwards

The Government bill to nationalize both the aircraft and shipbuilding industries was eventually passed into law in March 1977. Thus from 29 April 1977, Hawker Siddeley Aviation and Hawker Siddeley Dynamics, the British Aircraft Corporation and Scottish Aviation joined together to become British Aerospace. The Government paid a total of £115m compensation to the Hawker Siddeley Group for nationalization of the HSA and HSD. Hawker Siddeley unsuccessfully contested this settlement, which the Group held to be unfair.

In the last complete year prior to nationalization – 1976 – Hawker Siddeley Aviation and Dynamics had combined sales of £242m (2013 = £1.7bn) and announced a profit after tax of £13.7m (2013 = £97m), which was a fall from the previous year. Total Group sales were £732m and total net profits were £37.5m.

The Hawker Siddeley Group continued as a major international mechanical and electrical engineering group with some 50,000 employees. Principal member companies included Hawker Siddeley Canada, the Brush Group, Crompton Parkinson, Petter and Mirrlees Blackstone. Group companies with aerospace products and equipment that were not nationalized included Hawker Siddeley Dynamics Engineering, Gloster Saro, High Duty Alloys and Hawker de Havilland Australia.

Sir Arnold Hall remained as Chairman of Hawker Siddeley until 1986, relinquishing the role of Managing Director in 1984. The last tie with the past was the death of Sir Tom Sopwith, the founder of the company, in 1989 at age 101. Only two years later the industrial conglomerate BTR acquired Hawker Siddeley for £1.55bn, and in 1999 BTR and Seibe merged to form Invensys, a British multinational engineering and information technology company. At the end of July 2013 the takeover of Invensys by the French Schneider Electric for £3.4bn was announced. The company's name still survives in Hawker Siddeley Switchgear, a British manufacturer of electrical switchgear and overhead line equipment for the railways. However, this seems a terribly sad epitaph.

CHAPTER THREE

Legacy Military Aircraft Programmes

Hawker Sea Hawk

The basic design of the Hawker P1040, which was later named the Sea Hawk, was supervised by Sir Sydney Camm in 1944. Initial hopes of a RAF order were misplaced, but in December 1945 the Royal Navy issued specification N7/46 for a carrier-borne interceptor; an order was placed two months later for three prototypes and one structural-test example.

In those early years of jet flight there was doubt in some quarters as to the suitability of Hawker's placing the air intakes for the Rolls-Royce Nene turbojet in the stub-wing leading edges, discharging at low velocity into a plenum chamber. Immediately aft of the turbine the jet-pipe was 'bifurcated' (divided), the two exhausts carefully faired-in aft of the trailing edge. Hawker claimed that this arrangement greatly reduced the frictional loss associated with long intake and exhaust systems, and at the same time afforded valuable space for equipment and fuel tanks fore and aft of the engine. After rigorous testing the configuration was proved acceptable, and by contrast all other features of the design were conventional.

The prototype P1040, VP401, was first flown from Boscombe Down on 2 September 1947 by Bill Humble, Hawker's chief test pilot. The first prototype N7/46 – which was navalized with folding wings and cannon – was VP413, which first flew on 31 August 1948. During 1949 this aircraft twice carried out deck landing trials on an aircraft carrier. A further prototype, VP422, flew in 1949 and in November 1951 the first production Sea Hawk, WF143 with a higher-powered 5,000lb thrust Nene, took to the air, with the wingspan widened from 36ft 6in (11.13m) to 39ft (11.89m), a revised cockpit hood and other refinements. Trials continued with other early aircraft, and other modifications were introduced, which included an acorn fairing at the front of the vertical and horizontal tail to smooth out a flow irregularity.

Production Transferred to Armstrong Whitworth

During 1952 with the Hunter ordered into 'super-priority' production by the Government, Hawker's Kingston and Langley factories were so overloaded that all production of the Sea Hawk was passed to Armstrong Whitworth, another Hawker Siddeley company, which had capacity to take on this work; by August 1952, all jigs and parts had been transferred to Armstrong Whitworth at Baginton and Bitteswell. Owing to the urgent need for these aircraft, rear fuselage manufacture was sub-contracted to Flight Refuelling in Wimborne. Only thirty-five Sea Hawks were completed by Hawker, and the first Baginton-built and Bitteswell-assembled Sea Hawk, WF162, emerged in December 1952. During the first half of 1953, sixty Sea Hawk F.1s were flown from Bitteswell. The F.1s were followed by forty F.2s.

The F.2 was soon superseded by the FB.3 fighter/bomber. Externally, the FB.3 resembled the previous marks with a built-in armament of four 20mm cannon, but it was also capable of carrying bombs. Next came the FGA.4 fighter/ground attack variant, which had attachments for underwing bombs, rockets and other offensive stores, in addition to the guns. The FGA.4 was the first mark with powered ailerons and was a popular machine among pilots of the Fleet Air Arm for its docility, comfort and quietness.

The final development was the FGA.6 with a higher-powered 5,200lb Nene and the ability to carry a greater complement of stores than the earlier versions. The FGA.6 could carry a 75gal fuel tank mounted on the pylon inboard of the wing fold and further pylons, outboard of the fold, could carry 500lb bombs or 60lb air-to-ground rockets. The four fuselage-mounted 20mm cannon were retained. Bitteswell assembled eighty-seven new FGA.6s and converted many of the ninety-seven FGA.4s to FGA.6 standard.

The third prototype and second navalized Sea Hawk, VP422, being flown by Hawker's chief test pilot 'Wimpey' Wade, who took over from Bill Humble and carried out the aircraft's initial testing. BAE Systems

NATO 'Off-Shore' Contracts

At the height of the Cold War in the early 1950s the USA, anxious to ensure that NATO countries in Western Europe could defend themselves from possible Soviet aggression, placed orders with aircraft firms in NATO countries to supply their aircraft to the armed forces of their own or other NATO countries, and the cost was paid in dollars by the USA – American manufacturers were so overstretched that they could not fulfil this demand themselves. Hawker Siddeley was a beneficiary of these 'off-shore' contracts, to supply both Sea Hawks and Hunters.

In late 1952 Hawker Siddeley received the first of these orders, a $13m (£4.6m) contract for more than 100 Sea Hawks for the Royal Navy. A further off-shore contract worth $5m (£1.9m) was signed in June 1954, then another worth $6.4m (£2.4m) in May 1956; at the time the recipients of these aircraft were unspecified, but they proved to be Holland and West Germany.

XE456, a Sea Hawk FGA.6 built at Baginton and flown from Bitteswell in January 1956. It was exhibited at the 1956 Farnborough Air Show. It remained with the manufacturer for trials. BAE Systems

The last of twenty-two Sea Hawk F.50s for the Dutch Navy at Bitteswell in January 1958; it was delivered later that month. Ray Williams

Exports

The Sea Hawk production lines at Baginton and Bitteswell closed at the end of 1955 but the third US 'offshore' order in 1956 resulted in a new lease of life and the first of twenty-two Sea Hawk F.50s – equivalent to the FGA.6 – was delivered to the Dutch Navy in May 1957. The sixty-eight German machines that followed on the production line were designated the F.100 – basically the latest FGA.6 type – and the F.101, which could carry radar in a specially developed underwing pod. All the German machines had a taller fin to improve handling. They carried full deck-landing equipment and retained the folding wing so that their pilots could use the aircraft carriers of other NATO nations (as Germany had none of its own). These navies were not the last to order the Sea Hawk, however, as in December 1958 the Indian Navy bought fourteen new aircraft, delivered in 1961, and sixteen refurbished ex-Royal Navy FB.3s, delivery of which was only completed in 1963.

Sea Hawks in Service

The first Sea Hawk squadron was No. 806, which was formed in spring 1953 at Brawdy in Pembrokeshire. Emblazoned with the Ace of Diamonds insignia, they made a vivid impression at the Coronation Fleet Review at Spithead in June 1953, flying in company with prototype Sea Venoms at the rear of the flypast.

It was not long before the Sea Hawk had the opportunity to show its mettle, especially in the ground-attack role. During the

Specification – Hawker Sea Hawk FGA.6	
Length	39ft 8in (12.09m)
Wingspan	39ft 0in (11.89m)
Height	8ft 8in (2.64m)
MTOW	16,150lb (7,320kg)
Max speed	600mph (965km/h)
Powerplant	1 × Rolls-Royce Nene 103 turbojet, 5,200lb thrust
Armament	4 × 20mm cannon; bombs, rockets, fuel tanks

One of the German Navy's Sea Hawk 100s delivered in May 1958 photographed during a test flight from Bitteswell. Note the heightened fin introduced to improve handling. Ray Williams

Following the wartime success of the Lancaster there had been high expectations for the Tudor airliner. However, the Tudor was not a success, which put pressure on the Avro design team to produce a successful and profitable aircraft. Their return to the proven military market with the Shackleton was to provide a steady income stream to Hawker Siddeley over many years.

Maiden Flight

The Avro 696 Shackleton MR.1 prototype, VW126, made its first flight from Woodford on 9 March 1949, piloted by Chief Test Pilot Jimmy Orrell. It was airborne for Thirty-three minutes on its maiden flight, and a further flight of forty-five minutes followed later the same day. The test programme ensued and six months later it was displayed at the annual Farnborough Air Show, where it was the largest aircraft there with its 120ft span. At the time it was Britain's largest aircraft, though soon to be overtaken by the Bristol Brabazon.

The Shackleton evolved from an interest expressed by the Air Staff in 1945 for a version of the Lincoln bomber – itself a development of the Lancaster – for general reconnaissance and air/sea rescue duties. A design study concluded that a wider and deeper fuselage was necessary for the radar, comfort of the large crew, weapons and other equipment demanded for its duties. The specification was issued in April 1946 and by May of the following year the design had been finalized. To a marked extent, tooling and design costs were defrayed, and delivery expedited, by utilizing components of the Lincoln bomber and failed Tudor airliner, either in their original or somewhat modified form. The wings, tailplane and

Suez imbroglio many sorties were flown by the six squadrons of Sea Hawks on HMS *Eagle*, *Albion* and *Bulwark*. Airfields attacked included Cairo West, Cairo Almaza, Inchas, Dekheila, Bilbeis and Gamil. On the second and third days the major effort was switched to other targets such as Gamil Bridge, finally destroyed in dive bombing by Sea Hawks.

Royal Navy service ended in the mid-1960s, though a small number continued flying with the Airwork-operated Fleet Requirements Unit at Hurn until 1969. The Dutch Sea Hawks flew from the carrier *Karel Doorman* and in their later years were equipped with missiles. The Indian Sea Hawks flew from the *Vikrant*, remaining in service until replacement by Sea Harriers in 1983. They flew offensive missions during the Indo-Pakistan Wars of 1965 and 1971, where they destroyed Pakistani warships and merchant vessels.

Avro Shackleton

When the Shackleton made its first flight in 1949, no-one would have believed that the design would still be in service with the RAF in 1991. In those days developments in aviation were very rapid, and aircraft became obsolete and were replaced within a few years of entering service. The Shackleton was the exception and only began to be displaced from its original role of maritime reconnaissance when the Nimrod entered service in 1969; some continued in service in the airborne early warning role until 1991.

The third prototype MR.1, VW135, which first flew 29 March 1950, was used on armament trials. As with the second prototype, VW131, all of the anti-aircraft armament bar the dorsal turret had been removed. Avro Heritage

undercarriage were basically those of the Lincoln, but the increased all-up weight and the higher aerodynamic drag of the new high-capacity fuselage necessitated the adoption of Rolls-Royce Griffon 67s driving de Havilland six-blade contra-rotating propellers. The Griffon was the last of Rolls-Royce's classic V12 aero engines; it followed the general lines of earlier engines such as the Kestrel and Merlin, but physically it is a much bigger unit, with a cubic capacity of 37 litres. The growth of the basic Lancaster/Lincoln concept can be gauged from the Lancaster's empty weight of 36,700lb and loaded weight of 70,000lb; the ultimate Shackleton weighed 57,800lb empty and 108,000lb maximum.

VW126 originally had two cannon mounted in 'cheeks' either side of the nose, and a rear turret and an upper dorsal turret both fitted with machine guns. From the second prototype onwards, only the latter guns remained. Following the three prototypes, seventy-six MR.1s and MR.1As with uprated Griffons were assembled at Woodford. In the post-war austerity years, the Shackleton proved to be a steady earner for Hawker Siddeley's Avro plants.

In the meantime there was plenty of other work for the Avro factories and test pilots, with the testing of the four Avro 707s built to research the delta planform of the Vulcan, and the construction of Lancasters for the French navy.

Shackleton Developments

Even as the Shackleton MR.1 was preparing to enter service, Avro's designers were working on the MR.2 variant to rectify some of the problems found in the early aircraft. The main problem was the positioning of the search radar in a chin fairing under the nose, where it was vulnerable to bird strikes and was not ideal for a 360-degree sweep.

The MR.2 had a lengthened nose with two remotely controlled 20mm guns, aimed by a gunner sitting above the bomb-aimer. The chin radome was replaced by a retractable radome aft of the bomb bay and the extreme tail portion of the fuselage was

RIGHT: **During 1951 the first Shackleton, VW126, was heavily rebuilt as the aerodynamic prototype for the Shackleton MR.2. It had the new nose section, new tail section and the retractable radar 'dustbin'.** Avro Heritage

BELOW: **Production Shackleton WL796 at the 1953 Farnborough Air Show showing the nose cannon installation and with an airborne lifeboat fitted partly into the bomb bay. During the same Farnborough Show the Shackleton made a flypast with three engines feathered.** Avro Heritage

tapered off into a transparent cone to provide an additional look-out position. Instead of the single fixed tailwheel of the MR.1 there were twin retractable wheels to make taxiing easier. Additional equipment was added to improve the type's performance, and to accommodate this new equipment and improve crew space the mid-upper turret was dispensed with.

The first Shackleton prototype, VW126, was rebuilt as the MR.2 aerodynamic prototype in 1950–51 and first flew in its new form on 19 April 1951. MR.1 WB833 was removed from the production line and completed as a fully functioning MR.2 prototype, first flying on 17 June 1952. The MR.2 proved to be a substantial improvement on the MR.1 and sixty-nine were built, of which nine were taken from the MR.1 production line. They regularly returned to Hawker Siddeley's Avro works at Woodford, Bracebridge Heath and Langar for equipment updates.

With a large fleet of maritime reconnaissance aircraft there was an ongoing need to train radar operators, so in 1957 some seventeen MR.1s were converted into T.4s; these were later augmented by ten MR.2s that were redesignated as T.2s.

Though the design had been improved with the MR.2, crews continued to complain about the noise and attendant fatigue. Their concerns were listened to and factored into the redesign put in train in 1954, which resulted in the MR.3. This much improved design incorporated a nosewheel undercarriage and had increased fuel capacity by virtue of auxiliary tanks at the wing-tips. The pilots' canopy was of a wrap-around type improving vision and various changes were made in internal equipment. The dorsal turret was deleted though the forward guns were retained and low-speed handling benefited from ailerons of a modified design. A total of forty-two MR.3s was produced for the RAF and eight were sold to the South African Air Force.

Strictly speaking, there was no prototype MR.3. The first MR.3, WR970, took to the air on the 2 September 1955, just in time for that year's Farnborough Air Show, the sixth consecutive year when the Shackleton was demonstrated and also the last. The flight test programme proved challenging as the low-speed handling left much to be desired. During stalling trials from Woodford the aircraft turned upside down and crashed, killing the crew. The handling trials were restarted with WR971 and a spoiler was fitted to the inner wing leading edge,

The Shackleton MR.3 production line at Woodford. This final new-build version of the aircraft had a tricycle undercarriage, new outer wings and ailerons, improved soundproofing, greater fuel capacity and no dorsal turret. Avro Heritage

The MR.3 Phase 3 trials aircraft, WR973, at Woodford in 1965. The major element of the Phase 3 modifications was the installation of a Viper engine in the lower part of each outboard Griffon nacelle. Avro Heritage

which cured the poor stalling performance. The third MR.3, WR972, never entered squadron service and based at the A&AEE Boscombe Down engaged in research tasks, initially trialling updates for the type and later serving at Farnborough with the RAE for towing and drag testing parachutes, such as Concorde's braking parachutes.

Shackleton MR.3s typically had a crew of ten comprising a captain, co-pilot, two navigators, an engineer and five signallers.

Crew-members could rest in a soundproofed wardroom and use a galley. The weapon load could consist of up to five torpedoes or bombs, depth charges, sonobuoys and flares. Provision was made for an air/sea rescue lifeboat, though this was later superseded by Lindholme gear (a nine-man life raft).

Like the MR.2, the MR.3 received updates to its electronic equipment: Phase 1 was an update of the radar and Phase 2 was the installation of electronic counter measures (ECM). The Phase 3 modification was a far more substantial makeover with a redesigned nosewheel, larger tip tanks and much new internal equipment. The weight of the aircraft was now so great that its performance at higher temperatures and higher altitudes was inadequate. As the Griffon engines could not be uprated, a Viper turbojet offering 2,700lb of thrust was very neatly fitted into the rear of each of the outboard engines nacelles.

The MR.3s sold to South Africa received all of the Phase 3 modifications, but did not have the Viper turbojet engines fitted. This proved to be wise, as the RAF was to later to discover that addition of the turbojets led to premature fatigue of the main spars and shortened the aircraft's service life, so much so that many of them were prematurely withdrawn from service owing to metal fatigue.

Maritime Shackletons in Service

The Shackleton boasted an impressive endurance that enabled it to fly halfway across the Atlantic and, with its high-powered radar equipment, to search an area of some 200,000 square miles of sea in the course of a single sortie. To demonstrate to taxpayers and spectators the hard work put in by the Shackletons and their crews, an operational flavour was injected into the 1960 Farnborough Air Show when one of No. 201 Sqn's aircraft departed daily from the show, returning twenty-two hours later after an all-night NATO sortie.

Special assignments often required crews to fly their aircraft to almost any part of the world; for example 224 Squadron, operating from Gibraltar, circumnavigated most of South America on a goodwill and training mission. To demonstrate their versatility they were employed as troop carriers on

several occasions, the first time in 1956 during troubles in Cyprus.

They were also used in anger several times; for example, on anti-submarine patrols in the 1956 Suez conflict, in 1958 dropping bombs on Dhala in the Arabian Gulf, during the Malayan insurgency, during the Borneo confrontation in the early-1960s, and in Aden.

Shackleton squadrons took part in 'showing the flag' around the world as a hangover from Britain's imperial role, and often operated from bases in the USA, Canada, Malta and Gibraltar as well as in the UK on maritime exercises. In addition to their maritime activities, Shackletons were detached to the Arabian Peninsula, Gan and the Caribbean. Goodwill visits and demonstration flights to the Caribbean were a regular feature of Coastal Command's training programme.

For Those in Peril on the Seas

In 1963 Shackletons demonstrated their life-saving capability. Following distress calls from the Greek liner *Lakonia*, two 224 Sqn Shackletons took off from RAF Gibraltar early on 23 December and dropped Lindholme gear to survivors in the water near the burning liner. Another Shackleton, of 42 Sqn, flew from St Mawgan to drop more dinghies and then landed at Gibraltar to deliver additional survival gear. This aircraft returned to Britain the following day, Christmas Eve, visiting the rescue scene on the return journey.

Oil Watch

Following the Unilateral Declaration of Independence by the Rhodesian Government of Ian Smith on 11 November 1965, Shackletons were deployed from Aden and

Malta to watch the seaward approaches to Beira – the port in Mozambique that served landlocked Rhodesia – for tankers that might be running oil to the Smith regime. On Wednesday 3 March 1966, the first Shackleton arrived in the Malagasy Republic. Three aircraft operated from Majunga, on the north-west coast of Madagascar, which was very well situated for the purpose, and kept the Mozambique Channel under surveillance in cooperation with the Royal Navy forces. Eighteen months later the Shackleton MR.2s of 38 Sqn were relieved by MR.3s of 42 Sqn, which arrived in the Malagasy Republic from the Far East, where they had been on detachment from their home station at St Mawgan.

The patrolling Shackletons of 42 Sqn located and identified over 1,600 ships during the blockade. They visually checked all radar contacts, passing each ship's name, port of registry, course and speed to the RN surface force commander. Each sortie covered over 200,000 square miles and patrols were normally flown at 6,000ft, reduced to 100ft for visual identification.

South African Shackletons

The eight South African aircraft were used to monitor shipping lanes, for fishery protection and for border control; they were also able to pinpoint the crew of a South African Buccaneer that crashed during its delivery flight from the UK. Hawker Siddeley brought South Africa's seven surviving Shackletons – the eighth had crashed into a mountain in 1963 – up to Phase 3 standard, though without the Viper. However, from 1964 the arms embargo introduced by Harold Wilson's Labour Government meant that spares became unobtainable. Over the years Shackleton numbers were reduced, the final four remaining in service until 1984.

The fifth Shackleton for the South African Air Force flew in September 1957 and was delivered in February 1958. In the background is Avro Ashton WB490. Avro Heritage

The AEW Shackleton

In 1969 the MoD decided that the Royal Air Force was to take over maritime airborne early warning (AEW) duties from the Fleet Air Arm after the Royal Navy's aircraft carriers and their Fairey Gannet AEW aircraft were phased out of service during the 1970s. The Gannets' radar would be fitted to Shackletons, then being withdrawn from the RAF maritime reconnaissance role as the Nimrod – described in Chapter 15 – came into service. An advantage of this plan was the low cost involved in modifying existing aircraft instead of buying new equipment.

As the fatigue life of Shackleton MR.3s had been prematurely shortened by the Viper engine installation, it fell to the MR.2s to be converted into the AEW role. The best twelve machines with the lowest hours were selected for conversion by Hawker Siddeley. The first prototype conversion, of WL745, was made at the aircraft's birthplace at Woodford, while the production conversions were handled at Bitteswell; following the completion of the latter, WL745 was brought up to production standard at Bitteswell. The aircraft joined No. 8 Sqn at RAF Kinloss in January 1972, later moving to Lossiemouth.

Their role was much extended from that of the Gannets, whose only role had been to provide the fleet with airborne early warning. The Shackleton had a much wider role including AEW for UK air defence, direction of strike/attack aircraft, reporting of surface forces through electronic surveillance measures (ESM), and limited search and rescue as each aircraft carried Lindholme gear. The normal crew complement in the AEW.2 was nine: captain, co-pilot, radio navigator, 'navigating' navigator, engineer and four radar operators. The AN/APS-20F (Improved) radar dated back to the 1940s and had originally been fitted to the Royal Navy's Douglas Skyraiders before being passed on to the Gannets and, with substantial upgrade, to the Shackletons. Contemporary AEW systems had computer assistance, automatic target detection and tracking, datalinks for information transfer and improved display formats, all of which served to enhance capability in the role.

It had been intended that the AEW.2s would be replaced by another Woodford product, the Nimrod AEW.3. However, after long delays to the new aircraft's entry into service – outlined in Chapter 15 – the entire project was cancelled in 1986. As a result, the Shackletons had to continue in service until they could be replaced by the Boeing E.3 Sentry AWACS that were now ordered in place of the AEW Nimrods. Half of the fleet had been scrapped in 1981, but the six survivors remained in use until July 1991 when they were finally replaced by the Sentry; tragically, one was lost with its entire crew in an accident in April 1990. In recognition of the length of their service, the Queen's Birthday flypast on 15 June 1991 was led by three Shackleton AEW.2s leading eight Tornado F.3s.

Gloster Javelin

The Gloster Aircraft Company, founded in 1917, had prospered during World War One. However, in the immediate post-war years it was beset with problems similar to those faced by other aircraft manufacturers, and diversified into other areas of engineering while remaining predominantly in the aircraft industry. An ailing aircraft manufacturer was ripe for takeover and in May 1934 an offer was made by the board of Hawker Aircraft to purchase the company for £180,000. Gloster lost much of its autonomy and one of Hawker's directors, Frank Spriggs, became chairman.

Despite its loss of autonomy Gloster played a hugely significant part in British aviation, producing the first British jet aircraft, the E28/39, and then the first jet aircraft to enter service with the RAF, the Meteor. The E28/39, powered by an engine designed by jet pioneer Frank Whittle, was

Specification – Shackleton MR.3	
Length	92ft 6in (28.19m)
Wingspan	119ft 8in (36.47m)
Height	23ft 3in (7.09m)
MTOW	98,000lb (44,500kg)
Cruising speed	300mph (480kmh)
Range	2,250 miles (3,620km)
Crew	10
Powerplant	4 × 1,620hp Rolls-Royce Griffon 57
	2 × 2,700lb Bristol Siddeley Viper 203
Armament	2 × 20mm canon, bombs, torpedoes, depth charges

Now preserved in the Manchester Museum of Science and Industry, Shackleton AEW.2 WR960 flies with the Hawker Siddeley Nimrod AEW.3 XZ285, which was meant to replace it. In the event the Nimrod AEW.3 was cancelled and eight of the Shackletons were re-sparred as Bitteswell in 1978–81 so that they could continue in service. BAE Systems

ordered just before the outbreak of war in 1939. Owing to the challenge of this revolutionary powerplant, the aircraft itself was kept as a simple, conventional design to prove the suitability of jet-powered aircraft and not provide problems of its own. It had a tricycle undercarriage so that the jet exhaust did not damage the ground. The sole E28/39, W4041, first flew on 15 May 1941, proving the success of Whittle's invention.

As a single Whittle jet engine was insufficiently powerful for a fighter aircraft, Gloster designed a twin-jet aircraft, the Meteor, which like the E28/39 was not a revolutionary design. The engines were mounted in the wings, which was to prove a boon as other engines could easily be installed as needed.

The contract was awarded in February 1941 but completion of the prototypes was delayed by difficulties in the delivery of the engines.

The Meteor first flew in June 1942 and, after substantial trials, entered service with the RAF in July 1944. With the pressures of wartime the Meteor was quickly developed, and even with the end of hostilities was in much demand in the UK and abroad. The Meteor proved a great investment success for Hawker Siddeley, with sales to many countries. The demand was so strong that design and production of the trainer and night-fighter versions was passed to another HS subsidiary, Armstrong Whitworth, in 1949. Production ended in 1954, after 3,545 had been built.

The specification and design process that culminated in the Gloster GA5 was tortuous. Specification F.4/48 called for a high-performance night and all-weather fighter, with a long endurance and carrying heavy armament. Competition came from the de Havilland DH110, which was rejected by the RAF but later adopted by the Navy as the Sea Vixen.

The GA5 was a large delta-winged aircraft with a T-tail and powered by two Armstrong Siddeley Sapphires (so both airframe and engine manufacturers were part of Hawker Siddeley). The first prototype, WD804, was built at Gloster's experimental department at Bentham; chief test pilot Bill Waterton took it on its maiden flight from Moreton Valence airfield on 26 November 1951. Development flying continued until 29 June 1952, when on its ninety-ninth flight WD804 was afflicted by violent flutter and both elevators came adrift. Waterton was able to maintain some control via

the variable-incidence tailplane, and the subsequent crash-landing at Boscombe Down won Waterton the George Medal.

Despite this crash, in July 1952 the Air Ministry decided to order the GA5 in quantity, naming it the Javelin. Only a few weeks elapsed before the second prototype, WD808, was in the air, but in June 1953 it entered a deep stall and crashed, killing its test pilot, Peter Lawrence.

The first production Javelin FAW.1, XA544, flew in July 1954 and was followed by thirty-nine others, ten of which were held back for all manner of tests. In October 1954 another pilot died after FAW.1

XA546 entered a spin. The Javelin needed and correspondingly underwent many modifications during its development. During the early stages of testing in the prototype stage, a decrease in sweep-back on the outer wing leading edges was engineered to give a better fineness ratio over the ailerons, and a clear-view canopy was adopted.

Criticisms of the Javelin

In July 1955 the *Sunday Express* carried a critical front-page article entitled 'New Fighter Shock', claiming that the Javelin

LEFT: **An advertisement for the Javelin from *Aeroplane* in 1953.** Author's collection

BELOW: **The 1954 Farnborough Air Show and Gloster exhibits five Javelins: the third, fourth and fifth prototypes, respectively WT827, WT830, WT836, and the first and third production aircraft, XA544 and XA546.** BAE Systems

'is displaying serious defects and, in its present form, could never be put into front-line service'. The fighter was said to have been given a few weeks' grace, then the Ministry would have to decide on its future. It was further reported that the Javelin had 'undesirable and sometimes alarming' characteristics at high altitudes and at Mach 1. Reference was made to the three test crashes.

This attack brought a sharp rejoinder from the Hawker Siddeley Group and the comment 'pure tripe' from Sir Frank Spriggs, Managing Director of the Group. A detailed statement from the Group asserted that 'there is absolutely no truth in the irresponsible, mischievous, and totally inaccurate report in the *Sunday Express* that there was a Javelin crisis'.

Conveniently disproving the press story about the Javelin's controllability at high speeds, a mysterious bang awakened many in south-east London in the early hours of 5 July: HSG issued a statement on the 7th that Gloster's new chief test pilot, Dicky Martin, had been testing a Javelin over the Home Counties at that time and had unintentionally exceeded the speed of sound while endeavouring to free an entangled oxygen tube.

A little over a year later the publication of Bill Waterton's book *The Quick and the Dead*, containing harsh criticisms of Gloster and the Javelin, brought swift repercussions. Waterton was a 'larger than life' character, who made his strong views on many matters pertaining to test flying very clear in his book. Again Hawker Siddeley had to issue a long statement defending the

Javelin. In the statement the Group took exception to Waterton's 'grave allegations of negligence and incompetence ... not substantiated by the facts'. The press release continued to give a detailed rebuttal to Waterton's comments on the crash of WD808 and the death of its pilot. Gloster's Dicky Martin also entered the fray, defending the Javelin against Waterton's slurs. Questions were also asked in Parliament, but eventually the storm died down.

The Javelin's Development

By late 1958 six marks of Javelin were with the RAF, forming the backbone of the country's interceptor force. The FAW.1s entered service with the RAF in the UK and Germany in 1956. The FAW.2's main innovation was an American radar instead of British equipment, though as it was an intermediate mark only thirty were supplied.

The Javelin T.3 prototype, WT841, first displayed at the Farnborough 1956 Show, was developed by a Hawker Siddeley subsidiary, Air Service Training at Hamble. It had increased internal fuel capacity, Sapphire 6 engines and an all-flying tail. The front fuselage was completely rearranged to accommodate pupil and instructor in tandem, and the instructor's ejection seat was considerably raised to provide forward view. In addition, the instructor was provided with a binocular periscope with lenses mounted on streamlined pylons projecting on either side of his cockpit. The search radar was replaced by a simple radar-ranging unit. Overall fuselage length was increased

by nearly 4ft (1.2m). Production of the T.3 took place at Gloster's Hucclecote works. Twenty-three were produced during 1958.

Marked Improvements

The next mark, the FAW.4, had a major improvement over its predecessors: an all-flying tailplane, as hitherto stick forces at high speed had been extremely high. The first production aircraft, XA629, flew in September 1955. The two subsequent marks had only minor improvements: the FAW.5 had an improved fuel capacity and the FAW.6 replaced a British for an American radar.

The most important advances came with the Javelin FAW.7, which was equipped

A dynamic shot of XA644.
BAE Systems

WT841, the Javelin T.3 prototype, with the longer fuselage, raised rear cockpit and sideways periscopes visible, in formation with XA644, a Javelin FAW.1. BAE Systems

with the much more powerful Sapphire 7 engines of 11,000lb thrust and could carry four de Havilland Firestreak missiles on underwing pylons. To accommodate the larger engines the intakes were enlarged and the tail was lengthened. The FAW.8 went one better, having reheat for its Sapphire 7R engines providing 12,390lb thrust. With this additional power, the performance – particularly the climb – was greatly improved, although even the FAW.4 had a

performance comparable with that of the Hunter. The FAW.8 was the final new-production version of the Javelin and the last aircraft, XJ165, completed in August 1960, was the final aircraft to be built by Gloster.

As the FAW.7's climb and altitude performance was noticeably poorer than the FAW.8's, a large number of them were modified at Moreton Valence to FAW.8 standard and redesignated as FAW.9s, the conversion programme remaining in full

swing until July 1961. Of the seventy-six converted, forty were FAW.9Rs with provision for flight-refuelling probes. Some of the Javelin FAW.7s completed by Armstrong Whitworth at Bitteswell actually flew straight to Moreton Valence for the FAW.9 upgrade.

Javelins in RAF Service

At its peak the Javelin equipped fourteen RAF squadrons; however, they only served for a short time before being replaced by the superior (though critically shorter-ranged) English Electric Lightning. Javelins flew with UK RAF squadrons from 1956 until 1964, in Germany until 1966 and in Cyprus and the Far East for a further year.

Javelin Production

Under the Hawker Siddeley Group system of sharing production contracts, Air Service Training at Hamble not only designed and constructed the front fuselage of the T.3 prototype but also built Javelin inner wings, tail units, rear fuselages, ventral tanks and other components that made up some 30 per cent of the complete airframe. As with the Meteor, Sea Hawk and later the Hunter, Armstrong Whitworth at Baginton and Bitteswell assembled Javelins, 133 out of the 435 completed.

Following the cancellation of the proposed supersonic 'thin-wing Javelin' project in 1956, the company had nothing to follow the Javelin on the production line. Though in 1960 750,000sq ft were engaged in aircraft work, Gloster's aircraft manufacturing capacity had been over-large for a

ABOVE: **Javelin FAW.7 XH712 armed with four Firestreak air-to-air missiles.** BAE Systems

RIGHT: **Javelin FAW.8 XH966 with a full load of Firestreak missiles taking off from Farnborough during the September 1958 Show. It has the Hawker Siddeley emblem just behind the air intake.** BAE Systems

Specification – Javelin FAW.9	
Length	56ft 3in (17.15m)
Wingspan	51ft (15.54m)
Height	10ft 9in (3.28m)
MTOW	31,580lb (14,320kg)
Max speed	Mach 0.92
Range	790 miles (1,270km)
Crew	2
Powerplant	2 × Armstrong Siddeley Sapphire ASSa6, 11,000lb with reheat
Armament	2 × 30mm cannon, 4 × Firestreak missiles

time, so other members of the Group outside of the aviation sector, such as Hawker Siddeley Brush Turbines, occupied surplus plant, and other areas were engaged in diversification outside of aircraft manufacture. The latter at first embraced such products as farm machinery and automatic vending equipment, but later formed Gloster Saro, engaged in the manufacture of vehicle bodies for airport support, fire engines and aircraft refuellers. In 1984 Gloster Saro acquired the fire tender business of the Chubb group, and in 1987 the company merged with Simon Engineering to form Simon Gloster Saro.

The Formation of Whitworth Gloster Aircraft

The writing was clearly on the wall for Gloster. First, in mid-1961 Hawker Siddeley Aviation announced a merger between Armstrong Whitworth Aircraft and Gloster Aircraft as Whitworth Gloster Aircraft, and then in November HSA made it clear that without the early receipt of Government orders of sufficient magnitude the Gloster works, employing 4,000 people, would be closed by the middle of the following year. This duly happened: in 1962 both the former de Havilland factory in Christchurch and the Gloster factory at Hucclecote were closed.

Hawker Hunter

On 20 July 1951 Neville Duke made the first flight of the Hawker P.1067 – which was to become the Hunter – at Boscombe Down. The Hunter handled well, and was technically sound and reliable. It became a great success and over the next nine years

1,972 were built, spread amongst the Hawker plants at Langley, Kingston, Dunsfold and Blackpool, Armstrong Whitworth's factories at Baginton and Bitteswell, and the Belgian and Dutch consortia of Fairey-Sabca and Fokker-Aviolanda. A total of 1,140 Hunters were delivered to the RAF and 829 were exported. The Belgian and Dutch production was funded by the USA, which was anxious that NATO countries would be ready to defend themselves and felt it had no time to do so itself.

The Hunter grew from the need to replace the Gloster Meteor and the de Havilland Vampire. Hawker's initial offering was the P.1040 with its 'bifurcated' jet pipe, which the RAF felt offered too little of an advance over its existing types and rejected, though an improved version served as the Sea Hawk with the Royal Navy and elsewhere. Hawker developed a swept-wing version of the Sea Hawk design, the P.1052; this led to the P.1081 with a swept wing and tail, and straight-through jet pipe, which first flew in June 1950. All of these jets had had centrifugal-flow turbojets, but the RAF realized that the newer axial-flow jets were slimmer so the aircraft's drag could be reduced and accordingly issued Specification F3/48. This sought a single-seat aircraft using the axial-flow Rolls-Royce Avon or Armstrong Siddeley

Sapphire, capable of attacking high-altitude bombers using 30mm Aden cannon. Initial designs centred on a straight-through intake, but this was discarded when the final configuration was achieved.

Hunters in the Air

Three prototypes were built, the first two with Avons and the third with a Sapphire engine. These aircraft were constructed at Hawker's Langley factory, but as it was unsuitable for test flying, WB188 flew from Boscombe Down. The other two prototypes, WB195 and WB202, flew in May and November 1952, respectively, from Dunsfold; each had four Aden cannon and gunsights. By then the RAF had inadvisably ordered 113 aircraft 'off the drawing board'. The aircraft were far from adequate, having critically poor range and no effective airbrake; also, while the cannon worked on the Sapphire-engined WB202, WB195's Avon repeatedly surged when the guns were fired. Unlike the Avon the Sapphire was virtually surge-free, provided more power and was more fuel-efficient. The Avon-engined Hunters were built at Hawker's Kingston and Blackpool factories while the Sapphire Hunters were built at Armstrong Whitworth's Coventry and Bitteswell works.

The prototype Hawker P.1076 Hunter, WB188, at Dunsfold. This aircraft won the world air speed record of 727.63mph on 7 September 1953, flown by Hawker's chief test pilot Neville Duke, pictured here. The record was exceeded by a Supermarine Swift F.4 flown by Mike Lithgow on 25 September. BAE Systems

G-APUX was Hawker Siddeley's Hunter demonstrator; it was a former crashed Belgian Air Force F.6 mated to a two-seat nose section and designated as a T.66. It flew around the world as a demonstrator and was loaned to several air forces before being finally sold to the Chilean Air Force as a T.72 in 1967. BAE Systems

The initial Avon F.1s and Sapphire F.2s were inadequate for the RAF but some at least earned their keep as test aircraft. A limited number of Hunter F.1s issued for service use were able to show their zest when they 'attacked' Canberras at altitudes where the bombers were previously thought invulnerable. The F.1s were, however, outclassed by the F.2s with their comparatively docile Sapphire engines, which also entered service with squadrons. However, the first use of the aircraft in an exercise revealed more problems: the need for an ammunition link collector as otherwise links jettisoned on firing damaged the rear fuselage, and the lack of an all-flying tail. Hawker was overloaded with modification work, aircraft being built but stored in various stages of modification while trials continued to rectify these problems.

Fortunately the Hunter's problems were being dealt with and the Avon-powered F.1s were superseded by the superior F.4s with all-flying tails and surge-free engines, so the gun-firing problems ceased. While the Avon aircraft were developed, the Sapphire F.2s were developed into F.5s with the improved tail design and with their better range in 1956 saw active service in the Suez imbroglio. The range issue was addressed by improving internal fuel capacity and making provision for underwing tanks. Hunter squadrons were still beset with problems, as aircraft arrived in various stages of modification, but by 1956 the number of squadrons operating Hunters had grown to eighteen.

The F.6

In 1951 work on the P.1083 supersonic Hunter, with wing sweep increased to 50 degrees, began. The Hunter's designer, Sir Sidney Camm, chose the new Avon Mk 200 for it: as a sister Hawker Siddeley Group firm, Armstrong Siddeley must have looked askance when an engine with surging problems, poorer fuel consumption and higher cost was chosen over their Sapphire. In the event the supersonic Hunter was cancelled, but development of the Avon 200 continued, for the F.6 variant. The new Avon made its first flight in January 1954 in the F.6 prototype XF833, and in the first few months was far from trouble-free. However, seven other early Hunter F.1s were converted into interim F.6s to speed development of the engine, and the aircraft and the problems were ironed out. Production F.6s were equipped with a 'saw-tooth' wing, which prevented a 'pitch-up' effect at higher speeds and made the aircraft easier to control in high-speed turns.

With the F.6 the RAF finally had a great aircraft with a high-powered, almost surge-free engine and extra fuel capacity. Re-equipment of squadrons began in 1956 and a total of 515 F.6s was ordered. However, production of the F.6 was brought to a halt by the 1957 Defence White Paper, which stated that the world was entering a missile age and that there was no need for more manned military aircraft. This policy proved to be a calamity for the British aircraft

industry: many promising projects were cancelled in one fell swoop and job losses immediately followed. Hunter F.6 production was cut by 100 aircraft and as a result Hawker Siddeley announced the closure of their Blackpool factory and the loss of 4,000 jobs; the Langley factory lost 700 staff and Hunter manufacture was concentrated at Kingston and Baginton, with final assembly at Dunsfold and Bitteswell, respectively. (Gloster Aircraft dismissed 700 employees in June that year as no further orders for the Javelin had been received.) In fact the cancellations had no immediate effect on Group finances, as other air forces took advantage of the chance of quick delivery with alacrity: large export orders for the F.6 from Sweden, India, Iraq, Jordan and Switzerland accounted for much of the production at the end of the 1950s.

Hunter Twins

With the need for a trainer version of the Hunter to replace the RAF's Meteor and Vampire trainers self-evident, Hawker set to work to design a two-seater based on the F.4. There were two prototypes: XJ615, based on the F.4, flew in July 1955 and XJ627, based on the F.6, flew in November 1956. Refining the shape of the two-seat canopy and the spine behind it to limit drag involved many costly temporary fixes and eventually required a total redesign. New production was forty-five T.7s for the RAF and ten T.8s for the Royal Navy. Production trainers had the F.6's dog-tooth wing and a braking parachute, but only a single cannon. RAF Hunter squadrons each received a single example; No. 229 Operational Conversion Unit at Chivenor was wholly equipped with them and remained so for sixteen years. Besides the RN, other early customers were the Netherlands, Denmark and Peru. Following new-build trainers, existing F.4s were converted for RAF and RN, and as research aircraft. A further version of the Hunter twin-seater was based on the F.6 with the more powerful Avon.

Ground Attack and Other Variants

A RAF requirement arose for a ground-attack variant of the Hunter to replace the Venom fighter-bombers in service in the Near, Middle and Far East. Hawker devised a development of the F.6, the FGA.9,

with an Avon 207 with 10,050lb thrust, improved avionics and a brake parachute. This variant could carry fuel tanks, rockets and missiles under its wings, and retained the internal fit of twin 30mm cannon. The FGA.9s were rebuilds of F.6s and proved to be potent machines equipping nine RAF squadrons. Though Hunters had ceased operating in the interdiction role long before, the ground attack role remained until replacement by Harriers and Jaguars in 1972.

New roles for the Hunter continued to arise, but as production had ceased in 1960, all new variants were conversions of existing aircraft, many 'one-offs' serving with the UK research establishments.

Though the Canberra PR.7 and PR.9 were excellent reconnaissance aircraft, there was a demand for a less sophisticated aircraft for short-range reconnaissance, so the Hunter FR.10 – another F.6 conversion – came into being. This version was based on the high-powered FGA.9 but had a five-camera nose fit and equipped two RAF squadrons. In addition to its twin-seater Hunter trainers, the Royal Navy also sought a single-seat tactical weapons trainer. Perhaps surprisingly, the cannon were removed as the aircraft were only needed to train pilots in the use of bombs and rockets; however, they were fitted with airfield arrestor hooks.

Refurbishment

Production of Hunters ended with the last Hunter T.66 for the Indian Air Force (BS490), which first flew on 21 October 1960. However, the Hunter was a truly remarkable aircraft and demand was such that after production had ceased, 354 were

ABOVE: **A Royal Navy Hunter T.8 trainer.** Ray Williams

RIGHT: **Hunter XG154 was built as an F.6 and was returned to Hawkers and converted to a FGA.9 in 1960. It is on display at the RAF Museum at Hendon.** BAE Systems

ABOVE: **A Hunter F.6 at Dunsfold displaying the aircraft's ability to carry a large range of weapons, including 230- and 100-gallon drop tanks, 1,000 and 500lb bombs, practice bombs, 3in and 2in rockets, Firestreak and Fireflash missiles (which were never actually carried operationally) and four 30mm cannon.** BAE Systems

RIGHT: **As part of the huge contract won by BAC to supply Lightnings and Strikemasters to Saudi Arabia, four F.60s were delivered in 1966. RSAF 60602 is seen here at Dunsfold.** BAE Systems

refurbished by Hawker Siddeley for further use. Many more would have followed this path, but supplies finally begun to run dry in the mid-1970s. A substantial proportion of the refurbished aircraft were straight F.6/FGA.9 and F.6/FR.10 conversions for the RAF. Others were F.4/GA.11 weapons trainers for the Royal Navy, a few were T.7s and T.8s converted from single-seaters for the RAF and Royal Navy respectively, but the majority were remanufactured aircraft that were exported around the world.

A large number of the early remanufactured Hunters were licence-built Hunter F.4s bought back from the Dutch and Belgian air forces by Hawker Siddeley; later conversions returned from all over the world. The Dutch Hunters had had greater use than the Belgian examples, but were still bought cheaply. HSA was able to buy back the Belgian aircraft, many of which had flown fewer than fifty hours, at unit cost of £16,000 in 1962 (£270,000 at 2012 prices): less than a sixth of what they had originally cost. In 1976 Hawker Siddeley was reselling the remanufactured aircraft at £500,000 each (£3.3m at 2012 prices).

There were several classes of Hunter conversion: modifying F.6s into FGA.9s was straightforward, but converting the F.4 was more complex as it meant a major rebuilding to accommodate the larger-diameter Avon 200. Customers for the refurbished machines received an aircraft with a life of up to 3,000 hours at a fraction of the cost of a new modern equivalent. The simple construction of the Hunter in five major pieces – three fuselage sections and two wings – eased the task of dismantling and refurbishment. For example, for the conversion of a single-seater into a two-seater trainer, the front fuselage section was removed and a newly built two-seater front fuselage was fitted to the existing airframe.

Most of the Hunters bought for remanufacture flew into Dunsfold, although some went to Bitteswell. On arrival they were dismantled and surveyed, the Avon engines were sent to Rolls-Royce for reconditioning, original parts went back to their respective manufacturers, all rear fuselages went to Bitteswell and tails to Hamble, which also made new canopies. The remainder of the airframe was processed at Kingston where

conversion assemblies and new forward fuselage for the two-seat variants were produced. The airframes were stripped and painted in primer and parts or sections changed as necessary. As this work was in progress the work necessary to alter an aircraft to its new customer's specification was planned and implemented for the rebuild, which took an average of three months.

Demand was such that for a time in late 1970 Hawker Siddeley considered reopening the Hunter production line as they foresaw that they would be unable to provide aircraft to fulfil demand. Perhaps not surprisingly this expensive option was dropped, but demand was such that approximately 25 per cent of the Hunters were rebuilt twice. However, by 1978 the number of airframes available for conversion had dwindled to nothing. The ill-considered Defence White Paper of 1957 was partly to blame for this as its assumption that manned aircraft would not be needed in the future prematurely checked Hunter production. The situation was exacerbated by the belief in the early 1960s that the cost of converting F.4s to F.6s would be too high, which had led to the scrapping of many serviceable airframes. Only a year after the forced nationalization of Hawker Siddeley's aerospace assets, in July 1978, the last re-manufactured Hunters for export – three for Lebanon – departed from the Bitteswell plant; other refurbishments for the RAF and Royal Navy continued for three more years. In the previous

twenty-one years more than 320 Hunters no longer required by their original owners were reworked and delivered to twelve nations.

Hunters in Foreign Service

Sweden was the first of several countries to fly the F.50 version of the F.4, ordering 120 in 1954. Denmark ordered Hunters just after Sweden, receiving thirty F.53s and two T.53s. After their withdrawal from service in 1974 HSA bought twenty, though they were only used for spares or for static display. Elsewhere in Europe, NATO had funded licence-production of Hunters in Belgium and Holland as already related. Under this scheme Belgium received 255 F.4s/F.6s, operating them from 1955 until 1966, and Holland had 199 and flew them until 1968. Both countries' aircraft provided HSA with a ready source of under-used aircraft for refurbishment.

The Swiss Air Force received 100 Hunter F.58s in its initial order, and twelve years later it still had ninety-four in service. With this sort of record it was not surprising that the Swiss took a further sixty, the last being delivered in July 1976, the Swiss Air Force four-Hunter aerobatic team celebrating the occasion. (This was the 629th fighter built by Hawker Siddeley and its predecessor companies delivered to Switzerland since 1946, as de Havilland Vampires and Venoms had preceded the Hunters.)

In 1972 Hawker Siddeley proposed a 'Super Hunter' to the Swiss with greater payload, fuel capacity and thrust, a more accurate and comprehensive weapon system and higher energy wheel brakes, but unfortunately this interesting development was rejected.

India was second largest user of the Hunter after the UK, ordering 160 F.56s and twenty-two T.66s, receiving the last of these, the last newly manufactured Hunter, in October 1960. In the years following, wars with Pakistan much reduced the Indian fleet so there were large orders for refurbished Hunters, sixty-one in all, some remaining in service until the end of the twentieth century.

The frequently warring countries of the Middle East were a fertile market for Hunters, Iraq, Jordan and Lebanon receiving small numbers of ex-RAF aircraft in the late-1950s. After production had ceased forty-six F.59s (FGA.9s) were delivered to

Refurbishment of Hunter F.58As for the Swiss Air Force at Dunsfold in 1972.
BAE Systems

ABOVE: **The penultimate Hunter bought by Switzerland, a T.68 delivered in 1974.** BAE Systems

BELOW: **Hawker Siddeley's Hunter demonstrator on the way to Farnborough 76 with the flags of the eighteen nations that operated Hunters painted on the nose.** BAE Systems

De Havilland Sea Vixen

The aircraft that finally became the Sea Vixen started life in 1951 as the de Havilland 110, the ultimate development of de Havilland's Vampire, Venom and DH.108. The Vampire was de Havilland's first jet aircraft and became the second jet to enter service with the RAF, following the Meteor. The Vampire sold widely around the world and de Havilland improved on the design with the Venom. The minuscule swept-wing DH.108, of which three were built, had been the first British aircraft to exceed Mach 1, achieved with the help of a steep dive. The DH.110 shared the Vampire and Venom's twin-boom planform, but possessed a swept wing and tail.

The DH.110/Sea Vixen took many years to evolve into an effective operational aircraft. Compared with the lengthy gestation of more recent projects such as the Eurofighter Typhoon, the thirteen-year development phase for the Sea Vixen from 1951 to 1964 does not seem excessive; but in the middle of the twentieth century, when wartime pressures had accelerated production time, it was unusually protracted. To some extent this was due to official vacillation, which at one point resulted in the entire programme being cancelled by the Royal Navy and subsequently by the RAF. However, with dogged determination to persevere with their design de Havilland persuaded the Ministry of Supply and the Royal Navy that the Sea Vixen was the answer to the needs of the Senior Service.

The DH.110 of 1951 and the Sea Vixen of 1964 were markedly different in their structure, equipment, weapons, flying controls, systems and in every other major respect. Moreover, during the years that the project was in abeyance there were tremendous advances in weapons, fire-control systems, radar and flight instrumentation and, above all, in the integrated weapon-system concept. Thus, when de Havilland was at last able to go ahead with the operational version, the Sea Vixen was equipped with a weapons system and was the first British aircraft to become operational with guided weapons, not merely an aircraft containing some off-the-shelf stores and equipment.

Development of the Sea Vixen

It was in mid-1946 that de Havilland first began discussions with the Royal Navy on the possibility of a carrier-based all-weather

Iraq and Lebanon had another six, three of which were the last refurbished Hunters for export. Jordan had a small Hunter fleet, most of which were destroyed in the Six-Day War of 1967, but received more from the RAF, Saudi Arabia and HSA. Other recipients were Abu Dhabi, Kuwait, Oman, Qatar and Saudi Arabia.

In Latin America, Chile received twenty-five from 1966 and replacements from differing sources. Chile had even hoped to buy some Swiss Hunters when these were finally retired in the 1990s, but in the event they were unable to do so and formally retired the type in 1996. Peru's Hunter experience was comparatively short with the sixteen delivered serving until 1976. Kenya received a small number of Hunters on independence. The Royal Rhodesian Air Force had twelve former RAF FGA.9s and there were reports that some of these were airworthy with what is now the Air Force of Zimbabwe as recently as 2000. Finally, after the UK's withdrawal from east of Suez, Singapore operated twenty single-seaters and trainers.

Specification – Hunter FGA.9	
Length	45ft 11in (14m)
Wingspan	33ft 8in (10.26m)
Height	13ft 2in (4.01m)
MTOW	26,600lb (12,100kg)
Max speed	Mach 0.93
Combat range	240 miles (386km)
Crew	1
Engine	1 × 10,000lb Rolls-Royce Avon Mk 207
Armament	1,000lb bombs, unguided rockets, drop tanks, napalm, Sidewinder missiles, 4 × 30mm cannon

The Hunter was clearly a money-spinner for Hawker Siddeley, for after the difficulties in sorting out the aircraft in the initial development stage there was no huge investment that would have eaten into profits and extended the break-even point. Even the early cessation of production was not a block on sales or the development of new variants, merely leading to a sensible reuse of previously under-used Hunters.

LEFT: **De Havilland's Chester factory on 15 March 1951 with a line-up of its recent production including the last three Hornets, Chipmunks for the RAF and an evaluation batch of Vampires for the Swedish Air Force.** BAE Systems

BELOW LEFT: **Swiss Air Force Vampire J-1008, which was flown back to Hatfield for preservation at the de Havilland Museum at Salisbury Hall, London Colney, Hertfordshire.** BAE Systems

By January 1949 the Ministry of Supply had agreed to place development contracts for seven RAF night-fighter and two long-range fighter prototypes, two naval night-fighters and two naval strike fighter prototypes. But later that year the Navy cancelled their order. Construction of the two RAF prototypes went ahead at de Havilland's main plant at Hatfield. The first, WG236, was rolled out in the autumn of 1951 and John Cunningham took it into the air for the first time on 26 September. Its behaviour was exemplary and performance even better than had been expected. The second aircraft, WG240, flew on 25 July 1952, painted silver like WG236. Each was powered by a pair of Rolls-Royce Avon RA.7s of some 7,500lb thrust. A conventional tailplane and elevator were fitted, and air brakes were provided above and below the jet tailpipes. No provision was made for underwing store carriage; at this time the aircraft can be described as 'proof of concept' prototypes, far removed from an aircraft for active service.

However, in 1952 the whole programme was put in jeopardy when the RAF chose the Gloster Javelin as the standard land-based all-weather fighter. De Havilland was left with no production orders at all, although the development contract was retained. The RAF's decision appeared fully justified when, on 6 September, WG236 broke up in the air at the Farnborough show, killing pilot John Derry, observer Tony Richards and twenty-nine spectators.

After the accident, de Havilland carried out extensive structural investigations. An analysis led the company to conclude that in certain manoeuvres the aircraft was undergoing an entirely unpredicted combination of high acceleration and rate of roll. To prove the point, during a wing structural test the wing failed in torsion at the leading edge, exactly reproducing what had happened at Farnborough. Modifications were put in hand on WG240 to give the necessary increase in torsional strength, and at

fighter of outstanding performance. For maximum radar and navigational efficiency it was decided that a crew of two should be carried. Since the aircraft was to operate over the sea, twin engines seemed desirable. For performance, the wing was given the unprecedented sweep angle of 45 degrees. The aircraft was to have a moderate wing loading, for manoeuvrability at altitude as well as for deck take-offs and landings, and for the latter purpose highly effective flaps were required. Folded dimensions had to

conform to the limitations imposed by lifts and hangars, and the twin-boom layout was chosen in order to reduce both length and, particularly, height.

From this broad specification the DH.110 was begun, and a short time later the RAF issued a requirement for a night-fighter to which de Havilland decided that a non-navalized version of the DH.110 could be the answer. Early in 1947 they submitted tenders to both the RAF and the RN, and both were favourably received.

the same time a number of other improvements were incorporated to give better control at near-supersonic speeds.

Late in 1952 the Royal Navy issued a requirement for a multi-purpose all-weather fighter and low-level attack aircraft to replace the Sea Venom. Although the specification called for a small, single-engined aircraft, de Havilland decided to see how well it could be met by the DH.110 with more powerful Avons installed. The airframe would require extensive modification, with increased strength, greater fuel capacity, folding wings, an undercarriage designed for carrier landings, arrester hook, catapult gear and other changes. Meanwhile, equipment suitable for the Sea Vixen was under development, GEC with its sophisticated AI radar and DH Propellers (later HS Dynamics) with the Blue Jay (later named the Firestreak) infra-red homing missile.

Early in 1953 the Navy placed a development contract. Development flying continued with WG240, which was used to prove the approach characteristics on HMS Albion with 'touch-and-goes'. A 'semi-navalized' prototype, XF828, designated Mk 20X, was built in the experimental shop at Christchurch to prove the aircraft for deck operation. It was fitted with a catapult and arrester hook, but not with wing folding or military equipment. The 20X flew in June 1955; the previous February de Havilland has been awarded a substantial contract for the navalized DH.110, now named Sea Vixen to reflect its naval connections.

So, by the time XF828 had satisfactorily completed deck trials on HMS Ark Royal in April 1956, production drawings were being issued, and the DH.110 story was taking a happier turn. Hatfield carried out the design of the wing fold, the revised tail unit and the longer stroke undercarriage, but the overall responsibility for the redesign was centred at Christchurch where the Sea Vixen FAW.1s were produced. The first ten were allocated to development flying and the first production machine, XJ474, flew on 20 March 1957.

The redesign proved extensive. The fuselage was largely redesigned to accommodate the new armament system. To assist with carrier operations the upper rear ends of the fins were cut off and the new pointed radome could be folded back. Nosewheel steering improved deck manoeuvring, and the tail booms were raised to increase ground clearance. In the prototypes the engines were installed from below, in the production version they are installed

ABOVE: **The first DH.110, WG236, which tragically and dramatically broke up in the air at the 1952 Farnborough Air Show killing the crew and many spectators.** BAE Systems

LEFT: **The 'semi-navalized' prototype, XF828, which was built to prove the aircraft for deck operation. It was fitted with a catapult and arrester hook, but not with wing folding or military equipment.** BAE Systems

The first production Sea Vixen FAW.1, XJ474, on 20 March 1957. BAE Systems

through removable panels in the top of the fuselage. Instead of the original upper and lower airbrakes a large single airbrake was fitted further forward, in the bottom of the fuselage.

The Sea Vixen carried out an intensive trials programme covering all aspects of its handling, aircraft systems, weapon systems and carrier operation, plus winterization and tropical trials. The final trials were

LEFT: **XJ474 with flaps out and armed with four Firestreak air-to-air missiles.** BAE Systems

BELOW LEFT: **A Sea Vixen used for Firestreak missile trials. This view shows how the pilot was on the left side of the fuselage and the navigator confined in the 'coal hole' (as it was referred to by some crew) on his right, with only a small window.** BAE Systems

carried out by No. 700 Trials Squadron, after which the Sea Vixen went into service in July 1959 when 892 Sqn was formally commissioned at RNAS Yeovilton.

The GEC interception radar required a wide fuselage, which allowed side-by-side seating for pilot and observer and so reduced fuselage length. The observer was enclosed at a lower level than the pilot with just one small window.

The Sea Vixen had a 40-degree swept wing fitted with Fowler flaps. The main undercarriage, stressed for severe carrier operation, retracted inwards; the hydraulically steerable nosewheel retracted rearwards. The catapult hooks were mounted forward and inboard of the wheel wells, and the hook retracted between the engine tailpipes.

As an interceptor the primary armament was four missiles: Firestreak in the FAW.1 and Red Top in the later FAW.2. It could carry any stores in the RN's offensive inventory: bombs, rockets, flight-refuelling pods, launchers or 200gal drop tanks could be carried under the wings. In addition, twin Microcell rocket packs housing fourteen 2in rockets hinged down hydraulically from the lower front fuselage.

Sea Vixen FAW.2

The main difference between the FAW.1 and the FAW.2 was that the latter's tail booms projected well forward of the wings, allowing a substantial increase in internal fuel capacity. Four Red Top infra-red homing missiles replaced Firestreaks as primary armament; unlike Firestreak, Red Top could attack targets head-on, not just from behind.

Though production was at Chester the flight development programme was carried out from Hatfield. Powered by a pair of 11,230lb Rolls-Royce Avons, the FAW.2 had a fine performance up to 40,000ft where its climb rate flattened out, and it was only supersonic in a shallow dive. It had been expected to remain the standard British

The final development of the Sea Vixen, the FAW.2 differed externally from the FAW.1 chiefly in having tail booms that projected well forward of the wings, allowing a substantial increase in internal fuel capacity. Its armament was improved with Red Top missiles replacing the Firestreaks. BAE Systems

fleet defence aircraft until the introduction of the two-seat naval version of the Hawker P.1154, but after the cancellation of that aircraft it remained in operational service until 1972, even after the arrival of the McDonnell Douglas Phantom.

Sea Vixen Production at Christchurch and Chester

In 1951, de Havilland had taken over Airspeed and decided that its factory at Christchurch (then in Hampshire, now Dorset) should curtail development of the Ambassador; the hangers were filled instead with assembly lines for Vampires, Venoms and Sea Venoms. In 1953, development of the DH.110 was transferred there from Hatfield, under the direction of the Chief Designer (Christchurch), W.A. Tamblin. Though final assembly was centred at Christchurch, the one-piece centre section and stub-wing assembly were built at Portsmouth, the other former Airspeed factory. In 1960 the process was reversed: the entire Christchurch design staff was transferred to Hatfield; although Sea Vixen production remained at Christchurch, in August 1962 the last of 118 FAW.1s flew

out, the factory closed and production of the Sea Vixen was transferred to the Chester factory, where forty FAW.2s were produced between 1962 and 1966.

Sea Vixens in Service

Carrier-borne Sea Vixens were used in a sabre-rattling role on several occasions when Britain still projected power 'East of Suez'. Their airborne presence deterred Iraq when it threatened Kuwait in 1961, and Tanganyika and Indonesia in 1964. During the late 1960s Royal Navy aircraft carriers led the oil blockade of Ian Smith's Rhodesian regime and Sea Vixens flew many sorties then observing ships that might be breaking the blockade. They and other naval aircraft helped cover the difficult withdrawal from Aden in 1967.

Nearer to home, on 18 March 1967 the tanker *Torrey Canyon* ran aground on the Seven Stones Reef, 16 miles from Land's End, and a gigantic operation was started to minimize the damage that over 100,000 tons of crude oil would do to the English coastline and its sea-bird and fish life. Abortive efforts to pull the stricken vessel were given up, and Sea Vixens from

Yeovilton, along with Buccaneers and RAF Hunters were deployed to drop bombs and napalm in an attempt to burn off the spilled oil. According to *Flight* magazine:

Altogether, some 165 1,000lb bombs, 30,000gal of napalm and 10,000gal of aviation fuel were deposited in and around the *Torrey Canyon* during the three-day operation. By the Thursday evening the wreck was hardly visible and oil had almost ceased to flow from it.

The Sea Vixens remained in active service until 1972 when they were withdrawn from service. Three prototypes and twenty-two production aircraft were converted as unmanned target aircraft by Flight Refuelling, a firm well versed in such work. The remote control equipment was located in the vacant observer's station while the pilot's position continued to provide control for conventional flying. The Sea Vixen D.3, as it was designated, was painfully slow to be authorized and funded, and in the event only the prototypes were completed before the whole programme was cancelled. Two of the prototypes were involved in target drone work at RAE Llanbedr, but were always manned. This flying finally came to an end in October 1994.

Sea Vixen FAW.2 XJ579 at Yeovilton. It served on HMS *Eagle* and with 766 Sqn. Author

Specification – Sea Vixen FAW.2	
Length	55ft 7in (16.94m)
Wingspan	51ft (15.54m)
Height	10ft 9in (3.28m)
MTOW	46,750lb (21,200kg)
Max speed	Mach 0.91
Range	790 miles (1,270km)
Powerplant	Rolls-Royce Avon 208, 11,000lb thrust
Armament	20 × unguided rockets, 4 × Red Top missiles, 1 × nuclear bomb

Regrettably the Sea Vixen was not further developed, nor did it have the opportunity to replicate the outstanding export sales success of the Vampire and the Venom.

Folland Gnat

Folland Aircraft was founded by Henry Folland in December 1937 when he took over the assets of the short-lived British Marine Aircraft at Hamble in Hampshire. Folland had left Gloster Aircraft as Chief Designer as he was unhappy at Gloster's takeover by Hawker Siddeley. During World War Two the company had flourished as a subcontractor to Bristol, de Havilland, Supermarine and Vickers-Armstrongs. The end of hostilities was a challenge to the company and, like many others, it diversified into the manufacture of other products, including electric trucks and refrigerators.

Teddy Petter and the Gnat

In October 1950 W.E.W. 'Teddy' Petter left English Electric, where he had designed the Canberra and the P1, the progenitor of the Lightning, and invested his savings in Folland, which he joined as Deputy Managing Director. In July 1951, on Henry Folland's retirement, Petter became Managing Director and, in early 1954, he also became Chief Engineer.

Petter had tried to interest English Electric in a lightweight fighter but to no avail, and now proposed that Folland build it. The RAF also had a requirement for a lightweight fighter but were concentrating on the Hunter and Swift that were then being developed. However, Petter persuaded the Folland board to develop the design as a private venture and to build two prototypes powered by the new Bristol Saturn engine. Unfortunately, while the prototypes were being designed the powerplant was cancelled: to maintain impetus the first aircraft was adapted to fly with a lower-powered Armstrong Siddeley Viper of 1,640lb thrust. It became known as the Folland Midge, a 'proof of concept' aircraft

ABOVE: The Folland Midge, registered G-36-1, which flew in August 1954 and was the 'proof of concept' for Teddy Petter's lightweight fighter design. It crashed in September 1955.
BAE Systems

RIGHT: The Farnborough Air Show 1956 and XK724 on display, the first of the six Gnat F.1s ordered by the Ministry of Supply for evaluation. This Gnat was used in the development of the Indian Air Force aircraft and is now preserved at the RAF Museum at Cosford.
Peter Berry

56

for the design. As a replacement for the Saturn, Bristol Engines and Folland worked together on a private venture engine called the Orpheus to power the Gnat. As a result the second aircraft became the Gnat prototype, fitted with the new Orpheus that gave 3,285lb thrust.

The Midge, registered G-39-1, was assembled at Hamble and ground tested there before being transferred to Boscombe Down where it first flew on 11 August 1954. After further flights that same day it flew to Folland's flight test base at Chilbolton airfield in Hampshire. Sufficient flying was accomplished for the Midge to appear only a few weeks later at the Farnborough show. The tiny Midge was only 29ft long with a 21ft wide, 40-degree swept wing and proved supersonic in a dive. Flight testing proved satisfactory, though as the angle of attack on approach was found to be too high, drooped ailerons were fitted to make landings more manageable. The slightly larger and more powerful Gnat, registered G-39-2, joined the Midge in the air on 18 July 1955 and was demonstrated at Farnborough. Unfortunately the Midge crashed on its 221st flight in September 1955.

The Gnat was evaluated for the NATO fighter competition but was not selected, so Folland had no orders for the Gnat except from the Ministry of Supply, which had ordered six for evaluation. However Indian Air Force pilots who had evaluated the Hawker Hunter, Supermarine Swift and the Midge had been impressed with it and had recommended the Gnat should also be trialled. Following further tests the IAF acted speedily and by November 1955 had indicated their interest in ordering the Gnat F.1 and licence producing both it and the Orpheus engine.

The Gnat and the Indian Air Force

In Delhi on 15 September 1957, Mrs Gandhi, Chief of Staff to the Indian Prime Minister Jawaharlal Nehru, signed a contract in the presence of Teddy Petter for forty Gnat F.1s, twenty-five to be built and assembled in Hamble and fifteen as major sub-assemblies delivered to Hindustan Aircraft (HAL) at Kanpur for assembly with assistance from Folland engineers based there. In addition to the shipment of components, the contract stipulated the transport of jigs and tooling to HAL. Following the delivery of the UK-built aircraft, the IAF ordered 100 Gnats that were entirely constructed in Kanpur. These Gnats were powered by an uprated Orpheus offering 4,705lb thrust.

As the largest initial operator of the Gnat, it was to be expected that various improvements would be introduced by the IAF to refine the aircraft's performance and to facilitate ease of maintenance. The Indian aircraft bore the distinction of being the only Gnats used in anger, when they were used in the Indo-Pakistan wars of 1967 and 1971, acquitting themselves well against the Pakistani Sabres. The small size and manoeuvrability of the Gnat paid dividends in dog-fighting between the two types.

The standard armament fit on the Gnat F.1 was two 30mm Aden guns and 240 rounds of ammunition. Alternatively the Gnat could carry two 500lb bombs and two 66gal tanks, or two 500lb bombs and six 3in rockets, or eighteen 3in rockets alone, or twelve 3in rockets and two drop tanks. For reconnaissance it could transport a camera pod and a drop tank or several other combinations of stores.

In 1977 HAL started to deliver an indigenous development of the Gnat called the Ajeet. This had Martin-Baker ejector seats replacing Folland's lightweight seat, better avionics and hydraulics, a slab tailplane plus improved wing fuel tankage. Ajeets continued to serve until 1991.

Other Gnat F.1 Sales

Elsewhere the Gnat F.1 failed to gather sales, despite interest. Even before the finalization of the Indian contract, the Finnish Air Force had ordered twelve with an option to manufacture twenty aircraft under licence, though the licence production come to nought. The Finnish Gnats were delivered 1958–60; following the loss of one of them, Folland supplied a replacement from one of the original six built for evaluation by the RAF. They served until 1972. Two more Gnats were ordered by Yugoslavia for evaluation and shipped there by rail in 1958. Unfortunately one crashed soon after arrival and no more were ordered.

RAF Trainer

Having been very unenthusiastic about the Gnat in the early 1950s, the RAF recognized in 1956 that it needed to replace its Vampire trainers and obtain an aircraft with performance similar to contemporary jets. Petter speedily prepared a proposal for a tandem-two-seater. The fuselage was to be lengthened by 9 inches, the instructor occupying space previously used for equipment and fuel: the latter were moved into, respectively, the nose and the former gun compartments. The front windscreen was altered

Six Gnats at Chilbolton in early 1959; the three camouflaged aircraft including GN-107 are destined for Finland, the two unpainted ones for the Indian Air Force and the last was the Ministry of Supply's XK724. Author

from a fighter-type to a conventional shape. To make allowance for student pilots and to facilitate operation from smaller airfields, the wing was considerably altered by extending its area and by providing split flaps in conjunction with outboard ailerons. The controls remained the same as those of the F.1, but the area of the tail surfaces was increased. The Gnat T.1 had a high performance: it could exceed Mach 1 in a dive, reach Mach 0.97 in level flight and climb to 40,000ft in ten minutes, besides which it was cleared for spinning with drop-tanks in place. In March 1958 a £2.5m order was placed for a development batch of fourteen aircraft and the first of these, XM691, flew from Chilbolton on the contract date of 31 August 1959.

Hawker Siddeley Takeover

Folland then waited for a production order, but that was only forthcoming after it was taken over by Hawker Siddeley in September 1959. It was ironic that the Folland Company was founded by Henry Folland when he departed Goster after its takeover by Hawker Siddeley in 1937, and that twenty-two years later that same combine took over this small firm. In a similar manner Teddy Petter, who bitterly opposed the merger, left the firm on its takeover and retired to a monastery near Lausanne with his French-speaking Swiss wife.

Production of the Gnat continued at Hamble after the takeover, but in spring 1961 production test flying was moved to Dunsfold and the last Gnat flew out of Chilbolton in January 1962. The design office, while still offering Gnat developments, was tasked with designing and developing a trainer version of the P.1127, which led to the Harrier trainer following the RAF order. From July 1963 Hamble became part of the Hawker Siddeley Kingston Brough Division, and in 1965 purely Hawker Siddeley Hamble. The design office moved to Kingston, bringing to an end any further Gnat developments.

RAF and the Red Arrows

The production order for the Gnat trainer was placed in February 1960 with further orders in July 1961 and the final one in March 1962, bringing the total order to 105. The RAF Central Flying School received their first aircraft in November 1962 and the type settled in to serve as the RAF's trainer with the delivery of the final aircraft, XS111, in April 1965.

In many ways it was a complex aircraft and some pilots felt that Hunter trainers with their side-by-side layout would have been a far better (but also far more expensive) choice. Instructors found considerable difficulty in seeing ahead from behind the trainee, as the tight fit of the canopy in the rear of the cockpit restricted side-to-side head movement. However, re-manufacture of the canopies improved their shape and ameliorated this difficulty.

The month after Gnat production ended the Red Arrows were formed, flying seven Gnats as the RAF's sole display team and based at Kemble in Gloucestershire. They became immensely popular for the panache of their displays and were expanded to nine aircraft, always performing at Farnborough and regularly at venues in the UK and overseas. With the replacement of the RAF's Gnats by the Hawk in the training role, from 1979 the Red Arrows also replaced their machines with the Hawk.

Now as part of the Hawker Siddeley Group, the Gnat trainer XM691 is exhibited next to Vulcan XH534 at the 1960 Farnborough Show. BAE Systems

XM706, which joined the Central Flying School in 1965, in formation with another Gnat T.1. BAE Systems

Specification – Gnat T.1	
Length	31ft 9in (9.68m)
Wingspan	24ft 7.31m)
Height	9ft 7in (2.92m)
MTOW	9,520lb (4,320kg)
Max speed	Mach 0.95
Range	1,150 miles (1,850km)
Crew	2
Powerplant	Bristol Siddeley Orpheus 101, 4,520lb thrust

RIGHT: **The RAF's XP506 showing off its manoeuvrability at low level.** BAE Systems

BELOW: **Gnats of the Red Arrows saluting a Hawk at Hawker Siddeley Bitteswell in 1979. Through the 1960s and 1970s many Gnats, including those of the Red Arrows, passed through Bitteswell for overhaul and repair. The same plant took on the repair of Hawks and later assembled thirty-nine of them there.** BAE Systems

Hamble Sub-Contract

Though production of entire aircraft at Hamble ceased with the delivery of the last Gnat in 1965, as in the past the factory engaged in sub-contracting for other aircraft. The factory produced tails and wings for the Trident, 748 wings, Harrier tail sections and Airbus A300 components.

Unlike most Hawker Siddeley Aviation factories, Hamble is thankfully still functioning and engaged in aerospace work. In 1991 as part of British Aerospace it was renamed Aerostructures Hamble and sold off; it is now part of GE Aviation, an aerospace sub-contractor.

CHAPTER FOUR

Legacy Civil Aircraft Programmes

De Havilland Dove and Heron

In the period leading up to World War Two, de Havilland was a very successful manufacturer of light and larger types of aircraft. Many of the light aircraft were single or twin-engined; among the latter were the Dragon and Dragon Rapide, which could each carry six passengers and were used as airliners on British internal flights in the 1930s. A military version of the Rapide called the Dominie flew for the RAF on communications and training roles during the war.

As the war drew to a close and victory became certain, the British government and aircraft industry made plans for civil types that could fill the production lines and avoid a repetition of the great slump in aircraft manufacturing after World War One. A committee under the chairmanship of Lord Brabazon identified various types that would be needed, and the de Havilland DH.104 Dove was Hatfield's offering to conform to the Brabazon Committee's 5B specification for a new feederliner. Constructed of metal, this low-wing monoplane with a tricycle landing gear and reversible-pitch braking propellers was a substantial departure from the Dragon Rapide it was designed to replace.

Work on the design had begun in 1944 and the prototype G-AGPJ made its first flight from Hatfield just after the end of the war on 25 September 1945, but production was slow to gain momentum, with the second prototype only airborne in June 1946. However, substantial improvements had taken place during this time, a dorsal fin being added to improve directional stability and the overall size increased twice until a final satisfactory aesthetic and aerodynamic shape was achieved.

Initial versions powered by the de Havilland 330hp Gipsy Queen were the 7–11-seater Dove Mk 1 and the executive 6-seater Mk 2. The development of the Dove was driven by the installation of increasingly powerful engines and correspondingly higher operating weights, yet the overall dimensions remained unchanged throughout its production run.

The Dove found ready custom from airlines: fifty-five were still flying with worldwide airlines in 1960, and with firms such as Vickers-Armstrongs, English Electric, Hawker Siddeley, David Brown, Short Brothers, Dunlop, Shell and de Havilland themselves as executive transports. The RAF and Royal Navy ordered a military version of the Dove Mk 4 called the Devon, and a number of foreign air forces including

Geoffrey Pike made the first flight of the prototype Dove G-AGPJ from Hatfield on 25 September 1945. It is seen here some time later, after alterations to the dorsal fin to improve directional stability. BAE Systems

Dove CS-TAB was delivered to SATA, a Portuguese airline based in the Azores in May 1947. The Doves were used for inter-island flights. BAE Systems

ABOVE: **VR-NAB was delivered new to West African Airways in August 1947. Just beyond it is the first Dove prototype, G-AGPJ. Also visible on the Hatfield apron are three Mosquitoes and an early Vampire.** BAE Systems

LEFT: **Dove 1 VT-CQA on a publicity photo sortie with a full load of DH's lady employees. It was delivered to Airways (India) Ltd on 7 January 1948, but crashed into Mt Urbanu, 40 miles from Rome, whilst on its delivery flight.** BAE Systems

BELOW: **Although Hawker Siddeley had been nationalized and become part of British Aerospace, at this gathering of the company's Doves at Hatfield in December 1977 the aircraft still bear HSA markings.** BAE Systems

those of Argentina, India and New Zealand also operated Devons or Doves.

In 1953 the Dove 1 and 2 (many of which had been re-engined with 340hp Gipsy Queens as Dove 1Bs and 2Bs) were superseded by the Dove 5 airliner and Dove 6 executive transport with twin 380hp Gipsy Queen engines. These versions continued very successfully in production until 1960, when improved 400hp Gipsy Queen engines led to the introduction of the final variants, the Dove 7 Mk 8 for the airline and executive markets. These two marks had improved performance and also introduced the domed cockpit roof as fitted to the de Havilland Heron, a four-engined development of the Dove. In 1966 the Dove Mk 8 could be bought for £73,000 (2012 prices: £1.1m).

Production was shared between Hatfield and Chester, with the former completing 298, but by the mid-1950s it was based at Chester where 242 were built. The final Dove was completed in 1967 by Executive

Air Engineering at Baginton using components partially built by Hawker Siddeley Chester and was then delivered to Martin-Baker.

From Dove to Heron

Often in aeronautical engineering, a manufacturer will scale up a successful design to appeal to a wider market, profiting from the research and investment put in to the original. Before World War Two the Dragon and Dragon Rapide had led to the four-engined Express. The Express had not had the great success of the twin-engined types, but did sell reasonably well in return for the small investment de Havilland made in developing it.

The enlarged version of the Dove was the four-engined DH.114 Heron, which offered airliner standards for feeder-line routes. A rugged fourteen to seventeen-seat airliner with Gipsy Queen 30 engines and a fixed undercarriage for short to medium range services into unsophisticated airfields it was, like the Dove, of all-metal construction with fabric-covered control surfaces.

The prototype Heron, G-ALZL, was built largely from existing components, including Dove outer wing panels, nose and tail units. It flew on 10 May 1950 and completed its first 100 hours flying daily demonstrations at the 1950 Farnborough Air Show. During testing the original straight tailplane was replaced with a dihedral tailplane and the cockpit roof was reconfigured with a prominent bulge. The type received its Certificate of Airworthiness in November 1950. Following the prototype, six Heron Mk 1s and then the prototype Heron Mk2 were built at Hatfield, after which production was transferred to de Havilland's Chester plant. On 14 December 1952 the Heron Mk 2 took to the air,

ABOVE: **Vickers-Armstrongs' Dove and Heron fleet at Wisley in the early 1960s. The Dove G-AKSV is in BAC livery, while G-ANNO a Heron 1 and G-AOGW a Heron 2 still carry Vickers' livery, though without titling.** BAE Systems

LEFT: **On 10 May 1950 de Havilland test pilot Geoffrey Pike took the unpainted Heron prototype G-ALZL aloft on its first flight from Hatfield. The following summer British European Airways trialled the Heron on its Scottish and Channel Island services in BEA colours, and it was demonstrated at the September 1951 Farnborough Show. At the 1952 Farnborough display it appeared in Japan Air Lines livery. It is preserved in a poor state at the RAAF Association Aviation Heritage Museum of Western Australia.** BAE Systems

featuring a retractable undercarriage, which gave a 20mph increase in cruising speed and improved fuel consumption. Of the 149 Herons built, fifty-one were Mk 1s and the remainder Mk 2s.

The first services were flown by Braathens in Norway in August 1952 and Herons rapidly spread around the world operating in Australasia, South America, and the Middle and Far East. Herons also flew with the air forces of West Germany, Ghana, Iraq, Jordan, Kuwait, Malaysia, Saudi Arabia, South Africa and Sri Lanka, and with the RAF (including the Queen's Flight) and the Royal Navy. Production of Mk 1 Herons ceased on 12 April 1956 but the Mk 2 continued in production until May 1961.

Post-Production Developments of the Dove and Heron

Following the closure of the Dove production line a number of aircraft were heavily modified by US aviation firms to further improve their performance and marketability. The Riley Aeronautics Corporation replaced the Gipsy Queens with Avco Lycoming engines and fitted a large swept tail. In 1966 this was topped by an even more substantial development when Carstadt introduced the Carstadt Jet Liner 600, fitted with 600shp Garrett-AiResearch TPE331 turboprops and with a lengthened fuselage seating eighteen passengers.

Riley also re-engined the Heron with 290hp Lycomings to create the Riley Heron, and later made the turboprop-powered Riley Turbo Skyliner. In 1969 Saunders Aircraft of Manitoba carried out a far more extensive conversion by replacing the four piston engines with twin United Aircraft turboprops, and altering the flight deck and cabin window shape.

Conclusion

Through its innovative design and ability to fill a specific market, the Dove must be regarded as one of the successes of the Brabazon Committee for it made large sales: a total of 541 constructed by the time production ended in 1968. The Heron sold a little more than a quarter of this figure, but both amply repaid their investment.

A Heron 2 for Sicilian Airlines, I-AOVI on a test flight from Chester.
BAE Systems

Specification – Dove 7 and 8, Heron 2		
	Dove 7 & 8	*Heron*
Length	39ft 4in (11.99m)	48ft 6in (14.78m)
Wingspan	57ft (17.37m)	71ft 6in (21.79m)
Height	13ft 4in (4.06m)	15ft 7in (4.75m)
MTOW	8,950lb (3,900kg)	12,500lb (5,670kg)
Empty weight	6,580lb (2,985kg)	7,900lb (3,580kg)
Speed	162mph (260km/h)	163mph (262km/h)
Range	1,175 miles (1,890km)	805 miles (1,295km)
Passengers	8–14	14–17
Powerplant	2 × 400hp de Havilland Gipsy Queen 70 Mk 3	4 × 250hp de Havilland Gipsy Queen 30

Comet

When Hawker Siddeley took over de Havilland at the end of 1959 the Group inherited not just the Sea Vixen, Dove and Heron, but also the famous Comet, the world's first jetliner. With its own Argosy and 748 entering service and the Trident and the 125 on the horizon, Hawker Siddeley was transformed from a mainly military aircraft producer to one with an appreciable range of civil machines.

The Comet was designed to meet the Brabazon Committee's Type 4 specification for a jet-powered mail carrier. Though the design team under R.E. Bishop considered several unusual configurations, they finally decided on a classic design with a moderately (20 degrees) swept wing and four de Havilland Ghost engines embedded in the wing roots. The Ministry of Supply placed an order for two prototypes in September 1946, and in January 1947 ordered fourteen Comets on behalf of BOAC and British South American Airways. Construction began under strict security at de Havilland's Hatfield plant.

Maiden Flight

Less than three years after the finalization of the design, Comet prototype G-5-1 made its maiden flight on 27 July 1949; re-registered as G-ALVG and piloted by John Cunningham, it went on to impress the crowds at Farnborough in September that year.

It was soon decided that the original single mainwheel undercarriage was inadequate for production aircraft, and from December 1949 to February 1950 trials were conducted with a four-wheel bogie undercarriage that became standard on production Comet 1s. The prototype also embarked on a number of overseas flights to test both the aircraft's systems and its endurance. In eleven months 324 hours of testing were achieved, and on the first anniversary of the maiden flight of G-ALVG the second prototype, G-ALZK, took to the air. Early indications were that the Comet met most of its design specifications. It could cruise at 490mph at 40,000ft and, with an all-up weight of 105,000lb, could carry thirty-six passengers over 2,600 miles. Tropical trials took place at Nairobi

The two Comet 1 prototypes in the air. Unfortunately neither was preserved as both were used for structural tests at Farnborough. BAE Systems

and Khartoum in early to mid-1950, and in September 1950 G-ALVG returned to the Farnborough Show to make its second appearance, now bedecked in the livery of the Comet's premier customer, BOAC.

Production of Comet 1s for BOAC only slowly built up, with just three of BOAC's Comet 1s taking to the air from Hatfield during 1951. The world's first Certificate of Airworthiness for a commercial jet passenger aircraft was granted on the 22 January 1952 and on 2 May that year BOAC's Comet 1 G-ALYP operated the first jet airliner service from London to Johannesburg. A route to Tokyo was soon added, and the Comet with its high speeds and comfort was regarded as the acme of fashionable travel. Air France's Comets flew to Beirut while its French partner UAT (Union Aéromaritime de Transport) served Africa.

De Havilland engineers strove to improve their design and created the Comet 1A using a modified Ghost engine with water injection, which improved 'hot and high' airfield performance. This improved aircraft soon attracted orders from Canadian Pacific, Air France, UAT and the Royal Canadian Air Force. The first Comet 1A was CF-CUM for Canadian Pacific, but following a take-off crash on its delivery flight it remained with de Havilland and was used in take-off trials.

Comet 2

To the dismay of the de Havilland Engine Company's engineers the next mark of the Comet – the Comet 2 – incorporated a far superior engine, the Rolls-Royce Avon, which showed great potential. Its increase in thrust allowed for an increase in payload and range, and with a 3ft fuselage extension and reorganization of the cabin, accommodation grew to 44–48 passengers. The Comet 2 immediately attracted orders from BOAC, Japan Air Lines, LAV, National Airlines (USA) and Panair do Brasil.

One of BOAC's Comet 1s (G-ALYT) was diverted from the airline to become the prototype Avon-powered Comet. Though designated as a Comet 2X, this aircraft was built to Comet 1 dimensions. With the growth in demand, de Havilland established a production line at its large factory in Chester for the Comet 2 and 3, and Shorts at Belfast also became a manufacturing partner.

The Crashes

The Concorde-like glamour associated with the Comet was soon diminished when two crashed during take-off. De Havilland established that the cause was that pilots were

raising the aircraft's nose too soon, causing a ground stall, so introduced a drooped leading edge to stop its re-occurrence.

Whereas the cause of the take-off accidents had been easy to diagnose, the crashes that followed were far more difficult to analyse. On the anniversary of the first service, BOAC's G-ALYV crashed into the sea en route from Colombo bound for Delhi. Then disaster struck in a similar manner on 10 January 1954, with G-ALYP departing Rome, which crashed into the Mediterranean off Elba. All Comets were temporarily grounded but there was huge pressure from the airlines for the Comet to return to service. There was a baseless view that these accidents were caused by engine fire, so more than fifty modifications were introduced around the engines and the airliner returned to the skies. Just over two weeks later, on 8 April 1954 G-ALYY crashed into the sea after departing Rome and the Comet's Certificate of Airworthiness was withdrawn. The Comets made their way back to their bases without passengers, and were grounded.

Investigation into the Crashes

Even before the third mysterious crash, Royal Navy ships had been at work retrieving pieces of G-ALYP from the seabed off Elba. Most of the aircraft was brought to the surface and flown to RAE Farnborough where a brilliant investigation was led by the Director, Arnold Hall, who was knighted for the efficacy of this investigation. The pieces of wreckage were reconstructed on a wooden frame and it was clearly evident that there had been an explosive decompression. A large water tank was constructed and G-ALYU placed in it, and the fuselage was then filled with water, which was increased and decreased in pressure to simulate the strain of an actual flight. As the fuselage was surrounded by water, it would not cause a violent explosion if it ruptured. After only 3,000 simulated flights the fuselage split open and the investigation established that metal fatigue had grown from the corners of the riveted escape hatches, where the stresses were far greater than de Havilland had understood.

The Aftermath

These events caused de Havilland major problems: orders evaporated and airlines already using Comets demanded compensation. The twenty-one Comet 1s completed and the Comet 2s coming off the production lines would need either substantial re-manufacture to allow safe use or would have to be scrapped. The Government assisted de Havilland by ordering eight Comet 2s rebuilt with heavier-gauge fuselage skins and oval windows, even though it was uneconomical, and these eventually entered RAF service in a transport role – a strengthened Comet 2 was water-tank tested at Hatfield to ensure that the rebuild was effective. Three early Comet 2s were not rebuilt but, designated Comet 2R, were engaged in an electronic reconnaissance

role. Two of the earlier Comet 1s were also rebuilt with heavier-gauge fuselage skins for the RCAF, and two others for experiment purposes by the RAE.

The Public Enquiry into the crashes in November 1954 laid no blame with de Havilland, which was very fortunate for the manufacturer. Some commentators were critical that de Havilland had used square apertures for windows and other hatches, as it was known that holes in a pressure vessel should ideally be circular or elliptical. However, four days after the publication of the Enquiry report on 12 February 1955, BOAC gave a resounding vote of confidence to the aircraft and announced it would order a new fleet of Comets. A month later BOAC confirmed this as an order for nineteen Comet 4s.

Comet 3

During the hiatus caused by the accidents the sole Comet 3, G-ANLO, flew on 19 July 1954 and took on the mantle of ambassador for the Comet so that airlines and potential passengers should not imagine that the type was finished. The Comet 3 possessed the classic look of the Comet but was enhanced by the 15ft 5in longer fuselage and pinion tanks on each wing providing a streamlined, elegant profile.

In July 1956 it was rebuilt to incorporate many aspects of the Comet 4, enabling 80 per cent of the work needed for certification of that mark to be carried out by it. To expedite testing of the Comet 4B it was modified to represent the aerodynamic aspects of the 4B by the reduction of its wing span by 7ft and the removal of wing pods. It flew in this configuration on 21 August 1958 as the Comet 3B, and was exhibited at Farnborough in BEA livery the following month.

Comet 4

The Comet 4 was built to the same dimensions of the Comet 3 but had more powerful Avon 524 engines of 10,500lb thrust each. G-APDA was the first Comet 4, there being no prototype, and made its maiden flight on 27 April 1958, just over four years after the Comet 1s were withdrawn from service. The initial flight test evaluation by de Havilland of the Comet 4 required just a small number of flying hours owing to G-ANLO's major contribution. To ensure a safe-life for the Comet 4, de Havilland used the test programme set up to investigate the fatigue failures on the Comet 1 to test new components, and could guarantee the life of a Comet 4 up to 30,000 hours.

In September 1958 the Comet 4 received a Certificate of Airworthiness and on 4 October BOAC transatlantic services began, just ahead of Pan Am's introduction of transatlantic services with Boeing 707s. However, the Comets were only destined to ply the North Atlantic for two years as a refuelling stop was necessary on most westbound flights. BOAC's Comets also flew on Far East routes, but the Comet 4's career with BOAC was short as their last service was in November 1965 and the fleet was offered for sale. Further examples of the Comet 4 were purchased by Aerolineas Argentinas and East African Airways.

The basic Comet 4 design was adapted to offer the medium-range Comet 4B with the fuselage stretched by 6ft 6in, and with the wing cropped by 7ft and the pinion tanks deleted. As G-ANLO had flown with this wing (but not the extended fuselage), test flying of the Comet 4B was comparatively short. BEA ordered fourteen of this version and Olympic Airways operated four, though they were actually purchased by BEA. The final Comet, the 4C,

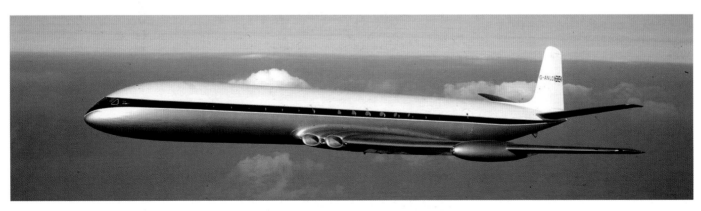

The Comet 3 prototype G-ANLO, which was demonstrated at Farnborough in September 1954, 1955 and 1957. BAE Systems

LEFT: **The first Comet 4B, G-APMA, in October 1959. It was delivered to BEA in December 1959 and conducted BEA's last Comet flight on 31 October 1971.** BAE Systems

BELOW: **Comet 4C ST-AAW was delivered to Sudan Airways in November 1962.** BAE Systems

BOTTOM: **A former BOAC Comet 4, G-APDG was sold to Kuwait Airways in 1966 and purchased by Dan-Air in 1970. It is seen here at Heathrow.** BAE Systems

had the longer fuselage of the 4B together with the broader span wing of the Comet 4. Mexicana was the launch customer and among others to fly it were Kuwait Airways, Middle East Airlines, the RAF, Sudan Airways and – in an executive version – the King of Saudi Arabia.

As the Comets were displaced by newer, more economical jets in the late 1960s and 1970s, Dan-Air snapped up a large proportion of the survivors and at its peak had

over half the Comet 4s of all marks ever built. The last commercial service was flown in 1980, though the A&AEE's XS235 continued flying in a research role until 1997. Though only sixty-five Comet 4s of all marks were sold, a profit was reportedly made on its production.

The Royal Air Force's Nimrod maritime patrol aircraft – described in detail in Chapter 15 – was based on the Comet, and served from 1969 until 2011.

Specification – Comet 4C	
Length	118ft (35.97m)
Wingspan	115ft (35.05m)
Height	28ft 6in (8.69m)
MTOW	162,000lb (73,500kg)
Max cruise speed	500mph (800km/h)
Range	2,570 miles (4,135km)
Passengers	72–106
Powerplant	4 × 10,500lb Rolls-Royce Avon 525

CHAPTER FIVE

From the Argosy to the Hawker Siddeley 681

Introduction

Armstrong Whitworth's first aircraft works in the Coventry area was established at Whitley Abbey Airfield in 1920, just after the RAF had vacated the site, where the firm ran a flying school alongside its manufacturing base. In 1931 the flying school moved to Hamble and was renamed Air Service Training (AST).

As a wholly owned part of Hawker Siddeley Group from 1935, Armstrong Whitworth built the large, four-engined Ensign airliner, the Whitley bomber and the Albemarle transport/glider tug. In 1936 Armstrong Whitworth had expanded their operations by establishing a factory at Baginton airfield and this became the centre of aircraft manufacturing. During and after World War Two Armstrong Whitworth production mainly comprised the manufacture and development of aircraft for other Group companies such as the Gloster Meteor and Hawker Sea Hawk. There were minor exceptions in the shape of the AW52 'flying wing' and the Apollo. The AW52 was a research aircraft that manifested itself as a glider and subsequently as a jet-powered research aircraft. The Apollo was built to the same specification as the Vickers Viscount airliner but proved a failure, largely due to the inadequate performance of the Armstrong Siddeley Mamba turboprop engines.

Owing to the lack of a hard runway at Baginton, the company leased two hangars at Bitteswell, Leicestershire for trials with the AW52G flying wing glider, purchasing the airfield outright in 1956; thereafter, final assembly and flight test were based at Bitteswell. The Armstrong Siddeley aero-engine test fleet was also based there from 1947 to 1959 when it was transferred to Filton following its merger with Bristol Aero-Engines to form Bristol Siddeley.

In the 1950s the Whitley factory took on the research and development into guided weapons, developing the Seaslug missile and doing the initial work on the Sea Dart. With the integration of the Group's holdings post-1960, this factory became part of Hawker Siddeley Dynamics. It was closed in 1968 and its work transferred to other HSD sites; the site was bought by Jaguar Cars in 1968.

Armstrong Whitworth Aircraft was eventually grouped with another Hawker Siddeley concern, the Gloster Aircraft Company, in October 1961 and the combined company was known as Whitworth Gloster Aircraft Ltd. On 1 July 1963 it was joined by Avro and became the Avro Whitworth Division of Hawker Siddeley Aviation. The last Armstrong Whitworth Design, the AW681 Transport, now became the HS681. When the Government axed many major aerospace programmes, including the HS681, in 1965, the closure of Baginton that July was inevitable. Bitteswell continued as an overhaul and repair facility until 1983, when British Aerospace closed the site.

Bitteswell had a remarkable and varied record of work, with the assembly and flight test of Meteors, Sea Hawks, Hunters, Javelins, Argosies and finally Hawks. Gnats, Vulcans and Buccaneers were regularly maintained there, while seven Shackletons were converted to AEW.2 standard and six Victors' flight decks were refitted during their conversion into K.2s at Woodford. Other aircraft that received attention at Bitteswell included Tridents, Nimrods and Harriers.

Argosy

The Argosy was the second commercial aircraft from Armstrong Whitworth Aircraft (AWA) to be so named, the first being a passenger aircraft of the 1920s and 1930s.

In the autumn of 1955 the Air Ministry formulated operational requirement OR323 for a new transport for passengers or heavy freight. The specification was for a machine of a size roughly midway between the Vickers Valetta and the Blackburn Beverley, and with a performance surpassing that of either of the earlier aircraft. It was suggested to tendering companies that particular consideration be given to an aircraft designed to appeal to commercial operators as well.

By the mid-1950s Armstrong Whitworth was acutely aware that its military work was in decline. During late 1955 the company began a campaign to rectify their shrinking circumstances, holding discussions with air forces and civil operators throughout the world. Europe was covered by the AWA sales staff at Baginton and London, while prospective customers further afield were interviewed by the regional executives of the Hawker Siddeley Group.

These discussions soon confirmed what the company had been hoping, that the projected RAF aircraft was of a size and character likely to interest a very large number of operators throughout the world. Then as now, most civil freight aircraft were versions of airliners built as dedicated or passenger/freight convertible aircraft, or were converted to this role after passenger service (such as the many freighter versions of Airbuses and Boeings). This does rather question the veracity of Hawker Siddeley's market research in the mid-1950s.

A submission to the Ministry of Supply was made with a high-wing aircraft as the AW66 with a gross weight of 65,000lb and two 3,000hp turboprop engines. The fuselage had a 'beaver' tail with a loading ramp and doors to permit truck-bed loading and heavy dropping to meet an obvious military requirement. Narrow appendages extended from the rear fuselage, ending in a pair of vertical tail surfaces mounted on the horizontal tail. However, this design was soon totally revised as it became clear that to achieve the maximum possible operational flexibility, the aircraft would need to be capable of rapid turn-round with any kind of load – passengers or freight. In the freight role it is a great advantage to have a full-section door at both ends of the hold, so that cargo can be loaded and unloaded rapidly from both ends. These large doors posed a major design problem and so a twin-boom tail was adopted, allowing for a more satisfactory and flexible layout.

By 1956 the funding available for the purchase of new military aircraft was being curtailed, and the Air Ministry requirement evaporated. However, Armstrong-Whitworth was so convinced of the correctness of its design and of its commercial potential that work was allowed to continue. By the autumn of 1956 the design had settled down as a firm project, bearing the designation AW650. It was regarded as primarily a civil aircraft with obvious military applications, instead of the other way round.

Designed specifically to bring down the cost of air freight, the Argosy was designed from the start to embody the most advantageous aspects of a modern freighter: front and rear direct loading, strong floors and lashing points at vehicle height, a large volume (3,680cu ft) and floor area, and pressurization. Aware that the airline industry was not generally inclined towards freight-only aircraft the Argosy was designed to be readily adaptable to passenger-carrying work, and comfortable accommodation could be provided for up to eighty-three passengers. The intensive market survey carried out in 1955–56 had shown that four Rolls-Royce Dart engines should be used, but it was planned to offer a version with two Rolls-Royce Tynes, the AW651. The Tynes, with their lower installed drag and greater efficiency, would have been suitable for longer stage-lengths.

Hawker Siddeley's aim was to produce a range of freight aircraft using the same basic wing, powerplant, twin-boom, fin and

Argosy production at the Baginton factory on the outskirts of Coventry. Ray Williams

tailplane, but using them with a variety of fuselages according to the required role. The military freighter development of the AW650 – with an integral rear beaver tail ramp for dropping stores – was designated the AW660. A similar version with Tyne engines, the AW661, was also projected. The AW670 was a further project with a larger unpressurized double-deck fuselage and a floor-level width of 174in: it could have been a car ferry accommodating six cars and thirty passengers or a short-range passenger aircraft with 130 seats.

Hawker Siddeley Group Board Approval

The board of the Hawker Siddeley Group authorized a complete programme on 11 September 1956. Putting into production the only firmly established civil aircraft in the Group without any orders was a calcu-

lated gamble as it was wholly financed by the Group without any Government support. The projected cost of the Argosy programme, which included the manufacture of ten production aircraft, was £10m at 1956 prices (£206.5m at 2012 prices). The Government provided support of £130,000.

It was anticipated that deliveries of the fully certificated production aircraft would be made in early 1960. Hawker Siddeley managing director Sir Roy Dobson had insisted that to save money the Avro Shackleton MR.3 wing should be used in place of the more modern design that the AWA team had designed for the Argosy. However, in order to provide adequate clearance for the projected twin Tyne versions with their larger propellers, the inboard engines and therefore the tail booms were moved further outboard than they had been in the original Shackleton. The resulting modifications to the Shackleton wing negated any cost saving and the aircraft was disadvantaged by having a wing that was 1,500lb heavier, reducing payload and causing additional drag that cut the cruising speed by 20kt. Initially given the name Freightliner or Freighter-Coach, it was formally named the Argosy in July 1958.

Production

Instead of cautiously constructing a single prototype, the Group agreed to the manufacture of a batch of ten aircraft in production jigs plus two complete airframes for static and fatigue testing, which were at the

The prototype Argosy 100, G-AOZZ, in its initial livery on the tarmac at Armstrong Whitworth's airfield at Bitteswell. Ray Williams

company's design centre at Whitley. Work began on constructing ten aircraft at Baginton with final assembly at Bitteswell, where the prototype was due to fly in October 1958. Armstrong Whitworth was then employing 8,000 at its three factories.

Early interest by Riddle Airlines encouraged the manufacturer to forge ahead with construction. With Argosies on order Riddle was able to steal a march on others tendering for Logair, a scheduled cargo airlift service operated on behalf of the USAF. It was the biggest cargo airlift in the world.

In the UK, BEA and Silver City were the two airlines bidding for the Argosy at this early stage – the latter seeking the ultra-wide-hold version to carry six cars parked two abreast on its cross-Channel services. The exorbitant cost of conversion put an end to this project, but BEA's plans materialized and the airline ordered three aircraft for freight carriage.

To achieve the tightest possible schedule the workload was spread widely amongst the Group companies, which became involved in the ground testing, design and the production of the Argosy. In addition to the wind tunnels at Whitley, Avro's at Woodford and Armstrong Siddeley Motors' low-speed tunnel at Anstey all took part in the test programmes. Whereas Armstrong Whitworth undertook the design and manufacture of the complete fuselage, the tail booms, the wing trailing edge, the double-slotted flaps and the basic design of the empennage, Avro assumed responsibility for the extensive redesign and manufacture of the Shackleton wing. Gloster handled the detail design of the side doors, flaps, outer nacelles and tail unit, and Air Service Training contributed numerous small parts. From outside the Group there were many suppliers, most notably Rolls-Royce and Vickers-Armstrongs (Aircraft) who provided the complete powerplant package, and Dowty, which manufactured the undercarriage.

The decision to have a completely unobstructed cargo hold with full-section doors at either end dictated much of design. The flight deck was sited above the hold and the configuration of the aircraft was largely determined by the height of the main undercarriage and the height of the fins. Accordingly, the wing spars were sunk into the upper part of the fuselage, giving an interior hold height of 80in and width of 120in; the floor area was 426sq ft. The roof of the flight deck swept down to the rear to meet the basic fuselage at the leading-edge of the wing. The airframe was built up from conventional light-alloy sheet and sections fabricated by riveting and Redux bonding.

For manufacturing purposes the open-ended monocoque fuselage was divided into logical sections: the floor and under-floor structure, side panels, flight-deck floor, and superstructure over the flight deck and equipment bay. Continuing the philosophy of conventional construction and proven systems, all flying control surfaces were manually operated by a mixture of push/pull-rods and cables. The three units of the undercarriage retracted rearwards; the main gear was extended by controlled free-fall action following hydraulic release of the up-locks, while the small, steerable nose gear was lowered by positive hydraulic power. The Rolls-Royce Dart engine installation was in essence a copy of that for the Viscount, and Vickers was contracted to provide the nacelles for the aircraft.

Flight Test

The first Argosy, G-AOZZ, installed with an extensive amount of flight test equipment, was rolled out on 20 December 1958 from the Bitteswell flight shed; then followed vibration tests, ground running of the four Rolls-Royce Darts and a pre-flight

Publicity shot of an Argosy demonstrating its Mini-carrying capabilities. Ray Williams

The second Argosy built, G-APRL, flying with a beaver tail to trial it for the RAF's Argosy C.1. This tail could be opened in flight to allow air dropping of supplies. G-APRL was converted back to Argosy 100 configuration and delivered to Riddle as N6507R. It returned to the British register and is now preserved at Baginton. Ray Williams

inspection. It completed its weighing and compass-swinging checks and two days of taxiing trials on the snow-cleared runway before being taken into the air on 8 January 1959 by Armstrong Whitworth's chief test pilot, Eric Franklin.

Several other Argosies took part in the flight testing and the second, G-APRL, was temporarily converted to become the aerodynamic prototype of the military Argosy: it was fitted with a new rear fuselage with clamshell rear loading doors and flew on 28 July 1960 from Bitteswell. It was later converted back to the normal civil configuration and delivered to Riddle. Armstrong Whitworth laid down a rigorous schedule for the completion of all flight-testing for both the FAA and ARB certificates, and as a result these were awarded in December 1960.

Argosy Series 200

Following on from the production of the civil series 100 and military Argosies, Hawker Siddeley decided that the Argosy should have more payload and a better climb and terrain-clearance performance. To this end the upgraded Argosy 200 was developed. The major change was the structural design of the wing: the original two-spar mass-boom wing developed from the Shackleton had fatigue life limited to about 30,000 hours, while the series 200's box-spar wing was fail-safe and had an infinite fatigue life. A useful bonus conferred by the new wing was a reduction of the total airframe weight by 380lb, by eliminating the bag-type fuel tanks by sealing the intermediate portions of the wing to make integral tanks, and by removing two of the fuselage frames by a

new method of wing attachment. The new design permitted an all-round increase in permissible weights and had provision for any foreseeable increase in power from the Roll-Royce Dart engine, though this never transpired. Though 3,060eshp Dart 10s would have been desirable, the likely development expense was judged too costly, so uprated versions of the existing engine were chosen instead. Even so, the Series 220 had around 12 per cent more power and the chief performance objectives were realized with a 5,000lb higher gross weight. This was achieved without an increase in the empty weight, so the new Argosy became a much more capable aircraft. Compared with the 100 series, this version offered costs per ton mile some 10 per cent less, and also doubled range with maximum payload (31,170lb over 500 miles).

The prototype Argosy 200, G-ASKZ. In this photo from early in the test programme it is yet to receive the wing fences fitted to cure problems at the stall. Ray Williams

At the time the aircraft entered BEA service in November 1961 it became clear that the 108 × 88in freight pallet would become the international standard. This size had already been chosen by USAF Military Air Transport Service and adopted for long-haul civil freighters such as the CL-44, DC-8F and 707-320C. The Argosy could accept the big pallet only by fitting a ball mat inside the door (in order that the pallets could be moved to one side of centre to allow an access gangway down one side). So for the 200 the end-loading openings were widened to the maximum – necessitating highly stressed steel inserts at the narrow point of the frames – to allow straight-in loading of the pallet.

Hawker Siddeley laid down ten Series 200 on the Baginton production line for delivery starting in late 1964. Though there was an appreciation of the aircraft in many parts of Europe and North America, at approximately £725,000 each without spares, most operators viewed the investment with some trepidation. The 200 series development incurred high development costs that were never recouped by Hawker Siddeley from the sale of just six aircraft.

Argosy 200 Flight Test

With chief test pilot Eric Franklin at the controls, the first Argosy 200, G-ASKZ, flew from Bitteswell on 11 March 1964. The new wing produced unexpected stalling and low-speed handling difficulties due to its different flexing characteristics, changing the aircraft's stalling qualities and causing aileron snatch. A small leading-edge wedge placed inboard of the inner nacelles was the classic cure for the tip stalling, and the aileron difficulty was cured by a large fence. Elevator buffet (bothersome on the original 100 Series, cured by vortex generators behind the cockpit) reappeared and was overcome by tying together the two servo-tab-operated elevator sections.

BEA ordered five Series 200s to replace their three 100s in September 1964, designated as Series 222. One of these 222s, G-ASXL, soon crashed and was replaced by another, G-ATTC, but no more were sold even though BEA lost another machine soon after. G-ASKZ and one another partly assembled aircraft were dismantled, while parts for the final two were used for spares. All seventy-three civil and military Argosies were assembled at the Bitteswell plant and made their maiden flights from there.

The Argosy in Civilian Service

The first US operator of the Argosy was Riddle, which negotiated a £12m/four-year financing agreement with HSA for purchase of seven Argosy 101s. The largest part of its business was transport for the USAF in the form of the Logair contract supplying eighty-nine USAF stations in the USA with equipment and stores.

The first Argosy was delivered by Armstrong Whitworth to Riddle on 8 December 1960 and made its first revenue flight on Logair work on 15 January 1961. However, the aircraft was grounded only ten days later, due to skin cracking in the vertical and horizontal tail surfaces. This was soon rectified and the aircraft operated at very high utilization of 10–11 hours per day on Logair schedules. HSA compensated Riddle for the loss in service owing to the cracking, but in mid-1962 Riddle lost their Logair contract and sold the Argosies back to HSA. In the event the seven former Riddle Series 100s continued to serve with Capitol and Zantop, earning money on USAF Logair contracts and general freighting, though one Argosy crashed in 1965.

G-AOZZ was refurbished after flight trials and brought up to production standard for delivery to BEA on 21 December 1961 joining G-APRM and G-APRN, which were delivered the previous month. BEA's three Argosy 102s achieved an impressive reliability record with the airline despite the large freight capacity of the Vanguard fleet: the Argosies with their large capacity were soon handling 33 per cent of BEA's total freight traffic. They served on domestic and continental services, typically flying 1,475 miles a day on seven routes; for example, from London to Frankfurt, Frankfurt to Düsseldorf, Düsseldorf to London, London to Guernsey, Guernsey to London and London to Manchester and back to London. By taking advantage of the Argosy's unique double-end loading, turnarounds were easily accomplished in thirty minutes and sometimes as little as twenty minutes.

As BEA's improved series 222s arrived during 1965, the earlier 102s were returned to HSA. After G-ASXL crashed into a mountain in Italy in July 1965 one of the 102s, G-APRM, was chartered to fill the gap and a replacement was ordered. No replacement was ordered after a further write-off

N6501R, an Argosy for Riddle employed on the Logair contract and delivered in December 1960. Ray Williams

when G-ASXP cartwheeled at Stansted. Meanwhile, the three returned Argosy 102s lingered unused for a time; after three years G-AOZZ and G-APRN were sold to Universal in the USA, while G-APRM was employed by Rolls-Royce for transporting engines and other services from 1969 until 1980 and was scrapped at Castle Donington in 1982.

LEFT: The rear-loading door on a BEA Argosy 100. Author's collection

BELOW: A BEA Argosy 222 with the large wing fence needed to improve the stalling characteristics of the aircraft. BEA received five Argosy 222s but soon lost one, so ordered a replacement. Ray Williams

BEA's four remaining Argosy 222s were only employed until 1970 when they were replaced by the Merchantmen freighter conversion of the Vickers Vanguard. These four redundant Argosies flew off to serve with Midwest Airlines in Canada; two of them eventually went to serve on a New Zealand Post Office contract with Safe Air. Eventually the eight remaining Argosy 101s were bought by Universal, which went bankrupt in 1972: four remained in the USA, three joined Sagittair and one joined Shackleton Aviation in the UK. One of these, G-APRN, was leased by the British Aircraft Corporation to support a tour of the Middle East in 1975. These Argosies and two of the retired RAF aircraft gradually disappeared from the UK to fly in Australia, Congo and the Philippines.

Argosies remained in service in Australia and New Zealand until 1990, which was a remarkable achievement for this elderly design.

The RAF's Argosies

The RAF's Argosy AW660 was derived from the AW650, but differed considerably from it with its clamshell rear loading doors to admit bulky stores and vehicles. These doors could be opened in flight to permit air-dropping of almost any item of equipment up to a weight of 31,000lb. Inexplicably, the one-piece swinging nose of the civil Argosy was not fitted to the RAF's aircraft. Like many other military developments of civil transports, the AW660 had more power, a higher wing loading and a greater payload capacity than its precursor. The military Argosy had a higher rate of climb than the civil version owing to its Dart RDa8 military-rated turboprops, enabling it to quickly regain cruising altitude and resume pressurization after a heavy drop.

Basically a freighter, it also had applications as a VIP or troop transport, for casualty evacuation, as a mobile battle headquarters or for paratroop dropping. Full pressurization gave it the ability to cruise over trunk routes, providing more comfort

ABOVE: XN814, the first of fifty-six Argosy C.1s for the RAF. Ray Williams

RIGHT: XN814 with its beaver-tail open. BAE Systems

LEFT: **A rare photo of XN814 engaged in flight-refuelling trials.**
Avro Heritage

BELOW: **XN817 at HSA Woodford in April 1976 while employed on air-dropping trials with the A&AEE.**
BAE Systems

than soldiers had previously. In the event of a 'hot' situation the RAF version could go to the scene of operations, parachuting men and equipment or landing them at forward airstrips. Housed in the extreme nose there was a cloud-collision radar scanner with a prone viewing position below it for the parachute drop controller.

With fifty-six Argosy C.1s ordered, the first were delivered to RAF Transport Command: Nos 114 and 267 Squadrons at Benson and No. 105 at Aden. No. 215 Squadron at Changi, Singapore was next, and there was an Argosy Operational Conversion Unit at Thorney Island.

The Argosy was employed as a transport for supply dropping and parachuting. Though it was very well-equipped, the manual controls were heavy and the fitting of heavy freight floor and especially the beaver tail made the aircraft very heavy. As a result the payload was comparatively small given the aircraft's weight, so it could not go very far, fast or high when fully loaded. Indeed

its speed, payload and cruising altitude were not much better than the Hastings, an aircraft it was meant to replace and substantially surpass. The Argosy was underpowered and proved too slow to formate with the Victor for flight refuelling, so Argosies had to be specially equipped as flight-refuelling tankers to refuel other Argosies, a far from satisfactory situation. Owing to these factors, most Transport Command Argosies only had a short life before being replaced by Andovers or Hercules.

Nine Argosies were converted into E.1 radar calibration aircraft to assess airfields in 1971 and remained with this task until replaced by the Andover in 1978. A plan to use fourteen redundant aircraft as Argosy T.2s for navigational training, replacing Vickers Varsities, only progressed to the prototype conversion stage before it was abandoned. Five Argosies were sold for civil use: one for spares, two to ORAS in Zaire, one to Philippines Airlines and two in the USA.

Conclusions

The civil Argosy clearly failed to realize Hawker Siddeley's expectations from their research data and was a commercial failure, the company losing more than £6m (£105m at 2013 prices). At the initial price of under £400,000 per aircraft, the Argosy was often beaten by converted second-hand piston-engined ex-airliners such as the DC-6, DC-7C and Super Constellation. Airline interest waned when it was realized that the initial price had been very optimistic and that the Argosy cost approximately four times as much as comparable second-hand equipment.

In Europe the traffic potential existed, but it was thinly spread and among a multitude of competing carriers. With airlines receiving new jets with a vast increase in hold capacity used on the shorter inter-city sectors of long-haul routes, there was no need for the Argosy. BEA's three 100s only ever managed to break even and their more

Specification – Argosy 220	
Length	86ft 9in (26.43m)
Wingspan	115ft (35.05m)
Height	29ft 3in (8.92m)
MTOW	93,000lb (42,180kg)
Empty weight	48,830lb (22,145kg)
Max cruise speed	285mph (460km/h)
Range	1,850 miles (2,980km)
Passengers	83
Powerplant	4 × 2,230shp Rolls-Royce Dart 532/1

efficient Argosy 222s only remained in service until 1970 when they were replaced by the Merchantman.

The RAF's Argosy C.1 had only a short career with the RAF due to its indifferent performance and it was soon replaced by Lockheed Hercules, some of which remain in RAF service at the time of writing.

HS681

As the production of the Argosy passed its peak at the Baginton and Bitteswell factories the workforce could feel confident of continuing work as on 5 March 1963 the contract for the Hawker Siddeley 681 was announced by Julian Amery, the Minister

of Aviation. The Air Staff had formulated Operational Requirement 351 at least eighteen months earlier and in March 1962 Interavia reported:

The requirement would be for thirty aircraft, but R & D and production for aircraft such as the BAC.208 or the AW.681 would cost about £100m. Reluctance to spend such a sum, when an STOL Belfast or Lockheed C-130 could be bought very much more cheaply, appears to have been the principal reason for the prolonged delay in coming to a decision.

The 681 had grown from Air Ministry Operational Requirement 351 issued in 1961 calling for a large STOL transport, capable of taking nearly every type of British military equipment to relatively inaccessible overseas locations and replacing both the Hastings and Beverley. The specification asked for an aircraft capable of delivering a 35,000lb load 1,000 miles, make a STOL landing and return without refuelling. A key requirement was to transport 45,000lb 1,200 miles using a full-length runway.

The three short-listed contestants were the BAC 208 and BAC 222, the Hawker Siddeley 681 and the Shorts SC.5/21 Belfast. After dismissing the HS680, a four Rolls-Royce Tyne development of the

Argosy, the designers proposed the HS681 with a moderately swept high-aspect-ratio high wing with powerful flaps plus boundary-layer control, a 'T' tail design with a highly swept up tail with clamshell doors and a ramp for loading and air dropping. It was projected to have Bristol Siddeley Pegasus vector-thrust engines (as fitted to the HS P.1127/Harrier) and provision for as many as eighteen lift engines for VTOL. The BAC 208 was similar to the 681, powered by Pegasuses, while the 222 was a joint Lockheed/BAC version of the Hercules with a lowered floor, re-engined with Rolls-Royce Tynes and auxiliary compressors required for flap-blowing which the USAF had some interest in. Not to be outdone, Shorts proposed a STOL version of the Belfast with flap-blowing.

The specification was very exacting: the aircraft was required to have a payload of about 40,000lb, with a range of some 1,800 miles at 500kt. The HS681 had a capacious fuselage, 108ft 9in long, with a cabin 43ft 5in long, 10ft 6in wide and 10ft 2in high with rear loading under the high tail, and could take most current and projected military vehicles. There was provision for air dropping sixty paratroops, or carrying sixty-four casualties and six attendants or eighty-two passengers. The 681 was intended to be an exceedingly flexible aircraft, carrying very heavy loads when flying from runways, yet able to operate with reduced payload into unpaved strips only a few hundred feet in length. There was provision for in-flight refuelling and VTOL operation using lift-jet packages under the wings.

There would be twelve lift engines supplied either by Bristol Siddeley (50 per cent owned by HS) or Rolls-Royce. To test the actual use of lift pods on a large aircraft, the HS690 testbed was projected in conjunction with France and Germany, which was a Nord Noratlas fitted with lift pods.

A civil version of the 681, the HS682, was also projected with conventional jet powerplant and a longer 123ft fuselage. In the light of the firm's experience with the civil Argosy it is unlikely that this would have been proceeded with.

An artist's impression of the HS681 with optional pods for vertical lift engines fitted on its wings. Author's collection

Go-Ahead

The two-year delay in deciding on which firm should build the military jet airlifter was mainly due to concerns over funding the £70m (£1bn at 2013 prices) project. A number of avenues were investigated to

The wooden mock-up of the HS681 at Baginton. Ray Williams

reduce costs, including a collaboration with the USAF that was attempted but failed to develop, and the notion of designing versions to replace the Shackleton was briefly entertained in an attempt to bring down overheads.

When OR351/2 was eventually issued requirements had been eased and as a result the HS681 was scaled down: fuselage length was reduced and the cabin downsized to 40ft long and 9ft high. A second reason for the delay was Rolls-Royce's determination to install Medway engines, in direct opposition to the RAF's wishes for either the Pegasus or the BS100 intended for the P.1154.

In the event Hawker Siddeley's Avro Whitworth Division received the contract for the aircraft, powered by Medways. These engines would have switch-in thrust deflectors and with the addition of lift-jet pods on the wing the aircraft could achieve VTOL with an appreciable payload. The Medway engine thrust deflectors, two either side of the rear of the engine, allowed for thrust to be deflected to give STOL and could be turned to act as reversers. The contract was finally received in September 1963 and as Armstrong Whitworth and Avro had now been formed into the Hawker Siddeley Avro Whitworth Division, design work originally shared between Baginton and Kingston was now shared between Baginton and Woodford with the latter taking on the major role. The former Gloster team also handled detail design of the rear fuselage and loading ramp.

Production

The Chadderton and Woodford sites were to construct 45 per cent of the aircraft including final assembly and flight test. Baginton would make 39 per cent, including the fuselage and wings while Government-owned Shorts in Belfast would build 16 per cent. By the beginning of February 1965 detailed design was well underway and a full-scale fuselage mock up had been built at Baginton. RAF serials XT261–6 were issued for six development aircraft to fly in 1967–8 and an initial order for sixty-two aircraft was planned.

A Change of Government

On 15 October 1964 a General Election brought about the replacement of the Conservatives with a Labour Government who sought to carry out their election pledges and trim expenditure in the face of a weak economic position. In late October the new Government announced that, owing to the country's worsening economic situation, prestige projects including TSR2 and Concorde might have to be sacrificed. The new Minister of Defence, Denis Healey, was charged with capping expenditure and cutting costly new projects was a clear expedient. The Ministry of Defence examined alternatives to the HS681, easing the specification yet again and considered alternative aircraft such as the Franco-German Transall, a STOL version of the Belfast and the Hercules. The proven Hercules was clearly the best and was offered at a unit price of £800,000 in contrast with a projected price of £2.4m for the HS681. Furthermore, it would be available three years earlier than the HS681.

Cancellation

Aware of the threat to their project, workers from Hawker Siddeley plants in Coventry and Kingston together with colleagues from BAC protested in London on 14 January 1965. Less than two weeks later, on the 2 February 1965, having already announced the cancellation of the Hawker Siddeley P.1154, Prime Minister Harold Wilson cancelled the HS681 on the grounds that the RAF could replace it almost immediately with the Lockheed Hercules, which cost only one-third of the price of the 681. Subsequent to cancellation the Minister of Aviation, Roy Jenkins, stated in Parliament that expenditure on the HS681 had been £4m (1965 prices).

Redundancies

Only two days after the Prime Minister's announcement Charles Bayly, Avro Whitworth Director and General Manager, said that Coventry design teams, knowing that their jobs were in jeopardy, had devised a modified, utility version of the HS681. Known as HS802, this design would lack the short take-off and landing characteristics of the 681 but would cost only half as much. This incorporated the wing and engines of the Comet with the 681's fuselage and tail. However, these efforts were to no avail and on 10 February shop stewards met management at Baginton to be told that the closure of the factory was inevitable. On 12 February Hawker Siddeley announced that the remaining design-office team at Gloucester, employing about eighty men, would be closed down.

CHAPTER SIX

Hawker Siddeley's Bestseller – the 748

When the prototype Hawker Siddeley 748 took to the air on 24 June 1960 few would have predicted that over the next twenty-six years the 748 would prove so successful that a total of 380 would be manufactured, for both the civil and military markets.

The 748 came about as a result of the cutbacks in British military spending following the 1957 Defence White Paper, which wrongly concluded that no more military aircraft would be required. At that time Hawker Siddeley's aircraft companies were solely concerned with military aircraft manufacture so Avro (and Armstrong Whitworth) sought to re-enter the civil market. Following their disastrous experience with the Tudor after World War Two, Avro had stayed out of civil aircraft manufacture for almost a decade.

The two 748 Series 1 prototypes, G-APZV and G-ARAY, together on the occasion of G-ARAY's first flight on 10 April 1961. Avro Heritage

Go Ahead and Indian Licence-Production Contract

Avro began to examine the market and concluded that there was a large market for a 'DC-3 replacement', since approximately 3,000 DC-3s were still in service. The twin-Rolls-Royce Dart Avro 748 became the Hawker Siddeley Group's contender for this market, with a capacity for forty-four passengers, and was a direct competitor to the Handley Page Herald and Fokker Friendship.

At the 1958 Farnborough Air Show the aircraft was only a tentative project but in January 1959 the Hawker Siddeley Board gave the go-ahead and the 748 was launched as a private venture funded entirely by the Group. Construction of two prototypes began and first flight was scheduled for thirteen months later, setting the bar very high for both the production and flight test teams. In September 1959 basic

price of the 748, without radio and special customer equipment but with complete interior trim, was quoted as £168,000 (2013 = £3.3m).

In July 1959 the Indian Government signed a contract with Sir Roy Dobson, Managing Director of the Hawker Siddeley Group for a licence to manufacture the 748 for the Indian Air Force. This was probably the biggest export order ever placed for a British aircraft still on the drawing board. Hindustan Aeronautics would manufacture the 748s in a newly built factory at Kanpur.

First Flight

The prototype, G-APZV, powered by Dart 514s made a 2 hour 41 minute first flight from Woodford on 24 June 1960 piloted by Avro's Chief Test Pilot, Jimmy Harrison. It immediately set to work on the test programme and achieved sixty hours airborne in twenty flights in the four weeks after its

first flight. This was double the anticipated schedule of seven hours of test flying a week, testifying to the mechanical reliability of the first 748 and to the soundness of the design. In the first month the aircraft had been flown at its maximum weight of 35,100lb, up to 270kt, made over 200 stalls, flown to heights of 26,000ft and to within 80 per cent of the maximum design speeds with undercarriage and flaps down.

Four water-ballast tanks were installed fore and aft in the fuselage and these enabled the centre of gravity to be traversed through its full 14in travel in about three minutes. In individual tests, Avro test pilots checked: aileron, elevator and rudder balance, stalls in all configurations, minimum control speeds, engine out, roll rates, lateral stability and trim changes, and climb performance in four configurations of power, undercarriage and flap settings. Having achieved these milestones G-APZV was exhibited in the air at the Farnborough Air Show that September.

The second prototype, G-ARAY, was damaged during construction when owing to a fire a hangar roof collapsed on the fuselage at Chadderton in April 1960, so its much-delayed first flight did not take place until 10 April 1961. In July 1961 G-ARAY flew on tropical trials in Nicosia, Cyprus and Torrejon, Spain. In November G-ARAY was converted to the prototype 748 series 2 when it was fitted with higher-powered Dart 531s; these enabled it to fly at higher weights and at higher altitudes, which translated into either greater payload and/or longer range. During testing it was decided to extend the 748's wingspan by 3ft 6in and this was subsequently applied to both prototype aircraft. G-ARMV, the first production

aircraft destined for Skyways Coach-Air, made its maiden flight on 30 August 1961, joining the other two aircraft in the flight test programme. In November it completed the route proving trials for the certification programme, and on 9 January 1962 the 748 was granted a Certificate of Airworthiness.

G-ARAY took on the mantle of the Hawker Siddeley 748 demonstrator and in that role flew over 91,000 miles on sales tours around the world. Added to this role were periods on leases to airlines and these paid dividends as they resulted in sales of over thirty aircraft. At the end of April 1967 it was sold to Flacks Flyvetjeneste of Denmark. Four years later G-ARAY returned to the British register to fly with Dan-Air, finally being broken up in 1990. Following G-ARAY's sale Hawker Siddeley replaced it the following month with the first Series 2A G-AVRR, powered by uprated Dart 532 engines of 2,230shp. To take advantage of the improved performance most of the Series 2 aircraft were later modified to this standard. For five years G-AVRR was used as a 748 demonstrator and on lease to airlines. At the end of that period it was sold to Canada's Eastern Provincial Airways.

First Airline Services

In January 1961 came the first order, which was received when Aerolineas Argentinas ordered nine aircraft. By then the Board had authorized the establishment of a full-scale production line at the Chadderton factory with final assembly at Woodford. In May 1961 Skyways Coach Air ordered three aircraft, and these were the first production aircraft.

The 748's first airline services were with Aerolineas Argentinas in April 1962 and the airline's order was soon increased by three, making twelve in all. One of the reasons that the Argentine airline had purchased the 748 was because they needed an aircraft that offered airliner comfort but could operate from undeveloped, rough airstrips as there were plenty of these on their network. Their 748s were finally disposed of in 1977. As orders flowed in Hawker Siddeley Manchester Division became very busy with the 748 by 1963, turning out approximately two aircraft per month, for which there was a large order backlog, plus building the thirty-one for the RAF.

The 748s flown by Aerolineas Argentinas were later joined by others in South America, including AVIANCA, LAN-Chile, LAV of Venezuela and Varig of Brazil. On the opposite side of the world Thai Airways started operations in 1964 with three 748s and continued adding to their fleet. Philippines Air Lines followed suit, as did Aden Airways, Air Ceylon and Leeward Islands Air Transport, Merpati, Fiji Airways, New Zealand's Mount Cook and many more. The 748 sold well in Africa too, where there were eventually twenty-one operators.

The 748 made headway in the very competitive market conditions in Europe, earning orders from BKS, Austrian Airways and Channel Airways, Autair, British Airways and the UK's Dan-Air, which had a large fleet. Canada proved a market, too, and 748s flew with Midwest, Air Gaspe, Quebecair, Westwind and more. The last UK operator was Emerald, using the trusty 748s as freighters, until it ceased trading during 2006.

Argentina was well-accustomed to Avro aircraft. Here, an Aerolineas Argentinas 748 behind an Argentine Air Force Lincoln. Avro Heritage

Polynesian Airlines 5W-FAN, delivered in January 1972.
Avro Heritage

The Market Situation in 1970

In terms of numbers sold the Hawker Siddeley 748 ranked as Britain's most successful current commercial transport programme, with sales of 238 in July 1970. This total included sixty-nine ordered from Indian production at the Kanpur Division of Hindustan Aeronautics, of which forty-five were destined for the Indian Air Force and twenty-four for Indian Airlines. (Twenty more were eventually built in India.)

Production of commercial models covered two basic versions: the Series 1 certificated in January 1962, of which eighteen were built, and the Series 2, certificated in October 1962, for which the production run then totalled eighty-eight. The Series 2A then became the standard model with the first delivery made to Avianca in September 1968. This version employed the Rolls-Royce Dart 532-2L turboprop of 2,230eshp for improved airfield performance, but was otherwise similar to the Series 2.

In 1970 the Hawker Siddeley Board authorized production up to a total of 260 aircraft, including Indian assembly and manufacture, but excluding the thirty-one rear-loading Andover C.1 tactical transports built for the RAF. The Woodford production line was generally able to make a delivery within six months of contract signature and typical price for a fully equipped UK-produced aircraft was in the region of £500,000 (£6.5m at 2012 prices).

In the first six months of 1970 HSA booked twenty-four orders, one of the best half-yearly sales totals for the aircraft. US Federal Aviation Authority (FAA) certification of the aircraft was imminent as part of an HSA campaign to interest the fast-growing US third-level airline market in the type. Hawker Siddeley was rewarded for investing in FAA certification in 1971 when the HS748 made a major breakthrough into the US market with a sale to the commuter carrier Air Illinois.

Improved Interior and other Refinements in 1976

With more than 250 HS748s in service, flying hours built up rapidly and were well past the 2 million-hour mark. Aerolineas Argentinas had the lead aircraft, which had clocked up more than 30,000 hours. By 1976 the 748 was still selling well: production was then around eighteen per year, mainly for military customers and for government use. HS748s had been sold to some sixty military and civil operators, providing a firm base for re-orders.

To keep the aircraft competitive a completely redesigned interior was adopted for the latest passenger aircraft, with contemporary enclosed overhead lockers and indirect lighting matched to new design of seat giving greater comfort and spaciousness even in a high-density configuration. Seating arrangements with capacities varying from forty to sixty-two passengers provided ample space for baggage and freight. Conversion from passenger to an all-freight layout could be achieved in fifteen minutes by removal of the seats and the introduction of lightweight glassfibre screens to protect the cabin trim. Operating at its maximum take-off weight of 45,087lb, the 748 could carry its maximum payload of just over 11,000lb 540nm with fuel reserves for 188nm.

Hawker Siddeley 748MF

In the early 1960s the RAF had an urgent requirement for a short-range transport aircraft to replace the remaining Vickers Valetta C.1s in overseas commands and to relieve the elderly Beverley and Hastings fleet at home. There were two main competitors: the proposed military variants of the Avro 748 and the Handley Page Herald. G-ARAY took part in take-off, landing and taxiing trials for the RAF military transport contract against the Herald on a ploughed-up field at RAF Martlesham Heath, Suffolk on 29 January 1962. The Herald had already been tested and would have received the contract, but Handley Page's failure to join either BAC or Hawker Siddeley meant that Avro won the contract.

So Hawker Siddeley was awarded the contract and this led to the 748MF (Military Freighter), which was offered with a redesigned raised rear fuselage tail to permit rear loading and air-dropping, a strengthened freight floor and increased gross weight. It also had increased power from its Dart RDa12s, and a unique 'kneeling' undercarriage to facilitate the loading and unloading of freight.

The prototype G-APZV was dismantled at Woodford and returned to the Chadderton factory in August 1962 for conversion into aerodynamic prototype of the 748MF. Re-registered G-ARRV, it flew from Woodford on 21 December 1963 for 2 hours 5 minutes, again piloted by Jimmy Harrison. It was on public show at the following year's Farnborough and was demonstrated to the Indian Air Force in April/May 1965, though the Indians did not eventually purchase any. On return from India G-ARRV made its last flight on 27 May 1965.

By 1963 the name Andover had been chosen, and a contract signed for thirty-one production aircraft to be built at Chadderton and Woodford, with final assembly taking place at the latter. In addition, six basic 748s equipped to VIP standard were ordered as Andover CC.2s to replace the Herons of

ABOVE: Second prototype G-ARAY at RAF Martlesham Heath, Suffolk on 29 January 1962 during rough-field take-off and landing trials for the RAF military transport contract. The 748 was competing against the Handley Page Herald and won the contract for thirty-one aircraft. BAE Systems

LEFT: G-APZV was converted to become the aerodynamic prototype of the 748 Military Freighter with a high tail and rear-opening doors to allow for air dropping and straight-in loading. It was re-registered G-ARRV and flew in this form on 21 December 1963. It is seen here at the 1964 Farnborough Air Show. BAE Systems

BELOW: XS594, the first Andover C.1 for the RAF, demonstrating its 'kneeling' undercarriage at Woodford. This costly modification provided straight-through unloading onto a truck as shown. XS594 first flew on 15 July 1975 and was delivered to Boscombe Down for trials in December. Avro Heritage

the Queen's Flight and a couple of Valetta C.2s with the Metropolitan Communications Squadron.

The first Andover C.1 to fly, XS594, flew on 9 July 1965 and was delivered to the A&AEE before the end of that year, by which time the next two aircraft had flown. The production rate was two aircraft per month, with the last aircraft of the contract, XS647, flying in January 1968.

The Andover in Service

With acceptance trials completed, deliveries to Transport Command at Abingdon commenced in July 1966. Type conversion was handled with an eventual complement of six aircraft by the Andover Conversion Unit. In December the first two squadrons were formed. 46 Squadron inherited three of the ACU aircraft, and seven new deliveries

by mid-1967; and 52 Squadron, destined for service in Far East Air Force, worked up at Abingdon in the spring of 1967, with a complement of six aircraft.

Late in August 1967, 84 Squadron Middle East AF, later Air Forces Gulf, became the third and final squadron to re-equip with the type, using seven aircraft to replace the Beverley. At the end of 1969, No. 52 Squadron disbanded, followed in October

1971 by 84 Squadron. This led to an increase in 46 Squadron establishment, at one time in 1972 reaching a peak of nineteen aircraft, and the operation of a detachment at Masirah maintained until the squadron disbanded in August 1975, a victim of the defence cuts. In 1976 some twenty aircraft were in storage at 5MU Kemble following defence cuts. But its service life

was not over as some aircraft were retained in different roles. XS607 was temporarily registered as G-BEBY to Hawker Siddeley for a demonstration tour of India, but no sales were forthcoming.

Ten Andovers were sold to the RNZAF as a Bristol 170 replacement – in direct competition with the standard 748, which the manufacturers had hoped to sell – but they

were withdrawn in 1984. A number were prematurely scrapped while nine were converted at Woodford to become Andover E.3s for radio and airport navigation aid calibration. Others were employed in communications flying, at Boscombe Down and with the ETPS. The ETPS's Andover, XS606, was only withdrawn from use in December 2012 and has been put up for sale.

ABOVE: **XS605 was one of nine Andovers converted at Woodford to become an Andover E.3 for radio and airport navigation aid calibration.** Avro Heritage

BELOW: **The busy production line at Woodford in late 1970. There are twelve Hawker Siddeley 748s, ten Nimrods and a single Victor in the hanger.** Avro Heritage

Military HS748s

Besides the Andovers built for the RAF, a military freighter version of the standard HS748 entered production in the 1970s with a large side-opening freight door that could be opened in flight for paratroop or supply dropping, an optional strengthened floor and accommodation for up to fifty-eight troops. G-AZJH, the first aircraft with such a door, flew on 31 December 1971. The aircraft already had rapidly interchangeable passenger, passenger/cargo and all-cargo role capabilities, but the large cargo door allowed operators to load bulkier cargo items and light vehicles. It was designed for possible retrofit to existing aircraft. The cargo door incorporated the passenger door, which opened rearwards, and a large air-openable

LEFT: **The first Hawker Siddeley 748MF, G-AZJH, with a large side-opening freight door that could be opened in flight for paratroop or supply dropping and with accommodation for up to fifty-eight troops. Many other air forces bought this version of the 748.** Avro Heritage

BELOW: **Four 748s for the Columbian Air Force at Woodford, which were all delivered in March 1972. In the background is Hawker Siddeley's 748 demonstrator, G-AVRR, and two Victors awaiting conversion to tankers.** Avro Heritage

forward section that opened outwards and ran forward, parallel to the fuselage.

Many other military roles were undertaken by the HS748, including aeromedical evacuation and communications flying. The Royal Australian Air Force used eight 748s as navigation and air electronics flying classrooms for the training of aircrew for Australian military aircraft. The Royal Australian Navy also used two 748s in similar roles to the RAAF's.

The 748 proved very popular as a VIP and executive transport, and was used as a personal aircraft by the heads of state of Argentina, Brazil, Chile, India, Thailand, Venezuela, Zambia and the UK. It was also used as a VIP/communications aircraft by the air forces of Brazil, Australia, India and the UK.

Military 748 operators were Argentina, Australia, Brunei, Belgium, Brazil, Colombia, Ecuador, India Nepal, New Zealand, South Korea, Thailand, the UK and Zambia.

The Licence-Built Indian 748s

The first Indian 748, BH572, flew on 1 November 1961 from Kandahar. The first four aircraft, which were Series 1s, were assembled from parts made in Britain but as production developed in India a greater and greater proportion of the aircraft (Series 2s) was made there. The final twenty aircraft

were built with the large freight door. Both the Indian Air Force and Indian Airways Corporation were recipients of the aircraft and eighty-nine were licence-built in India between 1961 and 1984. Production rates were very variable with differing numbers built each year, but it was a profitable venture for Hawker Siddeley and then British Aerospace.

The Coastguarder and Multi-Role 748

The Coastguarder was Hawker Siddeley's answer to the problem of how to provide low-cost maritime surveillance and search and rescue over large areas. The prototype G-BCDZ first flew on 18 February 1977, staying airborne for about two hours. It took off from HSA Chester, where it had been rebuilt from a standard 748, and landed at Woodford. It had a radome slung beneath the forward fuselage and blister windows for observers in the rear fuselage. Its underslung radar antenna scanned through 360 degrees and could search out to a range of 210nm. Normal crew complement was six: two pilots, navigator, radar operator and two observers/store dispatchers. The Coastguarder could carry stores, flares and life rafts. Optional twin wing hardpoints would carry weapons, ECM and a pylon-mounted searchlight.

Following its maiden flight it carried out demonstration tours in Europe and South

The Indian Air Force's H-1144, a Hindustan Aeronautics-assembled 748. Author

The sole Hawker Siddeley Coastguarder, G-BCDZ, a sensible development of the 748 that surprisingly failed to make any sales. It flew in 1977 and was eventually converted back to a standard 748 in 1980.
Avro Heritage

Though the Coastguarder made no sales another secondhand aircraft, registered G-BDVH, fitted with a large freight door was modified with a radome and observer windows similar to the Coastguarder and dubbed the 'Multi-Role 748'. It is seen here at Hurn just by the former BAC flight shed. Chris Muir

America, and HS had estimates that there was a market for 200 aircraft in the Coastguarder class. In November 1979 it was converted back to a normal 748 configuration but fitted with Dart hush kits for trials. However, the company still felt there were possible sales for this type of aircraft and another second-hand aircraft, G-BDVH, was dubbed the 'Multi-Role 748'; it had a large freight door and subsequently received the radome and observer windows of the Coastguarder.

BAe entered the aircraft with a scratch crew in 'Sea Search 81', a Maritime Reconnaissance competition, against professional military crews and aircraft, beating them all and winning the Lockheed trophy, much to the chagrin of the professionals. Yet despite the obvious winning qualities of the aircraft (and crew), the Coastguarder never sold.

The HS748 Becomes the BAe 748

Just as the Avro 748 had become the Hawker Siddeley 748 following the Group's rationalization, with the nationalization (and later privatization) of British Aerospace in 1977 it was rebranded again as the BAe 748. In a competitive marketplace development had to continue and the basis for the BAe 748 2B was the uprated Dart 536 with 2,280shp and fitted with 12ft propellers. Wingspan was extended to 102ft 5in and avionics and soundproofing were upgraded. G-BGJV, the prototype 2B (which was also fitted with a large freight door), first flew on 22 June 1979 with Manchester chief test pilot Charles Masefield in command. Even

this development was not this sturdy airliner's last, for in 1983 BAe announced the Super 748 with yet more powerful Darts together with hush kits, greater fuel efficiency, an interior redesign and a more advanced flight deck. The first Super 748, G-BLGJ, flew on 30 June 1984 and was displayed at Farnborough. By this time the number of deliveries had slowed to a trickle and the final 748 delivery was to Makung Airlines of Taiwan on 24 January 1989. A total of 381 748s was built and all bar the first prototype were delivered to customers.

Conclusion

The 748 was a successful model of airliner development achieved by the hard work put in by their staff, prototypes and demonstrators to certify, develop and sell the aircraft, which flew with operators in all continents of the world. Its steady development and refinement maintained demand for the aircraft for as long as possible and amply repaid Hawker Siddeley, which had accurately assessed the demand and justifiably made profits from its investment.

ABOVE: **Bahamasair's C6-BED, delivered in July 1979.** Avro Heritage

LEFT: **The Empire Test Pilot School withdrew Andover XS608 from service in December 2012 and it was delivered to Hurn for onward sale.** Tony Guest

Specification – 748 Series 2B	
Length	67ft (20.42m)
Wingspan	98ft 6in (30.02m)
Height	24ft 10in (7.57m)
MTOW	46,500lb (21,100kg)
Cruising speed	281mph (452km/h)
Range	904 miles (1,455km)
Passengers	44–48
Powerplant	2 × 2,280shp Rolls-Royce Dart Rda 7 Mk 536-2

CHAPTER SEVEN

Airliners at Hatfield – from Trident to 146

The BEA Specification

The Trident grew from a BEA requirement for a short-range jet airliner issued in July 1956. The requirement called for an aircraft with three engines, a gross weight of about 120,000lb and accommodation for eighty tourist passengers or 100 in a high-density layout with a range of 1,000 miles. Six firms made proposals and after due consideration these were eventually reduced to three. The final shortlist competing for the BEA order and Government approval were the Avro 740, Bristol 200 and de Havilland 121. They were all similar, with a triple rear-engined layout. Whereas the Bristol and DH configurations were broadly the same, the Avro's could be distinguished by its 'V' tail.

As the programme had to be privately financed the Government viewed Bristol's and de Havilland's resources as insufficient to support the programme. As Avro had the resources of the Hawker Siddeley Group there was no such problem with their bid and they expected to invest £20m (equivalent to £380m in 2012 prices) and recoup these costs through substantial sales. Bristol did not want to lose the contract so they entered into discussion with HSA, which agreed to drop the Avro 740 and to co-operate with Bristol on the 200. HSA would command the lion's share of the project with 65 per cent, leaving Bristol with 35 per cent. The combined talents would bring Hawker Siddeley's high-speed jet experience matched to Bristol's knowledge of the civil market: Hawker Siddeley's Avro factories would build the aircraft while Bristol handled the systems and the engines.

Had this Bristol/Hawker Siddeley grouping won the contract then Bristol would have become a natural bedfellow for Hawker Siddeley while de Havilland would probably have joined forces with Vickers and English Electric during the formation of the British Aircraft Corporation in 1960. The ramifications of such a different result

from the major groupings of the companies in 1959–60 would probably have continued to be felt even today.

Similar to the Bristol/HS arrangement, de Havilland set up Airco (Aircraft Manufacturing Co. Ltd) with Fairey and Hunting to design, manufacture and develop the DH121. De Havilland held a majority 67.5 per cent share, Fairey 22.5 per cent and Hunting 10 per cent, with four, two and one member of each firm, respectively, representing their interests on the board of directors.

The Award of the Contract

Although the Government strongly favoured the Bristol/Hawker Siddeley bid, whose combined resources they regarded as much stronger than de Havilland's, BEA had become more enamoured with the de Havilland offering and were mindful of the firm's Comet experience. As a result in August 1958 the Minister of Transport and Civil Aviation agreed that BEA could order twenty-four de Havilland 121s and Airco began refining the project, which was now planned as a 111-seater with a maximum take-off weight of 123,000lb, powered by three Rolls-Royce RB141 Medways of 12,000lb each.

BEA's Reassessment of its Needs

After more than eighteen months of active project and detail design, in May 1959 BEA made quite radical changes in the specification for the 121. BEA now believed that the original estimates of size and weight were some 20 per cent overly optimistic. What was really needed the airline argued, was an aircraft with the same performance as the earlier 121, but weighing 100,000lb or less and with a maximum of eighty seats.

The airline's planners maintained that the design could then be stretched as extra capacity was required, but this did not in fact prove to be the case. In the face of these demands de Havilland and its consortium had to revise the design around three Rolls-Royce RB163 Speys of 9,850lb static thrust each, with a maximum weight of 105,000lb and seating reduced to a maximum of 100. This change of powerplant from the Medway to the smaller Spey stymied later efforts to lengthen the Trident and improve its performance.

Strangely, the de Havilland management offered little resistance to this major change of specification; although it appears that some staff protested, as BEA was then the only customer and certain to place a large order, their changes went ahead. Nowadays it is widely held that this decision crippled the sales potential of the aircraft, which was outsold by the larger and superior performing Boeing 727.

Awarding the Contract

A firm contract for twenty-four aircraft for delivery to BEA valued at £28m with spares was only finally signed on 12 August 1959, and in July 1960 the Government granted financial help to Airco to be repaid by a levy on sales. All twenty-four aircraft in the contract were to be delivered by September 1965 and first flight was planned for December 1961. Owing to its triplicated engines and systems, the 121 was appropriately named the Trident in September 1960. From the outset the Trident was designed for autoflare, with full automatic landing envisaged by 1970.

Change of Ownership

In December 1959 de Havilland was bought by Hawker Siddeley Group, which was a huge shock to this proud organization. The wholesale purchase of de Havilland by Hawker Siddeley had major ramifications for Airco as its three member companies now found themselves members of different camps, with de Havilland part of Hawker Siddeley, Hunting part of BAC and Fairey's aviation interests now owned by Westland. In February 1960 de Havilland announced Airco was to be wound up as the whole programme was now a Hawker Siddeley Group venture, for which de Havilland was technically responsible with Fairey Engineering and Hunting Aircraft remaining in the short-term as subcontractors.

At that time no other manufacturer in the world had as much hard-won knowledge of jet-transport structures and every part of this knowledge was needed for an airliner intended to fly short stages in dense air at very high speed for twenty years or more. The basic philosophy of the Trident was fail-safe. The fuselage comprised a pressure shell extending to the rear and a tail section carrying the engines, fin and tailplane. The fin section was more or less the same with all versions of the Trident: the only variance was with the 3B where the boost engine displaced the APU to the front of the fin. The variance in the wing between the 1C, 1E and 2E was a gradual increase in span and improvements in the high-lift devices, for the 3B the basic 2E wing was used but its incidence was increased by more than 2 degrees to provide for ground clearance during take-off. Where the leading edge of

the 1C's wing had an inboard Krüger flap and leading edge droop, the other marks had leading edge slats instead of droops. The trailing edge of the Trident wing had conventional flaps, airbrakes, lift dumpers and ailerons.

The Trident's flying controls were entirely hydraulic, without manual reversion. An entirely new feature, designed to eliminate both immediate pilot action in the event of power failure, was that each surface was driven by three jacks, each served by a separate hydraulic system. This triplex system was served by the three main engines, providing for full control throughout the flight envelope with any hydraulic system inoperative, and satisfactory control to complete a flight and land safely with any two systems failed.

In the Trident a really dramatic step forward was taken in planning the aircraft from its inception for 'Autoflare' and later for full 'Autoland'. Autoflare improved service by enabling weather minima to be reduced but Autoland was an even more remarkable advance, providing exactly what it said and enabling the Trident to land when other airliners were grounded.

Each main undercarriage unit had a single leg carrying four wheels. The steerable nose unit was unconventional because in order to save space it was offset 24in to the left of the centreline and retracted sideways.

The Rolls-Royce Speys installed in the Trident were developed in power from 9,850lb thrust for the 1C to 12,000lb for

the Trident 3B. However, the latter additionally carried the 5,400lb RB162 booster engine devised from a VTOL engine.

Flight Testing the Trident

The first aircraft, G-ARPA, was rolled out at 17.30 at Hatfield on 4 August 1961. It appeared complete but a great deal of work was necessary before the aircraft was ready for its first flight. Engine runs with two non-flight Speys were carried out soon after the roll-out, these engines being installed in the central and left pod, the right pod remaining incomplete. These engines were switched from one bay to the other with particular attention to the performance of the novel central installation. Meanwhile, structural testing was well advanced on test fuselage specimens while rig testing had cleared many of the systems and control issues.

A large amount of flight test instrumentation was installed after the roll-out, and the entire aircraft was subjected to the routine preflight tests including sedate taxiing, steering and braking trials. These indicated that some alterations to undercarriage suspension were necessary. Flight engines were installed in mid-December. Although the aircraft was finally cleared for flight on 21 December, to the schedule agreed more than two years previously, the maiden flight was delayed by snow. The first flight, made on 9 January 1962, lasted eighty minutes

The first Trident G-ARPA, only partly complete, undergoing ground testing in August 1961 at Hatfield. BAE Systems

G-ARPA bearing the colours of BEA during its maiden flight on 9 January 1962, piloted by Hatfield's Chief Test Pilot, John Cunningham. BAE Systems

and, though this was not made public at the time, it was not without drama. During retraction tests one of the main undercarriage legs could not retract as the under-fuselage door did not open and the main wheels jammed against it. This critical situation was resolved by the flight engineer depressurizing the relevant hydraulic system, allowing the gear and door to open – fortunately the landing gear locked into place by freefall.

Low-Speed Handling Trials

The first aircraft spent the following eight months mainly engaged on low-speed handling trials, which indicated that major changes to the design of the droop leading edge would be required to improve low-speed handling and performance. The third aircraft also shared the low-speed handling trials with the first machine.

The Civil Airworthiness Certification requirements were that at the stall there should be a clear warning of an imminent stall; the aircraft's nose should pitch down so strongly that the pilot could keep the wing stalled by nose-up elevator; and there should be no tendency for a wing drop.

The low-speed performance was initially unsatisfactory because of early flow separation over the outer wings and a lack of definition of the stall. Various temporary cures were employed and finally a Krüger-type flap was fitted at the wing root. The shape and angle and sealing of the wing droop, vortex generators and positioning of the wing fences also required considerable refinement to achieve a satisfactory performance. These trial alterations were made as speedily as possible, using vast quantities of balsawood ply, dope, fabric and plastic sealer! In spite of a programme of over 3,000 stalls, it was finally concluded that the aircraft's stalling characteristics would not be acceptable to Civil Airworthiness authorities and that a stick pusher would have to be installed to satisfy their requirements.

The stick pusher was activated by twin vanes either side of the aircraft's nose to measure the angle of incidence of the aircraft. If the incidence rose too high then the stick pusher pushed the control column forward, pitching the aircraft's nose down with a force of 80lb when the aircraft reached

The second and third Tridents, G-ARPC closer with its dark wings covered in wool tufting and G-ARPB further away. Just visible on the Manor Road side of the airfield is the Blue Streak test tower, Hastings TE580 used for propeller trials and a Lightning employed on missile tests. BAE Systems

an incidence of 17 degrees with droop leading edge down, or 11 degrees 'clean', in slow approaches to the stall.

G-ARPA completed more than 500 hours' testing and, following low-speed testing, also bore the brunt of the high-speed flying, which included flutter artificially induced by hydraulic exciters. G-ARPB, the second aircraft tasked with systems development, flew in May 1962 and the third, G-ARPC, primarily intended for performance testing, in mid-July. G-ARPD flew in January 1963 fitted with the fixed full-span wing slats of the later Trident 1E in place of the droops of the Trident 1 and tested these for ten months.

G-ARPE was delayed on the production line so that it could fly with the first set of low-speed modifications in production form in May 1963, and was later brought up to near production standard for the 35,000-mile, eighty-hour route proving and sales demonstration to All Nippon Airways in Japan in October 1963. The remainder of the 200-hour route proving was flown on BEA routes by the same aircraft, including a Middle East sales tour in January 1964. As part of Hawker Siddeley Woodford's proposals for a Maritime Reconnaissance aircraft development of Trident prior to the decision to go ahead with the Nimrod, G-ARPE flew evaluation trials from RAF St Mawgan in February 1964.

As the programme drew to an end and with the need to get test aircraft up to production standard some of the Tridents, for example G-ARPA, -C, -D and -E went to Bitteswell for lengthy periods of refurbishing and modification to delivery standard.

Approximately 2,300 hours were flown on the Trident 1 test programme, of which just under 1,600 hours were for direct development, as follows:

- Autopilot and flight systems 18 per cent
- Low- and high-speed handling, structural loads, flutter, etc 31 per cent
- Performance 22 per cent
- Systems and engineering tests, radio, etc. 29 per cent.

The Trident's Certificate of Airworthiness was finally granted on 18 February 1964 and on 11 March the Trident entered service with BEA; one year later fourteen were flying on BEA routes. Instead of the Trident 1's maximum take off weight of 107,000lb, all of BEA's were delivered as Trident 1Cs with

Five of the first six Trident 1s in the Hatfield flight hanger during the test programme. Clockwise from top left: G-ARPB, -F, -E, -C and -D. G-ARPB was employed on Autoland trials, G-ARPE carried out sales demonstrations in the Far East and G-ARPD trialled the leading edge slats devised for the Trident 1E. Though Hatfield Airfield is no longer in existence, the flight test hanger is preserved. BAE Systems

a MTOW of 115,000lb. The low specified excess thrust of the early Speys caused payload restrictions in order to comply with noise abatement climb procedures out of certain occasionally used runways, but was overcome when uprated engines were fitted to the Trident 1Cs. To improve working conditions for ground crew troubled by the heat and exhaust of the Bristol Siddeley Artouste APU under the wing centre-section, it was relocated to between the rudder and the centre engine exhaust; the space thus freed was used as additional tankage on later variants.

The Stick Pusher and G-ARPY's Crash

The definite need for a stick pusher was demonstrated when G-ARPY, a late production Trident 1C for BEA, was on its maiden flight from Hatfield. Having found that a small number of Tridents had a wing drop at or near the stick push, the Airworthiness authorities agreed with the manufacturers that to test for this eventuality an additional test was introduced at the stall. So following stall tests with the stick shaker and stick pusher (the stall recovery systems) functioning and a careful log of the incidence and speeds at which it operated, the stall recovery systems were switched off and an approach to stall flown using a specially calibrated air speed indicator. At 3–4kt below the speed at which these systems operated, the pilot was to immediately recover from the stall.

Captained by Peter Barlow, with the well-known former Airspeed chief test pilot George Errington as co-pilot, G-ARPY was airborne from Hatfield at 16:51 on 3 June 1966 on its maiden flight. Three approaches to the stall were made in landing configuration with the stall recovery systems operative, and then a fourth with the systems inoperative as required by the flight test schedule. However, as explained in the Accident Report, Peter Barlow delayed carrying out full stall recovery action at the required speed and G-ARPY entered a deep or 'super' stall. As the Trident descended Peter Barlow radioed Hatfield and informed them that the aircraft was in a superstall. Eyewitnesses observed it enter a spin as it descended and – clearly stalled – struck the ground in a flat attitude with little forward momentum, killing all four crew. Subsequently Trident flight tests were only flown with the stall recovery systems operative, and incidence meters were installed.

The Trident 1E Development

The first development of the Trident from the basic type was the Trident 1E. To give the improved airfield performance necessary the wingspan was extended by 5ft, the flap span and area were increased, and the droop leading-edge of the 1C was replaced by a leading-edge slat. The inboard end of the slat was faired by a simple Krüger flap operating with the slat. The increased wingspan permitted the ailerons to be mounted 18in further outboard, contributing to the increase in flap area; the flaps operated in conjunction with differential spoiler movement after approximately the first 15 degrees of aileron deflection. The spoilers

RIGHT: **The first Trident 1E, registered as G-ASWU for testing, was destined for Kuwait Airways and flew in their attractive livery. Following its maiden flight on 2 November 1964 it embarked on a lengthy trials programme and was delivered to Kuwait Airways on 19 March 1966 as 9K-ACF.** BAE Systems

BELOW: **The first of three Trident 1Es for Iraqi Airways, YI-AEA, at Heathrow. It was delivered to Iraqi Airways in October 1965 and withdrawn from use in 1977.** BAE Systems

were mounted ahead of the outer flaps and operated in unison with air brakes or lift dumpers to aid wheel braking on landing.

The Trident 1E had the benefit of 10,680lb thrust Speys, 6.5 per cent more wing area, wing leading-edge slats (trialled in a truncated form on 1C G-ARPD), more fuel tankage and all-round higher operating weights and payload for very little increase in empty weight. Payload range was better too, and although take-off and landing performance was not very different from that of the Trident 1C, hot and high climb-out performance was significantly better. With comparable payloads and fuel for similar ranges, the new Trident could fly out of smaller airfields than the earlier aircraft.

Although the 1E's fuselage was the same length as the 1C, it accommodated more passengers through refinement of the cabin design, the removal of a service door and by rearrangement of the vestibules following the adoption of up-and-over doors instead of the poor use of space made by the 1C's inward-opening doors. The first Trident 1E, destined for Kuwait Airways, flew on 2 November 1964 temporarily registered as G-ASWU. Flight testing was completed satisfactorily in record time and during

high-Mach handling trials G-ASWU was flown at almost level flight at Mach 0.975.

With the Trident 1E designed for operations from hot and high airfields, Hawker Siddeley envisaged the Middle East as a fertile ground for sales, particularly as the firm enjoyed strong associations with major operators in the region. It was an ideal

opportunity to engage with its rival Boeing head-on. For the final major exercise in the 1E's certification programme from 13 to 30 April 1965 G-ASWU carried out proving and hot weather performance trials in Africa, the Middle East and Pakistan. Captained by John Cunningham, Hawker Siddeley executive director and chief test

AP-ATK, the first of four Trident 1Es for Pakistan international Airlines, delivered in March 1966 and sold to the Chinese Aviation Administration in 1970. BAE Systems

pilot, Hatfield, backed by the old team of Peter Bugge (test pilot), Tony Fairbrother (flight test manager) and others, the Trident began its trip with a record-breaking flight to Cairo. During all of the performance trials, which included several maximum gross-weight accelerate-stops, the Trident worked perfectly. The 113-seat Trident had similar capabilities both in range and airfield performance to the heavier 128-seat 727. A lighter aeroplane, with less thrust, and a lower basic price, the Trident had all the features that would make for a cost per aircraft mile lower than that of the 727. In the event, however, the 1E did not achieve many sales in this market, Kuwait Airways and Iraqi Airways each ordering three, while Pakistan International received four.

Having laid down fifteen Trident 1Es and sold ten, all of which had been delivered by October 1966, HSA was understandably very eager to sell the five unsold and virtually complete remaining aircraft by mid-1967. Though Channel Airways was never the most financially sound of operators negotiations began in August and speedily reached a conclusion. On 5 October 1967 an £8m contract was signed for the remaining aircraft, designated as Trident 1E-140s. At the time HSA was in negotiation with BEA over Trident 3B and at the signing ceremony Channel's founder and Chairman Sqn Ldr Jack Jones cheekily quipped to Sir Arnold Hall and Sir Harry Broadhurst of Hawker Siddeley 'If you can't get that Trident 3 order from BEA perhaps we can get together to talk about Trident 3-140s.'

Channel's Tridents differed from the standard Trident 1E in that seating was increased from 115 to 139. This remarkable increase in passenger capacity – cutting seat-mile costs by about 20 per cent – was achieved by the installation of a new seat at 31-inch pitch and the forward cabin had seats seven-abreast. As could be expected there was considerable comment about this at the news conference following the signing of the contract. To meet passenger emergency escape regulations an additional Type 1 over-wing escape exit was provided in the Trident 1E-140.

Channel's first Trident, G-AVYB, was delivered to the airline on 31 May 1968 and operated its first service on 13 June from Stansted; their second and in the event final Trident, G-AVYE, was delivered the month after. Not surprisingly Channel proved to have problems in financing the order, which was speedily reduced to only two aircraft. Channel Tridents primarily operated on inclusive tour services to the Canary Islands, Las Palmas, Ibiza and Rimini and a small number of scheduled services. In March 1971 Hawker Siddeley chartered G-AVYB for a sales tour of Peru and Ghana, but no sales materialized from this venture.

Two Trident 1Es originally included in the Channel order but not delivered, G-AVYC and G-AVYD, were sold to BKS (an airline 70 per cent owned by BEA) in March/April 1969. These also had a high-density seating arrangement with a maximum capacity of 126 passengers. They operated from BKS's Newcastle base on scheduled services to Heathrow and Dublin, and charter services from Newcastle to tourist destinations. In November 1970 the airline's name was changed to Northeast, reflecting its base in that part of England. At the end of 1971 Channel ceased operations due to financial difficulties and its two Tridents were acquired by BEA and passed to Northeast, which was fully merged into British Airways in March 1976.

LEFT: **The first of Channel Airways Trident 1Es, G-AVFYB in March 1968. It was sold to Northeast Airlines in 1971 and became part of British Airways' large fleet.** BAE Systems

BELOW: **Though originally allotted to Channel Airways, G-AVYD was delivered to BKS in March 1969. BKS became Northeast and was later subsumed in British Airways, which is why this aircraft has Northeast livery and BA titling.** BAE Systems

Air Ceylon had planned to purchase a Trident 2E but took up the one remaining Trident 1E ordered by Channel Airways at the price of £2.2m with an option on a 2E. The aircraft, registered 4R-ACN, left Hatfield on 19 July 1969 and was displayed in the static park at the Paris Air Show on its delivery flight. Air Ceylon operated it until July 1978 when it was transferred to instructional use.

Following the crash of one of Kuwait's aircraft, their remaining two Tridents were sold to Cyprus Airways where they joined two Trident 2Es. Most importantly for Hatfield, Pakistan International sold its Tridents to CAAC of China in 1970, which a short time later led to orders for the Trident 2E.

G-AVFI, one of BEA's fleet of fifteen Trident 2Es. BAE Systems

The Trident 2E

BEA had always envisaged buying developed versions of the Trident. In August 1965 the airline agreed with Hawker Siddeley to order a new version: the Trident 2E, similar to the Trident 1E but with higher thrust 11,930lb Speys, a fuel tank in the fin to increase its range and Küchemann wing tips, which slightly increased the wingspan. BEA ordered fifteen and Cyprus Airways had two. In 1971 CAAC ordered six 2Es, ultimately increased to a total of thirty-three. The first Trident 2E, G-AVFA, made a three and a half hour first flight from Hatfield in BEA livery on 27 July 1967. Following initial flight testing, G-AVFA left Hatfield on 5 November for a month's hot and high trials in Nairobi. On return

to the UK, G-AVFA was fitted with a nose probe for high-speed trials and flew up to a speed of Mach 0.97. G-AVFA was the penultimate 2E to be delivered to BEA on 23 December 1969 as it took over from G-ARPB on Autoland development, flying 170 hours of trials between June 1968 and May 1969.

China and the Trident

Pakistan International Airlines (PIA) placed an order for three Trident 1Es (later increased to four) in January 1964. One of the reasons that PIA opted for the Trident over the 727, One-Eleven and Super Caravelle was a desire to operate into Peking without raising the possibility of an American spares embargo owing to the USA's poor

relations with China. PIA's Karachi–Peking service had been one of the few into the Chinese capital.

Though some PIA officials suggested to Hawker Siddeley that this link with China might lead to sales of the Trident to the Civil Aviation Administration of China (CAAC), this idea was apparently discounted by the British company, though they might have recalled that CAAC had ordered six Viscounts in 1962. However, when PIA decided to sell its Tridents and replace them with bigger aircraft, CAAC decided to purchase them and received them in June 1970. This purchase resulted in relations developing between CAAC and Hawker Siddeley. A sales team arrived in China in March 1971, and in August CAAC made an initial order for six Trident 2Es. In August the following year China

The first Trident 2E for China, carrying British marks for test flying and delivery. It was delivered in November 1972. BAE Systems

ordered six more 2Es with options on a further six. These options were taken up three months later, along with an additional contract for two extended-range Trident Super 3Bs. Only a few days later, on 19 November 1972, the first 2E left for delivery for China and in December 1973 a further and final order for fifteen Trident 2Es was placed. These thirty-three Tridents were valued at £120 million.

The Hawker Siddeley 1974 Annual Report spoke optimistically of new Trident orders. As future employment at Hatfield very much depended on production for the Chinese, the negotiation of an order from North Korea, possibly for more than a dozen aircraft, would have extended production. In the event this order did not come to fruition because suitable financial terms could not be agreed, but the Chinese contracts kept the Trident production line open until April 1978 when the last Trident was delivered to China in the hands of Hatfield's famous test pilot team of John Cunningham and Peter Bugge.

Trident Production

Final assembly of the Trident was centred at Hatfield and as there had been expectations of substantial sales there were plans for a second production line at Chester but this was never needed. Other factories within Hawker Siddeley assisted in production; for example, the former Airspeed factory at Portsmouth built the nose and forward fuselages until 1968 when the site was closed. The former Blackburn works at Brough took over this work and built the remaining sixty-four nose and forward

fuselages, completing the last one in 1975, while the former Folland factory at Hamble built the wings and tailplanes.

The Final Trident Development – the 3B

During 1964 and 1965 studies had taken place into a number of Trident developments. The HS132 was a stretched version 160-seater with twin Rolls-Royce RB178s and led on to the 185-seat HS134, which was far removed from its Trident origins: a radically different design similar to the Boeing 757 with a low tail and twin underwing RB.207 engines. As Hawker Siddeley could not fund this project single-handedly it sought collaboration with a European partner, but none was forthcoming.

In 1966 BEA had sought Government approval to order Boeing 727-200s and 737s, which caused considerable anger within the British aircraft industry. The Labour Government refused to grant approval for these purchases and insisted that BEA buy British. The BAC One-Eleven 500 was developed for the 737 requirement; Hawker Siddeley for its part began to investigate how it could develop the Trident 2E to fulfil BEA's requirements, whilst keeping development costs to less than 33 per cent of those of the HS132/134.

The result was the Trident 3B with the fuselage lengthened by 8ft 5in forward and 8ft aft of the wing to provide accommodation for 146 passengers in a mixed-class layout or up to 180 in all-economy seating. The angle of incidence of the wing was altered to provide the correct angle of attack on rotation and the wing area was increased.

To provide power for this much heavier aircraft the three 11,960lb thrust Speys were augmented by a Rolls-Royce RB162 booster providing 5,230lb thrust for take-off and climb. The booster engine was installed where the APU had been above the centre engine exhaust, while the APU was moved in front of the fin. Employing this existing booster engine instead of costly development of the Spey was expedient as costs had to be kept down. The benefit was evident when comparing the 2E with the 3B, for the 3B had a 1,500ft shorter take-off distance despite a 6,500lb increase in gross weight.

The final mark of the Trident, the first Trident 3B, G-AWYZ, made its maiden flight of two hours and ten minutes in BEA livery on 12 November 1969. Only a mock-up of Trident's new booster engine was installed for initial flights. The first flight with the booster was in February 1970 and the first boosted take-off was from Bedford on 26 March 1970.

In the flight test programme the first Trident 3B was engaged in development of the booster engine and Autoland system evaluation, while the second investigated low-speed handling and stall performance. From August to September 1970 G-AWYZ was engaged on tropical trials in Madrid and Dubai. Originally it was planned to use three aircraft in the 500-hour development and certification programme, but because this proved to be trouble-free only the first two were employed.

The Trident 3B entered service with BEA on schedule on 1 March 1971. BEA was not the only customer; CAAC also received two Super 3Bs which had an 8,000lb increase in all-up weight, allowing a 25 per cent increase in maximum payload range,

The Hawker Siddeley Brough factory took over the manufacture of the Trident forward fuselage from the Portsmouth plant in 1968. The four fuselages in the photo were for BEA Trident 3Bs G-AWZK to G-AWZN.
Blackburn Archive

The first 3B, G-AWYZ, on the Hatfield apron. This final development of the Trident was substantially longer than the earlier marks and owing to its heavier weights required a Rolls-Royce RB.162 booster engine below the rudder to provide adequate take-off and climb performance. (The APU was relocated to the front of the fin.) BAE Systems

ABOVE: G-AWYZ on the apron at Nicosia, Cyprus. It was first flown on 12 November 1969 and was delivered to BEA in March 1972. It was only in service with BEA/British Airways until October 1983 and was scrapped in June 1984. BAE Systems

RIGHT: The second of two Trident Super 3Bs for China, temporarily registered G-BAJM, which became 270. Although similar to the Trident 3B, the Super 3B had an 8,000lb increase in all-up weight, allowing a 25 per cent increase in maximum payload range. Range was increased to 1,825nm and 152 passengers could be carried. BAE Systems

to 1,825nm. The manufacturer was hopeful that more sales of the Super 3B would be found in south-east Asia, but regrettably these did not materialize.

Autoland Pioneer

BEA had specified that the Trident should be able to land in zero visibility, fully automatically. To this end the second Trident 1, G-ARPB, was dedicated to testing this facility for more than three years. Appropriately its first Autoland was made at RAE Bedford (the home of the Blind Landing Experimental Unit) on 3 March 1964. On 30 June G-ARPB was delivered to BEA but immediately leased back to the manufacturer for continuing Autoland development.

The first automatic touchdown was made by a Trident at Heathrow on 10 June 1965. G-ARPB made the inaugural low-visibility Autoland at Heathrow on 4 November 1965 when the airport was closed to all other aircraft owing to poor visibility. By the end of 1968 BEA were making 300 Autolands per month; this ambitious programme led in May 1972 to approval for landings with operation in visibility of only 150ft. Autoland was also gradually introduced on BEA's Trident 2s and 3s as they entered service. The first Trident 2E for BEA, G-AVFA, was the penultimate 2E to be delivered to the airline as it took over Autoland development from G-ARPB, flying 170 hours of trials between June 1968 and May 1969. The first 2E was in turn replaced by G-AWYZ, the first 3B.

The benefit of this costly development was that the airline could save a huge amount of money by not having to cancel or divert its flights in adverse weather conditions. Other British airliners followed suit, as did foreign-built aircraft.

BEA/British Airways Service

With the delivery of this large fleet of sixty-four new Tridents between 1963 and 1974 (twenty-three Trident 1Cs, fifteen Trident 2Es and twenty-six Trident 3Bs) plus six second-hand examples (five 1Es and a single 2E), the aircraft became the backbone of BEA operations, giving BEA the advantage of an essentially homogenous fleet. The Trident 1Cs served on the main European routes and, with the arrival of the 2Es in 1968, began to fly to more distant places, such as Istanbul and Moscow.

Three years later the introduction of the 3B provided a higher-capacity aircraft for the airline's shorter routes.

BEA and BOAC merged in 1974 to form British Airways, and soon afterwards the joint airline launched a shuttle service between its major UK destinations and Heathrow. The Trident took on the lion's share of this task until its withdrawal from service in the mid-1980s.

Accidents

The Trident had more than its fair share of losses in addition to the test-flying crash of G-ARPY. In addition to the more commonplace losses, the first in service loss of a BEA Trident was when a BKS Ambassador carrying horses had a flap failure landing at Heathrow in July 1968 and cartwheeled, hitting two Tridents on the ground and killing the three crew and three grooms. One of these Tridents, G-ARPT, was a write-off but G-ARPI, whose tail was partly torn off, was expensively rebuilt.

Just less than four years later in June 1972 this same aircraft crashed, killing 118 passengers and crew in what remains the worst-ever British airliner accident. Taking off from Heathrow, G-ARPI stalled as the drooped leading edge was retracted prematurely. The crew did not respond to the stall warnings and stick pusher, and turned them off. The captain continued to fly the aircraft normally, but as no recovery action was taken the aircraft crashed near Staines a mere two and a half minutes after the brake release on the runway. The accident report was unable to establish who had retracted the leading edge droop, though it was clear from the post-mortem that the captain – who was flying the aircraft – was suffering from a serious heart condition and might have had a heart attack during take-off.

An unusual incident was the crash, possibly by shooting down, of a CAAC 1E (originally bought from Pakistan International) with Lin Biao, a renegade member of the Chinese Politburo, on board in September 1971.

Wing Cracks

In July 1977, as production was coming to an end, a Trident 3B was found to have critical wing cracks. An immediate fleet-wide check followed and ten of British Airways' twenty-five Trident 3s were grounded; only

In 1978 three British Airways Trident 3Bs, G-AWZN, G-AWZP and G-AWZM at the former BAC plant at Hurn for repairs to remedy cracks in their wings. BAE Systems

one Trident 3 was found to be completely crack-free, the remaining fourteen having cracks that were not critical but still needed repair. At the same time the Trident 1 and Trident 2 fleets were inspected, found to be without cracks and considered not at risk.

The initial repair for the Trident 3B took the form of four external doublers, and as the work was time-consuming the aircraft were dealt with by the airline, British Aerospace working parties and by BAe plants at Hatfield and Hurn. The later definitive repair involved clipping the wingtips by 3ft to reduce bending, re-jigging the ailerons slightly upwards to reduce incidence, and re-rigging the flaps slightly downward. Henceforth the fleet would be operated at reduced speeds and would have operating weight reductions of between 4,000lb and 7,000lb. British Airways estimated the total cost of grounding and repairs as £25–30m. The CAAC Trident fleet also showed some signs of cracks, and repairs were instituted on these aircraft too.

Hush-Kitting and the End of the Trident Operations

Even the Trident 3Bs had little re-sale value on the open market. Their market appeal was low and they were costly to run. The Tridents' advantages were that they could not depreciate, and that with their Cat 3 landing systems they were excellent in poor visibility.

The introduction of Chapter 2 noise legislation spelled the end of British Trident operations owing to the impossibility of adequately hush-kitting the aircraft's centre engine. Though the Spey-engined One-Eleven could be hush-kitted with a considerable performance penalty, the Trident could not meet the requirements unless re-engined with Spey 67s. This would have been a major engineering task and would have probably involved still using a standard Spey in the centre engine position because the intake could not handle the higher mass flow of the refanned engine. A straight hush-kitted Trident 2E would suffer a big performance penalty and would have been unable to fly from London to Athens, one of the design cases for the aircraft.

The last British Airways Trident flight took place on 31 December 1985 and out of its total Trident fleet only five Trident 3Bs were sold. These went to a most unlikely operator, Air Charter Service in Zaire, in 1983–84 and were in use until 1988. On

the other side of the globe, however, the Chinese Tridents continued in service well into the 1990s. The great majority of the British-registered Trident fleet went to UK airports for fire services training and a smaller number to museums; others were broken up at Prestwick and Heathrow.

Trident Developments

As development of the Trident was limited by the thrust growth of the Spey, the projected Rolls-Royce RB178 of 28,000lb thrust was considered with a number of fuselage sizes. These studies led on to the HS134, which evolved into an aircraft similar to the Boeing 757 with a low tail and underwing podded engines. As Hawker Siddeley could not fund it themselves, discussions took place with the French with a view to collaboration; eventually these discussions would lead on to Airbus.

By the early 1980s the Chinese had the largest Trident fleet in service and were planning to keep them in use for many years. In 1983 two GE/SNECMA CFM56-2s engines were purchased as part of a scheme to re-engine the aircraft: they were going to remove the centre engine and reinforce the area vacated. With two modern high-bypass-ratio turbofans each producing 24,000lb thrust replacing three 12,000lb Speys, take-off performance, payload and range would have been much improved. In the event, nothing more was heard about the project.

Conclusions

Trident production came to an end on 13 September 1978 when the 117th and last Trident was delivered, to CAAC. The great expectations held out for the Trident were never realized. It was modelled too closely to a specification set by BEA rather than to the original intention to build a larger aircraft approximately the same size as the Boeing 727. Had the original design been proceeded with, it is likely that more Tridents would have been sold.

Regrettably for the Trident (and the BAC One-Eleven) the Spey did not exhibit the thrust growth potential of other engines and this was one of the reasons that attempts to develop the design were stymied and led to the need of the Trident 3B to have a booster engine. Though the Trident flew 14 months before its rival the Boeing 727,

Specification – Trident 2E	
Length	114ft 9in (34.98m)
Wingspan	98ft (29.87m)
Height	27ft (8.23m)
MTOW	144,500lb (65,500kg)
Cruising speed	590mph (950km/h)
Range	2,700 miles (4,344km)
Passengers	115
Powerplant	3 × 11,930lb Rolls-Royce Spey 512

it was the American tri-jet that entered service first.

The Trident led the way in Autoland and its effectiveness saved BEA/British Airways substantial amounts of money. The only major operators were BEA and CAAC (which at that time could not buy American aircraft). Without China's order it is unlikely that Hawker Siddeley would have broken even on the aircraft.

HS146

Even while the Trident's design was being finalized, engineers at de Havilland were pursuing the elusive 'Dakota replacement' market. In the UK Hawker Siddeley's Avro subsidiary was already building the 748 and Handley Page had the Herald. On the mainland of Europe the Fokker Friendship was winning orders in this market. These three aircraft were all powered by twin Rolls-Royce Dart turboprops.

A Troubled Birth

De Havilland had much expertise with small airliners and wanted to build on their experience with the Dove and Heron. Initially projected as the DH123 with a high wing, two de Havilland Gnome turboprops and capacity for 32–40 passengers, one year later the project was re-thought as the DH126 fitted with twin 3,850lb thrust rear-mounted de Havilland PS92B jet engines, a 'T' tail and capacity for thirty passengers. A problem with the 126 project was the lack of a suitable powerplant from de Havilland Engines or any other firm – the PS92B engines were never built and so work on the project slowed through 1961, frustrating the designers.

After de Havilland's takeover by Hawker Siddeley, in order to reduce costs in 1964 the project was redesigned employing the front fuselage and systems of the HS748 married to a new, moderately swept wing, engines and 'T' tail. This project was designated the HS131. But, as a thirty-seater, this was still a small airliner and the justifiable feeling in the early 1960s was that jet-power was not viable for this size of aircraft. So this project grew into the larger HS136 with the same basic configuration as the HS131 but able to carry up to forty passengers. After the stall problems that the 'T'-tailed BAC One-Eleven and the Trident suffered from, the design was radically rethought and in 1967 took on another configuration – one that is common to many airliners today. The Boeing 737 and Airbus A320 configuration, twin 9,730lb Rolls-Royce Trents mounted on low wing with a conventional tail and capable of holding fifty-seven passengers.

Regrettably this conventional configuration fell from favour mainly because of concerns over debris ingestion into the engines when operating from unmetalled runways. During 1968 the design grew again with capacity for ninety-three passengers and powered by the Rolls-Royce Trent, but the project engineers returned to a rear-engined, high-tailed design, again known as the HS136, proposed in two versions seating either sixty to eighty or seventy to ninety passengers.

Meanwhile, at the Woodford factory the design team had proposed the HS860 as a jet development for the Avro (HS) 748. When the Hawker Siddeley board met they opted for a comparative evaluation of the HS136 and HS860. After the evaluation the Board

instructed the two teams to work together to develop a final design.

The fruition of the joint group's work was the HS144 of 1969, a revisionist proposal with a high tail and rear-mounted Rolls-Royce Trent engines. This came in two versions for either sixty-two or eighty passengers. With Rolls-Royce's bankruptcy in 1971 the Trent engine fell by the wayside and once again the project was without an engine. However, there was a powerplant available from a rather unlikely source: the American-built Avco Lycoming ALF502, also fitted to the Canadair 600 (the progenitor for the Canadair RJ). Whereas all the previous projects had been based on two engines, the modest 6,700lb thrust of the ALF502 meant that four engines were now needed. As a result the HS144 configuration developed to a manner similar to the actual 146 with a high swept wing, four podded engines and a high tail, and a faired 'double bubble' fuselage. Further refinement led to the HS146, which had a circular fuselage section.

Bob Grigg, the 146's chief designer, said that he had qualms about whether airlines would buy a four-engined short-haul jet. However, this layout provided good airfield performance, which meant that certain other costly features such as leading edge slats and thrust reversers could be omitted on the grounds of weight and complexity. The quietness of the engines was such that no hush kitting was needed, and in the years to come this was to be one of the aircraft's major selling points.

In researching the market to justify the substantial investment, the Hawker Siddeley marketing department employed desk research and fieldwork, visiting many airlines and utilizing data on all IATA airlines held on a computer at Hatfield. The HS146 was now identified as a replacement for turboprop feeder liners such as the Fokker F-27, Avro 748 and Convairs, providing jet comfort on short to medium sectors without prejudicing field performance. It was to be a simple design that could be managed by unsophisticated operators requiring the minimum of ground equipment. The aircraft could operate from noise-sensitive airfields close to communities and would require minimal ground facilities. It would have doors at each corner, optional airstairs, an APU (or batteries) for engine starting, and two freight holds with a low sill height.

HS146 Given the Green Light

On 29 August 1973 Hawker Siddeley announced the go-ahead of the project. In order to finance it the Government invested £46m, to be recovered from a levy on sales. This sum was matched by Hawker Siddeley, which would also bear any cost overruns. However, Sir Arnold Hall, Chairman of Hawker Siddeley, assured the media that cost overruns would not be incurred.

Two basic versions were on offer in two configurations: the 146-100 would seat seventy passengers five-abreast or eighty-eight six-abreast while the larger 146-200 could

The Hawker Siddeley 146 engineering mock-up built in 1974. BAE Systems

seat either eighty-two or 102 at five or six abreast, respectively. The 146-100 was 85ft 10in long; the 146-200 was 93ft 1in long. The wingspan of each was identical at 86ft 6in. As for the engine, there was some surprise at the launch that no British engine manufacturer was involved especially when the value of the powerplant represented 27 per cent of the machine. It was stated that talks were taking place between Avco and Rolls-Royce with a view to there being some cooperation at a later stage.

Design, final assembly and flight test of the 146 would be at the Hatfield plant. There would be three development aircraft, the first flying in December 1975 with entry into service in 1977. About 20,000 people in the Hawker Siddeley and supplier plants would be involved in production.

The Hatfield design team led by Bob Grigg designed the aircraft to meet the demanding requirements of the regional air transport market where heavy use over short sector lengths coupled with high reliability are paramount requirements. Outstanding airfield performance and whisper-jet noise levels were other attributes of the aircraft, which offered excellent profit potential on low-density routes. Target price was set at $4.4m for 1977 delivery, which compared with the twin-jet Fokker F28's price of $4m.

Michael Heseltine, Conservative Minister for Aerospace, commented at the launch press conference at the Department for Trade and Industry that he was impressed by Hawker Siddeley's commitment to the project and its willingness to invest heavily in it. However, when Sir Arnold Hall was asked if there was a launching order book he responded that the firm was yet to seek orders for the 146. He believed that British Airways might have a requirement for a lengthened 146 but that the main market was the global market. In response British Airways managing director, Henry Marking, stated that the airline might have a requirement for such an aircraft in the following decade.

At the press conference there was some surprise expressed that this was not an international collaborative project. The response was that Hawker Siddeley was well able to manage the production of a machine of this size without the added challenges of foreign partners. In support of this view, Michael Heseltine declared that it was important for Europe that Britain should maintain a strongly based national aerospace industry.

Financial Times Report

On 30 August the *Financial Times* reported the launch under the headline, 'Hawker unveils its good neighbour jet'. The article continued:

> Before launching the HS146, Hawker spent some years studying the market, with which it already has much experience in selling its twin-engined HS748 feeder liner turboprop, its HS125 executive jet and its Canadian Twin Otter. It is convinced that the sales potential is there and the initial volume of airline interest (including British Airways Regional Division) tends to confirm the fact. The overall cost of the HS146 is estimated at £80m including research and development, jigging and tooling and initial production. Progress payments should be flowing in from about 1975 onwards, if not earlier.

Towards the end of 1973 work on the 146 gathered momentum, as the firm was aiming for a first flight in December 1975 and certification in February 1977. A wooden mock-up was fabricated at Hatfield where design and final assembly work was centred. Other work was split between Hawker Siddeley factories at Hatfield, Brough and Woodford. Woodford was responsible for the wing surfaces, tail and rear fuselage while Brough would build the nose and Hatfield the forward fuselage. No decision was made about the fabrication of the wing, though discussions were held with Aérospatiale of France.

Costs Rise

The future for the project was looking good, but within a year events on the world stage – the oil crisis, a product of the Yom Kippur War, and the rampant inflation – signalled the worst economic recession since between the wars. The August 1974 HS146 Project Status Review indicated that the development costs would far surpass £92 million, how far was not known, but the figure might exceed £200 million and that the aircraft's unit cost would be similarly affected. Although the British Government's share in development costs was adjusted for inflation, Hawker Siddeley was not prepared to invest more in a project for which it saw no secure future as prototype construction moved ahead. It is also highly likely that the return to power of a Labour Government at the February 1974 General Election and their policy to nationalize the British

aerospace industry would have had a bearing on any decision made by the HSA Board.

On 17 September 1974 a meeting was held between the management and TASS (Technical, Administrative & Supervisory Staff) trades union at Hatfield where HSA's Managing Director, Mr Thorne, informed them that the board believed that the project was not financially viable. Four weeks later, TASS was told that the 146 would be cancelled and there would be redundancies. Union representatives met Tony Benn, the Labour Government's Secretary of State for Industry, and lobbied the Conservative and Liberal Parties for support.

The 146 is Shelved

HSA halted work on 21 October 1974 and informed the Government, but agreed with the union to withhold notice of redundancy while discussions continued between the union representatives and the Government. There were work-ins and demonstrations at Hatfield and Brough as workers sought to keep their jobs. Helen Hayman, Labour MP for Hatfield, strongly supported the workers whose factory was in her constituency and in her maiden speech to the House of Commons spoke in support of the project. The following day, 31 October, there was a mass lobby of the House by 500 staff and shop floor workers and a delegation visited Downing Street to present a petition. On 4 November in the House of Commons, Tony Benn said that Hawker Siddeley's decision to cease work was 'a breach of contract', breaking the agreement made between the company and the Government when the 146 was launched in 1973. The action did not stop there, for 2,000 workers from all HSA plants demonstrated at Speakers Corner on 6 November and a further petition was delivered to Downing Street. Further support was garnered from various local councils and the then Bishop of St Albans, Dr Runcie (later Archbishop of Canterbury), arranged a meeting for the union delegates with members of the House of Lords.

A Reprieve

On 9 December Tony Benn made a statement in the House that the Government accepted that 50–50 funding was no longer viable, but that they wanted to maintain this civil airliner capability when the aerospace industry was nationalized. Tony Benn said that Sir Arnold Hall had agreed to maintain the necessary jigs, tools, drawings and design capacity. The Hawker Siddeley Annual Report 1974 stated:

Meantime, keeping the design [of the 146] on the back burner has absorbed several million pounds of Government funding since October 1974, when Hawker Siddeley decided to stop spending on it. A small team has been kept working on the HS146 90/100-seat short-haul feeder-liner to give colour to Government statements that a nationalized corporation will retain the option of reactivating this project.

The Hawker Siddeley Board must have felt a sense of *déjà vu* at this point as in 1970 the Canadian Government had stepped in to financially support the de Havilland Canada DHC-7 that Hawker Siddeley had not wanted to proceed with; this difference of opinion between the Canadian Government and the Board resulted in the eventual nationalization of de Havilland Canada.

Tripartite talks took place between HSA, the Government and the union TASS (later part of MSF and now part of Unite) under the chairmanship of Tony Benn, and set up a working party to examine the options available. Benn took on an uphill task as the Treasury was also set against continuing with the project. Subsequently TASS had meetings with the Chancellor of the Exchequer and British Airways.

The workers were trying to convince everybody that without the 146 the state would be taking over an aerospace industry with a moribund Civil Aircraft Division. This view was not wholly accurate, as there was still the possibility for a further and probably cheaper development of the BAC One-Eleven, which had made over 200 sales but needed a new engine and other improvements to compete with the Boeing 737 and McDonnell Douglas MD-80.

In July 1976 the Government proposed terms to keep the project 'ticking over'. The cost of this was £3.75m and would finance additional design, research, development and structural testing while the union continued to press for full-scale continuation.

Aerospace Nationalization, Hesitation and then Resuscitation

Lord Beswick, Chairman Designate of the newly nationalized British Aerospace, and other members of the new Board arrived at Hatfield on 25 February 1977. He informed the union representatives that on the basis of what HSA had told him, he could not recommend the project to the Minister. In late March, 500 redundancies were announced at Hatfield, but after negotiations these numbers were reduced.

The nationalization Bill received the Royal Assent and on 29 April 1977 the state-owned British Aerospace came into being. But it was not the time for the unions to relax their pressure! More meetings were held with MPs, the Labour and Conservative aerospace committees and the British Aerospace Board. So on 10 July 1978 Gerald Kaufman, as Minister of State at the Department of Industry, announced in the Commons that the Government had given its approval to restart the BAe 146!

The BAe 146

The first 146, G-SSSH, made its maiden flight from Hatfield on 3 September 1981 and to hasten certification of the stretched version, the prototype 146-200, G-WISC, was the fourth aircraft to join the test programme following its maiden flight on 1 August 1982. Even before certification the 146 had flown into many small airfields on a sales tour of parts of India and the Far East that had previously never been frequented by jetliners. Comparative trials also demonstrated that it was the world's quietest jet airliner, beating others by a very substantial margin. The first service was in May 1983 with a Dan-Air service from Gatwick to Dublin. A month later services began in the USA, and airlines in Canada, Australia, New Zealand and the Far East followed suit.

146-300

To maintain momentum in the market place in 1984 the 146-300 was announced. This development was achieved by stretching the 146-100 fuselage by 15ft 9in, but employing the standard engine and wing of the earlier series without seriously degrading airfield performance. Initially envisaged as a six-abreast 120-seater, by the time the prototype 146-300 took to the air it was configured in a 100-seat five-abreast layout. This was chiefly as British Aerospace had re-focused the 146 series for the regional airline market, particularly in the USA, where the five-abreast layout on the type was already popular. As sales of the 146 developed, production of the larger models, the 146-200 and 146-300, predominated and demand for the 146-100 was far less.

The first BAe 146, G-SSSH, taking off on its first flight from Hatfield, on 3 September 1981. BAE Systems

In and out of the City

The first 146 demonstration at London City Airport in July 1988 proved a great success as the aircraft was able to fly the 5½-degree approach required and its quietness defied any opposition. Not only was the 146 instrumental in the development for London City, it is also used at similar city centre airports such as Stockholm–Bromma with difficult approaches and severe noise restrictions. To this day an appreciable number of the movements at London City are with the

RIGHT: **G-SSSH was later 'stretched' to become the first 146-300, re-registered G-LUXE. It first flew as the 146-300 prototype on 1 May 1987.**
BAE Systems

BELOW: **The success of BAe 146 and RJ operations into London City Airport is evidenced by this photo from the 1990s showing aircraft from Malmo, Lufthansa, Alitalia, Crossair and Air UK.** BAE Systems

146s and Avro Rjs (*see* below) of operators such as of Swiss and Cityjet.

Launch of the RJ Family

By 1990, with some 202 aircraft ordered and 157 delivered, British Aerospace could feel satisfied that the 146 had proved a success against the competition such as the Fokker 100. To maintain this position in 1990 BAe announced a number of major improvements to the 146 family. The aircraft would continue to be available in the three existing fuselage sizes but the most important change to this new version of the 146 was the introduction of digital avionics and the LF507 engine. This change was intended to lower engine maintenance costs, which had deterred some potential orders.

To emphasize the improvements the new aircraft were rebranded as Regional Jets, so each model would be identified by their passenger capacity with five-abreast seating:

RJ70 (former 146-100), RJ85 (former 146-200) and RJ100 (former 146-300). The RJ soon acquired a respectable order book and British Aerospace was justifiably proud of the fact that the RJs were ordered in the colours of 'blue chip' operators such as Lufthansa Cityline, Swissair, THY, Sabena, British Airways and Northwest Mesaba Airlines.

RJX – a Short-Lived Development

By 2000 the RJ was in need of further development as it had been in existence for eight years and new Bombardier and Embraer regional jets were gathering large orders. So in March 2000 BAE Systems launched the Avro RJX, revamped around an improved powerplant, the Honeywell AS977. In April 2000, Druk Air became the launch customer when it ordered a pair of RJX85s to replace its two BAe 146-100s

and in March 2001 British European – an established 146 operator – ordered twelve RJX100s.

Although the new engine and installation caused problems, the first flight of the Avro RJX85 prototype took place on 28 April 2001. The flight test programme then moved into full swing and the RJX100 prototype G-IRJX flew five months later. The aircraft had a noticeably better performance than the RJ, especially at high altitude.

But BAE Systems had long held doubts about the economic viability of civil aircraft programmes and had never made any money from the 146/RJ programme. On 27 November 2001 BAE made a surprise announcement closing the Regional Jet programme and 146/RJ/RJX production ended with a total of 394 having flown.

The final delivery of a British-made, essentially Hawker Siddeley-designed airliner took place at Woodford on 25 November 2003 when OH-SAP, a BAE RJ85, left for delivery to Blue 1.

LEFT: **The prototype RJX85, G-ORJX, together with the prototype RJX100, G-IRJX. Only three RJXs were completed before development was cancelled in November 2001.** BAE Systems

BELOW: **The final delivery of a British-made, essentially Hawker Siddeley-designed, airliner took place from Woodford on 26 November 2003 when OH-SAP, a BAE RJ85, left for delivery to Blue 1. Prior to its departure it had a photocall with the first BAE 146, G-LUXE (formerly G-SSSH), newly converted to be a meteorological research aircraft.** BAE Systems

CHAPTER EIGHT

Executive Jet Success –
the Hawker Siddeley 125

Following on from the sale of more than 500 de Havilland Doves and after considering turboprop conversions, the Hawker Siddeley Board was finally persuaded to give approval for work to proceed on an executive jet replacement in March 1961. This proved a very sound move as in the following five decades more nearly 1,700 125s were delivered and production only ceased in the USA following the bankruptcy of Hawker Beechcraft in 2012.

The 125 underwent many name changes. Originally 'de Havilland Jet Dragon', connecting it to the pre-war de Havilland biplane, was considered; this was quickly dropped and it first flew as the de Havilland 125. Following Hawker Siddeley Aircraft's rationalization in 1963 it became the HS125, following nationalization in 1977

the BAe 125 and, with the sale of the 125 programme to Raytheon in 1993, the 125 was renamed the Hawker, so the BAe 125-800 became the Hawker 800. In March 2007 Raytheon Aircraft was purchased from Raytheon by Beechcraft and the firm became known as Hawker Beechcraft.

The First 125s

The first two prototypes were built at Chester, as were all the others, but assembled in Hatfield so that a closer eye could be kept on them by the design team. The first aircraft, G-ARYA, flew from Hatfield on 13 August 1962 and the second, G-ARYB, in December 1962. Both aircraft were fully instrumented but had fuselages

1ft shorter than the standard production model. The first aircraft had wingspan of 3ft less than standard, so it returned to Chester in the winter of 1962–63 for modification to the production standard. G-ARYA was used on aircraft handling trials and G-ARYB for performance testing. Following these two prototypes came eight Series 1s with the standard full-length fuselage. The first of these (G-ARYC), which flew in February 1963, was the first 125 to be assembled and flown from Chester. It was painted in Bristol Siddeley Engines livery as was used by the manufacturer and Bristol Siddeley on a joint programme of airframe/engine development flying, plus business operations. The fourth aircraft, G-ASEC (amusingly known as 'Sausage, Egg and Chips'), joined the test programme in April

A close-up view of G-ARYA, the prototype de Havilland (later Hawker Siddeley) 125 having ground trials at Hatfield prior to its maiden flight on 13 August 1962. BAE Systems

The second prototype flew from Hatfield on 12 December 1962. The first two 125s were the only ones assembled at Hatfield.
Hawker 125 collection

1963. It was first employed on route-proving trials and was demonstrated at Farnborough 1964, by which time UK certification had already been granted, on 4 June. FAA certification followed on 28 September 1964.

Despite its high-tail layout the 125 achieved a straightforward stall purely through aerodynamic means and with no tendency to 'deep stall'. However, during testing it was found that rudder loads when flying in the engine-out case were too high and to rectify this an automatic rudder trimmer activated by a bleed from the engines was introduced, which meant that an engine could be taken from idle to full power while approaching to land without the pilot having to touch the rudder.

The HS125 was a conventional design whose fuselage sat almost entirely atop a low, moderately swept 47ft wing. Fitting the wing in this manner provided a flat cabin floor and aisle with headroom of 69 inches able to accommodate six to ten passengers. Entrance was via a single door that opened up and over on the inside. Optional airstairs could be fitted. Baggage was stowed opposite the doorway and was accessible in flight. The compact flightdeck had seating and controls for two pilots, but the 125 could be flown by one.

To maintain simplicity all the flying controls were manually operated and the wing had airbrakes and double-slotted flaps. The nosewheel retracted forward and the mainwheels inwards; doors were omitted over the mainwheels to save space. The twin Bristol Siddeley (later Rolls-Royce) Viper engines were carried on stub planes and the intakes were sited ahead of the trailing edge of the wing, which avoided debris damage during the take-off or landing roll.

The Bristol Siddeley Viper was 'stretched' in 1961 by adding an extra stage to meet the required 3,000lb thrust and became the Viper 520 installed in G-ARYA and G-ARYB in 1963 – these had originally flown with lower-rated engines. The 520 was soon superseded by the 521 offering 3,100lb thrust, which was fitted to the Series 3 aircraft, and then the 522 with 3,360lb thrust. To extend range additional fuel tanks were fitted under the rear fuselage and in the fin in addition to the fuel tanks in the wing box.

Orders Roll In

A year before certification in May 1963 the 125 already had thirty-six firm orders from the batch of sixty that had been laid down. Of these, the RAF was to receive twenty for navigational training. The Ministry of Aviation ordered two 125s for radar and navaid calibration, and Qantas bought two for crew training. Fully equipped price to full airline standard was then approximately £210,000 (2013 = £3.8m) although the basic cost for the unequipped aircraft was only about £170,000 (2013 = £3.1m); these prices were set too low and over time were increased to make the aircraft profitable. Production was then one aircraft per month, but was building up steadily.

The eighth 125, G-ASSI, became the first company demonstrator and embarked on a 105-day tour of North America in which it made over 500 demonstration flights. The tour was so successful that twenty-two orders were received. From January to March 1965 G-ASSI was sent on sales tours to Europe, the Middle East and South Africa. By this time 125s were being delivered and the first delivery was made in September 1964 to Chartag of Switzerland, which received the sixth aircraft, HB-VAG. Following the initial production run of eight Series 1s, these were succeeded by Series 1A for North America and Series 1B for the rest of the world; these

aircraft introduced minor refinements and increased operating weights and range. The RAF's Dominies were Series 2s, the next mark was the Series 3, which offered continuing improvement plus the option of an AiResearch APU.

RAF Dominies and Serving with Other Air Forces

The RAF's twenty 125s, which were named Dominies by the RAF, entered service in the autumn of 1965 at Stradishall as navigation trainers and the full fleet were in service by mid-1966. The first two aircraft, XS709 and XS710, flew in December 1964 and February 1965 respectively and were involved in trials at Hatfield and A&AEE Boscombe Down. The Dominies, fitted with Viper 301s of 3,310lb thrust, were specially equipped with a comprehensive navigation panel with appropriate avionics at the rear fuselage bulkhead. The aircraft was generally crewed by one pilot, one navigation trainer and two trainees. Dominies could be distinguished from the 125 by the enlarged forward wing-fuselage fairing required to accommodate the large Doppler aerial. Eleven aircraft from the original order of twenty were put through a mid-life update programme beginning in 1992 to make them more appropriate for training crews on modern fast-jet fleets. The update was also intended to extend the Dominie's service life to at least 2015, but as a result of the 2010 Strategic Defence Review it was withdrawn from use in January 2011.

Over twenty governments operated 125s in VIP or support roles including No. 32 Squadron based at RAF Northolt, which eventually had twelve aircraft. In the late 1990s 125s were also purchased as flight inspection aircraft by seven countries, including the USA and Japan.

ABOVE: **A fine view of HS125 Series 1 G-ASTY.**
BAE Systems

RIGHT: **The third RAF Dominie, XS711, at RIAT, Fairford 2004.** Author

Selling the 125 in North America

Although Hawker Siddeley had an established support organization in New York in the form of Hawker Siddeley International (formerly DH Inc.) it recognized that to sell the 125 in North America it would need an influential distributor and engaged in a series of negotiations with Pan Am about it taking on that role. As Pan Am wanted a larger, re-engined aircraft HSA backed away from an agreement, even though Pan Am would have ordered aircraft itself and sold them on. The company instead contracted AiResearch Aviation Services on the west coast of the USA and Atlantic Aviation on the east, which also oversaw Canada.

Those 125s destined for North America were completed at Chester in a very basic state. They were unpainted, unfurnished with bare walls and fitted with rudimentary

avionics for delivery to a distributor's completion centre on the other side of the Atlantic. For the trans-Atlantic delivery flight the 125s were equipped with a crate of ferry equipment with a life raft on top and a crate containing oil, de-icer, tools, a first-aid box and rations. The 'airstairs' supplied were a wooden box with a piece of string attached.

The typical route for a delivery to AiResearch in Los Angeles was from Chester to Prestwick, then to Keflavik in Iceland and on to Sonde Stromfiord in Greenland. The longest leg was then from Greenland to

Sept Isles at the mouth of the St Lawrence in Canada, onward to Buffalo and then across North America to the destination via Wichita. These 125s were supplied to the distributors at a cost of £300,000 (£4.7m = 2013) and the distributors painted them and fitted them out with furnishing and avionics adding some £75,000 (£1.8m = 2013) to their value. The equipment fit of the American 125s 1As gradually diverged from those of the 125 1Bs for the rest of the world, with different air conditioning systems and increasingly with an AiResearch APU.

Production of 125s and Nimrods at Hawker Siddeley Chester in 1968. BAE Systems

The First Developments and Extending the Range

The positive sales outlook for the 125 and the strength of American distributor network encouraged Hawker Siddeley to develop it further and produce a 125 Series 3. The main alterations to these aircraft were that, as on the 125s for North America, Hawker Siddeley replaced its own air conditioning system with the AiResearch system; it also offered the same firm's APU as an option on the 3B. Refinements were also made to the internal décor, seats and other fittings.

At that time the aircraft's range could not easily be increased as there was not an improved version of the Viper 522 available. However, driven by a demand for range improvements from the USA, HSA designed and trialled an external ventral fuel tank on a Series 1B, G-ATWH, at Hatfield, which fitted neatly under the rear fuselage; to maintain directional stability a small dorsal fin was introduced. Among other aerodynamic improvements was the introduction of mainwheel undercarriage doors to reduce drag. These versions of the Series 3 were designated Series 3A/RA and Series 3B/RA respectively. To promote the new variant Hatfield sent 3B/RA G-AVRG on a series of gruelling sales tours to South America, Europe, the Middle East and the Far East, including Australia.

A Facelift

With no immediate growth available from the Viper but the need to defend its market share in the highly competitive North American market, Hatfield's engineers set to work to improve their aircraft's looks and functionality. From these objectives the Series 400 was born. (Henceforward all new Series were in 100s.) The awkward inward opening, up and over door was replaced with a narrower door hinged at the bottom and opening outwards. As it was fitted with steps it provided a far better experience to the user besides freeing up space within the cabin. Other less immediately obvious alterations were the suppression of external aerials and an improved wing fuselage fairing that reduced drag. From the 173rd

G-AVPE, a HS125 Series 3, originally bought by the British Aircraft Corporation and still bearing their livery but carrying British Aerospace titling outside the flight shed at Hurn. BAE Systems

aircraft all 125s were completed as Series 400s. The first was G-AWMX, which flew in August 1968 and following a brief test programme was delivered to Atlantic Aviation for completion.

Sales of the HS125 in the Late 1960s

Five years after its first flight the sales of 125 had grown to 150. The devaluation of sterling in November 1966 raised import prices but correspondingly reduced export prices, so reducing the price of the HS125 and stimulating interest following a slow-down in sales earlier that year. Amongst the many sales that took place in 1967 were two aircraft delivered to BAC for communications flying on their collaborative programmes, one aircraft based at Filton flying daily to Toulouse for Concorde liaison and the other at Warton shuttling to Munich for Tornado cooperation.

Throughout 1968 and 1969 demand for the HS125 continued to be good. It was firmly established in the highly competitive marketplace. The 125 was one of only two European-built bizjets to have been widely adopted by North American operators, the other being the Dassault Falcon. In 1968 fifty 125s were sold and the following year, forty-four. By then sales had reached 228 and of these sales, 132 had

been to US and Canadian customers, representing 57 per cent of the total. Fifty-four were sold to other overseas countries, twenty-two to UK operators and twenty to the RAF as Dominies. The 125-400 remained in production until 1973 with 117 built. Notable buyers of the 125-400 were the Argentine Navy, which used it against the British forces during the 1982 Falklands War, and the J.C. Bamford of JCB, the British earth-moving equipment maker – Bamford said the 125 paid for itself in its first week.

Beechcraft Enters the Scene

In late 1969 HSA and Beechcraft entered into negotiations and in April 1970 announced that Beechcraft Hawker Corporation had been formed as a wholly owned subsidiary of Beechcraft to take over from Hawker Siddeley International, New York and manage the sales and marketing of HS125s in North America through its wide range of outlets now including AiResearch and Atlantic Aviation. Beechcraft took over much of the completion work itself. In the event this arrangement only continued until mid-1975 when the link was severed, and AiResearch and Atlantic Aviation went back to the previous position. Beechcraft was to return to the picture less than twenty years later.

More Thrust from the Viper and the 125-600

Having developed the 125-400 without being able to add to its thrust, matters were made easier for the engineers when Rolls-Royce squeezed 390lb more thrust from the engine with the Viper 600; regrettably it was noisier than the previous marks. Though HSA considered re-engining the 125-400 with the new engine to produce a 125-500, in the event the next version was the 125-600, which was a major development.

The 125-600 was some 2ft longer than the existing HS125-400, increasing maximum passenger capacity to fourteen and with an additional passenger window each side. The nose was increased in length by 6in and made more pointed, the cockpit roof contours were improved by the removal of the glassfibre cowl and the fin was heightened, all these alterations further improving the type's appearance. Fuel capacity was increased by the addition of a fin fuel tank, and with the more economical Viper 601s it had range of up to 1,875 miles. The 125-600 had better airfield performance and could cruise at slightly higher speeds.

Two 125-400s already on the production line were set aside for conversion as prototypes of the Series 600. The first, G-AYBH, made its maiden flight from Chester on 21 January 1971 landing at Hatfield, so that

Following the short-lived tie-up with Beechcraft in the early 1970s the 125 was marketed as the Beechcraft Hawker 125 in North America. Here is their demonstrator, 125-400 N125BH.
BAE Systems

The first 125-600, G-AYBH, was first flown unpainted from Broughton to Hatfield on 21 January 1971. It is pictured here by the Hatfield flight shed with the control tower above. The 125-600 was 2ft longer and also had a more pointed nose than the previous 125s. Hawker 125 collection

flight testing could begin immediately. The second was soon completed, but owing to Rolls-Royce's bankruptcy and subsequent nationalization by the Conservative Government all engine contracts were in disarray: the first flight of G-AZHS was delayed until 25 November 1971.

During high Mach number buffet trials with G-AYBH, both Vipers flamed out at 41,000ft over the North Sea and apparently took seventeen minutes to relight, by which time the aircraft had descended to 5,000ft. A quickly introduced modification was made to the combustion chamber, which cured this problem and made relighting acceptable. G-AYBH was also involved in tropical trials in August/September 1971. In late 1972 it became a demonstrator, visiting North and South America, the Far East and Australasia, besides finding time for the 1973 Paris Air Show.

Production and Sales of the 125-600

During 1971 Chester was building three HS125-400s or 125-600s per month and the Hawker Siddeley Board, confident of the success of the Series 600, authorized manufacture of thirty-eight well ahead of actual

sales. However, orders for the business jet during 1970–71 were disappointing with only thirty-two sales, mainly due to the difficult financial climate in the USA, which depressed the sales of all executive aircraft. Amongst buyers of the 125-600 were the RAF, which ordered two as executive transports based at Northolt, and the German Flight Safety Authority. In 1972 Hawker Beechcraft ordered more than twenty-three 125-600s for onward sale in North America, in addition to taking the last four 125-400s on the production line.

Following the introduction of noise regulations in the USA and Europe a 'hush kit' was fitted to the Viper 601s on some aircraft, with acoustic panels and an exhaust diffuser. However, it did not prove to be very effective. Owing to the noisiness of the Viper 601 and the increase in world oil prices the 600 series only made seventy-one sales. This indicated the need to introduce quieter, fuel-efficient turbofan engines embodying modern advanced technology, as some of the competition had already done. However, there was considerable resistance to the introduction of turbofan engines within HSA as it was calculated that the company would need to sell fifty aircraft per year at £2.1m (2013 = £23.5m) each to break even.

The Turbofan 125-700

Despite the firm's reservations about re-engining and the investment involved, from 1973 different turbofan engines were evaluated for the task. Unfortunately the development of the Rolls-Royce RB401 was too late for the firm's schedule for the 125-700, so the Hawker Siddeley engineers settled upon the American-built Garrett TFE731. This engine offered 3,700lb thrust, the noise footprint reduced by 80 per cent and greatly improved fuel consumption almost doubled the 125's range. Additional minor drag-reducing refinements were made to the airframe and even better avionics offered to customers.

Against the threat of nationalization of the aircraft industry by the Labour Government, Hawker Siddeley financed the project and the second prototype 125-600, G-AZHS, returned to Broughton to be re-engined as the Series 700 prototype. Suitably re-registered as G-BFAN, it flew on 28 July 1976. In September 1976 it was exhibited at Farnborough and in November 1976 there were tropical trials at Nairobi, followed by noise trials in Granada in February 1977. In May the 125-700 received its Certificate of Airworthiness from both the UK and US authorities. G-BFAN returned to Broughton on 15 July 1977 for refurbishment to F600 standard for flight deck modifications. More tropical trials followed in February 1978 in Nairobi and it was correctly rebranded as a BAe 125-F600 (i.e. a 600 Series with fan engines). The first production 125-700 was G-BEFZ, which made its maiden flight in November 1976 but suffered an engine failure. From December it was based at Hatfield test flying and then made sales tours worldwide. Though the aircraft were still designated as 125-700A for North America and 700B for the remainder of the world, gradually the specification of the latter had been brought up to the higher specification of the North American model and so the differences between them diminished.

A Spurt in Sales – 500 Up!

Following a two-year lull in sales from 1974 to 1976 the advent of the 125-700 resulted in a spurt in sales: the last six unsold 125-600s were sold while its successor became the best-selling model with 215 sales until the advent of the 800. Such was demand that potential customers had to join a nine-month waiting list. In 1979 sales exceeded targets and fifty-five were sold. On 29 October 1980 the nationalized British Aerospace celebrated the sale of the 500th 125, which also had the distinction of being the 300th sold in the USA.

ABOVE: To celebrate the sale of the 400th 125 there was a line-up of twelve 125s and a further one in the background outside the former Hawker Siddeley Chester plant on 20 April 1978. The 125s were G-BFAN, G-AVOI, G-5-13, G-BBEP, XS730, G-BSAA, XW791, unknown, XW930, G-BARB, G-BEFZ, G-AWWL and G-BJCB. The Dan-Air HS748 is G-ATMI. BAE Systems

BELOW: A HS125 Series 3A re-engined with the Garrett TFE731, N25MJ at Goose Bay, Newfoundland in June 1996. Derek Ferguson

Turbofan Re-Engining

Some operators of the 600 and 400 Series aircraft made it clear that they expected a retrofit programme so that they could derive the benefits of the TFE731 – greatly extended range and much less noise – without having to sell their aircraft. All the earlier aircraft could benefit from re-engining, bar the Series 1 where the amount of work needed made the cost prohibitive. British Aerospace stipulated that they would handle all B Series and all 125-600 conversions themselves and that Garrett AiResearch in Los Angeles would convert all A Series aircraft bar the 125-600s. The conversion demanded major fuselage alterations and aircraft systems. Owners often opted for additional improvements to the avionics and furnishings. The conversion increased range by 60–70 per cent and improved airfield performance. By the close of 1981 sixty-five conversions had been made, the great majority in the USA.

The Final British Developments – the 125-800 and 125-1000

Entering the 1980s, executive jet sales were booming and the 125 was third in the small executive jet market behind the American

The 125-800 prototype, G-BKTF, at Hatfield with a nose probe and a stall recovery parachute fitted for flight testing. The 800 differed from the 700 with a forward extension of the fin leading edge, greater wing span and deeper fuselage. The nose, windscreen and canopy were re-profiled while the ventral fin was removed. Hawker 125 archive

A Japanese Self-Defence Force U-125A, tasked as a search and rescue aircraft. Akira Uekaw

its 3,000-mile range the 125-800 could easily fly coast-to-coast across the USA or from the UK across the Atlantic to San Francisco with just one stop. To power the 800, a more powerful Garrett engine than that in the 125-700 was devised, the TFE-731-5R, which offered 600lb greater thrust – a total of 4,300lb. A modern EFIS flightdeck was fitted and a total redesign of the cabin trim capitalized on the space available.

The 125-800 Flight Test Programme

Two 700 series airframes were set aside at Broughton for conversion to become the 800 series prototypes. It had an anonymous first flight, unpainted as G-5-11, on 26 May 1983 from Broughton. In contrast, a week later for its public debut on 1 June there was a ceremonial roll-out and demonstration flight fully painted as N800BA. Then, registered as G-BKTF, it carried out the bulk of the 125-800's nine-month test programme from Hatfield; especially stability and handling, which included the fitting of special equipment such as a tail parachute for stall protection. During flight testing it was identified that unlike the earlier 125s the 125-800 did not exhibit the strong nose drop required at the stall for certification, so a stick pusher was installed. After appearing at Farnborough in September 1986 registered G-UWWB, it was sold to a South African customer.

The second prototype, G-DCCC (DCCC being 800 in Roman numerals), joined the first on the test programme on 24 June 1983 and was used on systems testing and the essential 'hot and high' trials, first at Sharjah in the United Arab Emirates and then at Harare in Zimbabwe. Following noise trials in Casablanca it was used as a BAe demonstrator and later sold. The first production 125-800, G-ABKUW, was employed on the natural icing trials and flight deck systems evaluation. Certification of the new 125 was granted in the spring of 1984.

From the start, Chester was tasked with produced twenty-eight aircraft per annum to meet demand, with approximately 60 per cent going to the USA, 20 per cent in the UK and the remainder around the world. Besides executive sales in 1988 the 125-800 won six sales from the USAF against serious competition as C-29A for the combat flight inspection and navigation role. The Japanese Air Self-Defence Force

Learjet and Cessna Citation. Determined to maintain their market share the next stage of development had already been under examination for a year, and two years later the BAe Board gave the go ahead for the 125-800. The 800 differed from the 700 with a redesigned tail, new outboard wings giving an increase in wingspan of 4½ft and deeper fuselage. Profile changes to the nose, windscreen and canopy improved pilot visibility and were also cosmetic in a market where looks counted. The dorsal fin was removed and ventral tank reshaped to increase capacity and reduce drag. Though the small tail fin fuel tank was removed the overall fuel capacity was greater and with

followed suit by ordering three U-125s for flight inspection. This order paved the way for an order for twenty-seven radically altered U-125As, which fulfilled a search and rescue role. These aircraft required the greatest number of modifications ever made to the design. Each had a large rectangular window ahead of the wing on both sides of the fuselage, and the ability to drop a life raft with an ingenious use of the wheel well. The aircraft descends to below 1,500ft and, inside the cabin, a cover over the left wheel is unscrewed and a raft placed in it; the U-125A flies at low level at 150kt over the dropping zone, the undercarriage is extended and the life raft drops, inflating on contact with the sea.

The Last British 125 Development – the 125-1000

British Aerospace decided it could exploit the 800 further and, by introducing a 33in stretch to the fuselage married to a new engine, the Pratt & Whitney PW305 of 5,225lb thrust, produced the BAe 125-1000 (there was no 125-900). The fuselage stretch improved the cabin dimensions, baggage space and galley, and allowed an additional forward fuel tank. It was identifiable from the 800 by an additional cabin window on each side, the improved fairing between the wing and the fuselage and thrust reversers, the first 125 to be so fitted.

The first BAe 125-1000 prototype, G-AEXLR, made its first flight on 16 June 1990 followed by a ceremonial 'first flight' from Chester to the new BAe Civil Flight Test Centre at Woodford on 28 June; it was used in flight trials until July 1992. The second 125-1000 development aircraft, G-OPFC, joined the test programme on 26 November 1990 but the first production aircraft – eventually registered G-ELRA – did not fly for another eight months and then it also took part in trials. There were aerodynamic problems discovered during the flight trials that took a long time to cure, but more importantly it was clear that the 1000 would not make its range estimates and eventually this shortfall was alleviated. In contrast to the popularity of the 800, only fifty-two BAe 125-1000s were built.

Raytheon

From the early 1990s British Aerospace was having problems with the cost base of its commercial aircraft programmes, especially the airliners, so a business restructuring took place where the 125 programme became a stand-alone company known as BAe Corporate Jets. This was making approximately £300m per year and employing 950 in the UK. BAe had considered that Corporate Jets' costs were too high and that it could not finance the next development for its 125 line. In 1992 the company was renamed Corporate Jets and offered for sale, but the unions raised objections aware of the threat to their members' livelihoods. BAe briefly withdrew it from sale, but then sold it to Raytheon, an American firm, the following year for £250m.

ABOVE: Two BAe 125 demonstrators in the summer of 1991: 125-800 N800BA and 125-1000 G-BTTX. BAE Systems

RIGHT: The third 125-1000, G-ELRA, at Saudokrokur, Iceland, in June 1992. Derek Ferguson

With the change in ownership, development of the 125 was placed in the hands of Raytheon. They branded the 125 as the Hawker and introduced the Hawker 800XP (Extended Performance), an 800 with essentially the wing of the 1000, Garrett TFE731-5BR turbofans, new systems and interior, increased fuel capacity and thrust reversers as standard. These features granted the 800XP an enhanced airfield performance. Subsequently the 800XP was developed by Raytheon into the 850XP with winglets, and further models came in the form of the Hawker 750 and 900XP.

The fuselage, wings and vertical tail were still assembled and partially equipped at Airbus's Chester (Broughton) plant but were then shipped to Wichita in the USA for final assembly. Work was only gradually transferred to Wichita and though the first US-built Hawker 800 flew on 5 November 1996, the last UK-built 800 did not fly until 29 April 1997. Final assembly of the 125-1000 was not transferred to the USA, and the final Hawker 1000 flew at Broughton on 18 March 1997.

In 1994 Raytheon merged its Hawker and Beechcraft lines into a single business valued at $1.7bn and in 2007 this was bought by Goldman Sachs Capital Partners and Onex Partners for $3.3bn. In May 2012 the company sought Chapter 11 bankruptcy. At the time of writing, Hawker Beechcraft continues to market its turboprop, piston and other non-jet aircraft, but has closed its executive jet business and thereby ended manufacture of the Hawker (or 125).

Conclusion – after Fifty Years in Production

Hawkers and 125s are in service with many international corporate customers, air forces and governments. With production terminated after fifty years and a grand total of 1,731 built, this is a tribute to the quality of the original design and the implementation of series of refinements in response to market needs over the years. Under American ownership 854 Hawkers were built, of which 481 were Hawker 800XPs. The American refinement of the design of the 125-800 and the 125-1000 was not so radical as British Aerospace's estimation, so it is disappointing that the project could not have remained in British ownership.

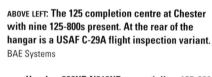

ABOVE LEFT: **The 125 completion centre at Chester with nine 125-800s present. At the rear of the hangar is a USAF C-29A flight inspection variant.**
BAE Systems

LEFT: **Hawker 800XP N313XP, essentially a 125-800 with the wing of the 1000, Garrett TFE731-5BR turbofans, new systems and interior, increased fuel capacity and thrust reversers as standard.**
Author

Specification – BAe 125-800	
Length	51ft 2in (15.6m)
Wingspan	51ft 5in (15.67m)
Height	17ft 7in (5.36m)
MTOW	27,400lb (12,430kg)
Cruising speed	510mph (820km/h)
Range	2,450 miles (3,940km)
Engine	2 × 4,300lb Garrett TFE731
Passengers	Up to 14

CHAPTER NINE

Airbus: From Partner to Subcontractor

Beginnings

In the immediate post-war period and for decades thereafter, American manufacturers dominated the civil airliner market, despite valiant attempts by European firms to adjust to new market conditions and with some notable successes such as the Vickers Viscount, Sud Aviation Caravelle and Fokker Friendship. By the mid-1960s British manufacturers were considering developments of the VC10, One-Eleven and Trident, demonstrating their commitment to civil aviation for the coming decades.

In the meantime, Hawker Siddeley Aviation had come up with the HS132/134 developments of the Trident, each powered by Rolls-Royce RB178 engines and, at the same time, in May 1965 the British and French Governments instigated a joint working party to develop a large (200–250 seater) short-haul civil aircraft.

Then, at the 1966 Hanover Air Show, to the surprise of many, the Hawker Siddeley, Breguet and Nord Aviation stands all displayed models of the previously unannounced 250-seat HBN (an alliance of Hawker Siddeley, Breguet, Nord Aviation) 100 twin-turbofan Airbus design, clear evidence of the newly formed alliance. Also on show at Hanover was a model of the Sud Aviation Galion proposal, outwardly similar to the HBN100. Germany then indicated its desire to collaborate with Britain and France on the Airbus project and talks took place between HSA, Sud and Arbeitsgemeinschaft Airbus (a grouping of German aircraft companies later known as Deutsche Airbus) at the 1966 Farnborough Air Show. A month later the three firms formally approached their Governments for support for the project, now formally 'Airbus'. At a tripartite Governmental meeting in London in December the French Government insisted that in return for Rolls-Royce's leadership on engine design and manufacture, Sud Aviation would be their French partner. HSA's initial chosen partners, Breguet and Nord Aviation, were ruthlessly excluded from the party and the Hawker Siddeley designers, engineers and technical staff now had to forge links with a new team at Toulouse.

The 1967 Hawker Siddeley Annual Report stated, 'Provided that the respective Governments agree late this year that the project should proceed, the Board is confident that a highly competitive and commercially successful aircraft will be produced as a result of this international co-operation.' Prescient words indeed, and evidence of the foresight and vision of those at the commanding heights of the British aviation industry at the time!

Go-Ahead

The Memorandum of Understanding on the European Airbus was duly signed in Bonn on 26 September 1967 by the British, French and German Governments. Sud Aviation had overall design leadership for the A300 and Rolls-Royce for the RB207 engine.

Britain and France each provided 37.5 per cent of the money and shared work in those proportions, while Germany provided the remaining 25 per cent of the finance and the work. Sud Aviation was to build the flight deck and the fuselage centre section, and final assembly and flight test were based at their factory and airfield at Toulouse. Hawker Siddeley would build the wing from tip to tip, including the high-lift devices and the engine attachment, at the Chester factory. The German group would build the remaining fuselage sections, the tail cone and empennage. Technical direction was centred at Toulouse, although in truth both the HBN100 and the A300 owed much of their genesis to Hatfield.

The wing for the A300B was designed and wind-tunnel tested at Hatfield. BAE Systems

By mid-1968 Rolls-Royce were concentrating their efforts on the RB211 engine for the Lockheed Tristar, which commanded substantial orders. As a consequence the RB207 engine for the Airbus was not being given due attention. At one point the Chairman of Hawker Siddeley, Sir Arnold Hall, warned the President of Airbus, Henri Ziegler, 'We are in serious danger of building the world's biggest glider.' As a result Airbus began considering other powerplants.

Not unexpectedly, costs escalated, and initial estimates were quickly exceeded. All three Governments expressed their dismay at the final £190m estimate plus at least £70m for the putative RB207, and obliged the Airbus consortium to come up with a cheaper version of their design. This was submitted at the end of 1968.

A new, smaller, 250-seater version of the Airbus was proposed, saving an estimated £100m and using a higher-powered version of the existing Rolls-Royce RB211, which was unimaginatively dubbed the A300B. However, Tony Benn, the British Minister of Technology, had become very unenthusiastic about the project and told his French and German colleagues that the A300B was a new project and that the Memorandum of Understanding on the A300 was dead.

Benn then tried to interest the French and Germans in the BAC Three-Eleven (a similar-sized aircraft designed by Hawker Siddeley's British rival, the British Aircraft Corporation) but the French and Germans would have nothing to do with it. Meanwhile Sud Aviation, as leaders of the A300B consortium, were discussing with the Germans and other European manufacturers the possibility of an Airbus without Britain, perhaps with Hawker Siddeley as a subcontractor and probably with American Pratt & Whitney JT9D engines.

British Government Withdrawal

French and German governmental irritation at the continued reluctance of the British Government to back the A300B Airbus reached a climax in London on 10 April 1969. After a meeting of the three ministers concerned, the French and Germans announced their decision to proceed alone. On 24 April 1969 *Flight* magazine stated, 'The Airbus agreement is dead as far as the British Government is concerned.' A long period of prevarication by the British Government ensued, with Tony Benn

stating in the House of Commons that Britain had not pulled out but was not convinced of the market prospects, development costs and the lack of a firm commitment to a European engine. The Minister also stated that the French and German Governments could pursue the project on a bilateral basis while keeping Britain informed. However, the French and German Governments were undeterred by the British withdrawal and indicated that they would proceed in partnership with the development. This left the British manufacturer, Hawker Siddeley, struggling to find a way to recoup the benefits of its extensive contribution of both technical and commercial knowledge to the project.

Hawker Siddeley Becomes a Subcontractor

Following in-depth discussions examining all the alternatives, in June 1969 the Hawker Siddeley Board expressed their firm desire to remain in the European Airbus programme and invest in it. France and Germany acknowledged they needed HSA, too. Manufacturing the largest wing ever fabricated in quantity in Britain required huge investment and understandably HSA was reluctant to hand over their well-designed Airbus wing to a foreign rival. To prevent this occurring and to seal their ambitious decision, in July 1969 HSA signed contracts with Sud Aviation and Deutsche Airbus for the supply of the four pairs of wing boxes for the two test specimens and two prototypes with an option on all the subsequent wings and continuing responsibility for wing design.

Thus, Hawker Siddeley's share of manufacturing now amounted to approximately 18 per cent of the A300, and this contribution now had to be funded without any Government support. The company's decision to remain in the programme demanded a huge investment in machine tools. For example, HSA bought a bespoke numerically controlled 60 × 12ft vacuum/air cushion to sculpt the aluminium billets that formed the skin panels, the largest high-speed wing-milling machines to produce 50ft-long wing skin panels and a 1,200-ton hydraulic horizontal press. All of these were British-made.

Airbus continued as a Franco-German-British programme with Hawker Siddeley investing £35m (£480m at 2013 prices) of the company's money as a major

subcontractor to Airbus Industrie, sharing in the design, manufacture, marketing and support of the aircraft.

The A300B wing design was the fruitful outcome of Hawker Siddeley's hard-won experience designing the Trident wing and its supercritical aerodynamics. While the Trident's high sweepback of 35 degrees had caused problems at low-speeds, the sweepback on the Airbus was reduced to 28 degrees to smooth out those problems. The product of these changes was the most advanced wing of the 1970s.

Britain's Losses – Far-Reaching Consequences

Following Britain's withdrawal, where HSA had previously been contracted to manufacture the whole wing, now production of all the moving parts of the wing, such as the slats, flaps, lift dumpers, etc was moved to other manufacturers outside the UK. Though HSA was still heavily involved in the project, British withdrawal from the programme was to have long-lasting effects on the British aviation's ancillary industries, since equipment decisions were now made by the French and German partners and the British contribution was much reduced. For example, Dowty designed and manufactured the undercarriage fitted to the Airbus A300B prototype but the production order went to Messier of France. Dunlop, which had pioneered carbon brakes for Concorde, only finally secured an Airbus order in 1999. British firms that would have profited and grown from the high production of the different Airbuses were severely handicapped in their bids to compete for work, while their French and German competitors gained.

HSA Airbus Work Progress

Hawker Siddeley's 1970 Annual Report reported:

Good progress was made in the design and development of the Airbus A300B with our European associates and manufacture of prototypes is now gathering impetus. There has been a big investment in Airbus tooling, but production will take some time to build up. The aircraft is planned to make its first flight in 1972, and enter service in 1974. Towards the end of the year [1970] it became evident that no European competitor to the A300B would emerge, and marketing efforts

A pair of A300B wings being loaded onto Super Guppy F-BPPA at Manchester Airport for transport to the Airbus Assembly Unit at Toulouse. BAE Systems

indicate that the aircraft has good prospects for substantial sales into the 1980s . . . Hatfield is also technical design centre for the company's participation in the A300B programme.

The Largest Wings ever Put into Production in Europe

Hawker Siddeley was responsible for the entire wing design and final assembly, and was contracted to deliver the first wing set to Toulouse on 1 November 1971. Several Hawker Siddeley plants were concerned with the design and manufacture of the A300B. Overall control of all wing design and detailing was at Hatfield, including the inboard leading edge, flying-control operating system and the hydraulic and fuel systems. Brough and Woodford managed the design and detailing of the fixed trailing-edge structure; Woodford had the same responsibility for the fixed leading-edge outboard of the engine pylon and other parts. Five factories shared manufacture of the mighty wings: Chester handled the major part with Woodford, with Hatfield and Brough and Hamble all participating. Final assembly of the A300B wing took place (and still takes place) at Chester and from there the entire wing, complete with leading and trailing edge flaps produced by Fokker-VFW, were taken by road to Manchester airport for airlift to Toulouse by Super Guppy.

First Wings Delivered

The first pair of wings built by HSA for the A300B was delivered by Super Guppy from Manchester Airport to the Airbus Assembly Unit at Toulouse on 23 November 1971. Hawker Siddeley engineers immediately started work on joining the wings to the fuselage, which were already equipped with fuel and hydraulic systems. The wings were the largest ever put into production in Europe, more than 70ft long and weighing 14 tons. Nearly 35 tons of fuel could be contained in the four integral fuel tanks of the two wings.

At a ceremony at Manchester Airport celebrating the handover, Airbus Industrie announced a further order for eight wing sets for production aircraft from Hawker Siddeley valued at £4m, together with authority for the procurement of raw material for future sets. Wing sets were already in production for the first six test and development aircraft and the new order ensured a year's work for 2,000 employees, half the Chester workforce.

The First Airline Order for Airbus

In November 1971 Airbus received its first firm order from Air France for six A300B2 with an option on a further ten. The initial production aircraft was for the A300B2, a short-haul model powered by two General Electric CF6-50As, each developing 49,000lb thrust, with a range of 1,700 miles and a typical payload of 280 passengers. In addition to the short-haul version there was a longer-range version, the A300B4 with a

F-WUAB, the first prototype, on its maiden flight from Aérospatiale Toulouse on 28 October 1972. BAE Systems

centre section wing fuel tank and 51,000lb static thrust GE CF6-50C engines and a range of over 3,000 miles.

Air France had been involved in the preparation of the detailed type specification of the A300B1, but as the engine had been developed to give more thrust called for an 8ft 6in increase in fuselage length to allow the inclusion of three extra rows of seats; this stretched variant was called the B2. Air France's order was valued at £45m, including spares of which £7m was accounted for by British components.

First Flight and into Service

The first prototype, F-WUAB, flew from Toulouse on 28 October 1972 and the second, F-WUAC, on 5 February the following year, both a little ahead of the programmed

schedule. Both were the shorter A300B1 model. The second and fourth airframes built were used for static testing. The B1 prototypes were succeeded in the air by two B2s, which were the first production aircraft. Excellent progress was made in the flight testing and with the accumulation of data required for the certification of the aircraft by the airworthiness authorities. The flight experience was satisfactory and no problems were encountered in bringing the aircraft to certification standard, or in meeting performance requirements.

The first prototype, re-registered F-OCAZ, made sales tours of the Americas, the Middle East and India in October 1973. A series of long-distance flight tests in January 1974 provided further evidence that the A300 was a very fuel-efficient aircraft, a characteristic of some importance in view of the scarcity and rising cost of fuel.

Certification followed in March 1974 and scheduled services were started by Air France on the London–Paris route in May that year, providing an exceptionally high degree of reliability and economy. Though FAA certification followed at the end of the month it was only of academic significance then as there was no American interest in the aircraft.

Lufthansa, Indian Airways, Korean Airlines and South African introduced small numbers of the type in 1976, but orders were extremely slow and in 1975 only four aircraft (to South African Airways) were sold, and just one in 1976. Though there were no competitors to the Airbus at that time, airlines appeared to have serious doubts about an aircraft constructed by a consortium and its customer service, and whether two engines were sufficiently reliable for the carriage of up to 300 passengers. Production

The first and second Airbus A300Bs together. The second Airbus F-WUAC flew in Air France livery on 5 February 1973. Both were the shorter A300B1 model. BAE Systems

continued at a slow rate and 'white tails' (unsold aircraft) were parked at Toulouse. Meanwhile, in an effort to make the aircraft more attractive to potential customers Airbus developed the A300B4 offering greater range, which was to sell in greater numbers than the B2.

Hawker Siddeley Breaks Even

Despite the slow sales in 1974, Hawker Siddeley received further orders for wing sets by which time there were orders and options covering over forty aircraft. The contract was worth more than £12m a year to HSA, which directly employed 3,000 people on it, not including indirect and administrative staff. By mid-1976 Hawker Siddeley had orders for 100 wing sets and authorization to purchase long-lead items for another thirty-two. It had been well worth the risk as HSA recouped its investment on delivery of the twenty-fifty set of wings.

British Aerospace becomes a Partner of Airbus

Airbus knew that if it was develop the Airbus concept it must set the development of the next aircraft planned in train. Aérospatiale (the former Sud Aviation) was keen on joining up with Boeing in 1975, while almost simultaneously the French and German Governments made approaches to the British Government to rejoin Airbus. To further muddy the waters, Boeing sought to entice BAe into its embrace as a subcontractor on the wing of the Boeing 757, powered by Rolls-Royce RB211s and ordered by British Airways, which showed no interest in Airbus. Rolls-Royce and some in the Labour Government were pressing for the Boeing–BAe deal while the Europhiles wanted BAe to be a full partner of Airbus, not just a subcontractor. In the talks between Governments, the French insisted that a condition of British re-admittance was an order by British Airways, but the airline remained intransigent.

ABOVE: **The third Airbus F-WUAD in Lufthansa livery at Toulouse. This aircraft was never delivered to an airline but retained for trials and demonstration of 'fly by wire'. Lufthansa and Air France were among the small number of initial operators of the A300B.** BAE Systems

RIGHT: **Laker Airways' second A300B, G-BIMB, temporarily registered F-WZEL for test flying. This Airbus was delivered to Laker in February 1981 but only flew with them for two years.** Airbus

HB-IPK was an Airbus A310 that flew with Balair of Switzerland for five years. The A310 was smaller than the A300 and proved more successful. Like the A300 it had British-built wings. Airbus

Negotiations trundled on but Airbus's position appeared weak and some still fought for a BAe tie up with Boeing. Then in May 1977 the Airbus order famine finally came to an end when Eastern Airways in the USA was enticed into trialling the aircraft. Airbus offered the large but financially insecure Eastern four aircraft for a six-month term free of charge. The trials proved a success for all concerned and Eastern ordered twenty-three A300Bs with an option on a further nine. To seal the deal Airbus even went to the lengths of organizing finance, knowing how important a toehold in the potentially lucrative US market would be. And so it came to pass; securing the deal with Eastern brought the first American customer, which soon attracted others.

News of the American order gave weight to those advocating Britain rejoin Airbus and the long period of prevarication came to an end. A deal was cobbled together whereby BA was permitted to order 757s while the Government announced on 31 August 1978 that BAe would join Airbus in January the following year. Although BA continued its 'Boeing Always' policy (inherited from BOAC, the 'Boeing Only Aircraft Corporation'), Britain's Laker Airways, which in the early 1960s had placed the first order for the BAC One-Eleven, ordered ten A300B4s, becoming the first UK Airbus operator.

Britain, once an equal partner with France in the consortium with Germany, now rejoined in third position with just a 20 per cent holding and without a role for Rolls-Royce. Spain was now a participant, albeit a small player with just a 4.2 per cent share, while France and Germany's share was cut to 37.9 per cent each to accommodate their new partner. This investment

by the British Government came with no guarantees of success, but following a slow first decade, sales were beginning to accelerate and in 1990 Airbus finally broke even.

Britain and Airbus After 1979

After the painfully slow uptake in sales during the first decade, Airbus sales began to climb steadily thereafter. Much of this success can be attributed to the decision, taken in mid-1978, to proceed with the A310, a medium- to long-range 200-seater that had very positive impact on sales figures in the coming years. Prior to 1978, there had been considerable debate within Airbus as to how such a plane could be achieved, and some believed that simply scaling down the A300 would suffice. Fortunately, reason prevailed, as such a machine would have had a wing too large and heavy for its size.

Design of the new wing was eventually passed to BAe, but not before an alternative design prepared by the French and German partners was put to the Board, and the final A310 wing was a combination of the two. The overall design was a winner. Orders soon rolled in from 'blue chip' carriers and even British Caledonian placed an order. The A310 was to prove the mainstay of production and went through continuous development. Production only ceased in 1998, after 255 had been manufactured.

The A320 and Later Airbuses

Both the A300 and A310 turned in very respectable sales but it was the next Airbus airliner that could best be described as a game changer. There had been pan-European proposals for a new 150-seat airliner

with the British Aircraft Corporation flying the flag for Britain as long ago as the 1970s and these passed through a series of metamorphoses until Airbus finally took the lead after the company had itself debated going for an aircraft larger than the A300. The result was the A320.

The project soon became mired in arguments about work share, with BAe at one stage proposing to make some of fuselage and handle final assembly at Filton, a former Bristol and then BAC plant. However, BAe won manufacture of the entire wing, unlike the A300 and A310 where the moving surfaces were built elsewhere. After intense politicking and very much against the views of Norman Tebbit, the Secretary of State for Industry, BAe managed to wrestle £250m from the Government, which was to be recouped by a levy on sales. This sum was not the total amount needed as BAe had to invest some £200m of its own for the project. Though the wing was designed in Britain, the design originated from the former BAC Weybridge plant rather than Hawker Siddeley Hatfield. Manufacture was shared between Chester (which under BAe became Broughton) and Filton. Broughton built the wing, which was then transported to Filton for completion, though from 1993 completion was dealt with at Broughton.

The A320 which flew in February 1987 introduced 'fly by wire' and sidesticks instead of the conventional flying controls on the flightdeck. These innovations stole a march on Boeing and attracted huge airline and media interest. There was no mechanical connection between the sidestick and the flying surfaces: the Flight Management System maintains the aircraft within its envelope, controlling angle of attack, airspeed and deflection of flight controls. If the pilot keeps the aircraft within the envelope there is no intervention in control.

At the time of writing the A320 family with its larger development the A321, the progressively smaller A319 and A318, and the improved A320NEO (New Engine Option) have achieved more than 9,000 sales, with production rates exceeding one aircraft per day, all flying on British-made wings. The A320 family has proved itself as a most successful competitor to the world's best-selling airliner, the Boeing 737.

For all its evident success Airbus continued to require huge investment, funded in part by Government loans. In May 1987 the Conservative Government agreed to a £450m loan to BAe for its involvement in the next Airbus project, the A330/340. The A330 was planned as a large-capacity, medium-range, twin-engined airliner and the four-engined A340 was the long- and ultra-long-range version. In essence the only difference between them was the number of engines. Both grew from original plans of Airbus at the time it was established. The wing was again manufactured at Chester and British Aerospace at Filton had overall design responsibility as the famous Hatfield site was shortly to close. The first A340 wings were completed in June 1990 and the first A330 wings in August the following year, all of which were sent to Bremen for completion. By February 1999 2,000 Airbus wing sets had been manufactured at Broughton. Investment continued in Airbus in the UK and in March 2000 the UK's was the first Government to invest in the huge A380 when it offered £530m to be repaid over seventeen years in order to safeguard wing manufacture at Filton and Broughton; the A380 received the go-ahead at the end of the year.

Previous wings had been flown out of Manchester Airport, and after Broughton's runways were lengthened could be flown from there, but the A380 wings could only be moved by road and sea. The A380 flew in April 2005 and should have been in service not much more than eighteen months later. However, it was beset by problems involving the electrical wiring and many aircraft had to be completely rewired, substantially delaying deliveries.

ABOVE: **In 1989 the 600th set of Airbus wings was delivered by British Aerospace Airbus Division; by this time the Chester and Filton factories were sharing the Airbus wing design and production work. Illustrated in this photo are wings for the A320, for which BAe Airbus completed not just the wing box but the complete wing, including the moving surfaces.** BAE Systems

BELOW: **One of the early production A320s, G-BUSC, was originally ordered by British Caledonian but following the airline's takeover it was delivered to British Airways.** BAE Systems

The world's largest airliner and Airbus flagship, the A380, at Farnborough International 2010. This is the fourth A380 built, registered F-WWDD, and retained by the manufacturer for testing and demonstrations. Author

F-WWDD in Emirates livery. Airbus

Airbus is not only involved in airliners but also has the A400M Atlas military freighter, which had a remarkably problematic gestation. The project was first set in train in 1982 and was beset by many vicissitudes, one of which was the difficulty in deciding on an engine. The Atlas finally flew in December 2009 and is due to enter service with the French Air Force in 2013; there are orders from eight other air forces including the RAF. Airbus claims the Atlas 'is able to perform both tactical missions directly to the point of need and long range strategic/logistic ones. And it can also serve as an air-to-air refuelling tanker.' The Atlas's wings are manufactured at Filton and are the largest composite wings ever made.

BAE Systems Sells its Stake in Airbus

In 1999 the ownership of Airbus changed when DASA bought CASA of Spain and then merged with Aérospatiale, coming together as EADS (European Aeronautic Defence and Space Company). The result

was that EADS now had a 80 per cent holding in Airbus and BAE Systems just 20 per cent, not a position from which it could exert much influence. Almost immediately BAE denied rumours that it had any intention of withdrawing from Airbus. In 2006, however, the BAE Board decided to sell this share and concentrate its activities on the defence market. Despite early expectations of raising £2.2bn from the sale of its stake to EADS, Airbus was hit by major problems with the A380 and its share price dropped sharply; as a result BAE Systems only realized £1.87m. After the sale, BAE's share price rose strongly, but many commentators took a contrary view and felt the sale was a dubious move and wondered why the Government had not intervened.

Though BAE Systems had exited from Airbus, thankfully the UK Government supported the continuing development of the latest development in the Airbus family, the A350. This new aircraft is being developed in response to Boeing's troubled 787 'Dreamliner'. The Government has invested £340 million ($563 million) in the programme, though the work share has

declined from previous aircraft and amounts to only 18 per cent of the total.

Conclusion

Without Hawker Siddeley's entrepreneurship, risk-taking and determination the UK would not have been part of Airbus. What a loss to the economy, to technology, to employment and the UK's position in the aviation world that would have been: at the time of writing the total number of Airbus civil and military aircraft built or on order is approaching 13,000.

Specification – Airbus A300B	
Length	176ft (53.64m)
Wingspan	147ft 1in (44.83m)
Height	54ft 6in (15.7m)
MTOW	360,000lb (163,300kg)
Max cruise speed	518mph (833km/h)
Range	4,200 miles (6,760km)
Passengers	220–375
Powerplant	2 × Pratt & Whitney JT9D

CHAPTER TEN

Avro Canada to de Havilland Canada

Avro Canada

At the Hawker Siddeley Group's twenty-first Annual General Meeting in 1957 the Chairman, Sir Thomas Sopwith, said that the largest single factor in the growth of the group was Avro Canada, formed in 1945 with only 300 employees, which had in the previous eleven years become one of Canada's major industrial units, employing some 20,000 people.

Britain had called on Canada for aid in World War Two, and by the end of 1944 Canadian shipyards had turned out almost 600 ships; forty-five aircraft companies, running 24 hours a day and employing 80,000 workers had produced over 16,000 aircraft. With the end of hostilities these Canadian firms all but collapsed as orders were cancelled and staff were laid off. One of these firms was Victory Aircraft of Malton, Ontario, which was owned by the Government and was mass-producing Avro Lancasters and Lincolns. In 1943 Sir Roy Dobson and Sir Frank Spriggs had visited the massive 800,000sq ft factory and had seen its potential.

The Canadian Government was anxious to offload the site and their responsibility for it. To make the purchase of the factory more attractive they issued a contract to the prospective purchaser for a home-grown fighter aircraft, as the Royal Canadian Air Force (RCAF) had already decided against ordering a British-made fighter. The Canadian Government also owned Turbo Research, an aeroengine company, and was anxious for it to cooperate with other major aero-engine firms, but these flatly rejected cooperation. The deal was sealed when Sir Roy Dobson offered to provide Armstrong Siddeley's turbine engine data and in return the Canadians reciprocated by offering the business to Hawker Siddeley free of charge, besides later loaning large sums of money to help the new company gain its feet. Sir Roy's argument convinced the Hawker Siddeley Board that there was a sound business case and on 2 November 1945 the deal was made. The new enterprise was named Avro Canada with Turbo Research becoming its Gas Turbine Division. Avro Canada was not a subsidiary of Avro in Manchester, but directly of Hawker Siddeley.

By 1955 Avro Canada included three other firms: Orenda Engines (formerly the Gas Turbine Division) producing powerful jet aero-engines; Canadian Car, which manufactured trains, trams, rail equipment and buses; and Canadian Steel Improvements involved in mining raw materials, forging, castings, producing basic steel products and materials, and fabricating finished and semi-finished products. Sir Roy Dobson's vigour had driven the establishment of Avro Canada to become far more than an aircraft and engine manufacturer, for he had the good sense to diversify the manufacturing range, while also encouraging the UK operation to do likewise.

By 1957 the Avro Canada group had grown so large that the member companies were separated into two major divisions. The Aeronautical Division of this Canadian Hawker Siddeley grouping comprised Avro Aircraft, Orenda Engines, Canadian Steel Improvement and Canadian Applied Research, while Canadian Car was included in the Industrial Division. The total number of companies in Canada owned by Avro Canada was forty-four, of which thirty-three were acquired with the taking-over of Dominion Steel and Coal the previous year.

Despite their large responsibilities at home, the Hawker Siddeley senior management maintained a tight control on their Canadian subsidiary and from Avro Canada's inception in 1945, Sir Roy Dobson was President with Sir Tom Sopwith and Sir Frank Spriggs as Directors. Sir Roy Dobson became Chairman in 1951.

Avro C-102 Jetliner

Within a few weeks of Avro Canada's establishment, Trans-Canada Airways (now Air Canada) invited the company to design a jet airliner powered by Rolls-Royce Avons. The design team set to work but the project was soon frustrated when the British Government refused to allow the export of the Avons: older Derwent engines had to be used. These had a higher fuel consumption, upsetting the profitability of the aircraft, and TCA later withdrew from the project,

The world's second jet airliner, the Avro Jetliner built by Hawker Siddeley's Canadian subsidiary Avro Canada. Registered CF-EJO-X, it made its maiden flight on 10 August 1949, not long after the de Havilland Comet. If it had had Avon engines like the Comet instead of Derwents, it might have been sold widely.
Avro Heritage

although the reasons for their withdrawal remain open to controversy. Unabashed, Avro continued with the project and the prototype Avro C-102 Jetliner flew on 10 August 1949, beaten into the air by the de Havilland Comet by a mere thirteen days, thereby becoming the second jet airliner in the world: a remarkable achievement for a company formed less than four years earlier.

As one of the few test pilots in the Hawker Siddeley fold to have piloted a large multi-engined jet aircraft, Jimmy Orrell, Avro's chief test pilot at Woodford, was deputed to make the maiden flight of the C-102. That went well but the second flight proved all too eventful as the main undercarriage would not extend and, with malfunctioning hydraulics, the challenge of this landing was exacerbated when the flaps could not be lowered to slow the aircraft down: Orrell landed the Jetliner on grass with only the nosewheel extended. Repairs were swift, as owing to the aircraft's design the engine nacelles bore the brunt of the damage, and it was soon back in the air. After a further fourteen flights in the Jetliner, Orrell left the test programme in the able hands of his Avro Canada colleagues.

Avro being eager to promote the Jetliner, it crossed the border to become the first jet transport aircraft to be seen in the USA when in April 1950 it landed at New York's Idlewild (now J.F. Kennedy) Airport. The aircraft was considered suitable for medium-range routes in the USA and garnered intense interest from Howard Hughes, who considered production under licence. Regrettably nothing came of this. Development of an improved version continued but repeated delays in the Avro CF-100 fighter (*see* below) led to an order from the Government to stop work in 1951; the prototype Jetliner was scrapped in 1956.

Avro CF-100

Meanwhile the CF-100 fighter aircraft project struggled on beset by numerous delays. Production versions of the large fighter were to be powered by Avro Canada Orenda engines but as these were still under development the two prototype Mk 1s were powered by Rolls-Royce Avons (which had been unavailable for the C-102). Just as Jimmy Orrell had been brought over from

Woodford to carry out the initial flight trials of the C-102, Sir Roy Dobson asked Bill Waterton, Gloster's Chief Test Pilot (and a Canadian), to make the initial flight trials of the CF-100. Taxiing trials began on the 17 January 1950 and two days later Waterton took the first Mk 1 prototype, registered 18101, into the air. After 15 months at Avro Canada, Waterton returned to Gloster in the UK and Avro Canada's chief test pilot, Donald Rogers, took over the test programme.

The first CF-100 to be powered by the 6,000lb thrust Orenda engine was the preproduction Mk2, which flew in June 1951 and showed a large improvement in performance. However, in November 1951 one of the first CF-100 Mk 2s delivered to the RCAF suffered a cracked centre-spar that put the whole programme in jeopardy. Earlier, during prototype testing, deficiencies had been detected in the wing design that were only temporarily fixed and no longterm solution had been implemented. Following redesign of the wing and its marked reinforcement, the problem was solved. With the fighter's structural problems sorted out, RCAF front-line squadrons began to receive seventy-one Mk 3As and 3Bs; these had a ventral pack with eight 0.50in machine guns and were the first CF-100s delivered in quantity.

The prototype CF-100 Mk 4, a rebuilt Mk 2 with a longer nose, made its first flight piloted by the well-known test pilot Jan Zurakowski on 11 October 1952. It was followed by 278 production versions, which were armed not only with guns but also with wing-tip rocket pods. The last variant to enter production was the Mk 5, which was also exported to the Belgian Air Force on

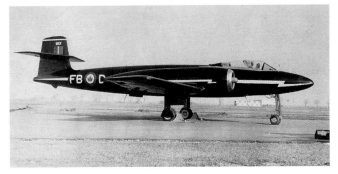

LEFT: **The prototype Avro Canada CF-100 18101 first flown by Gloster's Chief Test Pilot, Bill Waterton, on 19 January 1950.** Author

BELOW: **Four CF-100 Mk4s of the Royal Canadian Air Force. The RCAF's CF-100s were only finally withdrawn from service in 1981.** Author

very favourable terms, the USA paying 75 per cent of the price and the Canadians the balance. These Mk 5s had a much improved performance with greater ceiling and range owing to the 7,300lb Orenda engines, wing and tailplane extensions and weight saving with the removal of the guns. Altogether 332 CF-100s were built of which fifty-three were received by the Belgians. They served for almost thirty years as the last RCAF CF-100 was only withdrawn from service in 1981.

Avro CF-105 Arrow

At the RCAF's behest research into a supersonic interceptor to supersede the CF-100 began before the CF-100 flew. Initially the aircraft resembled a swept-wing CF-100, but as development proceeded the design made a radical departure from this configuration. In 1953 a specification was issued for a twin-crew, twin-engined, supersonic fighter with a 200-mile range capable of Mach 1.5 at 50,000ft.

The Arrow was a very large two-seater with a 55-degree sweptback delta planform designed to fly at a maximum speed of Mach 2.07, well beyond its specification. The initial Arrow Mk 1 development aircraft were powered by twin Pratt & Whitney J75 engines, which were to be replaced by the Orenda Iroquois under development for the production Arrow Mk 2. The Arrow was to carry Sparrow missiles mounted in a weapons pack in the lower fuselage.

Jan Zurakowski made the maiden flight of the Arrow, number 25201, from Malton on 25 March 1958 and its test programme began. On its third flight the Arrow reached Mch 1.1 in a climb and on the seventh flight Mach 1.52 at 49,000ft while it was still climbing. However, a major setback occurred on flight 11 when, owing to misalignment of the left undercarriage unit, the aircraft crashed on landing and was badly damaged. While it was being repaired the second Arrow prototype, 25202, flew on 1 August and only six weeks later reached Mach 1.86, a remarkable achievement so early in the programme. Unfortunately 25202 also had a landing accident, but despite these setbacks, testing and production was gathering pace and three more Arrows joined the testing while the sixth, a Mk2 powered by Iroquois engines, was very near completion.

In contrast to this success, powerful forces were gathering against the Arrow because,

ABOVE: **The ceremonial roll-out of the first Avro CF-105 Arrow on 4 October 1957 at Malton, Ontario.** Avro Heritage

BELOW: **Another view of the Arrow at roll-out.** Avro Heritage

as in the UK at that time, there were many who believed that the era of the manned military aircraft had passed and that they would all be replaced by missiles. With its budgeted cost at $387m by March 1959, politicians and senior members of the Canadian army and navy saw the Arrow as far too expensive for Canada or as a threat to

their own budgets. Talks ensued between Avro and the Government to find a solution to the mounting pressure against the aircraft and reduce costs, but no conclusion was reached even though it was clear that quite possibly only the initial order for thirty-seven Arrows would be completed.

Black Friday

Without warning, on Friday 20 February 1959 the Canadian Prime Minister John Diefenbaker announced in the House of Commons that the Arrow and Iroquois programmes were terminated with immediate effect. (This Friday became known as 'Black Friday' in Canadian aviation circles.) Crawford Gordon, President and General Manager Avro Canada, issued a statement to the workforce giving them all notice of the termination of their employment with immediate effect. The Government was infuriated by this action and bitterly criticized the company, but Sir Roy Dobson issued a statement that the dismissal of the 14,000 employees of Avro Aircraft and

LEFT: **The Arrow production line at Malton, Ontario with the sixth aircraft at the front. This aircraft never flew.** Author

BELOW: **The first Arrow, first flown by Jan Zurakowski on 25 March 1958. On 20 February 1959 the Arrow programme was cancelled and all the aircraft scrapped. This cancellation finished Avro Canada.** Author

Orenda Engines was not intended to embarrass the Canadian Government.

A late request by the British Government to purchase several Arrows for use in the development programme for a delta-winged supersonic commercial transport was likewise denied. So less than a year after the first flight all aircraft, parts, tooling and documentation were ordered to be destroyed, and little remains of this impressive and iconic aircraft.

For its defence Canada purchased American nuclear-tipped Bomarc surface-to-air missiles, but they proved ineffective and were soon phased out. To add insult to injury Canada acquired second-hand F-101 Voodoos from the US Air Force: an aircraft with an inferior performance that had been rejected by the RCAF as inadequate for the task.

Avro Canada – the Aftermath

Sir Roy Dobson tried to build something from the ashes and sought to relieve Hawker Siddeley's Canadian subsidiary of all management who were *persona non grata* with the Canadian Prime Minister. The company's president, Crawford Gordon, and other senior executives resigned as it was clear that Diefenbaker and Gordon had been at loggerheads and that Gordon's arbitrary action to dismiss all Avro Canada staff immediately after the Arrow's cancellations had worsened relations.

Avro Canada, which had the drive and expertise to lead the Canadian aviation industry to new heights having in a few years produced a jet airliner, an interceptor and a Mach 2 fighter at the cutting edge of aviation technology, was devastated by the cancellation of the Arrow. Canada, which had been establishing self-sufficiency in military aircraft, was now dependent on the USA. A skeleton staff continued at Malton, scrapping the Arrows, overhauling CF-100s, developing the Avrocar (see below), and making utensils and aluminium boats. Many of the engineers headed south to posts in the USA, some to de Havilland Canada and a few to the UK.

The two Avrocar testbeds – built under a contract from the US Army – were Avro's Canada's 'flying saucer', intended to be the forerunner of an amazing flying machine. This flying-saucer-shaped vehicle promised a major breakthrough in vertical take-off and landing technology, using a centrifugal system to bend a column of air to keep it aloft and accelerate. After two years of tests, the Avrocars proved they were unstable, could hover only 2 feet above the ground and move forward and backward at 35mph. Unsurprisingly, the programme was cancelled in 1961.

In his report to the Hawker Siddeley shareholders on 14 January 1960 Sir Tom Sopwith stated:

The cancellation of the Avro Arrow and Iroquois engine contracts was a severe blow ... coupled with the effects of the Canadian recession, resulted in a sharp fall in trading profit this year from £6,617,000 to £3,911,000. The profits in Canada next year will be even lower, but after that the worst should be over.

De Havilland Canada

When Hawker Siddeley bought de Havilland at the end of 1959 it also became the owners of de Havilland's overseas companies, of which the largest was de Havilland Canada with 4,000 employees. De Havilland Canada was established in 1928 in a tiny factory to assemble British-built members of the Moth family of aircraft. By 1937 the UK parent company was no longer able to maintain supply of Tiger Moths to Canada and the managing director, Phil Garratt, recognized that the time had come for the

firm to build its own aircraft. The RCAF ordered twenty-five Tiger Moths and the RAF followed suit. With the onset of war in 1939 large orders for Tiger Moths were placed and three years later the first of 1,135 Mosquitoes flew.

Chipmunk – DHC's First Home-Grown Design

From these times of frenetic activity, with peace in 1945 orders were cancelled and staff dismissed en masse. DHC took on refurbishment of Catalinas, Cansos,

Lancasters, Vampires and other types, besides restarting Fox Moth construction. Acustomed to trainers, DHC set to work on a low-wing, tandem-seat trainer powered by a de Havilland Gipsy Major, and Pat Fillingham, a Hatfield test pilot, crossed the Atlantic to manage the flight testing, taking the first DHC-1 Chipmunk on its maiden flight on 22 May 1946. A production line was soon established and the prototype sent to Hatfield for evaluation. After a hard-fought competition the Chipmunk was adopted as the RAF's primary training aircraft for new pilots and the RCAF later followed suit. The Chipmunk was also

One of the two Avrocar testbeds built for the US Army. The concept was a failure and the programme was cancelled in 1961. Author's collection

The prototype Chipmunk, CF-DIO-X, flown by Pat Fillingham. BAE Systems

exported and sixty were built in Portugal for the Portuguese Air Force. DHC built 217 but the UK production at Hatfield and Chester far outstripped this at 1,014.

Beaver and Turbo-Beaver – Rugged Simplicity

Where the name Chipmunk had been a bowdlerization and simplification of the designer's surname, Jakimiuk, subsequently it was decided that all subsequent DHC designs should have the names of Canadian animals. As the Chipmunk's design was being finalized the company was working on the DHC-2, which became the Beaver. This second indigenous design was prompted by the requirement of the Ontario Government for a bush plane to replace existing obsolescent types.

In December 1946 the go-ahead was given for the construction of a prototype, the specification of the new aircraft informed by market research that DHC instigated with the bush pilots. Just six weeks later it was flying with floats and later with skis. Following demonstrations the Ontario Government bought the sturdy-looking Beaver and a production line was laid down within a few years; the production rate was one a week. The great size of Canada made flying the only viable means of transport over long distances and DHC tapped into the demand for an economical means of travel providing an aircraft able to lift a half-ton load or seven people.

In 1950 the US Army took an interest in the Beaver, and though there was severe competition from several other types the Beaver saw them off; its STOL capabilities and the general ruggedness swayed the American forces. This was the first purchase since the war of a foreign aircraft by the US armed forces. The British Army also recognized the aircraft's capabilities and bought forty-six, which were assembled at Chester. During its twenty years of manufacture from 1947, a total 1,632 Beavers were sold, with sixty-two countries buying the civil version.

As demand for the Beaver tailed off in the mid-1960s, engineers projected a simple conversion with a Pratt & Whitney PT6 turboprop replacing the Wasp Junior, which could be produced as a new aircraft or sold in conversion kit. However, the design grew in complexity to include a fuselage extension, new fin and rudder, which made it far more costly than a second-hand example, many of which were on the market. The

Two Canadian-built Chipmunks were sent to Hatfield and assembled there. These two, G-AJVD and G-AKDN, were evaluated by the RAF and resulted in their acceptance by the service. G-AJVD is seen here with DHC Beaver G-ALOW, the thirty-sixth Beaver built and used by de Havilland as a demonstrator. The Beaver was put into production for the British Army. BAE Systems

Beaver XP769 at the Hawker Siddeley Chester factory in September 1960. BAE Systems

prototype flew on New Year's Eve 1963 but production was short-lived and only sixty had been sold when Hawker Siddeley closed DHC's production line in June 1968, a decision with which the local managers were very unhappy.

Otter – Building on the Beaver's Success

The success of the Beaver indicated that there was demand for a single-engined STOL aircraft, so in 1950 the DHC engineers set about devising a scaled-up version of the Beaver with the same STOL performance, double the payload and 150 per cent greater cabin volume. Initially called the King Beaver, the DHC-3 was soon renamed as the Otter. The prototype took off at Downsview airport, Toronto on 12 December 1951 using the same 600ft stretch of the runway that the Beaver normally used. To achieve this stunning airfield performance the Otter had double-slotted flaps and drooped ailerons. The test programme went smoothly and the aircraft was certified in less than eleven months.

Ordered straight into production, sales of the Otter soon grew. Pitted against an identically powered helicopter in US Army trials the Otter cleared a 50ft obstacle while carrying double the helicopter's load and orders from both the US Army and Navy soon followed, which finally totalled 200. Though it did not beat the Beaver's sales record a grand total of 466 had been built by the time production ended in 1967.

De Havilland Canada in 1960

In the de Havilland Canada (DHC) 1960 annual report its vice-president, Phil Garratt, reported on the merger with Hawker Siddeley (although in effect it was a takeover). He then continued to describe the large order book and deliveries to customers. Continuing production of the DHC-4 Caribou for the US Army and Ghana would take up most of the productive capacity in 1961–62 and there was strong expectation of further orders for this 2 ton load carrier, though it did not make a profit until 1962. The Beaver was in its thirteenth year of production and was being built at a modest rate; Beavers in kit form were being delivered to the de Havilland factory at Chester for final assembly to fulfil a British Army order. About 1,500 Beavers had been sold, its principal customer being the US Army. The Otter had been delivered during the year to the RCAF and US Army, making a total of approximately 400 deliveries at the end of 1960. Despite this progress with the firm's own designs, it was also making the last deliveries of licence-built Grumman Trackers to the Royal Canadian Navy.

DHC and Avro Canada

DHC found the change of ownership difficult to adjust to, but it was Hawker Siddeley that now ruled the roost and so the Board had to deal with Sir Roy Dobson. He was faced with a problem, namely what to do with Avro Canada, which, since the cancellation of the Avro Arrow, had struggled to exist. Diefenbaker's Canadian Government viewed it unfavourably owing to the dismissal of the workforce immediately following the cancellation and the once-vibrant firm struggled on, sorely crippled by events.

According to Fred Hotson,[4] after a Board meeting in mid-1961 Dobson told Garratt that he wanted DHC to buy Avro Canada. Garratt asked what the price was and Dobson replied 'book value'. Garratt asked what that was and Dobson enquired as to how much DHC had in the bank. When told that was CDN$12.5m, Dobson said that was book value. So the deal was done: now DHC owned the large former Avro site as well. Non-aviation elements of Avro Canada were hived off into the Industrial Division, then renamed Hawker Siddeley Canada.

The official transfer of the Avro Canada aviation business to DHC on 27 July 1962 was in many ways an accounting nicety as both were owned by the Hawker Siddeley Group, de Havilland's holding in DHC having been passed to the Group three weeks earlier. This transfer left DHC with a large and virtually unused plant at Malton, but fortunately in the following year the opportunity to manufacture aircraft components for Douglas Aircraft brought new life to the business: DHC entered into a joint venture with Douglas to manufacture wings and tail assemblies for the DC-9 jetliner.

Caribou

Building on the success of its brand as a manufacturer of rugged STOL types, the DHC designers considered a twin-engined Otter study in 1954, but this did not offer much increase in payload over the single-engined Otter so was not a viable proposition. As the US Army was its major customer for the Beaver and Otter, DHC had discussions with it about their requirements and learned that the Americans wanted a STOL aircraft capable of lifting 3 tons with a rear-loading capability.

In early 1957 a DHC specification was presented to the US Army, which responded with a proposal to order five when price and timescale was agreed; DHC immediately offered to sell them at $500,000 and deliver them in two years. A production line was set down to initially produce twenty aircraft, including the two prototypes and five evaluation aircraft, for the US Army.

The Caribou had a high wing and large tail and was powered by two Pratt & Whitney R-2000 piston engines. The aircraft's STOL performance was achieved by incorporating double-slotted flaps over the entire span, lowerable to a maximum of 50 degrees. These extended out to the wing fences, outboard of which was a fixed leading-edge camber. Double-slotted drooped ailerons were also fitted in two sections each side, with the rear parts of the outermost portions of the flaps serving as ailerons. There were doors each side for passengers, while an air-openable door under the very high tail allowed rapid loading of freight or vehicles. The aircraft was able to deliver twenty-two fully equipped paratroops, or carry twenty-four stretcher cases or thirty passengers on seats along the side of the cabin, which could be folded away to provide an uninterrupted cargo space of 1,150cu ft.

Flight Testing

On 30 July 1958 the prototype DHC-4 Caribou took off on a successful two-hour maiden flight. During testing it was decided to lengthen the forward fuselage by 42in to improve the centre of gravity; this was incorporated on the third aircraft and first for US Army evaluation. This aircraft crashed during test flying, when it suffered uncontrollable flutter and structural failure. Fortunately no-one was hurt and the problem easily solved. Stall clearance proved a problem for the aircraft, but after over 1,000 trial stalls and aerodynamic modifications the aircraft was cleared. These two problems delayed the programme and de Havilland Canada found themselves financially extended with only an order for five from the US Army, and Caribous under construction without any customers. Fortunately a RCAF order for four and the confidence of the banks tided the firm over until a dynamic demonstration of the Caribou in Washington sealed the US Army order, which were then ordered in fifties.

Sales Tours and in Service

Between 1959 and 1964 the Caribou was sent on three extensive world sales tours,

The ninth Caribou, CF-LVA, flew the first world sales tour from October 1959 to May 1960. It is seen here while based at Hatfield, when it was demonstrated to the British and NATO armies in December 1959. Author

deliberately operating from tiny runways normally the preserve of Beavers and Otters. The ninth Caribou, CF-LVA, began the first world tour from Hatfield on 12 December 1959, with a series of demonstrations to civil operators and both British and NATO forces. It showed off its STOL performance on grass, loaded with paratroops, a jeep and a trailer. It then departed on an extensive tour of Europe and the Middle and Far East, returning to Downsview five months later having made 479 demonstration flights. In October to December 1961 there was a tour of Latin America with CF-LAN and a final one in March to July 1964, when CF-OYE crossed the Pacific, toured south-east Asia, then Africa and back across the Atlantic.

The US Army flew Beavers in the Korean War while the Otters used in the Vietnam War were soon joined by their larger stablemates in 1962; eventually six squadrons served there. Some 15 per cent of all Caribou flight time has been logged in actual warfare, notably with the US Army and the RAAF in South Vietnam, where the type became the standard fixed-wing transport work horse. The RCAF put theirs to good work on a number of UN missions and many other air forces made good use of them. In 1967 Caribou production restarted to satisfy the small but continuing demand, and continued at a modest rate until it finally ceased in 1973 with the completion of the 307th machine.

DHC in 1965

In 1965 DHC made a loss, after Research and Development costs, of £1.1m. This position arose because the newer projects, the Turbo-Beaver, Twin Otter and Buffalo (which had flown in November that year) had incurred large R&D costs at a time when sales of older types had declined and sales of the new models were not yet replacing them.

DHC, as the largest subcontractors on the Douglas DC-9 programme, were employing 2,000 staff on the contract; a contract that was rising rapidly in size and complexity and was producing, both financially and technically, more than double that originally contemplated. As a result Douglas Aircraft of Canada was formed in 1965 and leased with an option to buy the DHC plant at Malton and purchased the equipment and machinery needed for their DC-9 work.

ABOVE: **A US Army Caribou being assembled at Downsview in October 1959.** BAE Systems

LEFT: **US Army trials at Downsview in October 1959.** BAE Systems

Buffalo

As production of the Caribou continued at the beginning of the 1960s, de Havilland Canada sought to capitalize on their invest-ment and develop an improved version, the DHC-5. The project's instigator, the US Army, wanted an aircraft in which the basic design and equipment was little changed from that of the Caribou but which would be bigger and better, with the same dimensions of the Chinook helicopter, capable of troop and stores airborne delivery. There was strenuous competition for this order, which DHC won, and development of the DHC-5 powered by twin General Electric T64 turboprops was financed by one-third shares from the US Army, Canadian Government and the manufacturer.

Now named the Buffalo, the prototype and the first of four evaluation aircraft for the US Army, registered 313686, flew on 9 April 1964. Testing went well and the Buffalo was certified a year later, whereupon the Canadian Forces ordered fifteen and a production line was established.

The US Army was impressed by the improvements the Buffalo offered over the Caribou and quickly employed two in Vietnam. A quantity order appeared a certainty, but this did not materialize as the in-fighting between the American armed forces resulted in the US Army being restricted to helicopters while the USAF took over all fixed-wing aircraft. Deliveries began to the Canadian forces and in 1967 the Brazilian Air Force chose the Buffalo, eventually becoming the largest customer and receiving twenty-four.

The Buffalo's cockpit was basically the same as that of the Caribou, with the distinctive sliding radio console in the centre and roof throttles above the two pilots' seats. Unlike its predecessor it not only had turboprop engines, but also an APU located at the rear of the left engine nacelle. The Buffalo could take off and clear a 50ft obstacle at gross weight of 41,000lb, while landing distance from over 50ft at maximum landing weight was 1,100ft and it could usually be halted in four lengths.

To achieve this startling airfield performance the Buffalo employed the flying surfaces of the Caribou with the addition of spoilers, just inboard of the drooped ailerons, which moved automatically with the ailerons immediately the latter reached 5 degrees of upward deflection. On landing the spoilers were actuated by undercarriage micro-switches and opened immediately on touchdown for very rapid lift dumping, which, combined with braking on all three wheels and reverse-pitch propellers, resulted in the incredibly short run. With a total volume of 1,580cu ft, forty-one troops or thirty-five paratroops could be carried, with standard fittings allowing quick conversion to a 24-stretcher casualty-evacuation layout.

Had the US Army ordered Buffalos in quantity then production costs and selling price could have been lowered, besides which there would have been continuous improvement to the design. In 1972 production ceased after fifty-nine deliveries; two years later production restarted and forty-three more were built, most of which were the improved DHC-5D with higher-rated engines and improved performance. The Buffalo continued to receive orders from the air forces of Mexico, Peru, UAE, Oman and seven in Africa, and 121 had been produced when the line closed in 1988.

Two Buffalos were heavily modified for research purposes: one with an air-cushion

ABOVE: The first Buffalo, one of four for US Army evaluation, flew on 9 April 1964 and seen here being demonstrated at Downsview. Registered 313686, it later served with the USAF and later still with NASA.
Author

RIGHT: A Zairian Air Force Buffalo outside the DHC plant.
Author

landing system, fitted with a large skirt similar to a hovercraft, and the other with jet engines and a new wing. The first was under the auspices of Bell to test its use on a STOL transport over all manner of rough terrain as half hovercraft, half aircraft. The other, the Augmentor Wing Buffalo, had Rolls-Royce Spey jet engines with vectored thrust replacing the turboprops, a new wing and boundary-layer control. The aircraft was modified by DHC and Boeing for joint Canadian/US research into improving take-off and landing performance, and showed a huge improvement on the standard Buffalo.

Hawker Siddeley in Competition with Itself – the Buffalo versus the Andover

DHC management must have been dismayed when in July 1966 Hawker Siddeley in the UK leased an Andover from the RAF for a demonstration to senior officers and civilians from the US Pentagon. In four days the aircraft made thirty-four demonstration STOL flights from Washington National Airport and attracted the interest of the USN, USAF, US Army and USMC. The US authorities were extremely impressed by the Andover's short-field performance and low-speed handling qualities. Such an aircraft could be used in the forward air support role by the USMC, or for shore-to-carrier deliveries by the USN. These demonstrations were clearly in direct competition to the DHC Buffalo, the only other STOL transport in the same payload/range class. The Andover had the advantage of pressurization over the unpressurized

Buffalo, but the US officials had reservations about the Andover's price and Hawker Siddeley's capacity to meet the delivery requirements. In the end these demonstrations proved fruitless as neither of Hawker Siddeley's large STOL aircraft received an order.

Star Performer – the Twin Otter

The Twin Otter flew in May 1965 and was an immediate success; it proved to be the mainstay of de Havilland Canada for many years. When the production line closed in 1988, 844 had been built and many remain in service today.

DHC was very busy in 1963 building Beavers, Otters and Caribous, while developing the Turbo-Beaver and the Buffalo. The US Army had expressed an interest in a twin-engined version of the Otter and de Havilland wanted to supply their prime customer of small STOL aircraft with one to suit them. The DHC designers had been considering a twin-engined version of the Otter and had already tested the Pratt & Whitney PT-6 turboprop in a Beech 18 in 1960; this was succeeded by trials with an Otter specially adapted for STOL research with a twin PT-6 installation. The engines exhibited startling performance so DHC had found the powerplant for the new aircraft: now they had to design it. After much deliberation they decided on a typical DHC configuration with a high wing and, for simplicity, a fixed nosewheel undercarriage. The wingspan was greater than the Otter's and the wing struts were located inboard of the nacelles. The fuselage cross-section

and wing centre-section were the same as the Otter's so a fair proportion of the parts and original tooling could be reused. A prototype and four pre-production aircraft were speedily ordered into production in late 1964. So confident was the company that ten production aircraft were soon added to the line and long lead items for a further forty-five aircraft were ordered; eventually 100 series 100s were built.

Sales

On 29 April 1965 the prototype was rolled out with Sir Roy Dobson and de Havilland Canada senior management present. Registered CF-DHC-X, it flew on 20 May just a day before the founder of the de Havilland Enterprise, Sir Geoffrey de Havilland, died. Less than a year later the Twin Otter was certified.

The US Army had continued to evince strong interest, as with the Buffalo, but the Twin Otter lost out to the Beechcraft King Air for this big order on price. The sales people got to work travelling the globe, Twin Otters demonstrating at the 1966 Farnborough and Hanover Air Shows, and orders rolled in. They were soon flying in small airlines into small airports in all continents.

Whereas the majority of customers for DHC's previous aircraft had been military or governmental, for the Twin Otter the company was at the mercy of the much more volatile civil market. In rejigging itself to this market DHC was surprised when – rather than the original emphasis on selling to bush operators – they were supplying commuter airlines at a price per aircraft of just under $300,000. Sales were initially

A DHC-6 Twin Otter delivered to the Royal Norwegian Air Force in July 1967. Author

strong, but by 1969 were at a reduced level especially in the USA, where a shortage of credit particularly affected operators of this class of aircraft. In reacting to this downturn DHC developed a new model, the Series 200 with a longer nose and improved rear compartment for luggage, which was well received. Typically for this manufacturer there were already floatplane and ski-equipped versions, and in 1969 the Twin Otter Series 300 was introduced with higher-powered engines and higher operating weights.

DHC at the End of the 1960s

By 1967 the company had moved back into substantial profitability ($5m) reflecting the receipt of income from McDonnell Douglas from the lease of the Malton plant for DC-9 wing manufacture and from sales of DHC's new aircraft, the Buffalo and Twin Otter. There were deliveries of 119 aircraft in 1967, including 66 Twin Otters, which then had an order book exceeding 190 from worldwide customers. Buffalo deliveries to the Canadian Defence Forces were in progress and the Brazilian Air Force had placed an order for twelve. Although the Buffalo had been intended to supersede the Caribou, demand for the Caribou had not flagged and in 1967 the Caribou production line was reopened. The amount of work and size of investment in Malton resulted in Douglas's purchasing De Havilland's buildings and surrounding property in 1968.

Showing the cyclical nature of the aircraft business, sales for 1969 were only $78m, substantially down from $108m in 1968. Profit before interest of $3m was depressed by the lower turnover and the reduced utilization of facilities. Owing to tight credit controls in Canada the amount of capital available for financing export orders, which had always represented an important part of the company's business, was seriously affected.

'There may be trouble ahead...'

In 1966 DHC began developing the 48-passenger DHC-7 STOL turboprop airliner for short-haul inter-city work, and as part of this organized operations of its Twin Otter and Buffalo into tiny STOL strips in Manhattan. A full-scale engineering mockup was completed in mid-1969, but in

December the Hawker Siddeley Board indicated their unwillingness to fund the project when they had their established the HS748 airliner and were developing the HS146 short-field airliner too, for which the DHC-7 could well be competition. The DHC-7 would have been dropped, but the Canadian Government stepped in so research and development were financed until 1971 at a limited rate. This impasse between the parent Board and the Canadian company was difficult to bridge.

...and into the 1970s

DHC's sales increased in 1971 due mainly to the higher volume of Twin Otter aircraft and spares deliveries, which more than offset the reduction in the number of Caribou and Buffalo aircraft delivered, so the company recorded a substantially improved result compared with 1970.

At a ceremony at the Downsview in April 1971 the 300th Twin Otter was delivered to Pakistan International, one of an order for six placed by PIA. Of the 300 Twin Otters sold, 170 were in use with commuter operators in the USA. Despite this milestone, by the latter half of the year the continuing problems of US commuter operators caused Twin Otter orders to lag and the assembly line was temporarily stopped until new orders justified restarting production.

The company's operations were hugely affected by a strike of the manufacturing employees from mid-January to mid-September 1972. Many orders were lost, but the managers and supervisors stepped into the breach and made outstanding efforts during this period by completing a number of aircraft and fulfilling orders for spares, and

were able to give valuable protection to the company's earnings. Once the plant was fully back in production, the order book for the Twin Otter rapidly increased. In contrast, orders for the Buffalo had dried up and the production line came to halt – it restarted the following year when three orders totalling fifteen aircraft were received for an improved version of the Buffalo and there were good prospects of further sales of this model.

Nationalization

Despite continued opposition from the Hawker Siddeley Board, work continued on the DHC-7 and in $75m funding was given for two pre-production aircraft, scheduled to fly in the autumn of 1974, though no decision had been made on whether to commit to production. As part of this agreement the Canadian Government took out an option to acquire the whole or part of the Hawker Siddeley Group's shareholding in DHC, which expired on 28 June 1974. A month ahead of that date the Government exercised their option and purchased DHC for $38m, and also sought an option to purchase Canadair, another Canadian aircraft manufacturer, for $32m.

In the Hawker Siddeley Annual Report for 1974 the company expressed a deep sense of injustice at the enforced nationalization of its aviation interests by the Canadian Government, though it still had substantial investment in engineering in Canada with Hawker Siddeley Canada. The Board reiterated to its shareholders that it was continuing hold a significant place in the mechanical and electrical engineering world.

A Scenic Air Lines Twin Otter N227SA, which offers flights over the Rockies. Mike Phipp

CHAPTER ELEVEN

Space and Missiles –
Hawker Siddeley Dynamics

Introduction

Prior to the takeover of the de Havilland enterprise and its associated companies at the end of 1959, the Hawker Siddeley companies' involvement in missiles and aerospace equipment was comparatively limited. The addition of the de Havilland Missile and Equipment Division (formerly de Havilland Propellers) substantially increased the proportion of these products to the Group's portfolio of products.

Formation of Hawker Siddeley Dynamics

From its inception in 1935 the companies of the Hawker Siddeley Group had been semi-autonomous and even competed for projects. Following the addition of Folland, de Havilland and Blackburn to the group there was a short period during which this approach continued, but then, simultaneously on 1 July 1963, all Hawker Siddeley Group airframe assets were formed into divisions and all of the Group's missiles, aerospace equipment and associated activities were formed into one company, to be known as Hawker Siddeley Dynamics (HSD). HSD also took over the design, development and production of propellers, air conditioning systems and electronic gear. This resulted in the rebranding of all products, for example, Hawker Siddeley Blue Streak, Hawker Siddeley Seaslug, Hawker Siddeley Firestreak and so on.

However, the Hawker Siddeley Group's major UK competitor, the British Aircraft Corporation, had pre-empted this manner of re-organization as it had grouped all its guided weapons and associated work into one division in March 1963, though it was only at the beginning of the following year that the trading names of its component companies vanished and were renamed as Divisions of BAC.

At that time HSD employed around 15,500 people and encompassed the missile, aerospace and associated products and the facilities of the former Avro, Whitworth Gloster and de Havilland companies, as follows:

Hatfield, Manor Road, Hertfordshire

The former de Havilland site was Headquarters, Administration and Sales Department for Hawker Siddeley Dynamics and Hawker Siddeley Dynamics Engineering. The site was responsible for design and development, electronics, engineering development of the Blue Streak satellite launcher (for which there were extensive facilities), missiles, air conditioning systems, Linescan, oceanographic systems, power supplies, propellers and undercarriages. The site was closed by British Aerospace in 1990.

Also based at Hatfield, Hawker Siddeley Dynamics Engineering (a subsidiary of HSD from 1971) was involved in design and development of automatic check-out equipment, gas turbine and electronic fuel controls, automatic controls for diesel engines and industrial turbines, electron-beam welding equipment, and automatic programmable handling devices.

Farnworth, Lancashire

Electronic equipment was produced at Farnworth including the TRACE tape-controlled recording and auto-check-out system for the rapid verification of aircraft avionics. This became a Hawker Siddeley Dynamics Engineering site.

Lakefield, Lancashire

The former de Havilland site was concerned with propeller repair and overhaul. It was closed in 1966.

London EC1 and WC1

Design and development of space systems, launch vehicles and weapons; closed in 1966.

Lostock, Bolton, Lancashire

Previously part of de Havilland, Lostock was the main production centre for manufacture of the Firestreak and Red Top air-to-air missiles, Seaslug and Sea Dart surface-to-air and Martel air-to-surface missiles, undercarriage components for HSA aircraft, air conditioning equipment for Concorde and HSA aircraft. Propellers were also manufactured for aircraft and hovercraft. This is currently an MBDA site.

Spadeadam Rocket Establishment, Cumbria

At the Ministry of Aviation Spadeadam Rocket Establishment a HSD and Rolls-Royce trials team carried out static firings on the complete Blue Streak rocket with their RZ2 power units duplicating the actual launching up to the moment of lift-off, before their long journey to Woomera, Australia. The last Blue Streak tests at Spadeadam ended in July 1971.

Stevenage, Hertfordshire

Blue Streak and satellite design and assembly was carried out at Stevenage. The factory developed and manufactured many

HSD satellites including ESRO 2, ESRO 4, X4, Intasat, Europa 1, Europa 2, Intelsat 3 OTS (Orbital Test Satellite) and Marots. With the MESH consortium it was a partner on the TD1, MAROTS, satellite receiving stations and automatic weather stations. HSD Stevenage also designed and manufactured pallets for NASA Space Shuttle. Stevenage was another former de Havilland facility, originally built to manufacture Comet spares in 1953. After nationalization in 1977 this site continued to specialize in space products and is now part of Airbus Defence and Space.

Whitley, Warwickshire

The former Armstrong Whitworth factory was the centre of development and production for the Seaslug Mk1 and Mk2 surface-to-air missile. Whitley was the initial centre of development of the CF-299 (later known as Sea Dart) surface-to-air missile. The Whitley site was closed by HSD in 1968 and Seaslug support was transferred to Hatfield. The site was purchased by Jaguar Cars in 1968.

Woodford, Cheshire

The former Avro facility was the centre of production and testing of the Blue Steel rocket-powered nuclear stand-off bomb and flight test of the weapon on the RAF Vulcan B.2s (built at Woodford) and Victor B.2s. The site was closed by BAE Systems in 2011.

Woomera, South Australia

HSD carried out flight trials of Blue Steel from V-bombers and Blue Streak launches as part of ELDO at the Weapons Research Establishment at Woomera. This work ended in 1972.

Seaslug

Research into a naval anti-aircraft missile for large RN warships began in 1949 at Armstrong Whitworth. GEC had responsibility for guidance and Sperry for control of the missile. To minimize the below-deck storage space the four boost motors were mounted on the forebody and their noses were squared off with the tip of the missile.

Hawker Siddeley Dynamics 1963

Site	Production in 1963	Present status
Hawker Siddeley Dynamics Headquarters Hatfield, Hertfordshire	Design and development of Blue Streak, missiles, satellites, propellers and other systems	Closed by BAe in 1992
Farnworth, Leicestershire	Electronic equipment production	Not nationalized, remained with Hawker Siddeley Dynamics Engineering after 1977
Lakefield, Lancashire	Propeller repair and overhaul	Closed by HSA in 1966
London	Design office	Closed by HSA in 1966
Lostock, Leicestershire	Firestreak, Red Top and Martel production, propellers & other systems	Currently an MBDA site
Spadeadam Rocket Establishment, Cumbria	Blue Streak trials	HSD work ended in 1971
Stevenage, Hertfordshire	Blue Streak production and satellite assembly	Currently an EADS Airbus Defence and Space site
Whitley, near Coventry, Warwickshire	Seaslug production and Sea Dart development	Closed by HSA in 1968
Woodford, Cheshire	Blue Steel production	Closed by BAE Systems in 2011
Woomera, South Australia	Blue Steel trials and Blue Streak support	HSD work ended in 1972

Royal Navy destroyer HMS *Devonshire* launching a Seaslug missile. Author's collection

The latter had a solid internal motor and was guided by radar beam to the target. Accuracy during trials was so high that steps were taken to prevent expensive targets from being destroyed.

Firing trials took place from shore establishments and from RFA *Girdle Ness*, a heavily converted Liberty ship. The latter successfully conducted firings in the Mediterranean. Armstrong Whitworth stated 'When a salvo of two Seaslugs was fired … the first missile hit the target aircraft …

Specification – Seaslug	
Length	20ft (6.1m)
Wingspan	4ft 9in (1.45m)
Max speed	Mach 2
Max range	20 miles (32km)
Powerplant	4 × ICI solid-propellant rocket motors
Warhead	200lb (90kg) high-explosive

the second veered off and hit the largest piece of the remaining wreckage.'

The only ships to use Seaslug were the eight large 'County' class destroyers, which each mounted a twin quarterdeck launcher automatically fed by a powered hoist system. The first four received the Seaslug Mk1 and all were due to receive the Mk2, but to save costs only the latter four ships received it. Seaslug Mk2 had greater range and speed, and improved performance against low-flying targets.

Seaslug saw its only operational use during the Falklands War of 1982. HMS *Antrim* fired one unguided Seaslug against an Argentine A-4 Skyhawk that was attacking it, just to clear the round from the launcher; it missed the attacker. In a role for which it was not designed, HMS *Glamorgan* fired four rounds at Port Stanley airfield, damaging the radar and the airfield, scattering debris over the runway.

Blue Steel

In September 1954 Air Staff Requirement OR.1132 was issued to the manufacturers of the three V-bombers, Avro, Handley Page and Vickers-Armstrongs. This was to have a range of 25nm (later increased to 100nm) carrying a warhead weighing 4,500lb and be used against heavily defended Soviet cities. It should be able to cruise at speeds between Mach 0.8 and Mach 2.5.

Vickers were favourites to win this contract owing to their guided weapons experience. Immediately post-war Barnes Wallis, who had designed many bombs in addition to 'Upkeep' (the Dam Busters' bomb) and 'Grand Slam', began work on a missile project. This became the Vickers Blue Boar, a family of TV-guided, unpowered glider bombs with extending wings, which would allow a bomber a degree of stand-off of 25nm, so a heavily defended target would not need to be overflown. Though substantial trials were carried out, the Blue Boar soon fell from favour as in poor visibility the target could not be seen, so it was cancelled in June 1954 after the expenditure of £3.1m.

Avro was a surprising choice for the programme as it had no previous guided weapons experience and had to set up a special department. Having won the contract Avro had to quickly recruit engineers and specialist technical staff and unsurprisingly the schedule began to slip as the new team strove to work together on unfamiliar territory. In August 1955 Avro's Weapons Research Department submitted a proposal and in May 1956 the MoS awarded a contract to the firm to produce a stand-off weapon. As prime contactor it

ABOVE: **A Blue Steel test round marked for photographic reference purposes, other rounds are also visible.** Avro Heritage

LEFT: **Blue Steel production at Chadderton in August 1959.** Avro Heritage

had to oversee the Armstrong Siddeley Motors (another Hawker Siddeley company – later Bristol Siddeley) rocket motor and the Elliotts-Automation inertial navigation system.

Blue Steel was larger than any other British missile until then. It was essentially a pilotless miniature aeroplane that could be launched from beneath a V-bomber and left to navigate by itself and deliver its thermonuclear payload. Constructed largely from stainless-steel honeycomb sandwich, the airframe was designed for a cruising speed of Mach 2.5, and to perform violent manoeuvres at all altitudes. Propulsion was provided by a Bristol Siddeley Stentor rocket engine fed with highly volatile HTP and kerosene from tankage within the fuselage. An upper fin and rudder, and a larger folding lower fin, provided directional control.

There had been an expectation that Blue Steel's rocket motor would prove troublesome, which proved not to be the case, but the real problems were the fabrication of the missile and the accuracy of inertial system, then in its infancy.

Blue Steel had a canard configuration giving high efficiency in cruising flight and could take evasive action through twist-and-steer manoeuvrability achieved by rear ailerons working in conjunction with a foreplane. Before release, the Elliott inertial navigation system of the missile checked all parameters with the bomber's system so at the moment of release the Blue Steel knew its position, heading and speed with extreme accuracy.

After release it fell freely for a few seconds, then the twin-chamber Stentor rocket engine started. The Blue Steel accelerated ahead, climbed to 70,000–80,000ft and homed on its target completely independently at high supersonic speed. Its radar cross-section was much less than that of a V-bomber, and it retained all the capability of a manned aeroplane to feint, manoeuvre and change its flight profile in any desired manner.

All Blue Steels were intended to be compatible with both the Vulcan B.2 and the Victor B.2. The missile had a folding ventral fin, which extended after the parent aircraft had taken off. Originally there was to have been an extended-range Blue Steel Mk.2, but this would not have been in service with RAF Bomber Command for several years and, as Blue Steel Mk.1 was behind schedule, the Ministry of Defence cancelled the project and ordered HSD to concentrate on getting the Mk1 into service.

Test Programme

The basic design, supplemented by a vast amount of system development, rig-testing and engineering refinement, were all conducted at the division's facilities on the company airfield at Woodford, Cheshire. Flight trials began with two-fifths scale models powered by twin liquid rocket motors, which were employed chiefly in the development of the missile's aerodynamics and autopilot. Most were dropped from early Valiants and Vulcans at the Aberporth range where, owing to the confines of Cardigan Bay, many hardly achieved cruising flight at all. In many cases the sole object of the trial was to investigate separation from the parent aircraft and the subsequent behaviour of the missile up to the point of light-up. Eventually full-scale test vehicles were employed for the same purposes, until a clean break could be guaranteed. The V-Bombers used at Woodford and in Australia were Valiant B.1s WP204, WZ370, WZ373 and WZ375, which were modified by Marshall of Cambridge for Vickers, Vulcan B.1s XA903, XH539, XL161 and Victor B.1s XH675, XL161.

Beginning in 1959, advanced testing designed to explore all the airborne subsystems took place at Woomera Weapons Research Establishment, Australia, where there were no geographical limitations. However, there were obvious severe logistic challenges to overcome in having to transport men and materials to Australia. All those test vehicles were powered by Double Spectre twin-barrel rocket engines by de Havilland Engines (later subsumed into Bristol Siddeley). A Services Trials Unit from RAF Bomber Command was also active at Woodford and Woomera, operating several V-bombers to assist in the development of the weapon. Following the successful completion of flight trials with the test vehicles, the Blue Steel Mk.1 was tested from V-bomber B.1s at Woomera.

Criticisms

In October 1959 Harold Watkinson succeeded Duncan Sandys as Minister of Defence and informed of expenditure of £60m and the constant delays with Blue Steel and cancellation was considered. The Ministry of Aviation regarded Avro's management of the Blue Steel programme as weak, but the Government could be criticized too for its choice of contractor. As

Blue Steel neared entry into service Avro tried to interest the MoD in further developments of the missile, but these were dismissed as it was expected that the Anglo-American Skybolt would replace it.

In Service

In February 1963 the press received a briefing at RAF Scampton on the capability of RAF Bomber Command as a nuclear deterrent force. Scampton was the first RAF Bomber Command station to be equipped for Blue Steel operations. No. 617 Sqn was already trained on the weapon, No. 27's training was well advanced and No. 83's followed. After Scampton, the Victor B.2s based at Wittering would be equipped for Blue Steel operations. Readying a Blue Steel-armed Vulcan for flight took four hours and then required careful tending owing to the unstable nature of the HTP rocket fuel. In the event of the temperature rising critically, the aircraft had to land and off-load the fuel. Following a week on standby the HTP tank had to be emptied and thoroughly cleaned.

Initially the weapon's capability was extremely limited. The missile could only be dropped inert, but release heights were progressively reduced, while readiness progressively increased and eventually Blue Steel became fully operational. The success rate of a Blue Steel hitting its target was low owing to the poor performance of the inertial program and in the event that the rocket motor did not fire the weapon could be dropped as a stand-off bomb with a range of 50nm.

Further development of the Blue Steel was believed unnecessary as it was due to be replaced by the Douglas Skybolt missile, which would be launched from Vulcans. However, Skybolt was cancelled by the US Government in 1962, and the USA offered the Polaris submarine nuclear missile system in its stead. As the submarines would take time to build, the Blue Steel was modified to allow operations at 1,000ft (below the radar): it was recognized that the V-bombers were increasingly vulnerable at high level to Soviet interception, which had been made abundantly clear by the shooting down of a U-2 reconnaissance aircraft over the USSR in 1960.

Scampton's Blue Steel Vulcan B.2s remained operational until December 1970, while Wittering's Victor B.2s, which entered service in October 1963, ceased operations in December 1968.

Handley Page Victor B2 XH674 with a Blue Steel missile. The RAF's Vulcan B.2s and Victor B.2s were armed with this nuclear weapon. BAE Systems

Specification – Blue Steel	
Length	35ft (10.67m)
Foreplane span	6ft 6in (1.98m)
Wingspan	13ft (3.96m)
Max speed	Mach 2.3
Max range	150 miles (240km)
Production	53 live rounds
Powerplant	Bristol Siddeley Stentor rocket
Warhead	Red Snow thermonuclear (1.1MT)

Blue Streak

Technically a great success, Blue Streak was planned as a long-range strategic missile able to deliver the UK independent nuclear deterrent to the Soviet Union. The firms for the project were chosen by the Ministry of Supply in 1955: de Havilland Propellers (later Hawker Siddeley Dynamics) was the prime contractor, Rolls-Royce provided the rocket motors and Sperry the guidance system. Management of Blue Streak was at best muddled, with the Ministries of Defence, Supply and Air Ministry all having a hand in it.

Development was rather slow even though Blue Streak proved to be quite the equal of both the US and Soviet ballistic missiles. However, in the process costs rose and development became far more costly and complicated, especially when it was decided that silos would need to be built to launch them. DH Propellers was tasked with building sixty of these, each of which would have been hugely expensive. (One silo was built at Thetford and remains there, full of vehicle tyres.) However, by 1970, besides being extremely costly to install, critics regarded the silos rather unfavourably as vulnerable to Soviet attack.

As costs continued to rise and estimates of the final costs seemed difficult to assess, competing pressure groups proposed American-built alternatives such as the air-launched Douglas Skybolt missile and the submarine-launched Polaris. The First Sea Lord, Admiral Lord Louis Mountbatten, who became Chief of Defence Staff in 1959, and wielded substantial influence in Whitehall, naturally favoured Polaris for the RN. The Army favoured a cheaper deterrent so that there would be more money available for their equipment while the RAF, though they would have had responsibility for Blue Streak, wanted to maintain a role for their V-bombers and were also intent on ordering VC10s to carry Skybolt missiles. On 5 February 1960 the combined Chiefs of Staff wrote to the Minister of Defence, Harold Watkinson, recommending cancellation. Whereas his predecessor, Duncan Sandys, had been strongly in favour of Blue Streak and would have resisted this, his successor did not.

On 13 April, Harold Watkinson made a lengthy statement in Parliament announcing that development of Blue Streak as a weapon would cease and that the Skybolt would be purchased. He recommended the Government consider whether the Blue Streak programme could be adapted for the development of a launcher for space satellites. The Government heeded Watkinson's recommendation and ordered Skybolt, but that project was cancelled by the Kennedy Administration in 1962; the UK then bought the Polaris system.

In the course of some five years until its cancellation as a military weapon in April 1960, approximately £65m had been spent on its development, financing not only the complete missile and launcher but also extensive static-test installations at Hatfield, Spadeadam in Cumbria and a launch emplacement and other installations at the Weapons Research Establishment at Woomera in South Australia. It was considered that £600m more (1960 prices) would have been spent to put it into service; thus a total of £665m (= £12.2bn 2012 prices)

Following cancellation, the design teams associated with the programme were not immediately dispersed, and many studies were carried out both within and outside the company to obtain accurate costings of space vehicles based on the same first stage. The Government considered total cancellation, but after toying with the development of a British satellite launcher programme with the Blue Streak as the first stage, the Saunders-Roe Black Knight or Black Arrow as the second and a third stage containing the payload, dismissed this proposal owing to cost. Somewhat surprisingly, the Government then elected to develop

Blue Streak as the first stage of a three-stage satellite-launcher, in conjunction with the major European nations and Australia.

Assembled at the HSD factory at Stevenage, the manufacture of Blue Streak, though related to aircraft building, also differed and required new skills. Blue Streak was 60ft high and 10ft in diameter. It had a balloon-type tank bay, fabricated by precision-welding very thin stainless-steel sheet, accommodating 60.8 tons of liquid oxygen and 26.3 tons of kerosene. At the lower end it was attached to a propulsion bay containing two gimballed Rolls-Royce RZ2 engines, each with a maximum thrust at sea level of 300,000lb. Lift off weight of Blue Streak was 185,000lb, the complete three-stage Europa satellite launcher weighing approximately 231,000lb.

Testing

There were substantial test facilities at Hatfield with a flow test tower and a launch test tower. Many other Government establishments were also involved in testing the launcher. Static firings for development of the engines, and tests of the complete rocket vehicle, were carried out at the Spadeadam Rocket Establishment in Cumbria. The flight test programme was at Woomera in Australia, which had the comprehensive range facilities necessary for such trials. First-stage preparation of Blue Streak at Woomera was handled by a Hawker Siddeley Dynamics trials team, under the head of the Satellite Launching Vehicles Division of the RAE Space Department.

Satellite Launcher

As part of the European Launcher Development organization (ELDO), Britain became responsible for the first-stage launcher, France for the second and Germany the third stage. The whole rocket was named Europa to reflect its European provenance, the more so as Italy, the Netherlands and Belgium were also involved while Australia provided the range and support facilities at Woomera. Problems soon arose as France wanted to move to a more sophisticated launcher capable of exploiting commercial satellite launchers, but the other countries did not seek this development. A compromise was agreed and Europa 1 continued while development of advanced

A Blue Streak at Spadeadam in Cumbria, where testing took place.
Author's collection

Europa with its Blue Streak first stage, and French and German second and third stages, on display at the Hanover Air Show in April 1966. BAE Systems

launch vehicles was planned. The aim was to place a 2,000lb satellite into a low circular orbit. The overall budget for a five-year development programme was £70 million (=£1.28bn).

A total of seventy-seven static firings and eleven launches took place between 1960 and 1973 without any serious accident – an impressive safety record. At Woomera there were ten flights between 1964 and 1970, of which the first three involved Blue Streak alone and these were successful. The fourth firing with dummy second and third stages was successful, but the next two were dogged by failure, initially with the French second stage Coralie. Matters did not improve on the following three flights as the German third stage Astris failed each time. More bad luck followed, as on the final flight from Woomera the fairing failed. There was a further and final firing of Blue Streak in Kourou in Guayana, where Blue Streak performed well but guidance control was lost.

The UK Withdraws from ELDO

Matters went critical on the project when it became clear that Europa could not carry sufficient payload high enough and a fourth stage was considered for Europa. By now the project budget had doubled and the UK Government, as a 40 per cent contributor, reviewed its involvement.

In what has been mooted as a retaliatory move following President de Gaulle's veto on the UK joining the European Union in 1967, in April 1968 Tony Benn, the Minister of Technology, told the House of Commons that the Government had decided it saw no economic justification for continuing investment in ELDO beyond the current programme's end in 1971–72. Though ELDO could have continued to employ Blue Streak, its contributing partners decided on a new first stage, which led to the very lucrative development of the French-built Ariane. By the end of 2012, the Ariane had made 199 successful launches.

Tony Benn maintained that the programme was costly and that Britain was not convinced of the necessity of having a European launcher for its space programme, so after £165m expenditure the UK withdrew. The Hawker Siddeley Board stated its regret at the decision, as this would result in the end of the development of space launcher vehicles.

LEFT: **A Europa test launch at Woomera, Australia.**
Author's collection

BELOW: **Blue Streak 14, preserved at the Deutsches Museum, Munich.**
Author's collection

Conclusions

The Government was right to cancel Blue Streak as a weapon in 1960 although with hindsight it would be fair to say that the decision to withdraw from ELDO seven years later was unwise, even though the financial contribution was very high. Britain lost much potential income from satellite launches, handing the market to the French. The technology and expertise were lost. Blue Streak remains a magnificent example of British aerospace engineering, which should be remembered.

Britain's First Missiles – Firestreak and Red Top

The Firestreak missile began life in 1951 when, as a DH Propellers project, it was given the code name of Blue Jay. In 1959 it was the first missile to enter British military service, with the final marks of the RAF's Javelins and the carrier-born Sea Vixens FAW.1s of the Royal Navy. It was also part of the Lightning F.1's armament suite when it joined the RAF the following year.

Firestreak was equipped with a single solid-propellant motor giving an exceedingly high thrust for a relatively short burning time. It was an infra-red guided homing missile, which means that it homed in on

sources of heat, such as the hot metal parts of the turbojets of an enemy aircraft; the warhead was detonated by a very sensitive proximity-fuse system. During the extensive testing phase hundred of rounds were fired from test aircraft and its exceptionally high performance was established.

The Firestreak (and its successor the Red Top) was exported to only two countries as part of the British Aircraft Corporation's major contracts, to supply Lightning F.53s and F.55s to Saudi Arabia and Kuwait.

When within range, 20 degrees either side of the stern of the target, the missile would lock on to the infra-red radiation of the target's engines and could be fired. Owing to this a Lightning with Firestreak could not engage a target flying faster than the aircraft's top speed of Mach 2, nor a Sea Vixen or Javelin one flying much above their maximum speeds of just under Mach 1.

Firestreak was followed on the production line by Red Top, which was unveiled at the Paris Air Show in June 1961. This refinement of Firestreak was a far more sophisticated and more powerful weapon with improved manoeuvrability at all altitudes. Unlike Firestreak, Red Top could lock onto its target from any direction, even from straight ahead, and intercept and destroy the latest types of enemy aircraft over a very wide altitude and speed range. Red Top supplemented Firestreak in service

with the RAF on Lighting F.3 and F.6, and Royal Navy's Sea Vixen FAW.2 from 1964, and was only retired with the last Lightnings in 1988.

Sea Dart

In August 1962 work began at Whitley on the CF299 missile by the team that had produced Seaslug. Later named Sea Dart, it was a ramjet-powered ship-to-air missile and an area-defence weapon, capable of

Specification – Firestreak	
Length	10ft 6in (3.2m)
Wingspan	2ft 6in (0.76m)
Max speed	Mach 2+
Max range	5 miles (8km)
Powerplant	solid-propellant rocket motor
Warhead	50lb (27kg) high explosive

Specification – Red Top	
Length	11ft 6in (3.5m)
Wingspan	3ft (0.91m)
Max speed	Mach 3
Max range	7 miles (11km)
Powerplant	solid-propellant rocket motor
Warhead	68lb (30kg) high explosive

BAC Lightning F6 XS933 at Warton with examples of its armament for training Saudi Air Force personnel. From the left are the Aden cannon, a missile launcher, the Hawker Siddeley Dynamics Firestreak missile and then the Red Top missile. BAE Systems

A Firestreak heads for its target. The Firestreak had to approach the target from astern. MBDA

RIGHT: **A Sea Dart mounted on its launcher. The magazine was vertically below the missile and could be speedily reloaded.** MBDA

FAR RIGHT: **A Sea Dart launch.** Author

intercepting aircraft and missiles at both very high and extremely low altitudes. The system was designed to simultaneously engage multiple targets, and also boasted a surface-to-surface capability.

The RN wanted a weapon that could be stored like a gun shell in a magazine and loaded vertically into the twin-launcher without the problem of large fins, as had been the case with Seaslug. HSD was in competition with BAC's Guided Weapons Division for the contract but the latter's proposal had too little range and HSD won the development contract.

Named Sea Dart, the new missile entered service on the Royal Navy's sole Type 82 destroyer HMS *Bristol*, and later with the sixteen Type 42 destroyers of the Royal Navy and the Argentine Navy's two Type 42s. The three 'Invincible' class aircraft carriers originally had Sea Dart, but these were removed at refit. Although a Sea Dart Mk 22 was cancelled, most of the planned improvements to the system except for much longer range were installed via incremental improvements and modifications.

Sea Dart in Active Service

Despite downing seven aircraft during the Falklands conflict there was criticism of its performance with its slowness and the poor performance of its radar. During the first Gulf War HMS *Gloucester* brought down an Iraqi 'Silkworm' missile with a Sea Dart, the first time a missile had shot down another missile. On 12 April 2012 HMS *Edinburgh*, the last serving Type 42 destroyer, fired seven Sea Darts at training targets, the last planned firing of a Sea Dart as the ship was decommissioned in the summer of 2013.

Specification – Sea Dart	
Length	14ft 4in (4.37m)
Max speed	Mach 2
Max range	20 miles (32km)
Powerplant	Rolls-Royce Odin ramjet and IMI solid-propellant booster
Warhead	High explosive with proximity fuse

Martel

Work on this air-to-surface missile began in 1964, with HSD leading on the AJ168 TV-guided anti-ship version and Matra on the AS37 anti-radar weapon; Martel was the first missile designed and developed as a cooperative venture between Britain and France. It was designed to arm the UK's Phantoms, Buccaneers and Nimrods and the French Air Force's Mirage IIIs, Jaguars and Breguet Atlantiques. The TV version followed a pre-programmed course immediately after launch, transmitting a direct TV picture of the target to a cockpit monitor, and completing its flight controlled from its launch aircraft by a mini joystick. The all-weather anti-radar version homed in on enemy search radars automatically.

After a successful series of firing trials, which confirmed the performance of the complete system and its accuracy in operation, quantity production was given the go-ahead in December 1968. Overall development costs were estimated as £70m and the production contract was valued at £30m. Whereas the French-developed AS37 was

A No. 12 Squadron Buccaneer armed with anti-radar and TV-guided Martel missiles. The outer pylons have the anti-radar version and the starboard inner the TV-guided example; the other inner pod contains the guidance system for the TV version.
BAE Systems

Specification – Martel	
Length	13ft 2in (4.01m)
Wingspan	3ft 8in (1.12m)
Max speed	Mach 0.9
Max range	40 miles (64km)
Powerplant	Solid propellant rocket
Warhead	High explosive

fitted to the Mirage, Jaguar, Buccaneer and Atlantique, the British TV-guided Martel was only fitted to the Buccaneer.

HSD from Rationalization to the Late 1960s

By 1968 after seven years of research into all fields of space technology, involving the development and production of the launch vehicles, satellites, ground support equipments and tracking stations, Hawker Siddeley Dynamics had developed a masterful understanding of European and international space programmes.

Clearly one of the most important programmes had been the success of Blue Streak as the reliable first stage booster for the ELDO launcher Europa 1. In collaboration with the other members of MESH (a powerful European consortium composed of MATRA of France, ERNO of Germany, SAAB of Sweden and HSD) the firm could satisfy the requirements of UK and international customers for the design, development and supply of spacecraft. Such spacecraft, which include scientific satellites, advanced communications satellites and earth resource satellites, was no mean capability. As part of the MESH in 1969 the Space Division saw its ESRO 2 launched and go into satisfactory operation and the development of the TD satellite for ESRO (European Space Research Organization). The 1,200-strong staff of the Space Division proved to be very productive and highly competitive in gaining contracts.

A major disappointment for HSD and the Group was the Government's decision to withdraw from ELDO in 1968, which meant though work would continue on Blue Streak as a satellite launch vehicle until 1971, thereafter further development would cease.

Production of guided weapons systems was continuing and development work began on Martel and Sea Dart. Despite this strong demand, HSD closed the former Armstrong Whitworth factory at Whitley in 1968. The rationalization of HSD in 1963 and the continuing reduction in defence expenditure had a profound effect on the workforce, and the number of HSD employees fell from 15,000 to just 10,000 in 1969.

Propellers continued to represent a major activity. The Franco-German Transall military transport's Rolls-Royce Tyne turboprops had HSD-designed (and their largest-ever) 18ft constant-speed propellers, which were then licence-built in France. Air conditioning equipment produced by HSD originated from a Hamilton Standard licence, and in 1965 the company won the contract for the Concorde system and had responsibility for the Trident, HS125 and Shorts Belfast aircraft.

HSD had many other products and applied its expertise and experience to other allied areas. For example it developed an Automatic Test Equipment (TRACE) giving efficient and reliable service to test aircraft systems, which was purchased by a number of important airline operators and manufacturers in Europe and the USA. The company also applied its technology to the field of security systems for intruder detection and Shorrock Developments, a company specializing in this field, was acquired in 1969.

The Industrial Automation Division of HSD achieved significant success in selling training simulators to the RAF, Royal

Australian Air Force, for Concorde and for the Boeing 747. It continued to progress its business of data transmission, data logging and computing. The electronic control division developed its business in railway traction and track-side equipment, in industrial gas turbine and diesel engine controls, and secured its first important entrance to the market in automatic gear change control for commercial vehicles. S.G. Brown Ltd was acquired, becoming a subsidiary of HSD, supplying specialized marine navigation systems and ships' gyroscopic compasses.

Taildog/SRAAM

HSD began developing the tube-launched, thrust-vectoring Taildog – later renamed SRAAM (Short-Range Anti-Aircraft Missile) – in 1968. There were high expectations for the sales of the missile, which was due to enter service with the Royal Air Force, but owing to defence cuts in 1974 it was relegated to a technology demonstrator programme. In 1980, the SRAAM project became the British Aerospace Dynamics contribution to the ASRAAM multinational missile project. This proved to be a very successful missile developed in many forms, and is now produced by MBDA as ASRAAM.

Linescan

In 1968 Hawker Siddeley Dynamics broke into the important and lucrative UAV (Unmanned Aerial Vehicle) market with its Linescan equipment when it was selected, after international competition, to develop the HSD Type 201 infra-red Linescan system as an alternative to cameras for the 400 Canadair CL-89 reconnaissance drones equipping the Canadian, British, West German and Italian armies. As all objects emit infra-red radiation according to their temperature, a comprehensive thermal picture of terrain can be obtained by day or by night by using Linescan.

The 8ft long, missile-like CL-89 drone would fly over the target, scan the ground with its 120-degree infra-red sensors at high speed at right angles to the flight path, to detect and record on film minute variations in infra-red radiation. It then homed in on its recovery site, the engine was cut and the drone floated down to earth on a parachute. Linescan provided all-weather reconnaissance, unlike optical cameras, as it used

Handley Page Hasting prototype TE580 was used by Hawker Siddeley Dynamics to trial different propellers and here it is seen with the propeller for the SRN4 Hovercraft, which were built by HSD. There is a water spray rig for icing tests just visible ahead of the propeller.
BAE Systems

infra-red, and it also functioned at night providing a clear image of the heat signatures of aircraft, vehicles and so on, through camouflage.

Following its success, HSD made an agreement with the Ministry of Aviation in 1971 to share the costs of a development of Linescan 201 on the expectation of export sales. The new model was Linescan 401, designed for near-supersonic missions at very low altitudes.

Hawker Siddeley Dynamics From 1970 to Nationalization

In 1970 HSD's results were depressed by the conjunction of a number of events and a refocusing of the business. Aware of the weakness of the defence market, HSD had undertaken the development of new products making use of the technology derived from guided weapon activity.

Guided weapons procurement was relatively low as changes in the UK defence programme took effect, and the costs of introducing new products were not yet covered by earnings. However, during the 1970s

export deliveries were made to the Argentine Navy and to the Kuwait Air Force. There was also a considerable amount of overhaul and repair work on weapons already in service. During the decade the position improved, with increasing orders for Linescan and Martel.

In the 1970s some commentators believed HSD's Space Division to be the most successful satellite-manufacturer in the Western world outside of the USA, evidenced by its heavily involvement in consortium manufacture of satellites. Notwithstanding the cancellation of the Blue Streak launch vehicle programme by the European Launcher Development organization in 1971, the level of activity in the Space Division continued steadily, particularly in the satellite field led by the production of a series of scientific satellites for the European Space Research organization.

In 1970 development of the air conditioning system for the Concorde aircraft was completed, in production and giving satisfactory service. Though this had been expected to be a very lucrative contract, Concorde's poor sales put paid to this expectation. British Rail placed a design and development contract for the suspension and braking system for the Advanced Passenger Train and here again there were few sales, as the train was not developed beyond the prototype stage. The level of business in the other products of the Mechanical Equipment and Systems Division, which included aircraft and hovercraft propellers, continued to be satisfactory. The vending machine business – originally with Group subsidiary Gloster-Saro – was transferred into Hawker Siddeley Dynamics so that it might have the benefit of the electronic and mechanical technology there.

Hawker Siddeley Dynamics Divided into Two Businesses

In January 1971, with the approval of the Group board, Hawker Siddeley Dynamics judged that the time had come to establish Hawker Siddeley Dynamics Holdings and establish two distinct businesses, as the number of its companies had recently increased with the addition of Shorrock Developments, S.G. Brown, Coin Acceptors and Gloster Vending. These two businesses were Hawker Siddeley Dynamics (missile, space, aircraft equipment, specialized mechanical equipment and systems) and Hawker Siddeley Dynamics Engineering (electron-beam welding, automatic handling, automatic test and electronic control equipments).

The setting up of Hawker Siddeley Dynamics Engineering was to prove a fortuitous move for the Group as a whole. Sir John Lidbury served as Chairman for the two businesses.

Sky Flash

In response to an Air Staff Target for an improved medium-range air-to-air missile to replace the American Sidewinder and Sparrow, a programme began in December 1973 to develop Sky Flash. At an early stage it was planned to use components of the well-proven AIM-7E Sparrow as the new weapon was to be compatible with the semi-recessed Sparrow installation on RAF Phantoms.

The Sparrow's development went back to 1951 but had been built in large quantities and much refined. Hawker Siddeley Dynamics made a licence agreement with Raytheon covering production of the basic missile airframe in the UK, designed a new

Tornado F.2 ZA524 at the Farnborough Air Show in 1982 with four Skyflash missiles under its fuselage. BAE Systems

autopilot and an active radar proximity fuse. By matching these components with new electronics Hawker Siddeley Dynamics could speedily and inexpensively produce an effective missile system for the 1980s. All trials were conducted in the USA involving firings from F-4J trials aircraft and it entered service with RAF Phantoms in 1978, later serving with Tornado F.2s and F.3s.

Satellites in the Late 1960s and 1970s

Design and development of ESRO 2 by Hawker Siddeley Dynamics as prime contractor and Société Engins Matra, principal subcontractor began in November 1964. ESRO's first satellite ESRO 2/IRIS was designed to carry out a twelve-month study of solar astronomy and cosmic rays. Hawker Siddeley Dynamics was the project leader with overall responsibility for coordination of the programme and integration of the systems engineering. Matra designed and developed the bulk of the electronic systems, aerials and ground equipment while the solar cells were produced by Ferranti.

Eight satellites were built, six for static trials and two identical flight models. The contract was valued at £1.3m (2012 prices

Specification – Sky Flash	
Length	13ft 2in (4.01m)
Wingspan	3ft 8in (1.12m)
Max speed	Mach 4
Max range	28 miles (45km)
Powerplant	Solid propellant rocket
Warhead	High explosive

= £21.5m). The satellite's planned tasks were to investigate the physical properties of the Earth's environment, in particular X-ray and ultra-violet radiation emanating from the sun. Following completion at Stevenage, the flight model satellites were transported by air to California and were launched at Vandenberg by a NASA Scout vehicle. Whereas the first flight model did not achieve orbit after its launch on 30 May 1967 the second was launched successfully on 17 May 1968, ESRO's first orbiting satellite and designed for a six-month life, and in successful orbit it was renamed IRIS.

HSD was exceptionally busy through the 1970s producing satellites, initially producing the external structure for ESRO's second satellite, TD1A which was successfully launched in March 1972 tasked with ultra-violet and infra-red measurements of the stars. Following on was ESRO 4, a product of the MESH consortium, comprising Matra, Erno, Saab, HSD and others. Its role was to examine near-Earth space phenomena. HSD was the leading light of this consortium and final assembly of the ESRO 4 prototype satellite took place at the

Stevenage factory. Two were constructed, the prototype which served as a test model, and the back-up spacecraft. The operational satellite was launched in September 1972.

In March 1974 the all-British X-4 experimental satellite was placed into an approximately 500-mile polar orbit by a Scout vehicle launched from the Western Test Range in California. It was originally planned to be launched on the British Black Arrow booster, but owing to cancellation of the launcher programme it was launched by an American Scout. Once established in orbit and renamed Miranda, the spacecraft began to transmit data showing it to be working normally. Throughout its operational life, Miranda was controlled by the RAE Satellite Control Centre at Farnborough, assisted by the RAE ground station at Lasham and by the Stadan (Space Tracking and Data Acquisition Network) system operated by NASA.

HSD's collaborations spread to working with Spain with which it developed Intasat, Spain's first satellite. It entered a 900-mile circular orbit on 15 November 1975 and contributed to studies of the density of the atmosphere.

The MESH consortium, led by Hawker Siddeley Dynamics, produced ESA's OTS and MAROTS communications satellites in a contract worth £25m. The OTS (Orbital Test Satellite) was a modular design that provided a template for future satellites. OTS was launched into geostationary orbit in June 1977, followed by MAROTS in October 1977 offering telephone/telex circuits and two TV channels. MAROTS (Maritime Orbital Test Satellite) was specifically designed for maritime communications and provided thirty communications channels of special significance to a maritime power like Britain. As a member of MESH, HSD's contribution to Spacelab was a £5m contract to manufacture pallets for the Spacelab, which were taken into orbit by the Space Shuttle.

Ikara

The Ikara anti-submarine missile was developed by Australian Government Aircraft Factory for the Australian Navy and when the Royal Navy purchased it the Australian Government entered into an agreement with HSD to act as sales agent and 'sister company' for the modified RN Ikara that was developed for the Royal Navy's Leander class frigates. In 1972 HSD sold the

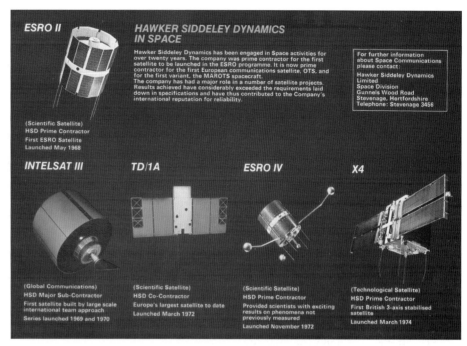

The impressive number and variety of satellites produced by the firm from 1968 to 1974. Astrium

An Orbital Test Satellite (OTS) having its antennae tested at Stevenage. Astrium

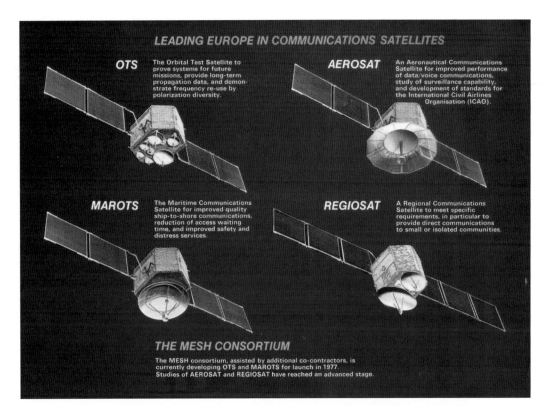

LEADING EUROPE IN COMMUNICATIONS SATELLITES

OTS The Orbital Test Satellite to prove systems for future missions, provide long-term propagation data, and demonstrate frequency re-use by polarization diversity.

AEROSAT An Aeronautical Communications Satellite for improved performance of data/voice communications, study of surveillance capability, and development of standards for the International Civil Airlines Organisation (ICAO).

MAROTS The Maritime Communications Satellite for improved quality ship-to-shore communications, reduction of access waiting time, and improved safety and distress services.

REGIOSAT A Regional Communications Satellite to meet specific requirements, in particular to provide direct communications to small or isolated communities.

THE MESH CONSORTIUM

The MESH consortium, assisted by additional co-contractors, is currently developing OTS and MAROTS for launch in 1977. Studies of AEROSAT and REGIOSAT have reached an advanced stage.

Hawker Siddeley Dynamics communications satellites, which were built on a modular basis to allow for different applications. These were produced by the MESH (Matra, Erno, Saab and Hawker Siddeley) consortium. Astrium

Ikara missile system for installation in four warships being built for Brazil. The value of this work amounted to approximately £10m, a large part of which was manufactured in Australia, but HSD provided the weapon system and were responsible for its installation and support.

Ikara had a cropped-delta aircraft configuration, with control surfaces and a rocket motor. Its actual weapon was a homing torpedo recessed into the bottom of its fuselage. After target location, Ikara was fired from the warship and having reached the target area, released the parachute-retarded homing torpedo, which searched for the submarine and then attacked.

Nationalization and Hawker Siddeley Dynamics Engineering

At the nationalization of HSA and HSD as part of the new British Aerospace in March 1977, one small part of the Group's aerospace empire was saved from this state control and this was Hawker Siddeley Dynamics Engineering (HSDE).

HSDE was sited at Hatfield with 700 employees and in 1977 it had a turnover of £6.5m, with approximately 30 per cent

Specification – Ikara	
Length	11ft 3in (3.43m)
Wingspan	5ft (1.52m)
Max speed	440mph (700km/h)
Max range	12 miles (20km)
Powerplant	Bristol Aerojet solid-propellant rocket
Warhead	Type 44 lightweight torpedo

generated by equipment and another 30 per cent defence related. A large part of HSDE's work could be traced to the Group's aerospace parents: HS Dynamics and before that de Havilland Propellers. But where these had originally been aerospace spin-offs, now its control-systems expertise in propulsion, coal-mining and even bottle-making had developed a momentum of its own.

Conclusion

By nationalization in 1977 Hawker Siddeley Dynamics had become a leading missile, space and equipment enterprise making a much larger than proportional contribution to the overall profitability of the Group than HSA. In 1963 the formation of HSD had been a bold move, not site specific, which

had to draw in staff and products from many sites. De Havilland Propellers' offerings dwarfed those of the other Group companies and integration of those with their new partners was a major challenge. Established with 15,500 staff in 1963, only ten years later the roll call had halved to just 7,700 employees.

In April 1977 Hawker Siddeley Dynamics together with their former rivals BAC Guided Weapons Division became part of the nationalized British Aerospace as British Aerospace Dynamics (BAe Dynamics). Partly privatized in 1981, by 1989 it was fully privately owned. Changes continued and BAe Dynamics established two subsidiaries, one dealing with Space Systems and the other Guided Weapons. In 1994 BAe Dynamics sold its subsidiary British Aerospace Space Systems to Matra Marconi Space and this is now Astrium (renamed Airbus Defence and Space in July 2013), and the former HSD Stevenage site is their spacecraft design and build facility. In 1996 the Guided Weapons subsidiary merged with Matra Defence to form Matra BAe Dynamics. Finally in 2001 it merged with Aérospatiale-Matra Missiles (now EADS) and Finmeccanica of Italy to create MBDA. The Hawker Siddeley connection continues as the former HSD Lostock site is one of their two factories.

CHAPTER TWELVE

Vulcans and Victors at Woodford

Avro

The famous firm of A.V. Roe owed its inception to the activities of a great British aviation pioneer, Alliott Verdon Roe. He formed A.V. Roe & Co. on 1 January 1910 at Ancoats, Manchester. The first aircraft was the Avro Triplane, whose flight trials took place some distance away at Brooklands in Surrey where the company rented a hanger. Roy Chadwick was hired in 1911 and became the Chief Designer at the end of the First World War. Three years later Roy Dobson joined the company, rising to manage Avro and to become Chairman of the Hawker Siddeley Group. Avro was initially financially insecure but the War in 1914 led to a huge boom in orders for the Avro 504K. However, with the cessation of hostilities there was a slump in orders and many aircraft companies went out of business. Avro as a business entity remained in being although its founder, A.V. Roe, had to sell a majority holding to Crossley Motors in 1920 giving them a holding of 60 per cent of the share capital. However, by 1928 Crossley Motors' car-manufacturing business was in serious trouble. In order to ease their difficulties, Avro was sold to Sir John Siddeley who owned the Armstrong Siddeley Development Company, which in turn controlled Armstrong Whitworth Aircraft and Armstrong Siddeley Motors.

In 1934 Tom Sopwith and his board of directors at Hawker Aircraft were researching new firms to acquire, reasoning that rearmament was in the air. This policy had borne fruit with the purchase of Gloster Aircraft and in 1935 Sir John Siddeley was offered £1m (= £60m 2013) to sell his companies to Hawker Aircraft. As a result Hawker Siddeley Aircraft was formed with Avro as one of its major enterprises. Avro was now a part of a large group of companies, although it continued to retain a large amount of autonomy until the late 1950s.

During the war its factories made a huge contribution to the war effort building Anson trainers and the Lancaster bomber, which was the great stalwart of Bomber Command throughout the war along with its successor, the Lincoln. From the Lancaster design evolved the Avro York, a large transport aircraft. Post-war, Avro designed the four-engined Tudor airliner. This proved to be a failure, so much so that many were never delivered and were scrapped at Chadderton and Woodford.

The Mighty Vulcan

The RAF instigated this project by issuing a specification in January 1947 for an aircraft with the capability to carry a nuclear bomb load over long ranges while flying at high altitude at near Mach 1 speeds and capable of operating from normal bomber airfields. The thinking that led to the Vulcan's configuration (known initially as the Avro 698) came from wartime German research into delta-winged aircraft as there was no research from British or American resources, and this proposal was officially put forward in March 1947. During the summer of that year the original concept of an all-wing design with a small bubble for the crew gave way to a new arrangement with a thinner wing and a full-length fuselage, which faired in well with the delta shape and with wingtip fins and rudders. To provide strength the wing was thick, seven feet deep at the wing roots merging into the nine foot wide fuselage containing a 29ft long weapons bay. Avro's tender for the 698 was accepted in November 1947, but during 1948 the aircraft's design was radically amended when the elevons were replaced by conventional elevators and ailerons and wingtip fins and rudders were replaced by a central fin and rudder.

Sir Roy Dobson, then Avro's Managing Director and a Hawker Siddeley Director, took personal responsibility for all the major aspects of the 698. Ray Chadwick was the Technical Director at the beginning of the project and after his death in an Avro Tudor accident at Woodford he was replaced by Sir William Farren.

The Avro 707

To test the concept of the tailless delta, a series of small single-seat research aircraft were built. Four of these Avro 707s flew; the first was built to explore low-speed characteristics, and first flew in September 1949

The second of the five Avro 707s built, 707B VX790 with a revised dorsal engine air intake. Roly Falk made its maiden flight in 6 September 1950 at Boscombe Down. After a landing accident it was broken up in 1956. BAE Systems

The prototype VX770 about to touch down at Woodford.
Avro Heritage

but was destroyed the following month killing the pilot Eric Esler. Modifications were incorporated in the second aircraft, the 707B high-speed machine, which Roly Falk flew for the first time in September 1950. Two further 707 variants were built, a 707A for further high-speed work and a twin-seater, the 707C.

Comprehensive ground-rig testing was completed on the 698 with a complete airframe built solely for ground-test purposes subjected to two years of thorough load-testing. Other rigs were constructed to test the hydraulic systems, pressurization and air conditioning, powered flying controls, fuel system and engine installation. Additional items of research equipment installed by the company included a transonic and supersonic wind-tunnel, high-altitude and low temperature pressure chamber, electronic flight simulator and a digital computer.

The Prototype Vulcans and a Farnborough Show-Stopper

In a rush to get the aircraft to the Farnborough Air Show ahead of their rivals Handley Page and their Victor, the Avro workers pulled out all the stops and 30 August 1952 the Avro 698 prototype VX770 made its maiden flight from Woodford powered by Rolls-Royce Avons. It was flown by Roly Falk alone with no other crew. Two more flights at Woodford followed before the aircraft flew south to Boscombe Down. From there it made daily flyovers at Farnborough in the company of two Avro 707s; the red 707A and the blue 707B. Only a month later the 698 was formally named the Vulcan. The previous month the twenty-five B.1s had been ordered and two years later thirty-seven more were added.

It was the intention of the designers to install Bristol Olympus engines, but as its development had lagged behind the Vulcan, VX770's initial trials took place with the Avons. These were exchanged for more powerful Armstrong Siddeley Sapphires in mid-1953, making it very much a Hawker Siddeley Group aircraft. Meanwhile the second prototype VX777 was completed with the Olympus engines and flew on 2 September 1953, just over a year after VX770. Stealing the show at Farnborough 1953 the two Vulcans flew in formation with the four Avro 707s, impressing all who witnessed it.

Flight Testing

During high-speed flight trials with the Olympus-powered VX777 and with 707A WD280 a high-speed buffet was very noticeable. Although this had been perceptible with the lower-powered Sapphire and Avons the buffeting was now a significant problem and would affect the stability of the aircraft during high-level bombing. Furthermore the constant buffeting would stress the wing structure and shorten the aircraft's fatigue life.

To counteract this, trials took place in the summer of 1954 with various fixes on WD280 though none provided the answer. RAE Farnborough was called in and proposed a kinked leading edge to the wing and this was tested on WD280. As this was found to be effective the modification was adopted and produced for retrofit to the prototypes and for the initial production aircraft.

On 27 July 1954 while flying on low-speed manoeuvres VX777's rudder jammed hard left when recovering from a stall. Roly Falk decided to make an emergency landing

at Farnborough. The aircraft became very difficult to control but with the two right-hand engines at full power and the left-hand engines at flight idle Roly managed to sideslip onto the runway. The braking parachute only partly worked and the left brake jammed so the aircraft ran off the runway and the undercarriage collapsed. Roy Dobson was reportedly extremely angry about this accident, especially when Hawker Siddeley was in competition with Handley Page for the RAF bomber order. It took six months to repair VX777, which was very seriously damaged. Under different circumstances the aircraft might well have been declared a write-off but in competitive situations companies are loath to give their rivals any political advantage that could arise from the adverse publicity attending a write-off. In order to deflect adverse criticism, therefore, a company might expend significant resources on a lengthy and costly repair.

The first production aircraft XA889 flew in February 1955 and the second in August. Neither had the new leading edge, and though XA889 received it later XA890 never did. Roly Falk made an indelible impression at that year's Farnborough Air Show by 'rolling' XA890 in front of the crowds. However, three days later he was stopped from repeating this manoeuvre as the SBAC President Sir Arnold Hall, who was later the Chairman of Hawker Siddeley Group, forbade such showmanship.

Production

Almost the entire airframe was manufactured within the Hawker Siddeley Group. Avro had two principal facilities for its airframe production. The main works at Chadderton, between Manchester and Oldham,

RIGHT: **Vulcan prototypes VX777 and VX770 with the four surviving Avro 707s at the Farnborough Air Show on 11 September 1953. VX777 had only made its maiden flight on 2 September.** BAE Systems

BELOW: **VX770 being towed past the Farnborough control tower during the 1957 Air Show. It appeared at Farnborough five times with three different powerplants. In 1952 and 1953 powered by Rolls-Royce Avons, in 1954 with Armstrong-Siddeley Sapphires, in 1957 and 1958 powered by Rolls-Royce Conways. It crashed on 20 September 1958.** Peter Berry

The first production Vulcan B.1, XA899, which flew on 4 February 1955. It is seen here at Filton during development work on the Olympus engine. Author

constructed the main parts of the airframe. These were then taken by road to Woodford, some 10 miles south of Manchester for final assembly and flight test. The largest part of the aircraft was the centre section and to accommodate this there were numerous hinged lamp-posts on the ring road around Manchester and through Stockport. Avro's factory at Langar, Nottinghamshire manufactured the fins and rudders while another Hawker Siddeley Group company, Armstrong Whitworth in Coventry produced elevators and ailerons.

50,000 special tools were required to put the first Vulcan squadron into service, each aircraft consisting of 167,063 separate parts (excluding engines, nuts, bolts, rivets, etc.). A total of 39,500 drawings were required for the Vulcan project from the start of the 707 to completion of the Vulcan B.1. Refinement of the Vulcan B.1 did not end with the advent of the B.2 and twenty-nine were fitted with Electronic Counter-Measures (ECM) gear, including tail warning radar in a much enlarged rear fuselage, fairing and these were redesignated as B.1As.

Vulcan B.2

As deliveries of the B.1s were made to the RAF in 1955 plans were afoot to further develop the Vulcan and improve all areas of its operating envelope. As the power of the Bristol Olympus engines grew, Avro proposed a development of the Vulcan with the totally redesigned (Phase 2c) wing, which would avoid any recurrence of the buffet problem when even more powerful Olympus engines were fitted to the aircraft.

The span of the new wing was 12ft wider and its thickness/chord ratio was much reduced. This new 15 per cent larger wing removed the regular triangular shape of the original wing as its trailing edge was no longer perpendicular to the fuselage.

The B.2s were also to be fitted with more powerful Olympus 201s, elevons instead of separate ailerons and elevators, a Rover APU, strengthened undercarriage to cater for higher weights, active ECM equipment and improved systems. Understandably in order to benefit from this much improved aircraft the final seventeen B.1s on the production line were completed as B.2s.

In the late 1950s when the Cold War was at its height, development of the improved Vulcan and its new wing was paramount, so to expedite trials VX777, the original second prototype, was rebuilt to aerodynamically represent the B.2. It flew on 31 August 1957 just in time to appear at the Farnborough Air Show. VX777 was one of five Vulcans at the Show. The RAF sent two, while Avro had VX770 flying with Rolls-Royce Conways, the first B.1, XA899, and VX777. This was not the only earlier mark of Vulcan to be called upon to ease development of the B.2. Four B.1s were involved testing new marks of the Olympus, the ECM and other systems. These were joined by eight B.2s testing handling and performance, service release, radio and radar, armament, Blue Steel and engines.

Trials indicated a large improvement in performance over the B.1. The first production B.2 XH533 demonstrated a range increase of more than 25 per cent and reached over 60,000ft on trials, yet it was powered by the original 16,000lb thrust

Bristol Olympuses that were standard on the Vulcan B.1. The second B.2 had the higher powered Olympus 201s, which offered 17,000lb thrust. As the engine was still being developed and went on to power Concorde, the even more powerful Olympus 301 offering 20,000lb of thrust was fitted to approximately half of the B.2s manufactured. XH557, a Vulcan B.2, was loaned to Bristol Siddeley in 1961 and flew initially with two Olympus 201s and two 301s. The 301 caused surging problems as the Vulcan had not been designed for it and during tests it became clear for the 301's greater demands of air the intakes of Vulcans needed to be the slightly deepened.

Vulcan Engine Testbeds

Certain Vulcans were loaned to Bristol Siddeley and Rolls-Royce as engine testbeds to carry out trials on different engines of radically different versions of the Olympus. The prototype Vulcan VX770 was loaned to Rolls-Royce and became the first aircraft to take the Rolls-Royce Conway airborne. It broke up in mid-air and crashed during an air display at RAF Syerston on 20 September 1958.

Another Vulcan engine testbed that met with an unfortunate demise was a B.1, XA894. It was loaned to Bristol Siddeley to test the 30,610lb thrust Olympus 320s devised for the TSR2. XA894 was delivered to Filton in July 1960 for the installation of a test engine in a custom nacelle on the underside of the aircraft, giving it a grand total of five Olympuses – the four generic Olympuses and the TSR2 trial Olympus under its centre section. A894 made its maiden flight with a development version of the Olympus 320 in February 1962 and embarked on a test programme.

On 3 December 1962 XA894 was positioned for a full power run of the trial engine on the ground. As the engine was run up to full power there was a flash of light, an explosion and the crew swiftly exited the Vulcan as fuel poured out onto the tarmac

The Olympus 320 engine was selected for the BAC TSR2 low-level strike aircraft and a test engine was installed in a custom nacelle on the underside of Vulcan XA894 giving it a grand total of five Olympuses – the four generic Olympuses and the TSR2 trial Olympus under its centre section. XA894 is seen here making a low pass at the 1962 Farnborough Air Show. Rolls-Royce Historical Trust

RIGHT: On 3 December 1962, during a full-power run on the ground of the TSR2 trial engine under the Vulcan Olympus testbed XA894, the engine exploded, fuel poured out and ignited, even setting fire to a new fire engine watching over the engine test. The explosion was caused by a low-pressure turbine disc that had shot out of the engine, travelled round the bomb bay puncturing the fuel tanks, bounced down on the ground, sending shrapnel through the wing fuel tank before careering across the airfield. Rolls-Royce Historical Trust

BELOW: Vulcan B.2 XH557 landing Filton in August 1961 during Olympus 301 trials. The Olympus 301 provided 20, 000lb of thrust and was installed in approximately half of the B.2s built. In service it was normally derated to 18,000lb. Author's collection

and ignited, even setting fire to a new fire engine positioned to watch over the engine test. The Vulcan then burned for several hours, creating a huge pall of dense, black smoke, which rose high into air above Bristol. The incident was caused by a low pressure turbine disc, which had shot out of the engine, travelled round the bomb bay puncturing the fuel tanks, and then bounced down on the ground, sending shrapnel through the wing fuel tank before careering across the airfield. From then until the maiden flight of the TSR2 at Boscombe Down in September 1964 all Olympus 320 testing was ground based.

As with the TSR2 Olympus an Avro Vulcan was selected to trial the Olympus 593 for Concorde together with the sophisticated engine intake in a nacelle similar to that destined for Concorde. On Concorde the Olympuses were mounted in twin nacelles

under each wing, but on the Vulcan testbed a specialist half-nacelle was fabricated underneath the bomb bay. Following a lengthy installation XA903 flew at Filton on 9 September 1966, the first occasion on which the Olympus 593 had been aloft and well prior to Concorde's maiden flight.

Following its tests with the Olympus 593 for Concorde, XA903 was called on to test the RB199 for the Panavia Tornado. The prototype engine made its first flight from Filton in April 1973 in XA903 in an accurately designed ventral nacelle representing the half fuselage of the Tornado. XA903 was unique amongst Vulcans as the ventral nacelle was even equipped with an accurately positioned Mauser 27mm cannon as installed on the Tornado so that gun gas ingestion trials could be carried out. The firing trials were carried out on the ground and, contrary to some sources, also in the air.

The Vulcan in RAF Service

The first production Vulcan XA899 was delivered for preliminary acceptance trials at Boscombe Down in March 1956. Range with a 10,000lb bomb load was 1,500nm, although performance was not fully satisfactory as engine power limited the operating ceiling at Mach 0.85 to 43,000ft and navigational and bombing systems serviceability was initially poor. However, the Vulcan was released for service and the first Vulcan squadrons were Nos 83 and 101 formed in 1957 with No. 617, the famous 'Dambuster' unit following the year after. These Vulcans then began to 'fly the flag' all over the world.

The RAF decided that No. 83 Sqn should be the first B.2 unit so its B.1s were passed to No. 10 Sqn. No. 27 and 617 followed suit passing their B.1s on. Squadrons new to the Vulcan that received the B.2 were Nos 9, 12 and 35 and by 1967 all the Vulcan units had B.2s and no B.1s remained in front line use. As there was little likelihood by the late 1950s that the RAF's V-bombers could successfully fly deep over enemy territory without interception, Avro had been contracted to design a strategic nuclear missile called Blue Steel (see Chapter 11) to be air launched by Vulcans and Victors. Valiants, Vulcans and Victors were all involved in Blue Steel trials at Woodford and at Woomera in Australia. Until the time when Blue Steel became fully operational the V-bombers would have dispersed to thirty-six airfields in the UK primed to be airborne within less than four minutes to attack Soviet airbases. During the Cuban missile crisis in 1962 the Vulcans and Victors were ready and armed, waiting to go at the RAF bases. The Vulcans had a limited operational capability with Blue Steel from 1963 and gradually other Vulcan and Victor squadrons were armed with it and its serviceability and reliability improved. Thankfully it was never used in anger and with the introduction of the Navy's nuclear Polaris submarines into service the nuclear deterrent became their responsiblity and the last Vulcan squadrons ceased to carry it from the end of 1970.

Before adopting the American Polaris missile system the British Government had been planning to develop the de Havilland/ Hawker Siddeley Blue Streak strategic missile programme and place these in silos around the UK (see Chapter 11). In April 1960 the Government cancelled this programme claiming that its huge cost and apparent vulnerability made it a poor choice. Talks had already taken place with the US Government about purchase of the Douglas Skybolt air-launched nuclear missile programme and agreement was reached that the UK could purchase them.

Hawker Siddeley quickly pressed ahead with the Ministry of Defence to develop the Vulcan B.2 as the Skybolt's primary launch vehicle ahead of Handley Page whose Victor was probably unsuitable for the task and BAC, which proposed a version of the VC10. Hawker Siddeley was instructed to strengthen the wings of the sixty-first aircraft on the line onwards with underwing hard points to be able to carry the American weapon. Trials took place with the dummy Skybolts mounted on XH537, XH538 and XL391. Whereas Blue Steel in its semi-recessed position under the fuselage had caused no aerodynamic difficulties, the two large Skybolts when mounted under the Vulcan's wings had some effect. Take-off with them was fine but on landing the two missiles and their pylons acted like endplates trapping the air and making it float, so pilots had to push the Vulcan down. Landing with just one missile was fine but during the take-off run the Vulcan needed substantial amounts of rudder to keep it straight. However, just as trials were proceeding the US Government cancelled the programme owing to its costs and poor performance during trials. Though the programme was offered to the UK, this offer was not accepted and submarine-launched Polaris missiles became the British nuclear weapon. If Skybolt had been adopted it is very likely the development of the Vulcan

would have proceeded beyond the B.2 to a larger B.3, so production ended on 21 December 1964 with the first flight of the eighty-ninth and last B.2, XH657.

In 1964 the Vulcans had to alter their mode of attack with Blue Steel as high altitude ceased to offer any invulnerability following the shooting down of a Lockheed U-2 reconnaissance aircraft over the USSR in 1962. The Vulcans would approach the target at low level, climbing briefly to launch the Blue Steel, which would climb to 17,000ft, accelerate to Mach 2 and attack

the target. For this low-level mode of attack they were fitted with terrain-avoidance radar in the extreme nose and passive ECM equipment in a rectangular fairing on the top of the fin. They also lost their virginal white and were camouflaged.

With the end of Blue Steel operations sixty Vulcans were maintained in service as strategic bombers. With the withdrawal of the Victor B(SR).2s for conversion to tankers in 1974 eight Vulcans were deputed to take over their task and were redesignated as Vulcan B.2 (MRR), for maritime

Vulcan B.2 XH539 carrying a Blue Steel missile in August 1961. It performed the first live firing of a Blue Steel at Woomera on 12 December 1961. BAE Systems

A camouflaged Vulcan B.2 carrying Blue Steel. BAE Systems

radar and reconnaissance. From then on the Vulcan squadrons were gradually run down as they were to be replaced by Tornados with the last squadrons expected to be disbanded in June 1982.

Black Buck – the Longest Bombing Mission in History

When Argentina invaded the Falkland Islands on 2 April 1982 there appeared little chance that the British could dislodge them. The only immediate possibility for Operation *Corporate* was for a Naval Task Force to set sail, but there was no expectation of bombing missions by land-based units as

RIGHT: **XH538 on trials from Woodford with two Douglas Skybolt missiles. As the Skybolt missile system was cancelled by the USA, the project went no further.** BAE Systems

BELOW: **XM575 flying over RAF Scampton with seven Vulcans on the ground.** BAE Systems

the nearest friendly landfall was on Ascension Island, more than 4,500 miles from the Falklands. However, Ascension was suitable as a staging post for the task force and had a USAF base there at Wideawake Airfield with a long runway.

While the Task Force mounted operations against the enemy in the vicinity of the Falklands the RAF determined to raid the islands and attack Port Stanley airfield with its Vulcans. Meanwhile back at RAF Waddington ten Vulcans had their flight refuelling systems reactivated and of these five, all with Olympus 301s and the Skybolt pylon attachments, were prepared for a conventional bombing mission. New inertial navigation systems were trialled and integrated while in-flight refuelling was hurriedly practised by day and by night with Victors and a radar jamming pod was mounted on one of the underwing pylons. XM598 and XM607 departed for Ascension on 29 April, refuelled in the air by Victors.

The following day a huge operation – Operation *Black Buck* – ensued to get one Vulcan to be able drop twenty-one 1,000lb bombs on Port Stanley airfield. Just before midnight the two Vulcans with their fuel tanks and bomb bays fully laden taxied out to take off accompanied by four Victors. XM598, the Vulcan chosen to lead the raid had a technical problem so it returned to Wideawake and its place was taken by XM607. During the long flight to the Falklands XM607 had to refuel from Victors six times, once more than scheduled as fuel consumption was greater than calculated.

The Woodford production line in May 1982 with three Vulcans, including XM571, being converted to K.2 tankers. Nearer to the camera are four Nimrod MR.2s. BAE Systems

A total of eleven Victors had to refuel each other and the Vulcan to get it to the target. Descending to just 250ft for the bombing run the twenty-one bombs were dropped over Port Stanley airfield and XM607 quickly climbed away and set course for Wideawake but short of fuel. Fortunately it rendezvoused with a Victor and was able to return safely.

The results of the raid were satisfactory, though the runway was still usable by Hercules and lighter aircraft. Some say it served as a deterrent to the placing of Argentine jets there. Of the six further *Black Bucks* planned, two were aborted and the other five were bombing or anti-radar attacks. One of these anti-radar operations, *Black Buck 6*, had the added complication that the Vulcan broke its refuelling probe on the way back to Wideawake and had to divert to Rio de Janeiro. The crew and XM597 were returned after nine days.

There has been much debate as to the effectiveness of the raids, their actual effect and their propaganda value, but the performance of the crews, the Vulcans and the Victors cannot be belittled.

The Vulcan's Final Role

After the Falkland Islands had been liberated from Argentina most of the RAF units, including the Vulcans, returned home. Now there seemed little need for the Vulcans any more despite their valiant deeds. However, as the Victor K.2s had been overworked during Operation *Corporate* there was an urgent need for more tanker capacity. Nine VC10 tankers were still being converted at Filton but additional aerial

The underside of the Vulcan K.2s was painted in white with red markings to assist aircraft refuelling from them. Avro Heritage

tanking capacity was paramount and it was decided that the Vulcan would fit the bill. So much so that after initial discussions on 30 April, the go ahead was given just a few days later on 4 May 1982.

It was decided to install a Hose Drum Unit (HDU) in the rear ECM bay when installation in the bomb bay was found to be unsuitable. As the bomb bay was not going to be used, a third bomb bay fuel tank could also be fitted giving the Vulcan an overall fuel capacity of 100,000lb. Six Vulcans were converted at Woodford; XH558, '560, '561, XJ825, XL445 and XM571. They flew with No.50 Squadron until the end of March 1984 when they were replaced by newly-rebuilt VC10 tankers.

Following the disbandment of No.50 Squadron XH558 and XL426 remained there as part of the station flight. XH558 was kept in use by the RAF for display flying until 1992 when it was delivered to Bruntingthorpe. However, the Vulcan to the Sky Trust was formed and through a huge amount of public and company support it took to the air again fifteen years later. It has appeared at many air displays to the

great joy of many since then, but whether it will be able to do so in the future is open to question.

Conclusion

Of the three V-bombers, the Vickers Valiant, Handley Page Victor and the Avro Vulcan, it was the Vulcan that remained longest in the bombing role. The Valiant was an earlier and more conventional aircraft, the Victor though a revolutionary aircraft with a fine performance did not have the structure to withstand the low-level role the V-bombers later had to adopt.

For Avro and Hawker Siddeley the Vulcan meant many years of hard work with production starting in 1950 and continuing until 1965. However, in the years following not only was there the production of spares but Vulcans regularly returned to Woodford for update and modification for additional roles, such as its final service task as an aerial tanker for which the work was only completed in 1982.

The Avro 698 Vulcan was a momentous leap forward, for Avro's preceding bomber had been the conventional Lincoln; with the Vulcan the company made a huge technological leap forward and produced a mighty bomb platform, which saw action in the twilight of its days and in the most challenging of circumstances.

The Victor K.2 Conversion Programme

The first of the three British V-bombers to act in the tanking role was the earliest of them, the Vickers Valiant. However, the Valiant's use in this role was cut short owing to wing spar fatigue, and they were replaced

by a conversion of the Handley Page Victor B.1, carried out by the makers of the Victor at their Hertfordshire factory in Radlett.

Following the success of the Victor K.1 tanker an obvious candidate for an even better and more powerful tanker was with the Conway-powered Victor B.2. With the end of the Vulcan's and Victor's strategic role in delivering the Blue Steel nuclear stand-off bomb the Vulcan B.2s with their superior low-level performance moved onto strategic conventional bombing. The Victors, despite their ability to carry more bombs, were not suited to low-level operations and were earmarked for conversion into tankers. Handley Page received a contract to design the work needed for conversion and twenty Victor B.2s flew in to Radlett for storage in late 1968. However, by that time Handley Page was in a parlous financial state, having run up huge costs on the Jetstream programme and no conversion contract was offered by the MoD as the Ministry was uncertain as to how long the firm could survive.

On Monday 2 March 1970 the Handley Page factories at Radlett were closed and the company's 2,500-strong work force, with the exception of about 200 essential personnel, was dismissed. That month the Ministry acted and Victor jigs were moved to Woodford while the first Victor XL188 flew in there in March. (In the early 1960s HS had bid to buy Handley Page but were unable to agree terms – *see* Chapter Two.) In the interim HS was tasked with spares support for all Victors and Handley Page Hastings in the RAF, though it was not until the following year that this was contractually finalized along with the go ahead to rebuild the Victors as three-point tankers. Following the Victors from Radlett, one more came from St Athan in 1972 and three from Wyton in 1974.

Specification – Vulcan B.2	
Length	99ft 11in (30.45m)
Wingspan	111ft (33.83m)
Height	27ft 1in (8.25m)
MTOW	195,000lb (88,450kg)
Max speed	Mach 0.93
Range	5,500 miles (8,850 km) with 10,000lb (4,500kg) load
Crew	5
Powerplant	4 × Bristol Siddeley Olympus 301, 20,000lb thrust
Armament	Nuclear/conventional bombs, Blue Steel missile, Shrike anti-radar missile

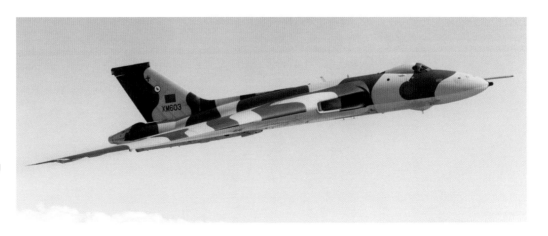

On 10 August 1982 XM603 returned to Woodford for preservation. Following the site's closure in 2011, its future looked uncertain but it is now to be refurbished as part of the Avro Heritage Centre. BAE Systems

The Tanker Conversion Programme

The tanker conversion was a major task, which Hawker Siddeley tackled in their own way, not following Handley Page's modification plan and deciding to rig the ailerons upwards by 3 degrees and reduce the wingspan by 3ft on each side.

The programme required changes involving the removal of all bombing and ECM equipment and structural work to strengthen the wing structure damaged in the previous low-level operations and increase the wing skin thickness in some places. Two underwing pylons were fitted with fuel hose drum units together with a retractable unit in the rear fuselage. The main refurbishment was handled at Woodford while the Chadderton and Bitteswell factories worked on the programme as well.

The Victor K.2 'prototype' XL231 with the aerodynamic alterations but otherwise only partially rebuilt flew in March 1972 and went through extensive trials at Woodford and Boscombe Down. The first fully modified K.2 flew in May 74 and was followed by twenty-three others with the last delivery in June 1978, including XL231, which had returned to the production line and had a full programme of modifications.

It is fortuitous that the Victors were modified to this role when full consideration is given to their remarkable service in the Falklands War with Argentina. There has been a greater than proportional amount of publicity given to the Vulcan's bombing missions, but the Victors had to fly great distances, refuel themselves and the Vulcans on those missions. Besides all their other refuelling tasks they were even engaged in reconnaissance flights. The Victor K.2s were the final V-bomber to remain in service and before their swansong in 1993 they had a large role to play in Operation *Desert Storm* supporting the RAF's operations.

ABOVE: Handley Page Victor K.2s on the production line at Woodford in June 1975 with XL188 at the front. HS748s and Nimrods are also visible.
BAE Systems

BELOW: Victor K.2 XL189 trailing all its flight refuelling hoses.
BAE Systems

CHAPTER THIRTEEN

Buccaneers and Phantoms at Brough

Blackburn Aircraft

Blackburn Aeroplane and Motor Co. set up a factory at Brough, Yorkshire on the Humber Estuary in 1916 for the final assembly of aircraft built at its Leeds factory. From its beginning the company was predominantly a manufacturer of seaplanes or land planes for the Royal Navy. It survived the post-First World War slump and during the Second World War built Navy attack aircraft such as the Blackburn Skua and Firebrand and Fairey Swordfishes and Short Sunderlands. In 1948 Blackburn expanded and took over General Aircraft of Feltham, Middlesex, becoming Blackburn & General Aircraft. With this move it inherited the GAL60 Universal Freighter, which was developed into the Blackburn Beverley for the RAF. Though primarily an airframe manufacturer the firm also manufactured small aero-engines and agricultural implements.

By late 1959 the directors of Blackburn Aircraft knew that they would have to join one of the larger groupings if they were to continue to exist. The Government's diktat had indicated that only those firms that were members of the two large groups would receive Government contracts or subsidy. As it was apparent that the Vickers-English Electric grouping that became the British Aircraft Corporation had little interest in them they opened talks with Hawker Siddeley where they felt they could maintain some autonomy, as this had previously been the case with the Group's companies. Unaware of Hawker Siddeley's negotiations with de Havilland, in early December Hawker Siddeley's bid for the ownership of the Blackburn Group was accepted. Subsequently the Blackburn management heard of Hawker Siddeley's bid for de Havilland and the directors realized that they would now have even less influence within the Group.

Initially Blackburn maintained some autonomy, but in October 1960 Sir Roy Dobson, Vice-Chairman and Managing Director of Hawker Siddeley, became Chairman of Blackburn Aircraft. On 1 July

A Blackburn Beverley flying over the company's headquarters in May 1957. BAE Systems

1963 Hawker Siddeley Aviation (HSA) was established as the parent body of the many aircraft firms within the Group and the firm became part of HSA's Hawker Blackburn Division. Less than two years later, on 1 April 1965, the historic names vanished and the Hawker Blackburn Division was henceforward the Kingston-Brough Division.

The Buccaneer

In August 1952 the Royal Navy issued requirement NA39 for a high subsonic speed twin-seat, twin-jet, carrier-borne strike aircraft intended to be able to penetrate beneath an enemy's radar cover in order to deliver nuclear or conventional weapons in all weathers. The threat was seen as coming from any escalation in the Cold War resulting in Soviet Navy attacks upon Britain's merchant fleet, then the largest in the world. To operate from the Royal Navy's aircraft carriers the maximum

weight was limited to 40,000lb and its dimensions were constrained by the need to fit the lifts and hangers.

Hawker Siddeley's subsidiary Armstrong Whitworth, and other companies, Blackburn, Fairey, Shorts and Westland, were all invited to tender. Late in the day another Hawker Siddeley subsidiary, Hawker was added to the list. However, Blackburn's proposal prevailed and in February 1955 the company was given the go-ahead.

The whole airframe was specifically designed for long life, despite the heavy stresses caused by continuous low-level flying. Extensive use was made of integrally machined panels, and the design of fuselage was dictated by area-ruling avoiding abrupt changes in contours and giving a 'waisted' effect. Pilot and navigator sat in tandem between the two 7,100lb thrust de Havilland Gyron Junior turbojets. The wings were moderately swept as was the 'T' tail. Weapons were carried internally on a large, quick rotating bomb door, which gave a good aero shape open or closed, and also on four underwing pylons. A wide variety of conventional and nuclear weapons could be carried but there were no guns. Navigational and aiming equipment included a special bombing, terrain-clearance and ground-mapping radar developed by Ferranti, a Doppler radar, radio altimeter, navigation computers with pictorial presentation and extensive radio equipment.

The NA39 had a number of features that were designed to ensure good handling at low speeds. The wing leading-edge, flaps and underside of the slab tailplane were blown by high-pressure bleed air to achieve

the performance necessary for carrier operation. In order to reduce residual thrust when the engines were operating at high power to provide bleed air on approach to landing, the complete fuselage tailcone split open to form large airbrakes.

The NA39 was a large aircraft and as it had to fit the RN's aircraft carriers' lifts and hangars, it had wings that folded upwards by 120 degrees, a folding nose and a dual purpose 'clamshell' tailcone that folded outwards to fit the restricted carrier dimensions and also acted as an airbrake. All of these features added to the aircraft's weight and complexity.

Flight Testing

The first of twenty development aircraft, XK486 was completed at Brough and carried out engine runs in February 1958. As Brough's runway was far too short for the NA39's testing, Blackburn reactivated a former Bomber Command airfield in the East Riding of Yorkshire at Holme-on-Spalding Moor for development flying activities. To simulate aircraft carrier conditions, arrestor gear and a mirror landing system was fitted at both ends of the operational runway.

As it was felt that even Holme's main 6,000ft runway might prove too short, the maiden flight was made from RAE Bedford, which possessed one of the longest runways in the UK at 11,000ft, and in April XK486 was transported there. During lengthy taxi trials prior to the first flight one of the tyres

LEFT: **The first, second and fifth Buccaneers, XK486, XK487 and XK490.** BAE Systems

BELOW: **Though at the time of the Farnborough Air Show in 1959 Blackburn was still an independent company, that was about to change. Perhaps foretelling what was to come Buccaneer XK490 was placed next to two Hawker Siddeley aircraft – Gloster Javelin FAW.8 XJ125 and Avro Vulcan B.2 XH536.** BAE Systems

burst and the air under high pressure caused serious damage to the inner wing. However, the Blackburn engineers at Bedford 'pulled out all the stops' and managed to have the aircraft ready to fly on 30 April 1958. So that day Blackburn's Chief Test Pilot, Derek Whitehead, took XK486 up for a 42-minute flight. After three months at Bedford the first XK486 flew to Holme-on-Spalding Moor in East Yorkshire. As flight tests were carried out and checked, the aircraft's parameters were extended. The subsequent development machines were completed at Brough and then towed backwards to Holme, a distance of 16 miles, on their own wheels with wings folded (an advantage accruing from the Naval design), and almost ready to fly. At Holme the aircraft was fitted with arrestor gear installations at both ends of the runway used by the NA39, which can be used either on landing or to prevent overshooting.

Gradually other development aircraft flew; the second trialling aerodynamics, the third for developing the de Havilland Gyron Junior engines. It crashed spectacularly into greenhouses at the end of the Hatfield runway when it failed to get airborne in July 1961, fortunately without injury to anyone. The following year, when Lightning XG332 caught fire and the controls jammed on approach, the test pilot ejected and landed in the same greenhouses.

The other development aircraft were allotted other tasks involving systems, armament handling, aircraft carrier clearance trials, for which early in 1960 two NA39s completed thirty take-offs and landings from HMS *Victorious* in weather conditions varying between gale and flat calm. From its dull nomenclature as the NA39 in

August 1960 it graduated to an inspiring name: the Buccaneer.

By the end of 1961 all twenty development aircraft were airborne. Though the third aircraft XK488 was rebuilt after hitting the Hatfield greenhouses, other development aircraft and crew were not so fortunate. The fifth development batch machine, XK490, was the first Buccaneer to be lost in October 1959 when it stalled at 10,000ft, entered a spin from which it could not recover and both crew members were killed. XK486 crashed after an instrument failure in July 1960 but the crew safely ejected. While engaged in catapult launch trials in August 1961 on HMS *Hermes* the thirteenth aircraft, XK529, stalled and crashed into the sea with the loss of the two crew.

Selling the Buccaneer

Although designed and tasked specifically for operation from aircraft carriers, the NA39 had an obvious capability as a land-based tactical strike aircraft, and the

manufacturers made many presentations to both the RAF and foreign governments. The RAF wanted a larger, supersonic strike aircraft and were disenchanted by the poor performance of the S.1, where the much improved S.2 would have been worthy of more consideration. The Buccaneer's export potential was held back by the RAF's lack of interest. In contrast, the German Navy took a great deal of initial interest, first expressed in 1960 with a demonstration in Germany in September 1961, but no order was forthcoming and the Navy copied the German Air Force by ordering Lockheed F-104 Starfighters. However, the Buccaneer did win one export order when in October 1962 the South African Air Force placed an order for an undisclosed number, which later proved to be sixteen. However, when South Africa attempted to place a repeat order for a further sixteen, the Labour Government refused an export licence owing to the international sanctions against the country at that time.

In the late 1960s Hawker Siddeley's Buccaneer marketing strategy was to identify

ABOVE: **XK489 and a XK488 on their way to the Farnborough Air Show 1960, by which time Blackburn Aircraft was part of the Hawker Siddeley Group.** Author

LEFT: **Six of the twenty development batch aircraft at Holme-on-Spalding-Moor in mid-1961. Nearest to the camera, XK525, then XK524, XK489, XK523, XK487 and XK488.** BAE Systems

and make presentations to operators of the English Electric Canberra who were seeking a replacement. Though many presentations were made no sales were made.

The Buccaneer S.1 in Royal Navy Service

Initial clearance for service operation was given in July 1961 and No. 700Z Sqn was formed with XK531–536 as the Buccaneer intensive trials unit in August 1961. The first operational RN squadron, No. 801 Squadron, was commissioned in July 1962 and embarked in HMS *Ark Royal* in February 1963. In January 1963 No. 801 Sqn was formed, and No. 809 later that year.

All these units' land base was at RNAS Lossiemouth, Moray in Scotland.

The Buccaneer S.1 was underpowered, particularly when 10 per cent of the power from the Gyron Juniors engines was drained off for the boundary layer control system. One major drawback to this lack of power limited the use of the Buccaneer as it could not take off with a full fuel load. To maintain its operational effectiveness the Buccaneer S.1 was launched from the aircraft carrier with a partial fuel load and then refuelled by a Supermarine Scimitar configured as a tanker. This was a totally unsatisfactory arrangement and had the Buccaneer S.2 not been developed then the aircraft's life would have been very limited. Only twenty development aircraft and forty S.1s were built,

and by the end of the 1960s the survivors had been relegated to training status. All were withdrawn from use at the end of 1970.

The Buccaneer S.2

The manufacturer was only too aware that the Gyron Junior's performance was marginal and that even a much improved version of that engine would not provide the increase in range needed. But Rolls-Royce had had a potent offering with a military version of the Spey already selected for the Trident and the One-Eleven airliners. The Spey offered far more thrust, 11,380lb for a small increase in weight. In addition the engine could fit through the existing spars, though the intakes would need to be enlarged.

Two of the development batch, XK526 and 527, were chosen for conversion to become the Spey-powered S.2 prototypes. Work commenced in November 1962 and Derek Whitehead, Chief Test Pilot at Holme-on-Spalding Moor, took XK526 into the air for a 70min maiden flight from Holme to RAE Bedford on 17 May 1963. The second S.2 prototype XK527 flew in August the same year. Sensibly the last ten S.1s on the Brough production line were completed as S.2s and several of those took part in the S.2 test programme. Several further detail improvements were made to the equipment fix, and the wingtips were given small extensions, which improved range though caused fatigue problems later.

In April 1965 XK526 completed its deck landing and catapult trials on HMS *Ark Royal* in one week instead of two. The Buccaneer was launched from the catapult, using a tested and successful hands-off technique with the tailplane in a neutral position and with various internal and external loads at its full gross weight. The Navy's Buccaneer S.2 Intensive Flying Trials Unit No. 700B was formed the same month. This was not the end of the type's trials, other British aircraft carrier and American aircraft carriers tests took place to allow for greater flexibility of operation. After the initial ten Buccaneer S.1s completed as S.2s, further contracts followed in a rather piecemeal fashion until the final number of Spey Buccaneers built for the Navy was eighty-two.

As the Intensive Flying Trials Unit was disbanded in October 1965, No. 801 Sqn was commissioned, closely followed by No. 809 Sqn formed at the beginning of 1966 and embarking on HMS *Hermes*. No. 800

XK489 being launched from a catapult on HMS *Victorious* during carrier trials in the English Channel in January 1960. Derek Whitehead

First flight of the Buccaneer S.2 XK526 from Holme-on-Spalding-Moor. XK526 was rebuilt from a Buccaneer S.1. BAE Systems

followed and served with HMS *Eagle*. The Navy found the greater power and equipment refinements provided a far superior aircraft to the earlier S.1. However, the aircraft's career with the Navy was very limited as owing to defence cuts the aircraft carriers were gradually scrapped. The Navy only used its Buccaneers in 'anger' once when they bombed the oil tanker *Torrey Canyon* on 18 March 1967 after it went aground on the Seven Sisters Reef between the Scilly Isles and Lands End. The Government ordered the Navy and the RAF to bomb the vessel and ignite the oil to avoid an ecological disaster. Attacks on the stricken vessel by the Buccaneers were very effective with forty-two 1,000lb bombs dropped of which thirty hit, some going down the ship's funnel. Hunters and Sea Vixens kept the fires burning by using napalm and rockets. Eventually, under this combined bombardment, the tanker sank and the oil slick diminished to a trickle.

The Buccaneer gave the Navy a powerful tool that could attack targets at high speed and low level, sweeping in below the

LEFT: **Final assembly of a Royal Navy S.2 at Brough.** BAE Systems

BELOW: **Royal Navy Buccaneer S.2s on HMS *Hermes*.** Derek Whitehead

An RN Buccaneer S.2 parked on a carrier's deck. Derek Whitehead

radar accurately tracking targets with its effective Blue Parrot radar, automatically releasing its weapons at the optimum moment. There were also more conventional means of bombing, for example in a shallow dive or toss bombing. Its ability to flight-refuel other aircraft added to its operational flexibility. Though it had no defensive armament during its time in the Senior Service it was built strongly enough to escape at high speed at low level and could evade attackers by opening its an airbrake which it could slow the aircraft down from 560 knots to 160 knots very quickly so that potential attackers would overshoot.

The Aircraft Cancellations of 1965

In February 1965 the Government cancelled contracts for two Hawker Siddeley aircraft that were then under development; the HS 681 tactical airlifter and the HS P1154 V/STOL supersonic attack aircraft. These cancellations struck the Group seriously and resulted in redundancies and plant closure. Brough was affected as it had been engaged in design work for the P1154. However, there was compensation as the Government ordered the Harrier, so the plant was involved in design work and later in production of its wings and fuselages for more than thirty years. As part of this Government strategy American-built Phantoms were also ordered for the RAF and Hawker Siddeley Brough was to benefit from this very much.

In April the Government cancelled a further project, the BAC TSR2, which caused serious problems for the British Aircraft Corporation. In its place the Government took out an option on fifty American General Dynamics F-111Ks, which was made into a definite order in February 1966. During the period between the placing of the option and the order BAC acted with alacrity and proposed a version of the Mirage 4A nuclear strike bomber. Hawker Siddeley countered with the Buccaneer 2*, a much improved version of the aircraft employing some of the systems developed for the TSR2. A plethora of spurious reasons were proffered as to why neither the Buccaneer nor Spey-Mirage proposed by BAC would do. Although the F-111K order was placed, the whole sorry saga was brought to a close in January 1968 when the Government cancelled it, incurring sizeable cancellation charges. The Government cited rising costs and a significant degradation in performance estimates as justification for this cancellation.

To extricate themselves from this mess, in July 1968 the MoD announced that the Canberra would stay in service and that the RAF, which had rejected the Buccaneer as a candidate for TSR2 specification, would now inherit sixty-four from the Fleet Air Arm made redundant by the scrapping of the aircraft carrier fleet along with twenty-six newly-built aircraft. This was an interim measure to reduce the gap in Britain's strike/reconnaissance capability following the F-111 cancellation. This 'interim measure' continued until 1994 when the Buccaneer

was replaced by the Tornado. Value of the new order was about £26m (2013 = £382m) of which about two-thirds went directly to Hawker Siddeley; the remainder went to Rolls-Royce for the engines and to equipment suppliers.

South Africa's Buccaneer

The sixteen Buccaneer S.50s ordered by the South African Air Force in 1962 were part of a much larger Simonstown Agreement. As the aircraft were being constructed in Brough in November 1964 the Prime Minster Harold Wilson announced that the Labour Government would agree to the delivery of the aircraft to South Africa but that no further orders would be accepted.

The South African Government lobbied hard for sixteen more aircraft to be delivered but the Labour Government would not be swayed as it was felt that the aircraft could be used to enforce the Republic's universally condemned apartheid policy. In 1967 the Group Board's report commented that the Labour Government's refusal to grant a further export order to South Africa of these sixteen Buccaneers had resulted in redundancies at Brough.

All sixteen aircraft were given British 'B' class registrations for test flying at Holme, G-2-1 to G-2-16. Their South African registrations were 411 to 426. The first S.50 flew in January 1965 and along with the second aircraft trialled the armament and special equipment for this variant. These special features included much larger underwing tanks than those fitted to the RN's aircraft and twin Bristol Siddeley BS605 Stentor rockets fitted in the lower rear fuselage to boost take-off performance in 'hot and high' conditions, but they proved unnecessary and in later years they were removed.

Training was handled by the South African Air Force's No. 24 Sqn at Lossiemouth and the first eight aircraft left on delivery by air in October 1965, but one crashed en route and the Labour Government refused to allow a replacement. The remaining eight machines were cocooned after test flying at Holme and shipped from Hull to Cape Town. The South African Buccaneers were based at Waterkloof, Pretoria and were frequently engaged in operations during their twenty-two years of service, twice bombing wrecked oil tankers off the coast or attacking insurgents into Namibia and South Africa.

LEFT: **The first of sixteen Buccaneer S.50s for the South African Air Force, temporarily registered G-2-1.** BAE Systems

BELOW: **A South African Buccaneer testing Nord AS30 missiles.** BAE Systems

BOTTOM: **Four of the second batch of eight Buccaneers for the South African Air Force on a South African freighter at Hull. To protect them from the salt water they were cocooned for the journey.** BAE Systems

The RAF Orders the Buccaneer

The Royal Navy's contracts had been fulfilled with completion of the 160th aircraft in December 1968 so the Government's decision to order the twenty-six Buccaneer S.2Bs for the RAF in October 1968 was fortuitous. The twenty-six came too late to ensure continuity in production as the line had just closed, so the order provided long-term prospects for work at Brough rather than an increase in the workforce, but increased the unit cost.

In parallel with this new production, a refurbishment programme at Brough converted some sixty-four ex-Royal Navy Buccaneer S.2As to RAF standards. The initial batch of these refurbished aircraft was delivered to the RAF in October 1969 and the first new S.2B flew in January 1970. Further orders kept the Hawker Siddeley Brough production line busy, for seventeen more aircraft ordered in October 1971 and two batches of three were ordered later, the first three as attrition replacements and the second three for trials purposes by the research establishments. These orders prolonged the production life to the end of 1977, by when 209 had built.

Hawker Siddeley Brough made a number of proposals to the RAF for major improvements to the aircraft but only a few of them were accepted due to budgetary considerations. The majority of ex-Royal Navy Buccaneer S.2As transferred to the RAF were ultimately modified to full S.2B standard with the ability to carry the Martel TV-guided air-to-surface missile and incorporating the bomb door fuel tank modification specifically requested by the RAF. This added another 425gal to the existing fuel capacity and gave a pronounced bulge on the Buccaneer's underbelly. As the RAF Buccaneers were not constrained by the

limitations of aircraft carrier operation they could operate at a gross weight of 59,000lb compared to the 45,000lb limit for RN, but this necessitated the strengthening of the undercarriage.

The first RAF unit formed was No.12 Sqn at Honington, Suffolk in October 1969.

Its role was maritime strike in the North Atlantic and North Sea, a task hitherto handled by the Fleet Air Arm. As the Navy had lost their aircraft the RAF was now tasked with Fleet support and attack and had to adjust to this new maritime role. Six months later the first new-build aircraft

LEFT: **An RAF S.2 firing Matra rockets.**
BAE Systems

BELOW: **RAF Buccaneer S.2 XV356 swooping very low over the hangars at Holme-on-Spalding-Moor.**
BAE Systems

at Lossiemouth. Weapons employed included the TV-guided and Anti-radar versions of Martel and the Paveway laser-guided system used to guide bombs onto target. It was recognized that this weapons suite was insufficient, so forty-two aircraft were earmarked for modification to carry the BAe Dynamics Sea Eagle and host of other improvements to keep the aircraft viable into the 1990s. As Brough was fully occupied with Harrier and Hawk work, the aircraft flew into the former Hawker Siddeley factory airfield at Woodford and were converted there by workers from Brough.

Gulf War and Finale

Following Saddam Hussein's invasion of Kuwait in 1990 and the instigation of Operation *Desert Shield*, the RAF deployed Tornados and Jaguars in the strike role. When the Tornados were needed to attack infrastructure in Iraq there was a problem as the TIALD (Thermal Imaging Airborne Laser Designator) targeting pod that illuminated the target was still under development for them. At short notice, twelve Buccaneers of Nos 12 and 208 Sqns were deployed to support the Tornados with their Paveway system and laser-guided bombs. Additionally they carried ECM (Electronic Counter-Measures) pods and as a first received defensive weaponry in the form of one Sidewinder missile. 212 sorties were flown and at the end of the war the aircraft returned to the UK in desert pink camouflage and with their 'gung ho' markings. Over the remaining three years of their service life, numbers gradually dwindled though the popularity of this great aircraft grew. In 31 March 1994 they were withdrawn from service. As a tribute to Brough's great aircraft, in a unique operation Buccaneer XV168 flew into the airfield, the only time one ever landed there, and it remains on display at the factory.

The Phantoms of Brough and Holme

McDonnell Douglas Phantoms were originally purchased for the Royal Navy in July 1964 after the RN rejected a naval version of the Hawker Siddeley P1154 (*see* Chapter Fourteen). Initially the changes to the Phantom were to be kept to a minimum but the Government insisted on as much British content as possible, which grew to a total of

were delivered forming 15 and 16 Sqn, which joined RAF Germany ready to face Warsaw Pact attack. The fourth and final operational unit formed was 216 Sqn, which joined No.12 at Honington, later moving to Lossiemouth.

Buccaneers Grounded and Returned to Service

In July 1979 one of 15 Sqn's aircraft crashed in northern Germany after its right wing separated. The cause was a small crack, so all the fleet were examined and a few other machines found to have similar cracks. These were repaired and the aircraft resumed flying.

Less than a year later, during a 'Red Flag' exercise at Nellis Air Force Base in Nevada in February 1980, a 15 Sqn Buccaneer crashed into the desert after its wing broke off. All operational machines were immediately grounded. The cause of the additional stress to the airframe was primarily because of the wing tip fairing extension fitted to the S.2s. Two Buccaneers with the greatest

flying hours were totally dismantled at Brough and examined minutely, with one tested to destruction. The repair was very complicated, requiring a dismantling of the aircraft down to its basic structure and either the shaving of 0.1 inch from a metal rib to remove the crack in the structure or the total removal and replacement of the front spar.

In the meantime the Buccaneers were grounded and the 'Red Flag' aircraft remained in Nevada. All the aircraft were assessed, some did not need modification, some did and some were scrapped. All bar two of the aircraft in Nevada flew back and the others were shipped back for repair. With a net loss to the fleet, 216 Sqn was disbanded and its aircraft dispersed to make up the numbers of the others. To keep the crews' flying hours current, a motley fleet of thirty-four Hunters was assembled so they could keep flying. After six months the Buccaneer flights slowly resumed.

By 1983 with the introduction of the Tornado into service the Buccaneers' roles were reduced to maritime strike and reconnaissance and all the squadrons were based

46 per cent by value. A major element was the replacement of the General Electric J79s by Rolls-Royce Speys and much American equipment was replaced by British examples. Some production work was contracted to British companies; Short Brothers was given the contract for the outer wings and BAC Preston the rear fuselage fabrication.

The installation of the Rolls-Royce Spey proved a costly mistake as the aircraft was slower, had greater fuel consumption and less range than the General Electric J79-powered aircraft. The cost of this re-engining greatly increased the unit cost of the aircraft to the UK. When additional Phantoms were needed to protect the Falkland Islands following the war with Argentina, second-hand standard US Phantoms were bought with their American engines and systems.

So that the Navy's Phantoms could operate from the catapults and confined landing area of British aircraft carriers they were fitted with an extendable nosewheel leg, drooped ailerons, a slotted tailplane and boundary layer control. Likewise to fit the hanger lifts they received foldable noses, a not uncommon feature of naval aircraft. The Navy's aircraft were designated as Phantom F-4K by the manufacturer and as FG.1 in the Navy. The aircraft for both services were intended to cover fighter and ground attack roles.

Following the cancellation of the Hawker Siddeley P1154 for the RAF on 2 February 1965 the Air Force ordered Phantoms on 1 July to replace them. The RAF would have been happy with aircraft powered by American J79 engines but had to follow the Navy's lead and take re-engined aircraft. Their aircraft were designated as Phantom FGR.2s by the RAF and were similar to the FG.1s but without the special aerodynamic and nosewheel modifications for operating from aircraft carriers. As the carriers were being taken out of service only fifty-two FG.1s were built and only twenty-nine of these served with the Navy. A total of 118 FGR.2 Phantoms were built for the RAF, which initially served with RAF Germany. Following the scrapping of the Royal Navy's only Phantom-capable carrier, HMS *Ark Royal*, their Phantoms flew with the RAF in the air defence role, taking over some of the duties of the Lightning.

In May 1965 Hawker Siddeley Brough was chosen as the sister design company for the airframe and weapons systems for the Phantom. In September 1966 this arrangement was regularized when McDonnell

ABOVE: **Buccaneers XV352 'FC' and XZ452 'HC' of 2370CU in 1986.** BAE Systems

LEFT: **An RN Phantom FG.1 at Holme-on-Spalding-Moor, with the Hawker Siddeley Brough chief test pilot, Derek Whitehead, on the left.** BAE Systems

BELOW: **Eight Phantoms at Holme-on-Spalding-Moor, most of them RAF FGR.2s; the one at left front is a Navy FG.1.** BAE Systems

Douglas signed a contract with HSA granting access to the information necessary to take on the responsibilities in overseeing the UK's aircraft and carrying out redesign of the aircraft. The first Phantom YF-4K XT595 flew on 27 June 1966 and following completion of trials at McDonnell Douglas's St Louis plant was delivered to Holme-on-Spalding Moor in 1968. (The two prototype F-4Ks for the Royal Navy were designated YF-4Ks and the first two F-4Ms for the RAF were likewise YF-4Ms.) Evaluation of the two prototype and nine production aircraft ensued at Brough, Rolls-Royce at Hucknall and UK test establishments until 1971. As part of Hawker Siddeley's responsibility for the Phantom under contract from EMI, the company designed, manufactured and tested the aerodynamics of the large reconnaissance pod, which combined cameras, radar and infra-red Linescan.

Throughout their years of operation with the UK forces from 1968 to 1991 many Phantoms returned to Holme-on-Spalding Moor for repairs to the airframe owing to fatigue problems and four machines had their centre wings replaced. As road transport of the large Phantom from Holme to Brough was more problematic than the Buccaneer, much of the work was carried out at Holme. The Phantoms had repairs to their wing fold ribs, main spars and four of them had replacement wings. Following the closure of Holme in 1983 the aircraft were flown into RAF Scampton and then were transported across the Humber Bridge to Brough.

The Last HSA Plant

BAE Systems Brough is the last Hawker Siddeley Aviation plant still open and hopefully will remain open to celebrate its centenary in 2016 and beyond.

As one of Hawker Siddeley's factories, the Brough factory benefited from the substantial amount of work within the Group. As part of the Kingston-Brough Division it shared in the design and production of the Harrier and Hawk. From 1965 wings and from 1969 fuselages for the Harrier 1 were manufactured at Brough and this work continued with the Harrier 2 until 1999. Overall Brough built more than 50 per cent of the Harrier.

Brough's continuing connection with Kingston manifested itself in manufacturing the Hawk wing and tailplane 1974 with the forward centre fuselages constructed from 1976. Following the closure of Kingston, Hawk design and final assembly was transferred to Brough and remained there until 2012.

Though Brough had typically always built military aircraft, with the closure of the factory at Portsmouth in 1968 fabrication of the Trident's 55ft long front fuselage was passed to Brough and sixty-four were built between 1968 and 1975. Airliner work increased when from 1971 the factory started to build parts for the Airbus A300 and until 1999 the factory turned out various parts for other Airbus airliners plus parts for the 146. More recently Brough also worked on manufacturing parts for the

Nimrod MRA.4 and fatigue testing a specimen fuselage

At the time of writing the workers at Brough are engaged in Hawk technical support, manufacturing parts for the F-35 and fatigue testing specimen fuselages for the Eurofighter Typhoon and F35 Lightning.

Conclusion

The Buccaneer, the last all-British strike aircraft, deserved better. It was the victim of inter-service rivalry and ineptitude, without which far more might have been sold. Instead of the costly error of TSR2, Spey-Buccaneers could have equipped both the RN and the RAF from the start. It was only ten years after its maiden flight that the RAF reluctantly received the aircraft, after the cancellation of its chosen TSR2 and replacement, the F-111. The RAF began to value it for its range, versatility and ability to deliver a multitude of weapons at low level. Selling of the Buccaneer would have been assisted if other air forces had seen the RAF operating it. Its naval use was less of a selling point to other navies as few of them had aircraft carriers to operate them. As its one foreign customer, South Africa, was a political pariah during this period, the aircraft won little credence with prospective purchasers elsewhere.

Budgetary restrictions hampered its development. There were plans for major improvements to its electronics and even a supersonic version. It was ironic that the Tornado that replaced the Buccaneer had a shorter range. The sole reason for its withdrawal the RAF's desire to rationalize the number of types and reduce costs.

Specification – Buccaneer S.2	
Length	63ft 5in (19.33m)
Wingspan	44ft (13.41m)
Height	16ft 3in (4.95m)
MTOW	62,000lb (28,000kg)
Max speed	630mph (1,000km/h) at sea level
Combat radius	580 miles (930km)
Crew	2
Engine	2 × 11,100lb Rolls-Royce RB168 Spey 101
Armament	Sidewinder, Martel and Sea Eagle missiles; nuclear and conventional freefall bombs, rocket pods

A RAF Phantom FGR.2 at the RAF Golden Jubilee at Abingdon, 15 June 1968. Author

CHAPTER FOURTEEN

Vertical Hawkers

Introduction

The publication of the Duncan Sandys' 1957 Defence White Paper resulted in the cancellation or abandonment of many aircraft projects due to the need to cut costs and the prediction that future wars would not be conventional but nuclear: the paper also introduced other major changes such as the ending of conscription and a commitment to the nuclear deterrent. Hawker at Kingston, Surrey was working on the P1121, a private venture supersonic fighter but work was initially slowed and in early 1958 was abandoned. In the aftermath of the White Paper Hawker Siddeley's Chief Designers examined alternative projects and vertical take-off was considered a viable avenue to explore. Through the 1950s and beyond there had many experimental types built to explore vertical flight, in the UK there was the Rolls-Royce Thrust Measuring Rig (the so-called 'Flying Bedstead') and the Short SC1. Both these had a number of lift engines, though the SC1 also had a single engine for forward propulsion. There was recognition within NATO that runways were vulnerable to attack so an attack aircraft with V/STOL (Vertical/Short Take-off and Landing) would have a substantial advantage over conventional aircraft and that V/STOL aircraft could function in areas close to potential Cold War battlefields in the Europe of the late twentieth century.

A French aircraft designer, Michel Wibault, had devised an aircraft around a Bristol Orion engine with four rotating nozzles either side of the centre of gravity, which when rotated down provided vertical lift and rotated backwards gave propulsion. Bristol Engines were examining this concept using an Orpheus engine instead of the Orion when Sir Sydney Camm, Hawker's Chief Designer, desperate for a new project asked Bristol what they were doing about vertical take-off engines. In June 1957 Bristol responded with the BE53 Pegasus for which Camm proposed a V/STOL close-support aircraft, the P1127. (Bristol Engines

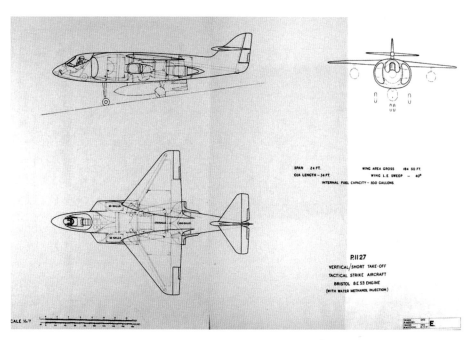

ABOVE: **One of the drawings from an October 1957 proposal for the P1127.** Hawker Archive

BELOW: **A Bristol Siddeley BE53 Pegasus engine with its four rotating nozzles.** Hawker Archive

ABOVE: The first P1127, XP831, having engine runs. Note the huge 'elephant ear' intakes initially used for hovering and slow speed flying. After trials of inflatable intakes providing larger and small intakes, a compromise intake made out of metal was accepted. Hawker Archive

LEFT: XP831's hovering trials on a special grid to absorb the engine efflux did not always go smoothly. Hawker Archive

BELOW: The second P1127, XP836, clearly showing its bicycle undercarriage with outriggers. The Pegasus's nozzles are in a near vertical position. Note that its engine intakes are different to those on XP831 and were considered the best shape for high speed flight, which was XP836's initial area of testing. Hawker Archive

merged with Armstrong Siddeley in 1959 to form Bristol Siddeley Engines, which was equally owned by Bristol and Hawker Siddeley; many of the Bristol Siddeley Board members sat on the Hawker Siddeley Board. In 1966 Bristol Siddeley was taken over by Rolls-Royce.)

Initial Development

The Ministry of Defence was not initially interested but the Hawker Siddeley Board had the vision to finance it as a private venture. In 1958 financial assistance was given by the MWDP (Mutual Weapons Defence Programme) for the development of the engine, and detailed design work started on the aircraft. (The MWDP was funded by the USA to help Western Europe develop weapons for the Cold War.) In May 1959 construction of two P1127s began at Kingston and in September 1959 the Pegasus ran for the first time at their factory at Patchway, Bristol.

Flight Development

Hawker's Chief Test Pilot Bill Bedford and his deputy, Hugh Merewether, trained assiduously for the challenging task of flying a revolutionary aircraft with an equally revolutionary engine; learning to fly helicopters, flying the Bell X14, an American VTOL aircraft, and the British-built Short SC1 VTOL aircraft.

On 21 October 1960 Bill Bedford made the first tethered hover in the prototype XP831. Other very short hovers followed and bit by bit the flight envelope was widened, untethered hovering following less than a month later. These hovers were of very short duration as the Pegasus only offered 11,000lb thrust, just slightly more thrust then the weight of the aircraft. Next the prototype was sent to RAE Bedford for conventional flying and the safety of its huge runway. The second aircraft, XP836 joined the programme on 7 July 1961 and on 12 September 1961, less than a year after the first tentative hover, the first transitions were made from vertical flight to wing-born flight. By this time Hawker Siddeley had signed a contract with the British Government where they were paid for the two already-constructed prototypes but in addition, four development aircraft were ordered. The first three of these development aircraft were the same as the prototypes but the final aircraft carried improvements; it was longer, had a redesigned wing and a more powerful Pegasus, representative of the Kestrel for the Tripartite Squadron.

There were many flight test development issues, the most notable of which was finding an optimum shape for the engine intake for both slow hovering and high-speed flight, which took a long time to define. Another major issue was refining the effectiveness of the reaction controls, which worked at the nose, the tail and at the wing tips during hovering to provide directional, attitude and roll control. There was also a need to improve high-speed flight performance, increase control sensitivity to maintain stability, refine the autostabilization system and improve the undercarriage.

Crashes and Demonstrations

In the development of such a revolutionary aircraft major problems were to be expected and the four that confronted the test pilots were all powerplant related. XP836 lost one of its Pegasus nozzles in flight forcing Bill Bedford to eject, Hugh Merewether crashlanded XP972 and later XP984 after suffering engine failures, and between those two incidents, Bill Bedford flying the first aircraft had to endure the humiliation of a crash landing at the 1963 Paris Air Show owing to a clogged filter blocking the nozzle activation.

The P1127 was only first seen by the British public at Farnborough 1962 where a pair of P1127s wowed the crowd with their balletic abilities and then did so for many a year thereafter. Hence the humiliation of the Paris Air Show the year after when the aircraft crashed. But demonstrations had been made to the RAF, and on 8 February 1963 the Navy first sampled the P1127 when XP831 made a vertical landing and take off from HMS *Ark Royal* steaming in the English Channel.

RIGHT: **An aircraft carrier first! The first landing and take-off by a vertical take-off aircraft from an aircraft carrier. XP831 piloted by Hawker Siddeley Kingston chief test pilot Bill Bedford (in the foreground) on 8 February 1963 on HMS *Ark Royal*.** Hawker Archive

BELOW: **Five of the nine Kestrels built for the joint USAF/Luftwaffe/RAF evaluation squadron. These aircraft had detail improvements based on the experience of the P1127s.** Hawker Archive

The Kestrel

A highlight of 1961 for the P1127 was funding to the tune of $30–35 million dollars for the airframe and engine from the USA and a condition of this was a tripartite operational evaluation in conjunction with Germany and the USA. For this evaluation Hawker Siddeley received an order for nine additional aircraft known as the Kestrels. Financed jointly by the UK and the USA, plus a lesser contribution from Germany, the tripartite 1127s had a number of modifications, including a more powerful Pegasus 5, longer fuselage, greater sweepback, a larger fin area and larger anhedral tailplane.

The Kestrel squadron was formed in October 1964 and its aircraft flew 1,200 sorties until the completion of evaluation flying in November 1965. Early in 1966 six aircraft, including the German Kestrels, were dispatched to America for further evaluation in the USA.

The P1154

Though testing of the P1127 was only in its infancy in early 1961, research began into a supersonic version of the P1127 under the P1150 project number. Later in the year NATO issued a requirement for a supersonic V/STOL single-seat strike aircraft. Many firms competed for the order and the Hawker proposed the P1154 using a Bristol Siddeley BS100 vectored thrust engine. The P1154 was declared the winner, but as NATO had insufficient funds for full development this proved a pyrrhic victory. However, the P1154 did receive some financial support from NATO for the BS100.

The RAF saw that the P1154 could lead to the kind of aircraft they needed to replace the Hawker Hunter from 1968, in contrast to the subsonic P1127. The Royal Navy also had a requirement for a Sea Vixen replacement, to enter service after 1970. Naturally the opportunity to develop the P1154 for both Services was attractive to the Government and Hawker Siddeley. But the two services needed very different aircraft, the RAF a single-seater strike aircraft and the Royal Navy wanted a two-seat, high altitude interceptor to operate from their carriers.

An initial joint proposal had the RAF and RN aircraft with 80 per cent in common. But as the designs were refined this commonality was hugely reduced between the two designs. While the RAF's requirements remained fairly constant, the Royal Navy's demands grew, leading to considerable weight growth, necessitating larger wings, while the catapult requirement led to a new undercarriage layout. While the naval aircraft design remained to be fixed, detailed design and construction of a mock-up began for the RAF variant. By mid-1963 this divergence was critical so the MoD tried to force the two services to agree to a common P1154, but this suited neither the RAF, nor the Navy. Various alternatives were investigated but so in February 1964, it was decided to adapt the Phantom with Spey engines for the Navy and to develop a version of the P1154 for the RAF alone. Hawker Siddeley could now concentrate on the P1154 for the Air Force and reductions in development costs, manufacture and flight-testing of the development batch aircraft could be envisaged.

Work was effectively agreed on the P1154 in July 1964 and Hawker Siddeley submitted their detailed design to the Ministry of Aviation and a development programme involving eight aircraft, with first flight in mid-1966. Bristol Siddeley started development work on the BS.100, including conversion of the Vulcan B.1A test-bed, XA896.

The P1154 had a length of 57ft 6in, span of 28ft 4in and height of 12ft 6 in, with a bicycle undercarriage with the outriggers similar to the P1127. Maximum speed was Mach 1.13 at sea level with plenum-chamber burning and with cold thrust the aircraft could achieve Mach 1.1 with two Red Tops. It was projected to have low-level combat range of 240 miles. Overall development costs were estimated at £170–200 million, with an additional £10 million for the two-seater. Unit costs were put at £1 million for the single-seat aircraft and £1.2 million for the trainer based on an order for 157 single-seater and 25 twin-seaters.

P1154 Cancelled, P1127 Ordered

With the change in Government in Britain on 15 October 1964 as a result of the General Election, costly aviation projects came under the spotlight as the Labour Government examined ways to cut expenditure in the face of a poor economic position.

On 2 February 1965 Prime Minister Harold Wilson announced the cancellation of two Hawker Siddeley aircraft. First the supersonic VTOL P1154 and then the HS681 heavy lifter were axed. The reasons giving for the cancellation of the P1154 were because its in service date was too late to replace the Hunter and owing to its high cost estimates. These cancellations were heavy blows to the Group but the blow was lessened by orders for the HS801 (which became the Nimrod) and for an operational version of the P1127 for use by the RAF as a close-support V/STOL weapon system.

By early 1965 over 5,000 men were directly employed on the P1154 at Hawker Siddeley and Bristol Siddeley plus the development aircraft under construction. Cancellation of the P1154 was probably a huge missed opportunity as the last all-British attempt for the key worldwide supersonic fighter market.

P1154 wing jig at the Hamble factory, just prior to the cancellation of the project in February 1965. BAE Systems

Harrier Development

Later in February 1965 Hawker Siddeley Aviation signed a contract to build six development aircraft and to modify the Kestrel to take the Pegasus 6 engine of 18,000/19,000lb thrust. This engine would power the P1127 (RAF) aircraft and a modified Kestrel fitted with this engine engaged on an engine development programme.

The P1127 (RAF) was the official designation until the official naming as the Harrier in 1967. The Harrier's close-support tasking was based upon the practical experience gained from six years' flying experience over both land and sea, by day and by night from the P1127 and Kestrel aircraft. Five development aircraft were ordered, the first XV276 flying from Dunsfold at the end of August 1966.

The Hawker Siddeley Harrier GR.1 had to be a minimum change from the Kestrel and was tightly constrained within a fixed price contract. Even so it was equipped with 30mm Aden guns and had the ability to carry a wide variety of stores on five external pylons (two on each wing and one on the centre fuselage). These pylons could carry bombs, rocket pods, reconnaissance pods, fuel tanks and flares. It also incorporated some of the avionics and weapon systems devised for the P1154, such as a Head-up Display, Weapon Aiming Computer and Moving Map Display.

In the course of development, the Harrier was tested in many different environments, including hot weather trials in Sicily and cold weather trials at Cold Lake in Canada. Trials were also made aboard aircraft carriers and other ships with suitable landing platforms. By 1970 Harrier family aircraft had completed some 25,000 vertical or short take-offs and landings and about 6,000 flying hours.

Early Harriers with the RAF

Harriers entered service with the RAF during 1969 only three years after the first development aircraft flew. However, before actual squadron service began and while the first aircraft were with the Operational Conversion Unit, the Air Force decided to enter them in the *Daily Mail* Transatlantic Air Race. The object was to set the fastest time from the Post Office Tower in London to the Empire State Building in New York using a combination of vehicles. The Air Force operated from RAF St Pancras

(a former coal yard next to the London railway terminus), landing on the Manhattan waterfront with Sqn Ldr Lecky-Thomson making the best time on the London–New York leg on 5 May 1969. As there was his Harrier and a spare in New York, Hawker Siddeley took advantage of this to demonstrate them to the US Navy, which was interested in buying them for the Marines. Sqn Ldr Lecky-Thomson and Hawker Siddeley's John Farley made several joint flying demonstrations and John landed one on a USN aircraft carrier.

The Harrier GR.1s, which were the initial production standard single-seaters, joined No. 1 Sqn at Wittering and three other squadrons with RAF Germany. The RAF also received thirteen T.2s, twin-seaters, which retained full operational capability. An additional squadron of Harriers was soon ordered for the RAF bringing total orders for this aircraft (including the US Marines' order) close to 200. Initially unenthusiastic about having the Harrier rather than the P1154 the RAF found themselves with a uniquely flexible aircraft, which could be dispersed close to the troops and provide quick effective response to incursions.

In November 1975 in their first out-of-theatre operational deployment, six Harrier

GR.1As were sent to Belize to deter the aggressive intentions of neighbouring Guatemala. As they were not granted landing rights in the USA they were supported by Victor tankers and flew via Goose Bay and Bermuda. The 1 Sqn Harriers were based at Belize Airport, which had a very short runway. They were withdrawn in April 1976, but the threat resurfaced in 1977 and in July that year Harrier GR.3s were again based in Belize and stayed there until 1993.

In another unexpected area of operations, Harrier GR.3s were deployed to the RN aircraft carriers as part of Operation *Corporate* and proved invaluable support to the UK's forces (*see* below).

As the aircraft matured in RAF service, refinements were introduced. For example, most of the GR.1s were fitted with the more powerful Pegasus 10 offering another 1,000lb thrust, becoming GR.1As. The aircraft were further improved and redesignated as GR.3s, with a noticeable extension to their noses to accommodate a LRMTS (Laser Ranger and Target Seeker) and a RWR (Radar Warning Receiver) fairing on the tail. These converted aircraft were reinforced by forty new-build Harrier GR.3s which received the Pegasus 11 with another 1,000lb thrust, and continuing

For the *Daily Mail* Trans-Atlantic Air Race in May 1969 the RAF entered the Harrier GR.1, which was just entering service. Here is XV741 piloted by Sqn Ldr Lecky-Thomson taking off from the temporary base at RAF St Pancras, adjacent to the London terminus. BAE Systems

modifications kept the work flowing to Hawker Siddeley's factories, principally at Kingston, which was primarily concerned with Harrier production, while component manufacture was dispersed to other plants in the group.

Harriers for Two

A twin-seat Harrier would have proved a real asset at the beginning of the programme when pilots just had to learn on the job. However, as the P1127 and Kestrel were specialist research aircraft, no such expense could be justified, besides which the initial power of the Pegasus was not enough to support the additional weight, so until the engine had developed there was no opportunity to build a twin-seater.

With the RAF GR.1 development there was a pressing need and with more engine power available the Harrier T.2 was devised. This had a tandem cockpit with a fuselage lengthened to accommodate the additional pilot. The front cockpit had to match the GR.1 while the rear had to give the instructor full authority over all controls.

The heavily-instrumented Harrier T.2 prototype XW174 made its maiden flight from Dunsfold on 24 April 1969 with Hugh Merewether at the controls. Following eight flights, one of Hugh's colleagues Duncan Simpson took it in the air and had an engine failure near Boscombe Down. He had no choice other than to eject, survived, broke his neck but made a return to test flying. Fortunately the second prototype XW175 flew a month later and testing resumed. Owing to directional stability problems the fin was increased in size several times but eventually a compromise solution was an

TOP: **Harrier XV738, a GR.3 conversion from a GR.1, firing its Matra rocket pods.** BAE Systems

ABOVE: **Hawker Siddeley's own Harrier trainer, appropriately registered G-VTOL and clearly flying in São Paulo, Brazil, carrying large underwing drop tanks. To counteract the lengthened nose to accommodate the two pilots, the tail boom had to be lengthened considerably to position the rear reaction control.** Hawker Archive

RIGHT: **A RAF Harrier T.4 now on display at the Farnborough Air Services Trust (FAST) museum.** BAE Systems

increase of 18in and the partial opening of airbrake at high angles of attack to remedy the situation.

Deliveries of Harrier T.2s began to the Harrier Conversion Unit at Wittering in July 1970. Further trials took place in the meantime so that the Harrier Trainer could carry the full range of stores. More Pegasus power meant that the T.2 soon became the T.2A. Further developments then followed to keep pace with the RAF's single-seaters, for example the T.4 becoming the trainer for the GR.3.

In 1970 HSA decided to build a company-owned demonstrator, doubtless remembering the success of the famous, company-owned Hunter demonstrator G-APUX and estimating that it would more than pay for itself in sales. It flew, as G-VTOL, on 16 September 1971 and appeared in countless demonstrations around the world operating on land and from carriers. This great example of the type has fortunately been preserved at the Brooklands Museum.

The US Marines Buy the Harrier

In December 1969 the United States Navy reached agreement with the UK Ministry of Technology for the purchase of 12 Hawker Siddeley Harriers for the US Marine Corps. This was the first export order for the Harrier and its significance cannot be underestimated: this was a breakthrough into the toughest market in the world. The initial order was estimated to be worth about £21m (2013 = £293m) with spares and support equipment. Other orders making a total of 110 aircraft soon followed.

At the same time Hawker Siddeley announced that they had entered into a cooperative production agreement with McDonnell Douglas of St Louis, Missouri, for the licensed manufacture of subsequent aircraft in America. Although in the event, all the 102 single-seater AV-8A and eight TAV-8A twin-seaters were manufactured at HSA plants in the UK. Both firms were already closely associated with one another as a result of the adoption of the Phantoms for the RAF and Royal Navy, for which aircraft HSA was nominated as the sister design firm. The USMC Harriers were designated AV-8A (the two initial letters standing for Attack, V/STOL). They were virtually identical to the RAF aircraft, except for the engine, which was the uprated Pegasus 11 of 22,500lb in place of the 19,500lb Pegasus 6.

This connection between HSA and McDonnell Douglas was to have major ramifications for the history and development of the Harrier as jointly funded work progressed with the company's American licensee, to define an advanced version of the Harrier embodying a more powerful engine.

ABOVE: **Harriers being built for the US Marine Corps at the Hawker Siddeley Kingston factory in May 1970.** BAE Systems

LEFT: **A Lockheed C-141 Super Starlifter at Dunsfold to collect Harriers for delivery to the US Marine Corps.** Hawker Archive

ABOVE: **Two US Marine Corps AV-8 Harriers.** Hawker Archive

BELOW: **A Spanish Navy AV-8. The sale of Harriers to the Spanish Navy followed on from the US Marines' experience with the aircraft.** Hawker Archive

Further Sales

With its mountainous terrain, Switzerland seemed an obvious market for the Harrier, a country looking to replace its elderly de Havilland Venoms. Hawker Siddeley's John Farley took XV742 to Switzerland, which had been demonstrated at the Farnborough Air Show in US Marines marking in 1970. It was loaned for the Swiss demonstration by the Ministry of Defence and registered as G-VSTO. Despite brilliant demonstrations by John Farley at several airfields in Switzerland, the customer did not bite and inexplicably no sales were forthcoming.

The Spanish Navy first showed interest in the Harrier in 1972, but, because of its continuing dispute with Britain over ownership of Gibraltar, it seemed a very challenging market. The UK's Labour Government had cancelled an order for frigates so there appeared little chance of achieving any sales. However, a demonstration by John Farley on their aircraft carrier clinched the issue and an order for six AV-8As and two TAV-8As named Matadors was placed in 1975 and these were produced on the UK production line. To avoid any possibility of cancellation the order was placed via the United States Navy and in 1977 an additional five aircraft were ordered. Those remaining serviceable were sold to the Royal Thai Navy in 1996 where they had only a limited life.

The Sea Harrier

When it became clear that there would no more big Royal Navy aircraft carriers the RN realized that if it were to maintain a fixed-wing element it had to use a version of the Harrier. So in 1971 a requirement was issued for a fighter, reconnaissance, and strike aircraft for operation from the new small 'Invincible' class vessels. Work on the Sea Harrier began and 24 FRS.1s were ordered for the Royal Navy in 1975. Despite both the US Marine Corps and the Spanish Navy operating their AV-8s from aircraft carriers, this was the first truly navalized version of the Harrier.

Though the Sea Harrier was to be a minimum design change from the RAF aircraft, significant alterations were nonetheless introduced. Most prominent among these were the raised cockpit to give the pilot a better rearward view, so necessary in combat, and the fitting of a nose-mounted radar. Invisible from the outside were improvements to the attack avionics and systems.

XZ438, the FRS.1, first flew on 20 August 1978, and in November of that year the first Sea Harrier carrier landing took place aboard HMS *Hermes*. The invention of the 'ski-jump' by Lt Cdr Taylor RN, which gave the aircraft extra lift on take-off and therefore an increased payload, was taken up by HSA, which was contracted to build an adjustable 'ski jump' for testing. The Sea Harrier and the 'ski jump' were simultaneously introduced on the carriers and proved their efficacy during Operation *Corporate*. Including replacements for aircraft lost in the Falklands War, a total of sixty-one Sea Harrier FRS.1s and two-seat T.4Ns based on the RAF trainers were purchased for the Royal Navy Fleet Air Arm.

By the mid-1970s the Indian Navy's elderly fleet of Hawker Sea Hawks operating from its carrier *Vikrant* needed replacement but only a limited number of the types were possible contenders. One of these was the Sea Harrier, which the Indian Navy had been enthusiastic about from the very beginning of its development and more so following a demonstration by John Farley on Hawker Siddeley's twin-seater demonstrator G-VTOL from the *Vikrant* in 1972. Six years later an order was placed for six FRS.51s and two T.60s to operate from the *Vikrant*. In 1986 India bought Britain's ski-jump-equipped *Hermes* for service and renamed it the *Viraat*. India bought a total of twenty-three Sea Harrier FRS.51s and four T.60 trainers to equip its two vessels, with the first FRS.51 delivery in December 1983.

ABOVE: **The first Sea Harrier FRS.1, XZ450, which made its maiden flight from Dunsfold on 20 August 1978. This aircraft was held back for development flying, but with the onset of hostilities between the UK and Argentina over the Falkland Islands, was called into service; it was shot down over Goose Green.** Hawker Archive

BELOW: **Harrier ski jump launch from one of the three 'Invincible' class aircraft carriers.** Hawker Archive

'Mission Impossible Without V/STOL'[5]

The effectiveness of the Harriers was well demonstrated during Operation *Corporate*, the 75-day war to recover the Falkland Islands from Argentina in 1982. The UK's forces were faced with an immense task as the nearest base was Ascension Island, some 4,000 miles distant.

The Royal Navy's two aircraft carriers, HMS *Hermes* and *Invincible*, and the fleet set sail from Portsmouth in the first week of April 1982 with Sea Harrier FRS.1s aboard after frantic efforts to get the ships ready. No. 800 Sqn's Harriers were embarked on *Hermes* and No. 801's on *Invincible*. Back at RNAS Yeovilton, Sea Harriers retrieved from store were brought up to the latest standard, pilot training was accelerated and RAF Harrier pilots were seconded to the RN for the duration.

In the longest-ever bombing raid in the RAF's history a Vulcan dropped bombs on Port Stanley airfield on 1 May and at dawn Sea Harriers followed suit with more bombs. Later in that same day a Harrier shot down

a Mirage and a Canberra, so the Argentine Air Force soon withdrew them from daily attacks. Another Vulcan raid on Port

Stanley airfield on 4 May and more Sea Harrier raids followed, but raiding Goose Green airfield the Navy lost its first Sea

An RAF Harrier GR.3 landing on HMS *Hermes* during the Falklands conflict. Hawker Archive

Harrier. Two days later there were further losses when two Harriers were lost, believed to have collided in cloud. Following these initial losses the Navy's aircraft increasingly concentrated its aircraft on air defence. The Sea Harriers had an immense task and during the hostilities in the South Atlantic flew over 1,200 sorties engaging enemy Daggers (an Israeli version of the Mirage) and Skyhawks.

In the meantime RAF Wittering's No. 1 Sqn RAF Harrier GR.3s were being readied for action in the South Atlantic. BAe at Kingston was immediately involved with the MoD in establishing the necessary modifications and provided detail drawings in a week. Initial modifications were alterations for aircraft carrier operation, others were major improvements to avionics and weapons fit even including kits to allow the

use of Sidewinder missiles and chaff dispensers. Many of these improvements had long been necessary but had been held back by Ministry indecision. While these modifications were being made the crews were frantically training on Yeovilton's ski jump, with weapons practice and interceptions with French Mirages and Super Etendards, aircraft types they might engage with during hostilities.

Fortunately No. 1's Harriers were already equipped with flight-refuelling probes and regularly engaged in air-to-air refuelling. To catch up with the fleet, they had to make a record tanker-supported transit to Ascension Island and join the *Atlantic Conveyor*, a merchant vessel requisitioned to transport the aircraft and helicopters to the proximity of the aircraft carriers. When they reached them, the RAF's Harriers flew on to the *Hermes* in the South Atlantic and almost immediately set to work.

On missions the RAF Harriers would have to endure withering ground fire and missiles as they engaged in close support. The RAF aircraft proved their worth, shooting down helicopters, bombing airfields, attacking Argentine ground stores, and reconnaissance. Following the Army's landing at San Carlos and as the British troops closed in on Port Stanley, the frantic pace of activities only accelerated with the Harriers supporting the British advance, which was driving the Argentines back, though as the enemy troops were more and more concentrated together, ground fire intensified and the Harriers became more vulnerable.

In all twenty-eight Sea Harriers and fourteen Harrier GR.3s took part in Operation *Corporate*. Altogether three of the original No. 1 Sqn aircraft were lost through enemy action in the course of 125 sorties, all thankfully without loss of life. Had the RAF aircraft arrived earlier they would have flown more sorties. Their attrition was far higher than the Sea Harriers, which lost only two from enemy action during 2,197 sorties and reflected the danger of close support operations in contrast with the Sea Harriers' air superiority role. Clearly without the Harrier the Falkland Islands would not have been regained.

A Sea Harrier launch from the packed deck of HMS *Hermes* during Operation *Corporate*. Hawker Archive

Sea Harrier 2

BAe was awarded a Sea Harrier mid-life update feasibility study in 1983 and Sea Harrier ZA195 was modified to be the

FRS.2 aerodynamic prototype and flew from Dunsfold on 19 September 1988. The second prototype XZ439 was tasked with radar and avionic development work and flew in March 1989. BAe also modified a BAe 125-600 to conduct FRS.2 weapon system integration work.

On 7 December 1988 the UK Ministry of Defence awarded British Aerospace a £170m contract to upgrade the Royal Navy's Sea Harriers with new radars, avionics, and weapons. The contract covered modification of all RN FRS.1s to FRS.2 standard. In 1990 a contract was awarded for new-build FRS.2s, which eventually grew to eighteen, making a total of sixty FRS.2s.

The FRS.1's Ferranti Blue Fox radar was replaced by the Blue Vixen radar in an enlarged and lengthened nose required for the AIM-120 AMRAAM (Advanced Medium-Range Air-to Air Missiles), which gave the Sea Harrier beyond-visual-range attack capability for the first time. Sea Eagle anti-ship and Alarm anti-radiation missiles could also be carried. Just as the nose was enlarged for the radar, a new 13.75in longer rear fuselage was constructed and the extra space was for an avionics bay. The Sea Harrier FRS.2 had four wing pylons and a centreline station, and the underbelly strakes could be replaced by gun packs or a pair of AIM-120 pylons. The inboard wing pylons were stressed to carry up to 2,000lb, the outboard wing pylons 1,000lb, and the centreline pylon a nominal 1,000lb.

Sea Harrier FRS.2 conversion work took place at BAe Kingston and at the Dunsfold flight test centre, supported by BAe Brough with conversion of each aircraft taking a year. The first production FRS.2, XZ497 flew in June 1991 and the first deliveries were made to the Fleet Air Arm in mid-1994. The Sea Harrier FRS.2s did not remain in service for long, as they were withdrawn in 2006. Altogether the Harrier had served for twenty-five years with the Navy.

The Harrier 2

Under their fifteen-year agreement made in 1969, both HSA Kingston and McDonnell Douglas in St Louis collaborated on further developments of the Harrier and in the early 1970s proposed the AV-16 Advanced Harrier and included a supersonic version for the UK, an AV-16S. The aim of the Advanced Harrier was to double the AV-8's payload and range capabilities, and was

ABOVE: **A Sea Harrier FA.2 launch from the RAE Bedford ski jump. The Sea Harrier FA.2 benefited from a much-improved radar in a larger, longer nose, which enabled it to carry better weapons, and a longer tail section offering space for improved avionics.**
Hawker Archive

LEFT: **This photo shows the large increase in the weapons capability of the Sea Harrier FA.2. It is carrying four ASRAAM missiles and fuel tanks.**
Hawker Archive

therefore unofficially named the AV-16. The British Labour Government was very concerned about the estimated $31bn cost, which would probably rise, and the small sixty aircraft requirement for the RAF, so in the 1975 Defence White Paper the UK was withdrawn from the project and ceased to be a partner of McDonnell Douglas. This withdrawal caused ructions in the UK, where Britain was seen to be selling its unique V/STOL heritage concept to the USA.

Unwisely for the UK as it transpired both HSA and McDonnell Douglas went their own ways in future developments of the Harrier. HSA proposed the GR5(K) and

McDonnell Douglas the AV-8B. Hawker Siddeley hoped that the McDonnell Douglas version would not be funded and then directly sell its own version to the USMC.

However, the USMC still desired an improved but much less costly aircraft than the AV-16, so McDonnell Douglas developed the Harrier 2 or AV-8B with a larger, composite wing, LERX (Leading Edge Extensions), lift refinements and raised cockpit. McDonnell Douglas began development of the AV-8B in 1975 and the first of two YAV-8B prototypes, modified AV-8As, flew in November 1978 to prove the modifications. The changes doubled the

AV-8's payload/range performance. Meanwhile Kingston worked on a larger metal-wing Harrier with six to eight pylons and wingtip missile rails. To maintain vertical landing performance with additional pylons, more internal fuel and retained missiles, the forward fuselage would have been extended 6in to improve intake recovery and thrust. As an alternative if the GR.5(K) proposal was not adopted, the big wing could have been developed for retrofit to Sea Harriers and export aircraft. To the manufacturer's disappointment the British Conservative Government did not support the Harrier GR.5(K) and Britain's V/STOL technology.

161397, the second prototype McDonnell Douglas AV-8B Harrier 2, with the new wing, LERX, lengthened fuselage and raised cockpit. Author

Two US Marine Corps Harrier 2 Plus. BAE Systems

GR.7

The US Department of Defense actively sought orders from the RAF for the Harrier 2 in order to lower production costs for the AV-8B. In August 1981 a Memorandum of Understanding was signed by the US and UK Governments whereby British Aerospace received a large workshare in the Harrier 2 programme. As the US Marine Corps was the prime customer and BAe was no longer a partner following withdrawal, it became a subcontractor to McDonnell Douglas building 40 per cent of the aircraft while Rolls-Royce produced 75 per cent of the engine with Pratt & Whitney building 25 per cent. That year McDonnell Douglas and British Aerospace signed a joint manufacturing agreement to build 390 Harrier 2s, 328 AV-8Bs for the USMC and sixty-two Harrier GR5s for the RAF.

The first AV-8B was handed over to the USMC in January 1984 and entered service in August 1985 and the two-seat TAV-8B flew in October 1986. The first UK GR.5 development aircraft ZD318 flew at Dunsfold on 30 April 1985. In April 1988 the UK announced a follow-on order for thirty-four Harrier 2s, the aircraft to be designated Harrier GR.7 and fitted with night-attack avionics and the Zeus electronic countermeasures system. The GR.5s were subsequently brought up to GR.7 standard. Though these RAF aircraft were similar to the AV-8B they had numerous differences including eight rather than six pylons to allow for the carriage of Sidewinder missiles, twin Aden cannon, a Martin-Baker ejection seat and different avionics. The initial trainer version for the RAF Harrier 2 was the T.10, which had a full operational capacity.

The final RAF versions of the Harrier were the GR.9 and its trainer, the T.12

which were upgrades of the GR.7 and T.10. These had a new rear fuselage, an upgraded Pegasus 107 offering 24,750lb thrust (almost 3,000lb more than GR.7) and 100 per cent LERX (Leading Edge Root Extension) in contrast to the 65 per cent extension on the GR.7. These improvements had a marked effect on the aircraft's performance as did further refinements to its avionics and weapons capabilities. The first conversion, ZD230, flew from Warton on 30 May 2003. With the completion of the final rear fuselages for the GR.9 in 2007, British manufacture of the Harrier came to an end.

Production

The P1127s and Kestrels were built at Kingston, assembled and flown from Dunsfold. Following the development of the Harrier for the RAF, Kingston built the forward fuselage and Brough the rear fuselage, taking over wing assembly from Hamble in 1969. Dunsfold continued to retain its role as the centre for final assembly and flight test. With the closure of the large, former Hawker Siddeley factory at Kingston in 1992, Harrier forward fuselage production was passed to Dunsfold, which closed when Harrier production ended in 2000.

Two RAF Harrier 2s; a T.10 and a GR.5. Hawker Archive

Harrier 2 Exports

The Spanish Navy ordered twelve EAV-8B Matadors in 1983, received the first three aircraft in October 1987 and these operated from the Spanish Navy carrier *Príncipe de Asturias*, which has a ski jump. In 1993 the Spanish aircraft saw action in Operation *Deny Flight* over Bosnia and Herzegovina. In 2003 its EAV-8Bs were modified by Boeing (which took over McDonnell Douglas in 1997) to become EAV-8B Plus Matadors.

After evaluating both the Sea Harrier and the AV-8B in 1989 the Italian Navy opted for the Harrier 2, placing an order for sixteen AV-8Bs and two TAV-8Bs. The first

This photo amplifies the differences between the first- and second-generation Harriers, here represented by a GR.7 and a GR.3. The larger wing, LERX, raised cockpit and eight underwing stores points can be clearly be seen on the GR.7. Hawker Archive

three AV-8Bs and the two TAV-8Bs were assembled in the USA and the remainder in Italy. The Harriers operated from the aircraft carrier *Garibaldi* and took part in the attack on Afghanistan in 2001–2. They also supported the military intervention in Libya in 2011, by which time the UK's Harrier fleet withdrawn.

Harrier 2 Plus

A further limited development of Harrier 2 Plus was developed for the USMC and ordered by Italy and Spain following a Tripartite Agreement made between the three countries in September 1990. The modifications were limited to new radar and improvements to the avionics, some aircraft having night-vision capability. The USMC received thirty-one new Harrier 2 Plus and its other Harrier 2s were altered to the same standard.

Harrier 2s in USMC and RAF Service

During Operation *Desert Storm*, the liberation of Kuwait in 1991, the USMC's Harrier 2s flew over 3,000 sorties and dropped almost 3,000 tons of ordnance. The Harrier 2 could do what it was designed to do, that is operate from a forward base, which traditional fixed-wing aircraft could not do. They were operated from a gravel runway only 100 miles from the Kuwaiti border and established a fleet of sixty-six aircraft there. In the same operational theatre, the USMC

Harrier 2s were heavily employed in Operation *Iraqi Freedom* in 2003 where they were more than 40 per cent of the Marines attack force and were based on four assault ships on the Arabian Gulf. More recently they have been in regular use in Afghanistan.

In 1999 a small number of USMC Harrier 2s were involved in the bombing of Yugoslavia and in 2011 in the bombing of Libya during the operation to overthrow Colonel Gaddafi. The first combat use of the RAF's Harrier GR.7 was in Operation *Deliberate Force*, the UN campaign over Bosnia in 1995. The Harrier GR.7 played a prominent role during the Iraq War in 2003, flying close air support missions, supporting advancing allied ground troops, carrying out reconnaissance and strike missions inside southern Iraq. The Harriers served in Afghanistan from 2004 until 2009, over five years of continuous operations, and flew over 22,000 hours in 8,500 sorties.

In the 1998 Strategic Defence Review it was decided to combine the RN Sea Harriers and the RAF Harriers into a single joint command with the aim of bringing the two Harrier communities together. However, full integration was impracticable as the two aircraft had less than 20 per cent commonality of airframe and avionics. The Review concluded that upgrading the Sea Harriers was not viable whereas all the GR.7 needed was a more powerful Pegasus engine. The GR.7s were upgraded to GR.9 standard and these aircraft were issued to two Fleet Air Arm squadrons as well as to the RAF. This resulted in the RN retaining fast jet expertise and the carriers having greatly enhanced offensive strike capability..

Most regrettably in the 2010 Strategic Defence Review the Harriers and the aircraft carriers were scrapped. So Hawker Siddeley's unique aircraft no longer flies with the British services, only foreign ones.

Conclusion

The Hawker Siddeley Board had the wisdom to proceed with the V/STOL aircraft concept at a time when defence budgets were being reduced. It proved a highly profitable investment for Hawker Siddeley and its successor firms and reaped large export earnings for the UK.

As some eminent aviation engineers argue that the P1154 would have been beset by problems, the decision to cancel may have been right and the production order for the Harrier for the RAF was correct as the aircraft soon proved its worth. Once it was in service the USMC could see its value and followed suit.

Its use by the RN and the RAF during the Falklands War confounded the critics of many air forces who had given up on the V/STOL and had thought it would be easy meat for aircraft such as the supersonic Mirage. Despite this its export potential was never truly achieved, as many air forces had long runways and still sought truly supersonic aircraft.

The US Marine Corps order and co-operation with McDonnell Douglas led to greater development than would have been the case if only Britain had been involved. It is most unfortunate that in the process the Americans came to lead the development. Most regrettably the Harrier no longer graces British skies but it does fly with the USMC and the Navies of India, Italy and Spain.

A Spanish Navy Harrier 2 Plus, which has improvements in its avionics and radar. These Harriers are operated from the Spanish Navy carrier *Príncipe de Asturias*, which has a ski jump. The American, Spanish and Italian Harrier 2s have only six underwing stores pylons. The large under-fuselage strakes assist hovering performance and can be replaced by twin cannon. BAE Systems

Specification – Harrier GR.9	
Length	46ft 4in (14.12m)
Wingspan	30ft 4in (9.25m)
Height	11ft 8in (3.56m)
MTOW (short take-off)	31,000lb (14,000kg)
Max speed	662mph (1,065km/h)
	at sea level
Combat range	380 miles (630km)
Crew	1
Engine	Rolls-Royce Pegasus 105, 21,750lb thrust
Armament	2 × 25mm Aden cannon, Sidewinder and Maverick missiles, guided and unguided bombs

CHAPTER FIFTEEN

The Mighty Hunter – Nimrod

Hawker Siddeley was dealt a body blow in February 1965 when the cancellation of its two major military programmes, the Hawker Siddeley P1154 supersonic V/STOL fighter and the 681 Tactical Airlifter, was announced by the Prime Minister, Harold Wilson. The pain was softened somewhat when in the same speech to the House of Commons, PM Wilson broke the news that a 'Maritime Comet' was to go ahead. This was the HS801, later named the Nimrod.

Despite the new order, proposed work on the 'Maritime Comet' was not enough to save the closure of the former Armstrong Whitworth plant at Baginton, Coventry and large-scale redundancies throughout Hawker Siddeley Aviation, involving 7,700 employees.

Genesis

In 1956 NATO member countries indicated a requirement for a replacement to the Lockheed Neptune Maritime Reconnaissance aircraft, while at the same time the RAF was seeking a Shackleton replacement. Many European companies including Avro entered proposals but the Breguet Atlantique beat the competition. It was bought by France, Germany and other NATO countries, but not the UK who rejected the Atlantique, claiming it was insufficiently advanced and likely to suffer from corrosion.

Having taken the step not to follow NATO's choice, the RAF was solicited by two companies, BAC and Hawker Siddeley, who each submitted designs employing four Rolls-Royce Tyne turboprops. The BAC example bore a distinct resemblance to the Vickers Vanguard. Neither company was successful at this stage, so in 1960 the RAF issued Operational Requirement (OR) 350 for an aircraft with a performance superior to the Breguet Atlantique with greater speed, endurance, range and payload. This produced two contenders: Avro responded with the Avro 776, based on a Trident fuselage with a redesigned and extended

wing, and thee RB179 turbofans giving 16,300lb thrust each. BAC offered a version of the VC10. The relatively high cost of the VC10 and the three-engined layout of the Trident militated against these two contenders, and turboprops were considered too complex and to lack the necessary speed.

However, a year later the RAF issued a less stringent requirement, OR381 calling for a Shackleton replacement to undertake the following tasks: to detect, fix and destroy surfaced and submerged submarines, both conventional and nuclear; to detect and shadow enemy surface units and forces; to conduct wide-area surveillance; to make limited air-to-surface strikes against individual vessels and to perform search and rescue.

The Hawker Siddeley team at Manchester set to work and conceived the HS801, a version of the Comet 4 with Rolls-Royce Speys instead of Avon engines. Both minimum and maximum speeds were well suited to the maritime task. The installation of Speys provided the required increased thrust and improved fuel consumption to optimize the range performance. Although in many ways a conservative offering, the HS801 made a great deal of commercial sense, since the tooling for the Comet, and two completed Comet airframes that had remained unsold on the Chester production line, could be utilized as prototypes.

Contract

Following approval in May 1965 HSA was asked to refine the HS801 proposal and on New Year's Eve 1965, a fixed-price contract for £95m (£1,517m = 2012 prices) was agreed between Hawker Siddeley and the British Government for the supply of two prototypes and thirty-eight production aircraft to replace the RAF's Shackleton MR.2s. (The newer Shackleton MR.3s were to soldier on without replacement.) As a fixed-price contract the burden of risk fell very heavily on the manufacturer, meaning that while HSA would receive an overall maximum profit there was theoretically no

limit to the losses the firm would have to bear should costs exceed estimates.

The basis for the Nimrod design was a Comet 4C airframe shortened by 6ft 6in forward of the wing, the centre section enlarged to take four Speys instead of Avons. Below the pressurized fuselage, an unpressurized pannier provided a 48ft long weapons and equipment bay and a large nose radome, ample in size to allow for existing and future radar scanners. In the pannier, weapons attachment points were placed at the strong points used to mount the floor and no strengthening of the basic Comet fuselage was needed.

The large weapons bay provided for the carriage of a variety of weapons; bombs as well as torpedoes and depth charges – or alternatively it housed air-sea rescue gear, long-range fuel tanks for global ferrying, or freight panniers. Due to the increased side area, a prominent dorsal fin was fitted and an ECM (Electronic Counter Measures) fairing at the top of the fin. To make the aircraft even more distinctive there was a MAD (Magnetic Anomaly Detector) mounted in a long tail boom. The pilots' windscreens were deepened to confer better visibility during search, and two eyebrow windows added in order to enable the crew to look into the turn when the aircraft was banked during manoeuvres at low altitude. In addition, two underwing pylons were introduced for external stores and a joystick, controlled 70 million candlepower searchlight was installed in the front of the starboard external wing tank.

Other operational equipment included two camera systems, one for low altitude and one for high altitude, and an electronic flash system for night photography. Owing to the increased weight of the machine the undercarriage had to be strengthened.

The Rolls-Royce Spey 250 was a military version of the civil Spey 25, initially rated at 11,500lb take-off thrust, with a modified accessory gearbox for driving the large alternators needed for Nimrod's electricity demands. Thrust reversers were fitted on the outboard tailpipes. In operation the

Nimrod could climb quickly to a transit altitude of about 30,000ft and cruise to about 400kt, descending to search altitude and shutting-down the outboard engines as required. For low-level searches, two engines were kept running at a fairly high thrust level to retain a low specific consumption. At high weights a third engine was kept idling to cover the possibility of an engine failure, but at average weights two engines were shut down. The aircraft could climb on one engine at normal search weights and on two engines at maximum weight. A Rover APU was carried to provide high-pressure air for engine starting on the ground. Fuel tanks were created from the Comet's original forward and rear under floor freight holds and in the wing root. Total fuel capacity was raised to 85,000lb.

The crew numbered eleven, consisting of two pilots, one flight engineer, two lookouts, a routine navigator, a tactical navigator, a radio operator, an ASV radar operator and two sonar operators.

Nimrod Prototypes

The first prototype to take to the air was the final aircraft remaining on the Comet production line at Chester. It was completed as the HS801 aerodynamic prototype and during modification had its wing centre section rebuilt to take the larger Spey engines and so its powerplant was representative of the production aircraft. Registered XV148 it flew from Chester to Woodford on 23 May 1967 piloted by John Cunningham and Jimmy Harrison, who took over the test programme from then on. That same month the HS801 was named Nimrod. Like all Nimrods the fuselage of

the Nimrod prototypes was 6ft shorter than the Comet 4C and as this alteration reduced the aircraft's directional stability the dorsal fin was enlarged in June 1967.

The penultimate Comet on the Chester production line was 75 per cent complete when the HS801 project began and it was decided to complete it as a Comet 4C and fly it to Woodford for conversion to become the Nimrod systems prototype. On 25 October 1965 registered XV147 it made the short flight from Chester to Woodford piloted by John Cunningham and Jimmy Harrison. As it would have been a costly task to version this partly-completed Comet to take Spey powerplant, it remained with its Rolls-Royce Avons. Following its rebuilding it flew as the second Nimrod prototype on 31 July 1967 with Jimmy Harrison in command.

RIGHT: **When the HS801 project began, the penultimate Comet on the Chester production line, which was 75 per cent assembled, was completed as a Comet 4C and flown to Woodford for conversion to become the Nimrod systems prototype. On 25 October 1965, registered XV147, it made the short flight from Chester to Woodford piloted by John Cunningham and Jimmy Harrison. After substantial rebuilding it flew as the second Nimrod prototype on 31 July 1967, though as it would have been costly to replace the Avon engines with Speys these remained.** Ray Williams

The final Comet on the production line was rebuilt as the first Nimrod prototype at Chester. Registered as XV148, it flew from Chester to Woodford on 23 May 1967. BAE Systems

The Flight Test Programme

The flight test programme started at the end of May 1967 with the maiden flight of the first prototype. Though it was aerodynamically representative of the production Nimrod, had the Spey engines and the completely new electrical system of the Nimrod, it was otherwise unrepresentative of the production aircraft as it still retained some other Comet systems.

The prototypes were fitted with comprehensive flight test instrumentation for test flying and crew carried parachutes on early flights for which the rear crew door would have been used to escape. The flight trials included engine re-lights, asymmetric power and aerodynamic handling with anti-spin parachute fitted. Certain aerodynamic aspects of the new aircraft remained akin to the Comet but tests were made of the lateral and directional characteristics, which, due to the completely changed side-elevation shape of the Nimrod, might be expected to be different from the Comet. In this way, after seven flights had been completed, a broad-brush picture emerged which confirmed that things were as expected longitudinally, but that lateral and directional behaviour warranted a more detailed investigation. In its first two months the XV148 flew nearly sixty hours. The first prototype continued testing these areas until January 1969 and then embarked on missile trials. Meantime the systems prototype XV147 tested the MR.1 systems and later the MR.2 systems. The first production aircraft XV226 flew on 28 June 1968 and was used for tropical and cold weather trials in 1969–70 and other systems development. The subsequent three production aircraft were all involved in test flying for armament, navigation and communication systems.

Production

Construction of the Nimrod was distributed extensively throughout Hawker Siddeley so that divisions of the company that had built Comet sub-assemblies initially also built the corresponding units for the Nimrod. Only where assemblies were peculiar to 801 was construction undertaken at Chadderton. Thus, the wing centre-section was built at Chester, which was also responsible for fuselage sections and outer wings, production of which had been transferred from Portsmouth following its closure in 1968. The tailplane and engine intakes were made at Hatfield. Final assembly and development flying was at Woodford.

The Nimrod MR.1 in Service

The first Nimrod was handed over to the RAF at the Woodford on 2 October 1969. Air Marshal Sir John Lapsley, AOC-in-C Coastal Command received it from Sir Harry Broadhurst, Deputy Managing Director of Hawker Siddeley Aviation. Later in the day an RAF crew flew XV230 to St Mawgan, Cornwall, where the Nimrod maritime operational training unit was being formed. The first fully operational Nimrod squadron was No. 201 formed at Kinloss in July 1970, closely followed by two more squadrons, Nos 206 and 42 at St Mawgan the following year. Finally No. 203

ABOVE: **The first production Nimrod fuselage on its way from Hawker Siddeley Chester nearly at the Woodford factory and passing the** *Rising Sun* **on Buxton Road, Hazel Grove in Stockport.** Avro Heritage

RIGHT: **Production Nimrod MR.1 XV236.** Avro Heritage

Squadron received the last of the Nimrod MR.1s and was based in Malta.

More Orders, and Attempts at Export

In a contract worth £35m the Ministry of Defence ordered an additional eight Nimrods and spares in January 1972. Views expressed in some quarters were that as deliveries of thirty-eight Nimrods from the original contract were coming to an end, this order was to avoid mass redundancies at HSA factories, especially Woodford. It is certainly the case that a delegation of twelve workers from Woodford, had presented their case for further Nimrod orders at the House of Commons in the weeks prior to the order. Part of their argument was:

> that the cost to the nation would not be just counted in the hard cash of paying out the unemployment pay, but in the loss of a vital industry which has developed some of the world's finest aircraft over the past fifty years ... amassing a wealth of knowledge which is used daily at our Manchester factories, to produce what is universally acclaimed the most progressive, effective and versatile maritime aircraft in the world today.

As a number of countries – Holland, Canada and Italy – had all expressed interest in the Nimrod at that time this RAF order appeared helpful in keeping the production line open for two further years. South Africa had already proclaimed an interest in the Nimrod to replace its Shackletons but had been turned down by the British Government. Other countries including Australia, Japan and India evaluated the Nimrod but no export orders were forthcoming.

In 1974 HSA bid against Lockheed to secure an order for maritime patrol aircraft to replace Australia's elderly Neptunes in the RAAF. Australia drove a hard bargain setting a price ceiling of $A109 million, and specified a minimum of 30 per cent in offset work for Australian industry. HSA offered $A32–37m in offset work covering parts and maintenance work if Nimrod were selected. However, the Hawker Siddeley bid was easily topped by Lockheed, which offered up to $A70m in offset for a P-3C Orion purchase and in 1975 the Australians ordered Orions. Three years later Hawker Siddeley offered Canada both the Nimrod MR.2 and an improved Nimrod but again Lockheed won the order with a version of the Orion.

Nimrod R.1

Following on from the thirty-eight Nimrod MR.1s on the HSA Woodford production were three more Nimrods, initially described as 'specialized trials aircraft for Ministry of Technology use'. (The Ministry of Aviation had been subsumed into the Ministry of Technology in 1967. In 1970 the Ministry became the Department for Trade and Industry.) In fact these aircraft – XW664, XW665 and XW666 – were destined to replace the three Comet R.2s of No. 51 Sqn at Wyton. The unequipped Nimrod R.1s were delivered to RAF Wyton from 1971 to 1973 where they were fitted with their equipment and operational flying only began in May 1974. They were externally distinguishable from the MR.1 as they had no MAD tail and were considerably different internally as the aircraft carried a large variety of electronic listening and recording equipment. Owing to the increasing complexity and demand for electronic intelligence these aircraft were frequently updated with new and additional equipment, stored in the fuselage and within the large under-fuselage structure. As more equipment was needed the number of crew burgeoned.

With the Argentine invasion of the Falkland Islands in March 1982 there was an urgent need for electronic intelligence gathering and the R.1s sprouted flight-refuelling probes. Though 51 Squadron's exact involvement is not public knowledge the Squadron received battle honours for its part in the conflict. During 1983 the R.1s were the first Nimrods to be fitted with ESM Loran pods at the wingtips and these were later fitted to MR.2s.

On 16 May 1995 Nimrod R.1 XW666 was on an air test from Kinloss when it suffered a fire in engine number 4 and then in number 3. The pilot immediately banked to return to base but one of his crewman reported that pieces of the wing structure were burning and falling off the aircraft and following two explosions he opted for a crash landing in Moray Firth; fortunately the seven crew all escaped. Clearly the Nimrod's configuration with twin engines contiguously mounted in the wing was exceptionally dangerous. When the wreckage was recovered it was discovered that the wing structure had been weakened by 25 per cent and might have broken away from the Nimrod causing a catastrophic accident.

As the Nimrod R.1s played an invaluable role and were being updated under the Starwindow programme with new sensors, receivers, databases and workstations, the Air Force decided that a MR.2 should be converted to replace it. XV249 was selected from four in store at Kinloss, overhauled and flown to Woodford for structural conversion to a R.1. The conversion programme was expedited and called 'Project Anneka', referring to Anneka Rice's TV programme then current. The programme began on 13 October 1995 and was completed on 19 December 1996 when it was delivered to RAF Waddington for equipment fit that took almost four months. XV249 was to prove a troublesome aircraft suffering from major fuel leak problems probably caused by a long period of outside storage, and no doubt exacerbated by its conversion to a R.1. Its whole fuel system had to be rebuilt. Despite these shortcomings, it remained in service until the protracted end of Nimrod R.1 operations along with XW664 in June 2011. They were to have been withdrawn from use in March 2011 but operations over Libya kept them flying a little longer.

Nimrod MR.2 and Operation *Corporate*

When the Hawker Siddeley Nimrod MR.1 entered service in 1970 it was accepted that there would be a regular upgrading of the electronic systems. In essence the upgrade to the MR.2 involved replacing analogue with digital systems, the replacement of the ASV radar inherited from the Shackleton with the Thorn-EMI Searchwater system and the installation of a Central Tactical System. The MR.2 upgrade was trialled by the Avon-powered Nimrod prototype XV147 beginning in April 1977. XV236, the first MR.2 conversion, flew in February 1979 and joined XV147 on trials to validate the new systems.

In total thirty-five Nimrod MR.1s were converted to MR.2s and more than half of these had been modified at the time of the Argentine invasion of the Falkland Islands and South Georgia in April 1982. The operation to regain the Falkland Islands was named Operation *Corporate*. The MoD was fired into action and required immediate improvements in the Nimrod's capabilities. Owing to the huge distances involved, flying almost 4,000 miles from the RAF base on Ascension Island to the Falklands, a flight refuelling capability was paramount. The MoD asked Woodford how quickly a Nimrod could be given a flight refuelling capability – the firm replied that it could be done within 30 days. The Woodford Design Office set to work with all speed and using a probe removed from a preserved Vulcan on the airfield fitted it to XV229 for aerodynamic tests. As expected the probe caused aerodynamic problems and the need for modifications to maintain directional stability – a small fin under the tail and finlets on the horizontal tail. The first completed 'wet' conversion of a Nimrod was XV238, which was delivered to Kinloss and cleared for day and night refuelling on 3 May.

Having speedily fitted the Nimrod with a flight refuelling ability, the MoD now demanded that Sidewinder missiles be trialled. The Nimrods had underwing hardpoints which had never been used, so mountings were quickly designed for twin

ABOVE: **Sidewinder self-defence for the Nimrod. During Operation** *Corporate* **Nimrods were hurriedly fitted with flight-refuelling probes and twin Sidewinder air-to-air missiles under each wing.** Avro Heritage

LEFT: **XV254 a Nimrod MR.2P in January 1983 with a flight-refuelling probe and Sidewinder air-to-air missiles. Small fins were added to the tailplane to maintain the aircraft's stability with these additions.** BAE Systems

Sidewinders and a trial firing was made. At the same time Harpoon missiles launched from the bomb bay were also tested. Typically, the exigencies of military conflict were a driver for a substantial improvement in the Nimrod's capabilities, which thereafter reaped the benefits of these improvements. Aircraft with these refinements were designated as Nimrod MR.2P.

MR.1s, MR.2s and R.1s took part in the Falklands conflict from the Ascension Island base. With flight refuelling capability the MR.2Ps were now able to fly exceedingly long missions and exceptionally one aircraft flew a 19-hour mission with refuelling from a Victor K.2. (The Victor originally built by Handley Page had been extensively modified for its flight refuelling role at Woodford.)

Post-Operation *Corporate*

Following *Corporate* and the ensuing peace, Woodford continued with the MR.2 work and the final MR.2, XZ284, was delivered to Kinloss in December 1985. It had been one of three Nimrods stored incomplete at Woodford and unlike the other MR.2s had never been a MR.1. Where Operation *Corporate* Nimrods had been involved in the maritime role for which they had been designed for the most part, with the end of the Cold War the role of MR.2 was extended to encompass land-based intelligence to ground forces.

Nimrod R.1 XV249 in July 2011, on one of its final flights. BAE Systems

During the two Gulf Wars the MR.2s and R.1s were heavily employed. In the war of 1990–91 five MR.2s were deployed to Seeb in Oman to record all movements in the sea lanes and assist coalition warships in their attacks on enemy shipping. Only eight years later the Nimrods were back in a role supporting NATO forces in Serbia. For the Second Gulf War in 2003 six Nimrod MR.2Ps received upgrades including a forward looking infra-red turret under the right wing to better support land forces and the capability to carry a BOZ pod under the left wing with a towed radar decoy.

In Afghanistan, the Nimrods were heavily involved in Afghan land operations to identify enemy forces until their withdrawal from use, which was brought about by two serious incidents. In September 2006 XV230 caught fire after refuelling in flight, broke up in the air and crashed killing fourteen people. A Board of Enquiry and an Independent Review concluded that there was vulnerability to the aircraft catching fire during or after in-flight refuelling and change of procedure was immediately introduced. Only fourteen months later, following flight refuelling XV235 the crew were alerted to a serious leak and it appeared that they were saved by the procedural change. As a result in-flight refuelling of the Nimrod was suspended.

AEW Nimrod

Following the demise of the Royal Navy's conventional aircraft carriers, the airborne early warning (AEW) role was maintained by the aged Shackleton AEW.2. There had been a continuing debate and discussion about a NATO order for twenty-seven Boeing E-3A AWACS delivered to major NATO countries, which would have filled this role. As no decision appeared likely in 1975 an Operational Requirement was issued for an AEW aircraft and Marconi and Hawker Siddeley offered the Nimrod. Though there had been consideration of a version with rotating scanner mounted above the fuselage, the project was finalized using a scanner mounted in the extreme nose and one in the tail sweeping 180° each, which was synchronized to provide 360° coverage. The forward radome was shaped and positioned by the constraints of aerial size, aerodynamics, pilot visibility and by ground clearance. The rear radome was mounted high on the tail to give sufficient clearance at take-off. HSA had hoped to use the same profile fore and aft, but the pointed shape of the forward radome had evolved to meet aerodynamic, bird strike and rain-erosion constraints and led to unsteady flow breakaway over a similarly shaped aft radome. As a result, a separate, more rounded radome profile was developed. Mounting the existing fin above the contours of the new rear fuselage improved the directional stability of Nimrod AEW in contrast with the other marks. As the bomb bay was not needed, it was used for additional fuel tanks, which could operate as heat exchangers for all the electronic

ABOVE: **XZ286 the first Nimrod AEW.3 being assembled at Woodford. This made its maiden flight on 16 July 1980. The HS748 in the background initially flew as G11-13 and was delivered to the Upper Volta Air Force in August 1981 as XT-MAN.** Avro Heritage

BELOW: **Nimrod AEW.3 XV263.** BAE Systems

equipment. The additional fuel thus carried naturally improved the aircraft's range.

In the continuing absence of agreement between the USA and European countries on a joint NATO purchase of Boeing E-3As, on 31 March 1977 the Labour Defence Secretary Fred Mulley gave the go-ahead to the AEW Nimrod. A development aircraft registered as XW826, a former BOAC Comet 4 originally bought by the MoD for radio trials work in mid-1972, was delivered to HSA Woodford and flew in June 1977 to test the new Marconi radar system for the AEW Nimrod. It was only partly representative of the projected aircraft as it only had the forward radar antenna installed.

Marconi-Elliott Avionics' role was to supply the radar and AEW systems, which were designed from the outset to work over land and water. It had automatic initiation and tracking of targets down to small boats. The data system could be linked to ships, fighters, ground stations, tankers or other AEW aircraft, including the AWACS. Hawker Siddeley's part was confined to providing the airframe but neither contractor was in total control of the project. The Royal Air Force requirement was for eleven aircraft but no new airframes were built. Instead they came from the squadron of aircraft withdrawn from Malta by 1979 and from the eight extra aircraft ordered for employment reasons in 1973, which had been in limbo at HSA Woodford for many months. The main changes from MR.1 to AEW involved the rear end structure, including an entirely new aft fuselage and a repositioned, heightened tail. The cooling system had four times the capacity of the MR Nimrod, with heat transferred to fuel in the wing. BAe-built ESM Loral electronic pods were mounted on the wingtips. The first aircraft was due to enter service with the RAF in 1982, though its equipment standard would have probably only been to an interim fit.

Three development AEW.3s flew designated as DB1, DB2 and DB3, respectively XZ286, XZ287 and XZ281. Charles Masefield made the first flight of DB1 on 16 July 1980 with over 2,000 employees watching and formated with the chase plane Nimrod prototype XV148. In September that year DB1 appeared at the Farnborough Air Show taking part in the flying programme every day. DB1 did not have the Mission System Avionics (MSA) and was for airframe and handling tests. However, the role of DB2 and DB3 was to test the MSA.

The first production aircraft, XZ285, flew in December 1981 but it did not have a fully functioning MSA. Four more AEW.3s were completed but by then the whole project was running late and costs were rising steeply. It had been hoped that the aged Shackleton AEW.2s could be retired and replaced by the Nimrods in 1982 but the Shackletons were still in service in 1985 and there was no clear indication of when they would be replaced. Questions were being raised in Parliament as to what was happening and there were stories in the media that the MSA did not match specification and that costs were out of control. In late 1985 work started on major overhauls of the six remaining Shackleton AEW.2s to keep them flying even longer.

Cancellation

On 18 December 1986 the whole project was cancelled. The RAF stated the radar and AEW systems were not functioning adequately and were unclear as to when it would work. However it was a very complex programme and the fact it was running late was not unsurprising. There are some who argue that had the programme continued, these problems would have been ironed out. The Nimrod AEW.3s were cannibalized for spares, then stored and then scrapped. For its part GEC Avionics (formerly Marconi) stated that the USA had applied pressure to force the UK to cancel the AEW.3 so that the Boeing E-3A Sentry could dominate the AWACS market. So after a considerable expense the RAF received the E-3, but had to wait five years for them to be delivered, while the Shackletons remained in use until July 1991.

Nimrod MRA.4

The Nimrod MRA.4's story is no better than the AEW.3's. In 1993 the MoD issued Staff Requirement (Air) SRA 420 for a Replacement Maritime Patrol Aircraft (replacing the Nimrod MR.2) with the intention of placing a production order in 1995–96. BAE Systems, previously British Aerospace, entered the fray with a bid based on the Nimrod. Its competitors were also offering revamps of existing aircraft: Lockheed Martin had its Orion2000, Lockheed Tactical Systems UK (formally Loral) another Orion rebuild while Breguet proposed a version of the Atlantique. The latter was soon dropped as the MoD made it plain that they would only accept a four-engined aircraft. By that time, after two rounds of defence cuts, the RAF had twenty-four Nimrods in service, plus two reserves and the expectation that twenty-five new aircraft would be ordered to replace these. Perhaps surprisingly the RAF's three Nimrod R.1s were not included in this replacement programme.

BAe won the UK's Replacement Maritime Patrol Aircraft competition in December 1996 with a bid based on a refurbished Nimrod MR.2 branded as Nimrod 2000. Using extensively refurbished aircraft was believed to be cheaper for the MoD, although BAe would probably have preferred to design a completely new aircraft.

The programme initially called for twenty-one aircraft employing refurbished Nimrod MR.2 fuselages mated to a new centre section, a new larger wing, undercarriage, pressure floor and entirely new systems. The plan was to re-engine the aircraft with four 15,500lb-thrust BMW Rolls-Royce BR710 turbofans and equip each with a Boeing mission system. While these engines consumed 30 per cent less fuel than the MR.2's Speys and produced 25 per cent more thrust, the BR710 had a diameter almost 50 per cent greater and introduced large aerodynamic changes to the inboard wing to accommodate the four new engines. Changes to the fuselage were much less significant; the most noticeable alteration was the addition of a ram-air turbine (RAT) in a teardrop fairing ahead of the port wing leading edge.

The flightdeck crew was reduced to two, as there was neither the flight engineer nor the en route navigator of the MR.2. Thales Avionics supplied the cockpit system based on the Airbus A330/A340 cockpit and Smiths Aerospace the flight management system, based on its unit for the Boeing 737. There were eight mission crew: two tactical coordinators, two acoustics operators, a communications manager and two dry operators – one for radar, one for electronic support measures (ESM) – and a crew member for additional tasks such as launching sonobuoys. The MRA.4 had three fewer crew than the MR.2.

Production Problems

The programme budgeted at £2.4bn soon ran into problems. In October 1999 BAE brought the rebuilding of the fuselages back in house from their subcontractors, Cobham at Hurn, Bournemouth and moved

LEFT: A Nimrod MR.2 fuselage being disgorged from a Heavy Lift Antonov An-124 at Woodford for conversion to become a Nimrod MRA.4. Avro Heritage

BELOW: A close up of the second MRA.4, ZJ518, showing the large intakes of its BMW Rolls-Royce BR710 turbofans. BAE Systems

BOTTOM: ZJ518 taking off from Woodford. BAE Systems

them to Woodford. As a result the programme slipped by two years pushing back the aircraft's in-service date from 2003 until at least 2005. BAE was forced to pay the government £46m in compensation. In 1999 the RAF had already cut its Nimrod MRA.4 order from twenty-one to eighteen, citing the reduced submarine threat and the aircraft's improved capability.

BAE had evidently bid too low for the project and had not appreciated the problems in mating fuselages built in the 1960s with new computer-designed wings built to precise dimensions. This attempt to match old with new may well have proved the Achilles heel of the whole project and led to its unfortunate cancellation. There are some at Woodford who feel that problems stemmed from design authority for the MRA.4 being passed from Woodford with its large aircraft expertise to Warton where different skills were prevalent.

BAE continued to hope that they might be able to offer the Nimrod MRA.4 to the United States Navy for their Multi-mission Maritime Aircraft (MMA) programme, and had examined the manufacture of new Nimrod fuselages for a possible USN order. At one point the British firm was teamed up with McDonnell Douglas, but this ended with its takeover by Boeing. As a result in 2002 BAE withdrew from the programme after failing to secure a US partner to support its proposed Nimrod MRA.4 offering. As it knew all too well, without a partner based in the USA, there was no likelihood of their bid being accepted.

Owing to the continuing delays in the programme in 2003 the MoD and BAE agreed to a new contract to produce three Nimrod MRA.4s to test the aircraft's aerodynamics and systems. These would be PA01, '02 and '03. PA01 (ZJ516) was not fitted with the Mission system but with

flight test equipment. PA02 (ZJ518) was tasked with hot/cold temperature and armament trials in addition to some Mission

system testing. It was the final test aircraft PA03 (ZJ517) that was the first to be fitted with the complete Mission system.

First Flight and Flight Testing

The first Nimrod MRA.4 was rolled out on 16 August 2002 and made its first flight on 26 August 2004 piloted by chief test pilot John Turner – the last maiden flight of a major new type from the historic Woodford site. The Nimrod was accompanied by a Tucano and a Hawk during its two-hour test flight and landed at Warton. The programme was primarily handled between Warton and Woodford. The flight test was centred at Warton, which monitored flights via telemetry, but all updates to the test aircraft took place at Woodford, which had the advantage of sufficient hangar space. The second test Nimrod, PA02, flew on 12 December 2004 and the third on 29 August 2005.

The Nimrod MRA.4 had several handling issue: an imbalance between the elevators and ailerons, a lack of stability (as with all the Nimrods they should have kept the longer Comet 4C fuselage rather than lopping 6ft off it), and a lack of a nose drop in some stalling configurations for which a stick pusher had to be introduced.

The MoD indicated that they were confident about the project and in July 2006 signed a production contract for twelve aircraft and thirty years of BAE support (which would allow the company to recoup the loss it had made at that point). In May 2009 the number of aircraft to be delivered was reduced again, this time to just nine, these would be from the fourth aircraft onwards; the three development Nimrods were to be scrapped. The fourth aircraft, ZJ514, flew in September 2009 and the fifth, ZJ515, followed in March 2010. At the same time ZJ514 was delivered to the RAF, though still based at Warton. ZJ515 only made two flights, from Woodford to Manchester Airport to be painted and back to Woodford for final completion.

Cancellation

When the new coalition government came into power in the UK in May 2010 it introduced swingeing cuts in expenditure. The Ministry of Defence was hugely overspent and seemed unable to control expenditure. Cuts were introduced in all three services; the RAF lost its Harriers, some of its Tornados and the Nimrod MRA.4 was also axed.

Many criticized the decision to scrap an aircraft with a superb capability just about to enter service and for which there was no apparent replacement. Supporting the Government's decision was a large amount of ill-informed comment on the MRA.4, which was tainted by its association with the terrible accident to XV230 and rumours that the new version was also vulnerable to the same problem. Ten of the eleven aircraft were scrapped at Woodford in January – February 2011 and ZJ514 at Warton in mid-February. The Woodford factory with its very long and great history of producing aircraft then closed for ever. The cost to the taxpayer for eighteen years of work resulting in nothing at all was *circa* £4bn.

TOP: The MRA.4's flight deck was radically different from the previous marks of the Nimrod, which had an essentially post-war four crew Comet flightdeck. The MRA.4 had a two-crew fly-by-wire glass flightdeck. BAE Systems

ABOVE: The interior of the Nimrod MRA.4. BAE Systems

Conclusions

The Nimrod MR.1, R.1 and MR.2 were delivered by HSA to the RAF on budget and on schedule. In contrast the AEW.3 procurement was poorly managed, it would appear to be a victim of not having a single contactor – HSA/BAe were responsible for the airframe and Marconi for the electronic systems, respectively. It is not clear but possibly if it had it been given more time it would have been successful.

The MRA.4 had the makings of a superb multi-role aircraft for the RAF for maritime and overland Combat-ISTAR (intelligence, surveillance target acquisition and reconnaissance) and as a bomber. There were many mistakes in its implementation: for example, the use of the original fuselages saved nothing and new-build examples would have precluded the difficulties with the mating to the wing centre-section. In the event it was cancelled when most of the money had already been spent.

Why was the Nimrod never exported? The Nimrod was praised by the RAF for its speed, endurance and payload so why was it unsuccessful in the export market? Several countries indicated their interest yet on almost every occasion Lockheed Orions were ordered and more than 700 Orions were sold. Australia chose the Orion over the Nimrod because it was cheaper and Lockheed offered more offset work in Australia. When BAE Systems tried to team up with a US firm to sell the Nimrod MRA.4 to the USN, they were unable to find a partner as the firms approached were convinced that either Lockheed or Boeing would win the contract – and Boeing did.

The Nimrod was truly the mighty hunter of the RAF for nigh on forty years and should have continued to serve.

ABOVE: **A view of the underside of ZJ518 showing the length of its weapons bay and the large number of aerials.** BAE Systems

BELOW: **The first development aircraft, ZJ516, at Woodford in January 2011. The wing of the second MRA.4, ZJ518, is just visible. Both were broken up in March 2011, In the background is engine-less Avro RJX85 G-ORJX.** Derek Ferguson

Specification – Nimrod MR.2	
Length	126ft 9in (38.63m)
Wingspan	114ft 10in (35m)
Height	31ft (9.45m)
MTOW	192,000lb (87,000kg)
Cruising speed	575mph (925km/h)
Range	5,755 miles (9,260km)
Crew	12
Powerplant	4 × Rolls-Royce Spey 250, 12,500lb
Armament	Sidewinder, Martel, Harpoon and Maverick missiles, Stingray torpedoes, depth charges

CHAPTER SIXTEEN

Hawk!

First Flight

The Hawker Siddeley Hawk's maiden flight took place from Dunsfold in Surrey on the evening of 21 August 1974. Chief test pilot Duncan Simpson flew the first Hawk, XX154, for 53 minutes before landing in the dusk. The first flight routine was typically cautious but the handling proved good with no untoward difficulties and a second flight was made the following afternoon. Hawker Siddeley was anxious to exhibit their new aircraft at the forthcoming Farnborough Air Show as the Dassault-Dornier Alpha Jet trainer would be on display there, so XX154 made seven more flights prior to the Show and the Hawk flew on each of the eight days. Though its display was necessarily muted, the Franco-German Alpha Jet had not been able to steal a march on the British aircraft. The Hawk was then grounded for the installation of full test instrumentation, which had been delayed to allow for the Farnborough appearance.

The first Hawk, XX154, having engine runs at Dunsfold prior to its maiden flight.
BAE Systems

The Origins of the Hawk

In the 1960s the RAF's advanced trainers were the Gnat and the Hunter. The first was to acquaint students with jets and the second for weapons training. The Gnat had many drawbacks that made it unsuitable for weapons training while the Hunter had a high fuel consumption. In 1962 the RAF formulated a requirement, Air Staff Target (AST) 362, to replace the Folland Gnat and the Hawker Hunter, specifying a supersonic aircraft with ground-attack capability. Hawker Siddeley offered two designs, the variable geometry Folland Fo147 and the Hawker P1173, while the British Air Corporation countered with two proposals, the Luton Division's H155 and Preston's supersonic, variable geometry P45. In the event none of these went ahead as the Labour Government was anxious to promote collaboration with France and both countries were keen to reduce costs and benefit from a larger order book.

In May 1965 the British and French Governments signed a Memorandum of Understanding on the development of two aircraft: an advanced trainer/strike aircraft and the Anglo-French Variable-Geometry aircraft for which all costs were to be shared equally. Roy Jenkins, Minister of Aviation, stated in his autobiography that the Government chose BAC over Hawker Siddeley, to compensate for the TSR2 cancellation. The strike/trainer was to be based on the Breguet 121 with the French firm granted design leadership for the airframe, putting BAC in a subordinate role. The product of this Breguet/BAC collaboration was the Jaguar, which, even before it entered service, was deemed too costly and demanding to operate in a training role.

By 1968 the RAF had produced AST 397, a requirement for a Jet Provost replacement. It specified a subsonic, single-engined, tandem-seat aircraft with a raised rear seat for the instructor. This was attractive to both HSA and BAC as a potentially huge order in the magnitude of 180 machines was at stake so both companies made strong proposals: BAC's P59, partly resembling an Alpha Jet with a mid-wing configuration, while the HSA contender had a low-wing.

In October 1971 Hawker Siddeley was chosen with its low-wing P1182 powered by the Rolls-Royce/Turbomeca Adour (the engine also installed in the Jaguar). Six months later HSA received a fixed price contract for 176 aircraft with one aircraft retained for development. Refinement of the design now began with a significant alteration to the shape of the intakes and negotiation with the RAF about different forms of equipment. The name Hawk was officially adopted in August 1973.

Flight Test

Besides XX154, the next five aircraft of the development batch of six were tasked with

ABOVE: **An early Hawk T.1, XX170.**
BAE Systems

LEFT: **The Hawker Siddeley Hawk T.50 company demonstrator, G-HAWK, in its original dark earth/mid stone/azure finish for Middle East demonstrations. It is loaded with a 30mm cannon pod and four bombs. The military serial ZA101 was carried for live weapons-firing demonstrations.** BAE Systems

different roles in the flight test programme. As these five were constructed on production jigs there was a delay until the next aircraft flew in April 1975, which was actually the third aircraft XX157. The second aircraft, XX156, was rolled out at Dunsfold in May for the press, carrying Matra rocket pods on all four wing pylons and resplendent in RAF camouflage. Two more flew in June and July, but the last one, XX160, only flew in November. As these five aircraft were built on production jigs, changes were kept to a rigid minimum in the knowledge that anything done to one aircraft would immediately have repercussions on the production line.

The initial faults discovered in the flight test programme were with the nose leg, which made taxiing difficult, poor aileron response and slow flap operation. All were soon remedied. Stalling required more work

to refine and to make the Hawk acceptable for a training role. The Hawk lacked a true stall warning, which was easily dealt with, and to avoid wing dropping at the stall a wing fence was introduced. A further difficulty was found under the extreme condition of stalling at altitude with the flaps at 50° and the undercarriage up – this manoeuvre completely stalled the tailplane and Duncan Simpson only managed to recover the aircraft, which was descending rapidly, after retracting the flaps. Though there would have been other remedies, as Hawker Siddeley was on a fixed price contract and the approach speed performance was better then estimated, removal of a length of flap vane adjusted the downwash over the tailplane tip and this cured the tailplane stall. Contrastingly, at the other range of the speed spectrum, slight control problems brought on by compressibility were rectified

by vortex generators both inside and outside of the wing fence. The last two aircraft, XX159 and XX160, flew only initial tests from Dunsfold before relocating to A&AEE Boscombe Down for acceptance trials with the RAF. Altogether the six test aircraft flew some 500 hours in the test programme in time for entry into service with the RAF in October 1976. All bar XX154 were refurbished and eventually delivered to the Air Force. The eighth Hawk built was Hawker Siddeley's company-funded demonstrator G-HAWK/ZA101, which first flew on 17 May 1976 and then joined the test programme. G-HAWK was already markedly different to the standard Hawk as it was fitted with a comprehensive navigational suite, fully dual controls and other refinements such as a braking parachute. During its long career it was to be substantially modified.

Four RAF Hawks in liveries of different units. From the top, a Red Arrows Hawk, the Flying Training School's XX164, No. 2 Tactical Weapons Unit's XX322 and the No. 1 Tactical Weapons Unit's XX324. BAE Systems

The Hawker test team flew the spinning test programme on specially instrumented XX158 and 350 spins were completed in four weeks. They concluded that the Hawk had to be flown deliberately into a spin and that regardless of the circumstances, recovery would start as soon as the pro-spin rudder had been reduced to less than half deflection. As the RAF required its Hawks for weapon training as well as advanced flying work, Hawker Siddeley was also responsible for testing the Hawk in the RAF Hawk standard weapon trainer configuration with two inboard wing pylons and the centre fuselage station for the Aden gun pod. Some of the most intensive weapon trials concerned the gun, with firings carried out from ground level up to 30,000ft and in turns as tight as 6g. On one day no fewer than ten gun-firing flights were made by a single aircraft. Also cleared by the manufacturer were Matra rocket firings, bomb release and jettison of CBLS (Carrier Bomb Light Store) units.

Delivery to the RAF

The first two Hawks for the Royal Air Force were delivered to RAF Valley, Anglesey, in November 1976 and these first deliveries were made to the schedule and cost specified by the original contract. A further eight aircraft reached the RAF before the end of the year and deliveries increased steadily as the production rate reached four a month for RAF in early 1978. The first students started in July 1977 with No. 4 Flying Training School, based at RAF Valley.

The RAF Controller of Aircraft (CA) release for service was granted at the beginning of October after one of the most successful trials programmes in many years. It was generally held that the handling report from A&AEE Boscombe Down showed all round satisfaction with the Hawk as an advanced trainer. The Service release cleared the aeroplane up to all specification figures apart from maximum Mach, which was higher than specified. One of several areas in which the Hawk exceeded specification was at the high-speed end of the envelope, with the manufacturer demonstrating Mach 1.16 and the RAF clearing

No. 4 Flying Training School's Hawks in the gloss black livery adopted in 1994, XX339 and XX185. Blackburn Archive

191

it up to Mach 1.05 for normal operations. Maximum level true Mach number was also up on specification at Mach 0.87 instead of Mach 0.84.

The Hawks replaced the RAF's Gnats and Hunters in the advanced training role at No. 4FTS at Valley, Anglesey, and for weapons training at the TWU at Brawdy, South Wales. Students graduated to the Hawk after 160 hours on Jet Provosts and after up to 130 hours on Hawk moved on to the operational conversion unit. The TWU's Hawks differed from the FTS aircraft in carrying a centreline gun pod and having two underwing pylons.

In August 1979 the Conservative Government, concerned about weaknesses in the UK's air defence, announced that an extra squadron of Lightnings was to be introduced to plug the gap in Britain's air defences. All Royal Air Force Phantoms were to receive weapons systems improvements and all Hawks would be modified to carry the Sidewinder AIM-9L air-to-air missile. Hawks would be used for local air defence of airfields, piloted by instructors from the weapons training unit at RAF Brawdy. As ever, the number of Hawks to be equipped was soon reduced and seventy-two aircraft received the additional armament in addition to the 30mm cannon. These were redesignated as Hawk T.1As.

Red Arrows

The Hawks took over from the Gnats in 1979 and the Red Arrows' Hawks (like the Gnats before) were modified and prepared for the team at Bitteswell. The ninth Hawk was formally handed over on 15 November in a ceremony at Bitteswell and a demonstration followed. Henceforth the Red Arrows regularly returned to the plant in the winter for overhaul.

The RAF aerobatic team was extremely pleased with the aircraft, which represented a twenty-year technological advance over the Gnat. The Hawks had clear advantages over the Gnats they replaced, not least with a fuel consumption 30 per cent less than the Gnats'. The Hawk was much more stable in formation, being better damped in all respects. Particularly pleasing was the new type's very good aileron control and the facility for 30 seconds of inverted flight, not possible with the Gnat.

In more than thirty years the excellence of the RAF Red Arrows flying team have been synonymous with their Hawks and have become a household name, performing acrobatic stunts of great skill and daring and wowing the crowds throughout the UK and many other countries. Not only do they represent the prowess of the team but also the excellence of the Hawk.

Sales Prospects

Hawker Siddeley believed it had a two-year delivery advantage over the Hawk's principal rival in the world market, the Dassault-Dornier Alpha Jet, and set to work to target markets and make sales. First export deliveries of the Hawk could be made in early to mid-1977 and the initial markets targeted were Australia and Egypt. Australia soon faded from the picture but in July 1975 XX156 spent four days being demonstrated to and flown by officers of the Egyptian Air Force; several years of negotiations followed but Egypt eventually placed an order for Alpha Jets.

HSA foresaw that offsets, finance deals and political manoeuvring would be necessary to clinch sales. They and the Ministry of Defence had also recognized the importance of other roles for the Hawk trainer and it was designed from the outset with an eye on the fighter/ground-attack market. The RAF contract recognized that the aircraft should be capable of conversion to the ground attack role. To promote this aspect of the aircraft's potential, the third aircraft to fly, XX156, was shown to the press camouflaged and carrying stores on all four wing hardpoints. As part of the expansion of this aspect of the Hawk, G-HAWK was employed in trialling and expanding the

The Red Arrows in action.
BAE Systems

First Sales

Just as the Hawk entered service with the RAF in November 1976 Finland became the first export customer and their Defence Ministry announced an order for up to fifty Hawks to be delivered in 1979. Selling aircraft in an overcrowded market was and is a matter of who can offer the best terms. For this sale to Finland Hawker Siddeley had to arrange offsets including an outlet for Finnish goods.

Licensed production was a fact of life in aircraft sales and off-loaded the production facilities of the parent company. All but the first four aircraft were assembled by Valmet in Finland. The Finnish company also manufactured some parts, such as the airbrake, from materials supplied by British Aerospace.

Other customers soon followed: Kenya ordered twelve while Indonesia initally ordered eight and later bought thirty more. These three overseas customers were the only recipients of the Hawk 50s, which were very similar to the Hawk T.1, but improvements in the Adour together with a refined wing design resulted in the introduction of the more powerful Hawk 60 as the standard export version. The Hawk 60s were powered by the Adour 861, producing 10 per cent more thrust at altitude and 20 per cent more at high speed at low level. The maximum lift of the wing was increased and the flap mechanism modified to allow full-flap take-offs to reduce the take-off distance. A braking parachute was an option were ground run could be critical.

As part of the sales effort during 1978 the Hawk demonstrator, G-HAWK, was painted in desert camouflage and made a month-long sales tour of eight Middle East countries during which forty-two service pilots from seven air forces carried out flying assessments. G-HAWK flew seventy-eight sorties on the tour, twenty-one more than planned, and travelled more than 20,000 miles. One potential customer asked for the aircraft to be flown around a 327nm circuit while carrying five 1,000lb bombs, with a high-speed dash in the final sector. Bombs and rockets were released against simulated targets, and strafing runs were made with the centreline 30mm cannon.

In the late 1980s orders continued to roll in from around the world. Zimbabwe

The first of many export customers for the Hawk was Finland, which received T.51s. These were broadly similar to the RAF's Hawk T.1s but had improved weapons-carrying facilities. BAE Systems

The first of the Saudi Arabian Air Force's thirty Hawk T.65s, 2110, at its roll out. The Hawk T.60 had an improved Adour engine offering performance benefits in both high- and low-level operations. BAE Systems

was the first customer for the Hawk 60, buying eight, and more orders came from Dubai, Abu Dhabi, Kuwait, Saudi Arabia and Switzerland. These twenty Swiss Hawks replaced elderly de Havilland Vampires and whereas the first Swiss Hawk was built in the UK, the remainder were assembled at the Swiss Air Force base at Emmen in Kanton Luzern. (The eighteen remaining Swiss aircraft were sold to Finland in 2002.) The final customer for the Hawk 60 was the Korean Air Force which ordered twenty,

LEFT: The first Hawk T.66 for Switzerland, U-1251 (the only one assembled in the UK), in a non-standard livery. It is in formation with a de Havilland Vampire U-1208 and a Northrop F-5. The Vampires were replaced by the Hawks. BAE Systems

BELOW: A USN Goshawk T-45. The Goshawk required a large number of major alterations before the US Navy accepted it. BAE Systems

these were hybrid aircraft, receiving some elements of the Hawk 200 (*see* below), including the lengthened nose.

The Hawk Becomes the Goshawk

In 1975 the United States Navy began formulating a requirement for a VTXTS jet trainer that could operate from its aircraft carriers. This became a specification in 1979 in which the broad configuration of the design was outlined and manufacturers were required to offer a complete package including a complete training programme including simulators.

British Aerospace received a US Navy contract to study navalization of the Hawk to meet the USN VTXTS (T-2 Buckeye/ TA-4 Skyhawk replacement) requirement. Apart from a strengthened undercarriage, twin nosewheel and arrestor hook modifications, new avionics including headup display were needed. Although cost was said to be a central issue governing the Navy's choice, BAe emphasized the saving on R&D should the service choose a proven type.

A number of US manufacturers expressed interest in teaming up with BAe and in 1980 BAe and McDonnell Douglas agreed to work together and offer two different aircraft to the USN, the D-7000 and the Hawk. In each case BAe would be the major subcontractor. To assist its sales effort G-HAWK was dispatched to USN bases in 1981 and 100 pilots sampled the aircraft. In order for the sampling to remain fair, no pilot involved in the selection process for

the USN contract was to take part in the handling trials.

Later that year the Hawk was selected by the US Navy and the contract was awarded to the Douglas division of McDonnell Douglas as VTXTS prime contractor, with BAe as major subcontractor, Rolls-Royce providing the Adour engines and Sperry the simulators.

The new machine was to be designated the T-45 and later became the Goshawk. With hindsight, when the number of airframe changes were measured and costed, it might seem that a totally new aircraft would have been a better route to have chosen. The aircraft had to be considerably modified and strengthened for carrier operation. The Goshawk required a much longer safe fatigue life than the Hawk and this demanded structural reinforcement.

As there were no prototypes, the first three YT-45As were allotted to flight testing. However, the USN felt that the aircraft had major deficiencies, namely high stalling speed, insufficient thrust, and poor

stability in various flight configurations. In order to counter these adverse characteristics, the airbrake operation was improved, the fin extended, nosewheel undercarriage doors closed after extension and the Adour's thrust increased. Even after this extensive range of modifications the Navy remained dissatisfied and so a full-span wing leading edge slat was introduced and a 'smurf', or small horizontal fin, positioned in front of the tailplane allowing an increase in the size of the flaps. This last feature related to the problem discovered during original Hawk testing. The heavily modified Goshawk was deemed satisfactory until problems were found in spinning, which required even further remedial work.

As can be seen the Goshawk was a very different aircraft to the Hawk and required costly and time-consuming modifications to suit the customer. The US Navy's original intention was to order over 300 but owing to budget cuts this was whittled down to only 187, which was still a sizeable fillip for the UK production lines.

Improved Hawks for Two – the Hawk 100

The Hawk 100 project was launched in 1982 and introduced a number of major aerodynamic improvements: the much improved Phase Three Combat Wing incorporating a slightly larger leading-edge radius and a very small amount of leading-edge droop, together a heightened fin with a RWR fairing and smurfs ahead of the tailplane, which allowed the reinstatement of the full-width double-slotted flaps. It also received aft-fuselage strakes that gave a 5–10 per cent increase in take-off lift and helped to stabilize the aircraft for weapon aiming. It had a lengthened nose to incorporate a much improved weapon avionics and the number of stores attachments was increased to seven and now included the wingtips.

G-HAWK/ZA101 was heavily altered to become the aerodynamic prototype for the Hawk 100 and flew for the first time as such in October 1987. It was not a Series 100 prototype in full, as the longer nose was mocked up out of alloy and plywood and it was only capable of carrying Series 50 avionics. The first fully-representative Series 100 Hawk prototype was ZJ100, which was the 359th Hawk built and flew in October 1991 at Warton. The first order for the 100 came from Abu Dhabi with an order for eighteen

the first of which were received in 1993 and others followed from Oman, which ordered thirty. More orders followed from Malaysia, Indonesia, Canada and Bahrain.

Hawk for One – the Hawk 200

A single-seat version of the Hawk was planned in 1975 but remained on the back burner for many years owing to the heavy costs of this investment. With nationalization in the offing HSA was not interested and British Aerospace only announced go-ahead nine years later. In the 100/200 series BAe managed to maintain the impressive 6,800lb carrying capacity on seven weapons stations while updating the leading and trailing edges of the wing to increase lift.

The new aircraft had a 30 per cent increase in lift through most of the flight envelope, and particularly in the combat areas.

The single-seater had a totally new nose section and repositioned nose wheel but in all other respects it aerodynamically represented the Hawk 100. The manufacturer envisaged that with its radar with air-to-air and air-to-surface modes it had a comprehensive range of roles, including airspace denial, close air support, battlefield interdiction, photo-reconnaissance and anti-shipping strike. The logic was that an air force could put four small, cheap aircraft on patrol for the same price as one large sophisticated type, presenting a powerful threat to an invader. The same logic applied in the case of anti-shipping strike, for when equipped with two 190 Imp gal wing tanks

ABOVE: **The short-lived Hawk 200 prototype ZG200, which made its maiden flight from Dunsfold on 19 May 1986 but crashed on 2 July.** BAE Systems

LEFT: **G-HAWK/ZA101 in its later form as the aerodynamic prototype of the Hawk 100, flying together with the second prototype Hawk 200, ZH200.** BAE Systems

and loaded with a Sea Eagle anti-ship missile, the Hawk 200 would have a loiter time of about four hours, 100 miles from base.

The first Hawk 200, ZG200, made its maiden flight from Dunsfold on 19 May 1986 but crashed, killing the pilot, at Dunsfold only six weeks later. The second prototype ZH200 was already on the stocks and its production was expedited so it could fly in April the following year. Despite the Hawk 200's multi-role ability only Indonesia, Malaysia and Oman purchased the aircraft, buying a total of sixty-two aircraft.

ABOVE: **ZJ201 was the first production standard Hawk 200 and first flown from Warton in February 1992.**
BAE Systems

LEFT: **The Malaysian Air Force operates a mixed fleet of both ten twin-seat Hawk 108s and eighteen single-seat Hawk 208s.**
BAE Systems

Producing the Hawk

As a Hawker design the Hawk was initially constructed mainly at Kingston, then transported by road to Dunsfold for flight testing. Brough manufactured the wing and tailplane from the start of the project. Owing to pressure of work at Dunsfold in assembling Harriers and Hawks, between late 1979 and early 1982 thirty-nine Hawks were assembled at Bitteswell, the last of these completing the RAF order. Goshawk production in the UK was shared between Samlesbury and Brough. With the closure of Kingston from 1991 complete production of the Hawk was passed to Brough and these aircraft were then roaded to Warton for assembly and flight test. Between 1991 and 1999 Warton carried out final assembly and flight test on 190 Hawk 100/200s.

On 31 January 2008 BAE's Hawk 120 demonstrator ZJ951 was the first Hawk ever to fly out of Brough despite Hawks having been assembled at the site for eighteen years. ZJ951 had been at Brough for a systems upgrade. Until then Hawks had always made the journey for flight testing at BAE Systems Warton in Lancashire by road. Following the Strategic Defence Review of 2010 several of BAE's programmes were axed and as a result Hawk production was transferred to Warton with Brough reduced to a technical support role.

Hawk 120

At the time of writing, the current production variant of the Hawk is the 120 and features a new wing, forward and centre fuselage, fin and tailplane. Though it resembles the Hawk it has less than 10 per cent commonality with the first generation aircraft. Only the canopy and the air brake are common with the RAF T.1s. The Series 120 has four times the fatigue life of the original aircraft.

Customers for the new version are the South African Air Force, the RAAF, the Indian Air Force, the RAF, the Omani and the Saudi Arabian Air Force. Most of the RAAF aircraft were assembled in Australia and India only received twenty-four from the UK production line with the remainder of their sixty-six aircraft order to be completed by Hindustan Aeronautics. In 2010 India increased its order by another fifty-seven aircraft. Just as with the Hawk's first order in 1976 to Finland no order comes without strings attached and increasingly that means some, or even a great deal of, local input.

The RAF continues to use over seventy of its elderly Hawk T.1s, but in 2009 it started receiving twenty-eight Hawk AJTs (Advanced Jet Trainer) into operation. Two pre-production aircraft ZK010 and ZK011 flew in 2004 and 2005 and the first production machine ZK012 in 2008. These Hawks are designated as Hawk T.2s and are very different to the T.1. The latter has an analogue cockpit whereas the new aircraft have a modern digital glass cockpit and have embedded simulation and emulation technologies that to quote BAE Systems, are 'capable of turning the skies into a hypothetical frontline warzone'. The Hawk has a datalink that can simulate threats from aircraft and weapons to which the pilot can respond by releasing virtual weapons.

Conclusion

The Hawk has been a highly successful and profitable programme for the UK, leading to very significant exports around the world. The facts of its success are especially comforting as it is a wholly British aircraft, not the result of any collaborative programme with any other country. The Hawk has been steadily improved in its forty plus years of development; a whole series of very small steps, rather than a few giant leaps, and these have paid dividends.

BAe owes a considerable debt to the personnel involved from HSA, the RAF and MoD who had the foresight to ensure that the Hawk would not simply be tailored to one specific role but would have development potential built in from the outset. The current success of the Hawk shows them to have been absolutely correct. As long as a steady stream of orders can be maintained then production may yet continue for many more years to come.

ABOVE: **Hawk 120 demonstrator ZJ951, the first Hawk with the new Adour 951 and FADEC (Full Authority Digital Engine Control). Following an update it was the first Hawk to fly out of Brough when the runway was reactivated in January 2008, saving the transport by road of the aircraft to Warton.** BAE Systems

Specification – Hawk T.2 AJT	
Length	40ft 9in (12.42m)
Wingspan	32ft 7in (9.93m)
Height	13ft 1in (3.99m)
MTOW	16,480lb (7,470kg)
Max speed	630mph (1,000km/h)
Range	1,565 miles (2,520km)
Crew	2
Powerplant	1 × Rolls-Royce Adour 951, 6,800lb

BELOW: **Three Hawk 127s of the Royal Australian Air Force.** BAE Systems

Conclusion

The Hawker Siddeley directors were justifiably aggrieved when in 1977 the Labour Government nationalized the highly profitable aviation and dynamics divisions of their organization for which they received a recompense they regarded as grossly inadequate. These divisions had a considerable sales potential, with the Airbus wing subcontract work, the 748 airliner, the Harrier and the Hawk and guided weapons and satellites. However, the company's hand was forced by the Government and on 29 April 1977 it nationalized Hawker Siddeley's aerospace divisions with its 36,000 employees, merging them with the smaller British Aircraft Corporation and comparatively tiny Scottish Aviation to form British Aerospace.

Hawker Siddeley's aviation firms had a remarkable history of innovation and success, looking as far back as to the Sopwith Camel, Hawker Hart, then the Hurricane, the Meteor, the Vulcan, the Hunter, the Harrier, the Nimrod and the Hawk. Here were fine aircraft and missiles provided to the British military services, which generally sold well abroad, not only providing export income but preventing imports, all to the betterment of the British economy and the prosperity of the nation.

Whereas BAC was the product of Government coercion based on their requirement for powerful contractors for the TSR2, there was no direct contractual incentive for Hawker Siddeley to take over other firms. However, once the Government had spelt out its policy of two large aviation groupings, Hawker Siddeley with its predominance was clearly destined to be the basis for one of those. Though Sir Tom Sopwith wrote of their being some reluctance to do the Government's bidding, the Group soon took advantage of the opportunity to add substantially to its portfolio.

Having taken over three aviation firms, one of them the powerful de Havilland Enterprise, the Group set out to absorb them

and to also end the partial autonomy hitherto enjoyed by its constituent holdings such as Avro. In 1963 the guided missiles, rocket, satellite and associated equipment were melded into one group while three aircraft divisions were formed in a manner that only partly preserved the former companies' names while all products became solely Hawker Siddeley products. This was a short-lived expedient as only two years later even those company names were swept away.

In 1960 the newly enlarged aerospace elements of Hawker Siddeley had a large number of older programmes in existence. While Vulcan deliveries were continuing to the RAF from Woodford, at Chester and Hatfield production of the Dove, Heron, Comet and Sea Vixen was past its peak. Elsewhere, at Kingston and at Dunsfold, although Hunter production was ending there was a very healthy demand for refurbished examples.

New types to replace these were the 748 airliner, Argosy turboprop freighter, the Trident jet airliner and the Buccaneer bomber for the Navy. Still in the early stages of development were the P1154 for the RAF and the HS681 V/STOL heavy lifter. Regrettably, these last two never flew as in 1965 both were cancelled by Government decree, with heavy redundancies and the closure of the Baginton factory. Contracts awarded for the Harrier and the Nimrod aircraft partly compensated for this blow and did prove profitable.

The acquisition of de Havilland in 1960 greatly increased the missiles and space product portfolio of the Group. Between then and 1977 Blue Streak was successfully employed as a launcher for ELDO until the Labour Government withdrew support and there was substantial further development in guided missiles and satellites and Hawker Siddeley Dynamics became a substantial world player.

At the time of writing, only three former Hawker Siddeley sites remain in use within the aerospace industry: Brough near Hull is still part of BAe Systems and provides support for the Hawk and at Stevenage the plant that constructed the Blue Streak is with Astrium, an EADS Airbus Defence and Space company. Another former de Havilland Propellers factory at Lostock, near Bolton is part of MBDA, which is owned by BAE Systems, EADS and Finmeccanica.

Hawker Siddeley's aerospace divisions prospered in a difficult and competitive market exacerbated by the lack of any consistent industrial strategy from British Governments. In 1965 when the Plowden Report concluded that all major aviation projects would have to be collaborative, Hawker Siddeley was one of the founders of Airbus, but with the Labour Government's decision to withdraw could only remain in the project as a subcontractor while the Government supported the BAC Three-Eleven, which never flew. Hawker Siddeley went on to invest privately in the project: that vision and investment led to the Airbus factory at Broughton (Chester) employing a large number of people in the UK.

If the Hawker Siddeley Group had not been eviscerated by the nationalization of its aerospace businesses where would British aviation be now? The Group continued on without them as a large engineering conglomerate for twenty-four years but has now disappeared.

Hawker Siddeley's aviation divisions created a number of great aircraft that will never be forgotten. The financing, designing, testing, production and selling of these aircraft, guided weapons and space vehicles were the result of the concerted endeavours by highly inventive, talented and creative individuals, who can be justly proud of their achievements.

The Top Men of Hawker Siddeley

Sir Thomas Sopwith
(1888–1989)

Sir Thomas Octave Murdoch Sopwith was born into a wealthy family in London in 1888. After an engineering education he pursued his already deep interest in early motor cars, motorcycles and sailing of which the latter remained a lifelong passion.

He taught himself to fly at Brooklands gaining aviator's certificate No. 31 in 1910. Between 1910 and 1912 he proved himself a proficient pilot, winning prizes in Britain, Europe and the USA, which provided the funds to found the Sopwith School of Flying and the Sopwith Aviation Company in 1912.

During the First World War the Sopwith Aviation Company became one of the leading early British aircraft manufacturers, supplying aircraft to both the Admiralty and the War Office. Between August 1914 and November 1918 more than 18,000 Sopwith aircraft, of thirty-two different types, were designed and built for the allied air forces.

With the slump in orders post-war, in 1920 Sopwith wisely put the company into liquidation while he was still able to pay off his creditors. He bounced back later the same year launching the H.G. Hawker Engineering Company Ltd, with himself as Chairman. In June 1928 the company's fortunes were secured, following the first flight at Brooklands of the outstanding Hawker Hart, a two-seat day bomber, designed by Sydney Camm.

In a dynamic move in 1935, Sopwith led the take over of the Armstrong Siddeley Development Company and with it, Armstrong Whitworth, Armstrong Siddeley Motors, Avro, and Air Service Training. These companies and Hawker and Gloster Aircraft together were established as the Hawker Siddeley Group, which became the largest grouping in British aviation. During the Second World War the Group delivered more than 40,000 aircraft ranging from Hurricane fighters to Lancaster bombers and to Meteor jet fighters.

Sir Thomas Sopwith 1888–1989, Chairman of the Hawker Siddeley Group from 1935 until 1963. President of the Group from 1963 until his death. BAE Systems

Sir Tom Sopwith was knighted in 1953 and oversaw the further expansion of Hawker Siddeley by taking over Folland, de Havilland and Blackburn in 1959 while also expanding the company's non-aviation interests. He remained as Chairman delegating his responsibilities to those he had wisely advanced, such as Sir Roy Dobson and Sir Arnold Hall until, in 1963 at the age of seventy-five, he resigned the Chairmanship but remained on the board until on his ninetieth birthday in 1978 when he was elected founder and life president.

He died in 1989, aged 101.

Sir Roy Hardy Dobson
(1891–1968)

Sir Roy Dobson was one of Britain's outstanding aviation pioneers and entrepreneurs. Born in 1891, he joined Avro as a fitter in 1914, soon qualifying as a pilot and doing some production test flying during and after the First World War. He rose rapidly to become Works Manager in 1919, then General Manager in 1934. Sir Roy was elected to the Avro Board in 1936 and was appointed Avro Managing Director in 1941. He oversaw the manufacture of 7,336 Lancaster bombers from the Manchester factories and shadow production lines and subcontractors throughout the country.

Known as 'Dobbie' throughout the aircraft industry, he was a forthright, outspoken Yorkshireman. In 1944, Sir Roy became a Director of the Hawker Siddeley Group Board and his war work was recognized by his Knighthood, conferred in 1945. With the aim of encouraging the future development of Hawker Siddeley, at the close of the war his vigour drove forward the establishment of Avro Canada and initiated the diversification of the Group with the establishment of an engineering combine, Hawker Siddeley Canada.

Sir Roy became Managing Director and Vice-Chairman of Hawker Siddeley Group in 1958 and took over from Sir Tom Sopwith as Chairman in 1963. In 1959–60 he led the negotiations that resulted in the enlargement of the Group with the takeover of Folland, Blackburn and de Havilland. His energy, drive and commercial acumen shaped the rationalization and widening of Hawker Siddeley's interests into a more coherent body in the 1960s to shape it for changing times. He retired as Chairman in 1967 and died the following year.

Sir Arnold Hall (1915–2000)

Born in Liverpool to parents who had left school at twelve, Arnold Hall grew up during the depression. His mathematical gifts and his potential in science and engineering emerged clearly at school. Sheer brilliance took him to Clare College, Cambridge, where, in addition to a first, he won prizes in Engineering, Aeronautics and Thermodynamics. On a post-graduate fellowship he worked with Frank Whittle and carried out the compressor stress calculations for Whittle's jet engine, the first in the world, to run in April 1937.

In 1938 he joined the staff of the Royal Aircraft Establishment, Farnborough and was there throughout the war. Appointed Director in 1951 he led the investigation into the Comet accidents, speedily establishing that metal fatigue was the cause of the problem. For this brilliant research he was honoured as a fellow of the Royal Society in 1953 and knighted in 1954.

The following year Hall joined Hawker Siddeley in a role created for him as Group Technical Director, then as Managing Director of Bristol Siddeley Engines and in 1967 as Chairman of the entire Hawker Siddeley Group. In the wake of the cancellation of the Hawker Siddeley P1154 and 681 he worked hard to limit the effects on the workforce and organization. Hall's perceptive decision to keep the company in the eventually highly successful Airbus project after the British Government had withdrawn emphasized his gifts and is a decision that has paid dividends to the UK economy and the country's engineering prowess.

Sir Arnold Hall was vigorously opposed to the Labour Government's nationalization and the enforced takeover of a third of his company. He continued as Chairman of the Group and retired in 1986. He died in 2000.

ABOVE: Sir Roy Hardy Dobson 1891–1968, Chairman of the Hawker Siddeley Group from 1962 until 1967. Author's collection

LEFT: Sir Arnold Hall 1915–2000, Chairman of the Hawker Siddeley Group from 1967 until 1986. Author's collection

High Duty Alloys

High Duty Alloys (HDA) was founded in 1928 on the Slough Trading Estate by Colonel Wallace Charles Devereux with funding of £30,000 from John Siddeley (who had a controlling interest) to forge aluminium alloys and to make pistons for Armstrong Siddeley cars. In 1935, with Hawker's takeover of Siddeley Deasy, HDA became a part of the Hawker Siddeley Group.

In 1929 HDA was appointed world licensee for a Rolls-Royce series of aluminium products, which were marketed under the name of HIDUMINIUM RR. These were high-strength, high temperature aluminium alloys for aero-engines. The company prospered and expanded, soon becoming a major manufacturer of aircraft pistons, and when World War Two broke out it was in a position to make an invaluable contribution to Britain's aircraft-production effort. The main site in Slough continued to expand, but even so in 1938 a further factory was opened at Redditch. This works boasted the Erie hammer, the largest forging hammer in the world, made in the USA and with a total weight of 455 tonnes. Despite the vast increases in productive capacity in the twelve years of HDA's existence, by 1940 it was still not enough to meet the demand for forgings and castings so a third works was opened at Distington, near Workington in Cumbria, well away from any possible German air raids.

The Slough forge suffered extensive bomb damage during war, so the two other sites took on a greater responsibility. During the war years HDA forged and machined 10 million aero-engine pistons, but even while these and other components were being fabricated, expansion plans were taking shape to forge parts for the new jet engines. Post-war restructuring led to Slough concentrating on casting while Redditch took over all forging. There was even further expansion when in 1954 HDA purchased a rolling mill at Briton Ferry for the production of high-quality aluminium alloy sheets, but this was sold in the 1960s. In an interesting diversion from its usual activities, High Duty Alloys made the 1,600 torches for the 1948 London Olympics.

HDA continued to supply the aircraft industry, supplying high-specification parts for jet engines, which demanded the invention of new materials such as Nimonic, and also fabricated the first aluminium compressor blades. From the 1950s onwards HDA continued to manufacture huge quantities of precision-forged jet engine turbine blades and sold them throughout the world.

In the same period HDA did not only supply materials for engines but manufactured titanium for military and civil aircraft structures. It was rewarded for its achievement in inventing and manufacturing HIDUMINIUM-RR58 aluminium alloy as the main structural material for Concorde, able to withstand the extreme temperatures and expansion and contraction stresses, when it received the Queen's Award to Industry for technological innovation in 1969. Thirty years on in 1999, HDA's efforts were further recognized with the Queen's Award for Export Achievement.

In the 1970s the HDA plants were rationalized with each plant specializing in certain processes: HDA's headquarters and HDA Castings were at Slough, HDA Forgings at Redditch and HDA Extrusions at

One of the 1,600 torches made by High Duty Alloys for the 1948 London Olympics.
Author

British Airways Concorde G-BOAE. Concorde's main structural material was HIDUMINIUM-RR58 aluminium alloy made by High Duty Alloys and able to withstand the extreme demands of Concorde's flight envelope.
Rob Ware

Distington. In March 1979, High Duty Extrusions at the Distington factory was sold to British Aluminium for £6.5m. In 1992 High Duty Alloys became part of BTR when it purchased the Hawker Siddeley Group, but this was short-lived for in 2000 the Mettis Group bought HDA for £42.5m. The Slough site was closed but the Redditch site continues and produces components for landing gear, airframe, flight controls and aero-engines in high-strength aluminium, titanium and steel alloys to major players such as Rolls-Royce, Boeing and Airbus.

APPENDIX III

Bristol Siddeley

In February 1959 Hawker Siddeley had already agreed that its aero-engine company, Armstrong Siddeley Motors, should merge with Bristol Engines to form Bristol Siddeley so that the joint firm could better compete with Rolls-Royce. This arrangement was in line with the Government's policy of concentrating aero-engine work into two companies, i.e. Rolls-Royce and Bristol Siddeley. HSG had a 50 per cent holding in the new Bristol Siddeley with Sir Roy Dobson as Vice-Chairman (succeeded by Sir Arnold Hall in January 1963) and Bristol's Sir Alliott Verdon-Roe was Chairman. In December 1961 Hawker Siddeley sold the newly acquired Blackburn Engines and the de Havilland Engines to Bristol Siddeley Engines whose range of engines was augmented by these acquisitions and could now offer powerplants ranging from the smallest to the largest.

In June 1966 Rolls-Royce entered into merger talks with Bristol Aeroplane, part-owner of Bristol Siddeley and a minority partner in British Aircraft Corporation (BAC). Following lengthy discussions Bristol's share was bought out by Rolls-Royce and in October Rolls-Royce paid the Hawker Siddeley Group £62.2m for its 50 per cent share of Bristol Siddeley.

Hawker Siddeley Group
Major Activities in 1969

HAWKER SIDDELEY Mechanical, electrical and aerospace equipment with world wide sales and service

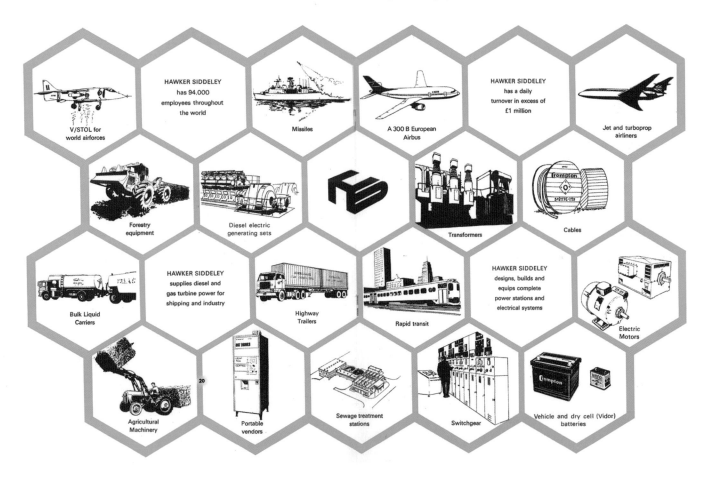

Bibliography and Notes

Air Accident Investigation Branch, *Civil Aircraft Accident Report on the Accident to G-ARPY near Felthorpe, Norwich on 3 June, 1966*

Aris, Stephen, *Close to the Sun* (Aurum, 2002)

BAE Systems, *From Blackburn to BAE Systems: Robert Blackburn and his legacy 1909–2005*

Barfield, Norman, *Broughton* (Tempus, 2001)

Bingham, Victor, *Folland Gnat – Sabre-Slayer & Red Arrow* (J & KH Publishing, 2000)

Blackman, Tony, and O'Keefe, Garry, *Victor Boys* (Grub St, 2012)

British Aerospace, *British Aerospace presents 75 years of Aviation in Kingston 1913–88*

Brown, David, *The Royal Navy & the Falklands War* (Arrow, 1989)

Buttler, Tony, *de Havilland Sea Vixen* (Air Britain, 2007)

Clegg, Peter V., *The Quiet Test Pilot – The story of Jimmy Orrell* (1989)

Comfort, Nicholas, *Surrender – How British Industry gave up the ghost 1952–2012* (Biteback, 2012)

Farley, John, *A View from the Hover* (Seager Publishing, 2008)

Gibson, Chris, *Vulcan's Hammer – V-Force Projects & Weapons since 1945* (Hikoki, 2011)

Gunston, Bill, *Airbus – the Complete Story* (Haynes, 2009)

Hill, C.N., *A Vertical Empire – The History of the UK Rocket & Space Programme, 1950–71* (Imperial College Press, 2001)

Hotson, Fred, *The de Havilland Canada Story* (CANAV Books, 1999)

Jenkins, Roy, *A Life at the Centre* (MacMillan, 1991)

Johnstone, Johnnie, *Finals – Three Greens* (Cirrus Publishing, 2000)

King, Peter, *Knights of the Air* (Constable, 1989)

Lapping, Brian, *The Labour Government 1964–70* (Penguin, 1970)

Longworth, James, *Triplane to Typhoon* (Lancashire County Developments, 2005)

Martin, Charles H., *de Havilland Blue Streak* (British Interplanetary Society, 2004)

Mason, Tim, *The Cold War Years – Flight Testing at Boscombe Down 1945–75* (Hikoki, 2001)

Merewether, Hugh, *Prelude to the Harrier – P1127: Prototype Flight Testing & Kestrel Evaluation* (X-Planes Books 3)

Molson & Taylor, *Canadian Aircraft since 1909* (Putnam, 1982)

Organ, Richard, *et al*, *Avro Arrow* (Boston Mills Press, 1980)

Pearse, Edward, *Denis Healey – a Life in Our Times* (Little, Brown, 2002)

Phipp, Mike, *Wessex Aviation Industry* (Amberley, 2011)

Reed, Arthur, *Britain's Aircraft Industry: What went right? What went wrong?* (Dent, 1973)

Skinner, Stephen, *BAe 146/RJ* (The History Press, 2005)

Skinner, Stephen, *British Aircraft Corporation* (Crowood, 2012)

Skinner, Stephen, *British Airliner Prototypes* (Midland Counties, 2008)

Gibson, Chris and Buttler, Tony, *British Secret Projects – Hypersonics, Ramjets & Missiles* (Midland Counties, 2007)

Skinner, Stephen, *Wisley – Vickers' Secret Airfield* (GMS Enterprises, 2005)

Smith, Bill, *Armstrong Siddeley Motors – The cars, the company and the people* (Veloce, 2006)

The RAF Harrier Story (Royal Air Force Historical Society, 2006)

Waterton, W.A., *The Quick and the Dead – The Story of a Chief Test Pilot* (Muller, 1956)

Zuk, Bill, *Janusz Zurakowski – Legend in the Skies* (Crecy, 2004)

Hawker Siddeley documents:
War Record, 1945
Hawker Siddeley Aviation Brochures 1960–77
Hawker Siddeley Dynamics Brochures 1960–77
Hawker Siddeley Group Annual Reports 1960–77
Hawker Siddeley Reviews 1948–70

Notes

1. Hawker Siddeley Aircraft Co Ltd, War Record 1945.
2. Harry Fraser-Mitchell, *Handley Page, Sixty Years of Achievement 1909–1970*
3. *Flight magazine*, 25 July 1974
4. Fred Hotson, *The de Havilland Canada Story*.
5. British Aerospace advertisement, April 1983.

Index

RELATED TITLES
FROM CROWOOD

American X & Y Planes Vol. 1
Experimental Aircraft to 1945

KEV DARLING

ISBN 978 1 84797 141 8
144pp, 100 illustrations

American X & Y Planes Vol. 2
Experimental Aircraft Since 1945

KEV DARLING

ISBN 978 1 84797 147 0
144pp, 100 illustrations

British Aircraft Corporation

STEPHEN SKINNER

ISBN 978 1 84797 318 4
160pp, 240 illustrations

British Experimental Turbojet Aircraft

BARRY JONES

ISBN 978 1 86126 860 0
208pp, 380 illustrations

English Electric Lightning

MARTIN W. BOWMAN

ISBN 978 1 86126 737 5
200pp, 190 illustrations

TSR2

DAMIEN BURKE

ISBN 978 1 84797 211 8
352pp, 450 illustrations

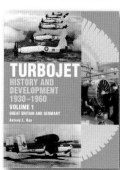

Turbojet History and Development 1930–1960
Vol. 1 Great Britain and Germany

ANTONY L. KAY

ISBN 978 1 86126 912 6
272pp, 300 illustrations

Turbojet History and Development 1930–1960
Vol. 2 USSR, USA, Japan, France, Canada, Sweden, Switzerland, Italy and Hungary

ANTONY L. KAY

ISBN 978 1 86126 939 3
272pp, 300 illustrations